PERSIAN
PILGRIMAGES

PERSIAN
PILGRIMAGES

Journeys across Iran

Afshin Molavi

W. W. Norton & Company

New York London

Excerpt from "Ending of the Shahnameh," from *Iranian Culture: A Persianist View* by Michael Hillman. Copyright © 1990 by University Press of American Inc. Reprinted by permission from University Press of America.

For information about permission to reproduce selections from this book, write to Permissions, W. W. Norton & Company, Inc., 500 Fifth Avenue, New York, NY 10110

The text of this book is composed in Guardi with the display set in Pompeijana
Composition by Claire Fontaine
Manufacturing by Maple-Vail Book Manufacturing Group
Book design by Blue Shoe Studio
Production manager: Julia Druskin

Library of Congress Cataloging-in-Publication Data

Molavi, Afshin.
Persian pilgrimages : journeys across Iran / Afshin Molavi.

p. cm.

Includes Index.

ISBN 0-393-05119-6

1. Iran—Description and travel. 2. Iran—Social life and customs—20th century. 3. Iran—Politics and government—1997– . 4. Molavi, Afshin—Journeys—Iran. I. Title.

DS259.2 .M65 2002

955.05'43—dc21   2002069211

W. W. Norton & Company, Inc., 500 Fifth Avenue, New York, N.Y. 10110
www.wwnorton.com

W. W. Norton & Company Ltd., Castle House, 75/76 Wells Street, London W1T 3QT

1 2 3 4 5 6 7 8 9 0

For my parents and for Sheila
who have given me the world
and for the people of Iran
who filled my journey with light and hope

CONTENTS

VII

VIII

IX

ACKNOWLEDGMENTS

In Persian, there is a saying, *yek donya mamnoon*. It means "a world of thanks." Sometimes I think "one world" may not be enough to thank all the people who supported this book.

I begin, appropriately, in Iran. Many of the Iranians I am most thankful to—friends, fellow travelers, sources, new acquaintances—have to remain nameless. I am uncertain how the book will be received in Iran, and I think it best to err on the side of caution. As a result, the names of many of the people in this book, the human voices that bring the following pages alive, have been changed to protect their identities. It is, in my view, a profoundly ungrateful act for the travel writer to endanger his sources, the very people who provide the light for the journey. Still, this book could not have been completed without this collection of nameless fellow travelers who shed light on my path. I shall thank each one personally on future visits.

Of course, public figures—government officials, journalists, public commentators—are a different matter. There is less cause for caution, so I can, and shall, thank them publicly. Firstly, I should like to thank Hossein Nosrat and Hossein Shiravi in the Foreign Press Section of the Ministry of Culture, both of whom helped arrange my press credentials. I should also thank Ali Reza Haghighi for his friendship and assistance in navigating Iran's political waters. In addition, I must thank Mr. Mohammadi from the Office of Foreign Residents and the other Mr. Mohammadi, from the Ministry of Culture, whose friendship and insights I valued. Journalists Dariush Sajjaddi, Shirzad Bozorgmehr, and Mehrdad Serjooie proved to be extremely knowledgeable guides to the Iranian political terrain. Haji Agha Abu Torabi offered me a rare glimpse into the life of a government-affiliated senior Muslim cleric, for which I am grateful. May he rest in peace.

I should like to thank the following people in Iran for sharing their insights with me in several conversations: political scientist Hadi Semati;

journalists Akbar Ganji, Mashallah Shamsolvaezin, and Mehdi Nassiri; economist Fariborz Raisdana; Caspian specialist Abbas Maleki; and chief of staff to the president Mohammad Ali Abtahi, who is currently the vice president of Iran.

I am deeply indebted to my extended Iranian family, who offered me love, warmth, and hospitality throughout my stay in Iran. Their presence made it feel as if I were reporting from home.

In the United States I should like to thank Ed Cody of the *Washington Post* for making a boyhood dream come true, giving me space in my "hometown paper" to write about Iran. Also at the *Post,* I have to thank Nora Boustany, who championed my cause and continues to be a source of inspiration. I am also grateful to the following editors who gave me space in their pages: Stanley Reed and Harry Mauer of *BusinessWeek,* Nicholas Nesson of *Arabies Trends,* Mark Strauss of *Foreign Policy,* Katrina vanden Heuvel and Karin Rothmyer of the *Nation,* and Justin Burke of EurasiaNet. My colleagues at the Reuters bureau in Dubai (1998-99) helped me grow as a journalist and observer of Iran. I especially thank Barry May and Firooz Sedarat.

I am immensely grateful to the fellowship support offered me by the Woodrow Wilson International Center for Scholars in the summer of 2001. Thanks to Mike Van Dusen, Robert Litwak, Janine Rowe, and the entire staff at the center for making me feel at home in an environment that is truly worthy of that great internationalist American president. At the center I benefited from the energy and skills of two uniquely talented interns, Justin Kahrl and Tiffany Darabi. Both provided excellent research and proved to be valuable chapter readers. Justin Kahrl often went above and beyond the call of duty in his work, for which I am very appreciative. Above all, I thank the formidable director of the Middle East Project at the center, Haleh Esfandiari. Ms. Esfandiari's support and insights were invaluable. I only hope the following pages vindicate her faith in the project.

In the summer of 2001 my manager at IFC, Joseph O'Keefe, generously granted me time away from my desk to do the heavy writing. My colleagues Ludwina Joseph, Adriana Gomez, and Sujani Eli helped cover my beat while I was away.

Over the years I have learned about Iran from so many scholars and specialists, many of whom I have had the privilege to get acquainted with. All their insights color the pages of this book, but the list would be too exhaustive to note here. Instead, I have confined myself to those whom I interviewed for this book. They are: Dr. R. K. Ramazani of the University of Virginia, Dr. Ahmad Karimi Hakkak of the University of Washington, Dr. Eric Hooglund of *Critique,* Dr. Seyyed Hossein Nasr of George Washington University, Dr. Jahangir Amuzegar, Dr. Homa Katouzian of Oxford University, Dr. Ramin Jahanbegloo of the University of Toronto, Dr. Haleh Esfandiari of the Woodrow Wilson Center, and Bill Royce of the Voice of America. I should also like to thank Dr. Gary Sick of Columbia University and my Gulf2000 colleagues whose almost daily comments on Iran read like a running interview.

One professor, a man whose works I admire greatly, played a critical role in the creation of this book. Dr. Fouad Ajami was my graduate school adviser at the Johns Hopkins School of Advanced International Studies, and he taught me the importance of probing beyond politics to the culture and history of the lands I cover. Over lunch at an Indian restaurant in New York City, we discussed the potential for this book. Three years later, with his support, it has become a reality.

My editor at Norton, Edwin Barber, helped transform my early disordered pages into an acceptable manuscript. His subsequent editing, with great skill and literary sense, substantively improved the book. I would also like to thank Nancy Palmquist, the managing editor of W. W. Norton, and my copy editors, Pearl Hanig and Mary Babcock, who cleaned, polished, and improved the language. Indeed, I am indebted to Ed Barber, Deirdre O'Dwyer, and everyone at W. W. Norton for taking a chance on a young, untested writer.

I am grateful to the following people who read and commented on all or parts of the manuscript: Dr. R. K. Ramazani, Dr. Ahmad Karimi Hakkak, Bill Royce, Dr. Fouad Ajami, Dr. Naghmeh Sohrabi, Karim Sadjadpour, Dokhi Fassihian, and my father, Dr. Hassan A. Molavi. Dr. Karimi Hakkak, in particular, proved to be an extraordinarily valuable critic who gave generously of his time and erudition.

My sister Yeganeh's interest in Iran nourished my own, and her encouragement to travel to Iran played no small role in my own journey. Hopefully, this book will guide her two-year-old son, Keyvan, to his own Iranian journey when he comes of age.

Sheila Shahriari, my wife and friend and valued reader, always reminded me to stay focused on the human aspect of the story, for she understands that, at the end of the day, human dignity is more important than fleeting political phenomena. She also read and commented wisely on the manuscript and provided much-needed emotional support. In many ways, this book is a joint venture. I shall always be grateful to her.

Above all, I must thank my parents. Their constant, unceasing love and devotion have cast a warm glow over my life. Their support for this book project has been unyielding. More than they will ever know, my attempt to understand Iran has been an effort to pay homage to them. For all that they have done for me, I am eternally grateful.

Afshin Molavi
Washington, D. C.

PROLOGUE

This is a book about Iran and Iranians. For more than a year, I traveled across this old and sophisticated and tormented land to observe, listen, discuss, think, and write. I logged thousands of miles and visited more than twenty cities and villages. In all my travels, I had one simple request of the thousands of Iranians I encountered. "Tell me your story," I asked. They did. The stories were edifying, enlightening, maddening, exhilarating, tragic, triumphant, sad, wonderful, and terrible. At times I felt overwhelmed, submerged, almost drowning in a sea of voices wanting to be heard. Often the interview subjects contacted me. "I hear you are a journalist and have come from America," one anonymous telephone caller said. "Well, perhaps my own story may interest you."

These voices formed the heart of my narrative; Iran's colorful and tormented twenty-six-hundred-year history formed the backbone. I began my journey with a pilgrimage to the tomb of Cyrus the Great, the sixth-century B.C. Persian king who founded the Persian Empire, a king who remains a cultural icon to this day. I ended it with two modern pilgrimages, to the shrine of Iran's war "martyrs," the nearly 300,000 young men killed in the 1980–88 Iran-Iraq war and to the Canadian embassy in Damascus, Syria, site of the Iranian youth "visa pilgrimage," an almost ritualized pattern of exit for young Iranians frustrated by the lack of job opportunities and the Islamic Republic's restrictions on personal and social freedoms.

The war martyrs' shrine, located in a scraggly dirt plain on the Iraqi border, is a haunting testament to a lost generation of Iranian youth and a sad reminder of the historical tendency for Iranian leaders to send their sons to death for hazy political causes. The visa pilgrimage shrine, especially the brain drain of Iran's young professional elite, displayed vividly, in Lenin's famous phrase, "a people voting with their feet." In between, I visited the shrines of saints, poets, clerics, and fallen political figures in an attempt to understand the Iranian history that so colors the present.

Understandably, the history presented in the following pages is not comprehensive. A land with nearly three thousand years of continuous recorded history cannot be encapsulated in an account of one traveler's journey. Still, any attempt to understand today's Iran demands a look back at yesterday's. In the following pages, I bring you a flavor of that history, particularly the moments that hold some resonance in today's Iran. Just as important, I also explore Iranians' perceptions of their own history, which animated a great deal of twentieth-century Iranian political discourse. In fact, a recurring theme of modern Iranian politics has been an attempt to define Iranian history to fit political agendas.

My journey was organized around a series of pilgrimages across the country, pilgrimages of my own choosing. Iranians are frequent pilgrims, visiting shrines of medieval poets, Sufi mystics, obscure clerics, and even fallen heroes of politics or culture like Mohammad Mossadeq, the late popular prime minister who was overthrown in a 1953 CIA-supported coup d'etat, or Gholam Reza Takhti, an Olympic champion wrestler buried in a Tehran cemetery. Some of the pilgrimages I chose were obvious because of their religious and cultural importance to all Iranians; others reflected a certain aspect of Iranian history or culture that I felt important to explore. Terence O'Donnell, a perceptive American who spent fourteen years living on a farm in Iran in the 1950s and 1960s, wrote this of the Iranian pilgrimage (in 1980, amid the fury of the revolution's early days):

From all that I know of the Iranians, I believe that in time the fanaticism of the revolution will pass. I can think of no better support for this than the nature of the Iranian pilgrimage and the shrines which are its object. Iranians are much prone to pilgrimage, for though they love the flesh, they love the spirit too—perhaps not quite the contradiction that some in the West might think. And they certainly have much opportunity for pilgrimage since Iran is covered with shrines, everything from little wayside places to the great edifices in the holy cities—some of the latter among the most dazzling buildings in the East. Not one of these thousands of shrines honors a soldier or a political figure. All are dedicated to either saints or poets. In the end, these, rather than the bullhorns, are the voices that Iranians heed and venerate.

I first began traveling to Iran as a journalist in 1997 to cover in a sense the "bullhorns," the politics and the public debate. It was an exciting moment in

Iran's history. A charismatic cleric, calling for democracy, the rule of law, and increased freedoms, captivated the country. President Mohammad Khatami, who won overwhelming election victories in 1997 and 2001, was treated like a rock star, his public appearances marked by cheering fans and banner-waving youths. Meanwhile a new breed of Iranian journalist probed the politics of the land, tackling subjects that were formerly taboo. Their pens blistered the still-entrenched ruling conservative clergy (to the delight of readers) and promoted heady ideas of democracy, freedom, and civil society. Iran's university campuses, dormant since playing a critical role in the thundering 1979 revolution, sprang alive once again, agitating for more social and political freedoms; student protests became a familiar feature of campus life. In the protests many of the students wore pictures of Khatami on their chests as they waved their newly beloved newspapers in the air. It seemed for a moment that the "bullhorns" had become interesting.

Today there is considerably less political excitement in Iran. Those tantalizing days have given way to a more sober reality: Iran's antidemocratic conservative ruling clerics, the real holders of power, are in little mood for change. A series of effective conservative-led assaults on reformist supporters of Khatami has left journalists in jail, newspapers shut down, parliamentarians groping to remain relevant, and Khatami's once-shining star darkening.

As a journalist I watched the politics closely. As a traveler and writer and student of Iranian history, I followed the culture trail. Although politics has the capacity to dominate the present, culture is a better guide for the future. The history of Iran is full of failed political enterprises; its culture is far more enduring. Indeed, the student of Iranian culture emerges with a different view of the land from that of the student of politics. Often he is more optimistic, more hopeful. After all, the student of culture can bask in the glories of an ancient civilization that has produced some of the world's most gifted poets and thinkers, stunning architecture, and exquisite art. Surely, such a formidable culture can weather the storms of politics, the culture scholar says. The student of politics has a more grim view. With rare exceptions, he has seen shortsighted, venal, and brutal leaders. He has witnessed exploitative and violent meddling by foreign powers. He has seen a colorful gallery of false messiahs, rogues, pretenders, and despots, with only short respites from a generally gloomy political picture.

In 1997, when I first began traveling to Iran as a journalist to write about the politics, it became easily apparent to me that there was far more to the Iranian universe than the reformist-conservative power struggle that captured world headlines. Unfortunately, my three-week visits felt hurried, unsatisfying, somehow artificial. Rushing from appointment to appointment, I had little time to linger over a cup of tea, get lost in the twisting bazaars, develop meaningful relationships with new friends. I met many officials of the Islamic Republic, but I found my conversations with taxi drivers, the butcher, the baker, or the trader more interesting and, indeed, more revealing. I learned more about Iran from a line of poetry than from hundreds of government briefings. After each visit I returned home to Washington or Dubai more perplexed than before, grasping the politics but failing to comprehend the seismic shifts taking place in Iranian society, hints of which I culled from my conversations with average Iranians, and groping to understand the culture and history that colors the Iranian canvas.

So in the middle of 1999 I decided to leave a settled position with an international news agency and head for Iran. It was a homecoming of sorts. I was born in Iran but moved to the United States at a young age, several years before the revolution. My memories of the land were hazy: soccer in the streets; saffron-flavored ice cream; a boy named Abdollah and his motorcycle rides. As a university student, I had traveled to other places: Europe, East Asia, the Arab world. As a journalist I had covered Arab lands and sought Arab truths for seven years: in Riyadh, in Cairo, in Dubai. It was, I thought, time for me to return to Iran, to experience the land of my ancestors, to tell an Iranian story, to seek Iranian truths.

It was a moving experience for me personally, but the following pages are not devoted to my own interior personal journey. They are devoted to a description, as best I could represent, of the history of this old civilization, of the current Iranian predicament, and, most of all, of the lives, fates, and hopes of Iranians I met along the way.

PERSIAN
PILGRIMAGES

1

Cities: Tehran, Shiraz, Persepolis, Pasargad

The Sleeping Guardian of the Islamic Books

The guardian of the Islamic books library was asleep. Slouched in a chair, his gray-bearded chin resting on his chest, he snored softly, his round stomach rising and falling. Two thin hairs poked out from his wide nose. On one of his gnarled brown hands, he wore a turquoise pinkie ring. His tattered white shirt revealed traces of what looked like soup stains. Behind him, above the large photograph of Ayatollah Khomeini, the clock read 8:30 A.M.

He perched there (when he was not asleep) to serve waiting passengers who might want to borrow a book. Conservative religious foundations linked to the government fund this library and many others in public spaces across the country. Usually, religious titles and the writings of prominent Muslim clerics, mostly written in Iran's national language of Farsi, stock their shelves. At this library, occupying a corner of the Mehrabad Airport domestic departure lounge, I saw titles, in Farsi, such as *The Book of Guidance, The Last Message of Imam Khomeini,* and *Youth and Morals in Islam.* I also spotted a few books in English and a couple in French: *The Rightly Guided Path, Dieu et Ses Attributes* and a translated volume, *Le Dernier Message d'Imam Khomeiny.*

I edged around the sleeping clerk to get a closer look at the books. His heaving stomach moved to the tune of his raspy snore as I browsed—alone. A thin layer of dust covered the books' jackets; no one else, among three hundred or so passengers waiting for flights to all parts of Iran, showed any interest.

"Don't wake him," a young man in blue jeans and a wide smirk said, noticing my interest in the books as the guardian slept. "The fellow usually sleeps all morning. You may give him a heart attack." He laughed and pulled a pack of cigarettes from his front shirt pocket. His black hair, with its front bangs hanging over his eyes, shone with the wet gloss of hair gel. He affected an air of cool disinterest in his surroundings, repeatedly fingering his hair and shrugging his shoulders in a "what's-the-use-anyway" manner. "Nobody is interested in those books," he said, flipping his hair back as he offered me a cigarette. "That's why the old man can sleep all morning."

He tapped his hands to his chest and ribs and searched the pockets of his blue Nike jacket for a match. "If you do wake him up, ask him for a lighter," the young man said. "I have seen him smoking. After all, he must pass the time, no?" He smiled and drifted away toward the gift shop that sold Barbie dolls, honey-soaked sweets, steaming tea, and foreign chocolates.

In fact, the airport Islamic library is one of the few public places in Iran where one can browse among books without a crowd. A miniboom raged in most bookstores across the country. Iranians avidly bought best-selling books by prodemocracy journalists, popular Persian romance novels, and biographies of American movie stars (Leonardo DiCaprio was especially in vogue at the time, though he has been eclipsed recently by the Backstreet Boys). But here there was no buzz, no jostling for space, no life, only a brown-eyed young man with a cigarette dangling from his lips, looking for a light.

I decided not to wake the sleeping clerk. I walked over to the newsstand instead. A large crowd had gathered, awaiting the morning newspapers, impatiently flipping through the weekly magazines. Every minute or so, someone approached the newspaper clerk: "Have the newspapers come?" "When will they be here?"

The newly freed press entranced Iran. Newsstands had been transformed into the most crowded places in Iranian cities; the newspaper vendor had become the most popular man in town. The newspapers, liberalized after the sweeping election victory of the reformist cleric Mohammad Khatami to the presidency in May 1997, served as a scorecard in the ongoing power struggle between reformers pushing political and social liberalization and their powerful hard-line opponents interested in maintaining the authoritarian status quo.

Every day Iranians rushed to the newsstands to read the latest news. The highly popular papers wrote breathlessly of democracy, civil society, dialogue, the rule of law, free speech, the rights of the individual. They lashed out at Iran's conservatives as autocrats hungry for power, using religion as a cover for their voracious appetites. They tackled formerly taboo subjects, questioning fundamental aspects of the Islamic Republic from the doctrine of clerical rule, known as the *velayat-e-faqih,* to the mandatory veil imposed upon women, *hijab,* to Iran's staunch opposition to the Middle East peace process.

The conservative-controlled judiciary regularly used its powers to shut down the reformist papers. Such actions hardly slowed the flow of reformist presses. As soon as the judiciary closed one paper, another sprang up, often controlled by the same editors of the newly banned daily. Conservative papers fought back, branding Iran's reformists as Western lackeys, morally corrupt, and unwitting supporters of "world Zionism." But few read them. Once, at a Tehran newsstand, a vendor furtively slipped a reformist daily inside the pages of a conservative one that I had brought. When I detected his subterfuge, he said: "You are a journalist. You write for foreign newspapers. You must not read that conservative garbage. You must read the reformist papers! That is what all Iranians are reading!" Government buildings and Iran Air distributed excess conservative dailies for free.

In April 2000 the conservative-controlled judiciary drew the line. Launching a wide-ranging crackdown, it closed nearly all of the reformist dailies and jailed leading journalists. Overnight the journalists became national heroes, their names on every Iranian's lips, their trials eagerly followed and buzzed about.

The press crackdown starkly reflected a fact that President Khatami had begun to realize in his first few months of office: his lack of real, substantive bureaucratic power within the system. In Iran, elections for the presidency and Parliament and some forms of civil society create pockets of "democratic space." President Khatami benefited from this limited democratic space. These pockets, however, must compete with sweeps of authoritarian space, mainly powerful conservative figures and bodies—the office of the Supreme Leader, Ayatollah Ali Khamenei (the successor to the late Ayatollah Khomeini), who has veto power on all matters of state; the conservative judiciary, which regularly shuts down newspapers and jails dissidents; a council of election supervisors known as the Guardian Council that vets all candidates for elective office; well-connected merchants who engage in corrupt business with leading officials, enriching both sides; and security services, ranging from Iran's elite Revolutionary Guards to the military leadership. The framers built this unequal struggle into the system. It turns the Islamic Republic into a confused political entity, a system that gives a small amount of power to the people and the decisive power to an alliance of conservative clerics and the security services that has little regard for democracy. To top it off, the mantle of religion and morality covers this authoritarian order. The conservative ruling clergy labels opponents not just political dissidents, but "unbelievers," "blasphemers."

I walked away from the vendor and sat down in one of the lounge's blue plastic chairs. Nearby a group of young men in blue jeans, clunky black shoes, and gelled hair joked with an Iran Air official, their backpacks slung casually over one shoulder. Two young women in red lipsticks and colorful head scarves, their hair jutting out defiantly against the Islamic Republic dress code, walked past, trailing a scent of perfume. The young men did a double take, stealing a glance at the women, then quickly looking away. An elderly woman in a wheelchair, plump and gray, with skin the color of withered green olives, drank tea the Iranian way: popping a sugar cube in her mouth before sipping the hot liquid, the cube melting upon impact and rushing down the throat in a burst of sugar and tea and warmth.

The early-morning sun streamed in through the tall airport windows. Red and orange neon signs blinked across the hall, advertising the Shandiz restaurant, a new ice-cream flavor, and a popular detergent. The Shandiz sign, a big strawberry dipped in chocolate, appeared to be dying, its red light flickering and flashing in shades of pink and red. Underneath the sign a toddler with big brown eyes scurried across the lounge, chased by his mother, her long black overcoat trailing the floor as she pleaded, "Ali! Ali! Slow down, Ali."

I returned to the lending library, where the guardian of the books still slept alone. I flipped through several books. In one nondescript pamphlet-style book, I came across the following sentence: "The *velayat-e-faqih* is our eternal system of government. May God bless Imam Khomeini for his foresight and wisdom."

The *velayat-e-faqih* essentially grants political power, the state's ruling apparatus, to Iran's clergy and gives one supreme clerical leader the role of head of state. This supreme clerical leader, the *faqih,* in theory would rule the country in a just manner according to his interpretation of Islamic law. The idea, first introduced in 1971 by the exiled Ayatollah Khomeini to a group of his clerical peers during a series of lectures in the Iraqi holy city of Najaf, argued that the clergy, as the most learned in Islamic law and the temporal representative of Shi'a Islam's messiah figure, should rule the majority Muslim Iranian people. This revolutionary idea not only disturbed the ruling Iranian government of the time—then ruled by an autocratic, modernizing, U.S.-backed monarch (Shah Mohammad Reza Pahlavi)—but also Khomeini's clerical peers. The classical Shi'a Muslim view in Iran and among other Shi'a communities opposed direct involvement in politics. The reasoning went like this: In the absence of the Shi'a messiah—the twelfth imam, who went into hiding more than a thousand years ago—all governments are profane, so taking part in government work would be deemed unworthy of the clergy. The Muslim cleric might *interact* with government officials, but must never get involved in governing. Of course, in practice, Shi'a clerics have formed an important power center in Iranian politics since the sixteenth-century rise of the Iranian Safavid dynasty that embraced Shi'ism and proclaimed it the new official faith of the then-majority Sunni Iran, but they never wielded direct political power.[1]

Ayatollah Khomeini, a Shi'a cleric, became a revolutionary figure in the early 1960s, defying the all-powerful Shah in stinging, religious-nationalist antigovernment speeches that led to his forced exile in Turkey, Iraq, and later France for three decisive months in 1977. Before his forced exile, Khomeini's brazen defiance also tapped into seething resentments against Iran's autocratic Shah (king), Mohammad Reza Pahlavi, from many quarters. Throughout the 1970s, a coalition of revolutionary forces—Marxists, Islamic socialists, nationalist democrats, leftist intellectuals, the underclass, students, writers, clerics, frustrated merchants—all agitated against the Shah, joining forces in creating a popular revolution that is inaccurately called Islamic. After all, economic grievances, longings for greater democracy, frustration

---

[1] The Shi'a-Sunni schism dates back to the early years of Islam and arose over succession rights to the Prophet Muhammad. Today the majority of the Muslim world is Sunni, 84 percent, but Iran is overwhelmingly Shi'a, 99 percent, as a result of the Safavid dynasty's actions. A full treatment of the schism is offered in chapter 2 and the Safavid Shi'atization in chapter 5.

with the Shah's secret police, leftist antiroyalism, the rising expectations of a growing middle class, and the sheer excitement of defying an all-powerful king played just as big a role in the revolution's gathering storm as did Khomeini's undefined Islamic utopianist visions.

After Iran's thundering 1979 revolution and Khomeini's triumphant return to Iran, a battle played out among leading revolutionary groups: chiefly the Khomeinists, the Islamic socialists (the Mojahedin-e-Khalq), the nationalists, and the radical Marxist anti-imperialist guerilla groups (the Fedayeen-e-Khalq). As is often the case with popular revolutions, the unity that ensures the revolution's success crumbles once victory has been achieved, and the most militant groups—not necessarily the most popular—emerge as leading contenders for the throne. In Iran's case, the most militant were the Khomeinists, the Mojahedin, and the Fedayeen. The Khomeinists, imbued with a messianic sense of right, the luster of a leader still viewed as a hero, manifestly higher popularity than the other two groups had, and more thugs per square mile than the other sides, won the battle. The victor usually writes the history, and here the victor called its revolution Islamic. And so did the rest of the world.

Thus the era of the Islamic republic arrived. Though legions of scholars will dispute the "Islamicness" of Iran's system (Islam, like other monotheistic religions, is open to multiple interpretations), and several high-ranking Iranian Shi'a clerics repudiated Khomeini's idea of an Islamic republic, Iran's government basically adhered to Khomeini's vision. In essence, this meant that the clergy should rule. This novel idea surprised many Iranians, who rose up against the Shah for a variety of reasons, many of them having nothing to do with Islam. Few had even heard of the term *velayat-e-faqih* before the revolution. A significant number had never heard of Khomeini himself until just a few months before the revolution's success.

Dialogue and protest on the subject, however, were muted as the initial euphoria of the revolution gave way to mob violence, reminiscent of other popular revolutions. Rival revolutionaries turned their guns on one another, on their former oppressors, often on innocents. The dead bodies of the latest "devilish officials" executed by the revolutionary firing squads covered the newspapers. Zeal reigned over reason, and the law of the street said simply: He who has the most guns wins. A frightening character, Ayatollah Sadeq

Khalkhali, became the "Hanging Judge," executing hundreds of former government officials on Inquisition-like charges of "spreading corruption on earth" and "warring against God." In a macabre moment, Khalkhali turned to a visiting Indian journalist, pointed to a group of imprisoned men, and said: "Pick any one of them. I'll execute him for you!" Even Khomeini lost control of the street. Revolutionaries ignored his demand to return all firearms. They still had scores to settle. Various leftist and Marxist groups said Khomeini had gone "soft." Khomeini responded, in effect, "I'll show you soft," and sanctioned more killings.

An alliance between the Khomeinists and the organizationally strong Communist Tudeh party (the Tudeh was the silent partner) sealed the Khomeinist victory. Khomeini's charisma as the defiant cleric who challenged the king and the unbending man of religion ensured victory for the setting up of an Islamic Republic. The Khomeinist revolutionaries, with the characteristic hubris of victorious revolutionaries, saw in their victory a chance to create a new world, a new way of thinking, new heroes, a new Iran. Learning from their Communist allies, they set up a propaganda machine similar in style, if not in scope, to Mao's China or Stalin's Russia. They pressed book publishers into their service, producing thousands of "revolutionary" books. These books preached adherence to Ayatollah Khomeini and the *velayat-e-faqih*. They told noble tales of Shi'a Muslim heroes, ignoring the pre-Islamic heroes of Persia's past. They attacked "imperialist powers" and "the Great Satan" of the United States. They reprimanded the "devilish" Shah. They preached a conservative social morality, heavy in patriarchy. Numerous books explained why women must wear the *hijab,* the Islamic veil.

Elegant, leather-bound volumes of Khomeini's speeches and writings, of prominent Shi'a religious tracts, of biographies of Shi'a religious figures, proliferated. In many cases, complex theological discourses, once confined only to seminaries and colleges, now took center stage in newsstands and airports. The new books of the "Islamic Revolution" were intended to cleanse Iranians of the Shah's regime and teach the flock the new way, the Rightly Guided Path, as one of the titles suggests.

The "revolutionary education" of Iranians spread beyond books. Billboards proclaiming the justness of *velayat-e-faqih* sprouted on highways. Clerics appeared on TV urging the faithful to pray, reminding them of the sacrifices of the revolutionary "martyrs," warning them against temptation. In an extraordinary act reminiscent of China's Cultural Revolution, Iran's universities were closed for three years in order to rewrite the curriculum, to "Islamicize" and "revolutionize" every subject from literature to science.

Ironically, in today's Iran, a country wounded by an anemic economy, the devastating 1980–88 war with Iraq, high unemployment, low wages, and social and political repression, the books of the Rightly Guided Path sit idle. Books about the former Shah (even censored ones) sell briskly, and clerics have trouble getting taxis to stop for them on the street.

All over the country Iranians of all classes openly blame the ruling clergy for everything from the weak economy to the stifling summer heat. In public protests, people chant, "The clerics are rich! We are poor!" Simple daily frustrations—airline delays, heavy traffic, a bad batch of fruit at the market—serve as launching points to wide-ranging attacks on the clergy and nostalgic reminiscences of "how things once were before the revolution." An Iranian taxi driver will rarely take you from point A to point B without filling your ear with a tirade against *akhoond-ha,* those clerics (usually these tirades refer to conservative clerics, not the reformists, like Khatami, who remain largely popular, even if widely acknowledged as weak). A friend, a young cleric in training, told me he tried to borrow money to buy a car because no taxi would pick him up. It is a familiar sight: clerics stranded by a road as empty taxis whiz by. "I guess that is the price of power," the young cleric said ruefully. Today, when he really needs a taxi, he puts on civilian clothes and stuffs his clerical robes into a bag.

Stepping quietly around the still-snoozing guardian of the Islamic books library, I put the pamphlet back on the dusty shelf, slipped a small bill in his shirt pocket, and walked across the lounge, past signs announcing departures to various Iranian cities: Mashad, Yazd, Tabriz, Isfahan. Underneath one of the signs, a small crowd had gathered around an Iran Air official, a young, slim, bearded man wearing the black slacks and white shirt of an airline steward. Their faces were taut and angry as he spoke. "There will be a slight delay," he said. "Please go back to your seats. We shall inform you. No need to keep approaching the desk." A heated exchange ensued, with two passengers, a middle-aged man and a college-age woman, berating the official in the pleading, angry tones heard from frustrated air travelers around the world. But this was Iran, and inevitably the argument turned to politics.

"This is the third delay I've experienced," the young woman said, her finger jabbing the air. "This is horrible! Simply horrible! And this is the airline of *your* Islamic Republic," she said, her voice dripping with sarcasm. "You should be ashamed!" The crowd craned their necks to hear the angry, finger-pointing diatribe and nodded their heads in support. Her anger seemed disproportionate, but the Iran Air official remained patient and apologetic. "Please," he said, cutting her off, "I'm very sorry for the delay. Why don't you go get a newspaper?" he said, pointing to the vendor. "I think they have arrived." Heads turned. Indeed, the papers had arrived. Most people trickled away toward the newsstand. The young woman stayed behind, continuing her tirade against the apologetic Iran Air official, who, shortly after the verbal beating ended, rushed to the newsstand to buy a paper.

Notes on a Pilgrimage: Cyrus the Great

Near the Islamic books library, in the comfortable chairs in the back of the departure lounge, I joined my travel partner, Davoud. He perused a copy of *Sobh-e-Emrooz,* one of the more daring reformist dailies. He wore black jeans and a blue shirt, cuffed at the elbows. He sported a three-day beard on his square jaw. In his early forties, he was fit, with broad shoulders and a long pink scar on his left arm, the result of a car accident. He was a good travel partner and friend, his knowledge ranging from Persian poetry and history to racy jokes and American rock music. We awaited a plane to Shiraz; our destination was the tomb of Cyrus, the sixth-century-B.C. king of Persia, known in history books as Cyrus the Great. When I first told Davoud of my travel plans, of my chronological journey through important moments in Iranian history, he said: "You must begin with Kurosh-e-Kabir [Cyrus the Great]. It all began with him." His tomb stands eighty miles outside Shiraz on a dusty, windswept plain ringed by honey-colored hills.

A millennium before Islam came to Persia in the seventh century A.D., Iran emerged as the world's first superpower, with lands from India in the east to present-day Macedonia, a landmass covering two million square miles. The story of the rise of the Persian Empire, one of the great stories of antiquity, begins with Cyrus, an ethnic Iranian prince from the province of Pars, today known as Fars, in south-central Iran. Cyrus descended from the Aryan tribes from Central Asia that migrated to Iran in the period 1500–850 B.C. These Aryan tribes spread through the Iranian plateau—comprising roughly today's Iran, Afghanistan, and parts of western Central Asia—and into India. The name Iran derives from this Aryan heritage, a fact of which many Iranians are quick to remind visitors who confuse them with Semitic Arabs.[2]

Cyrus conquered the northern Iranian tribes of Media in 550 B.C., joining the Medes with the Persians to form a powerful new country destined to become the center of the vast Persian Empire. This union of Medes and Persians went on to conquer nearby regional powers, first Babylonia and Assyria, then the lands of western China, and then west all the way to the edge of Macedonia. The Old Testament documents Cyrus's capture of Babylon because he freed the Jews from captivity, practiced religious tolerance, and financed the reconstruction of the destroyed Jewish temple in Jerusalem. The Old Testament refers to him as "the Lord's Anointed One." Scholars of antiquity also laud Cyrus as a trailblazing, progressive king, one who displayed unique levels of tolerance for conquered peoples. Even Plato, whose Greek compatriots expressed little love for their Persian foes, called Cyrus "a great man who gave his people the rights of free men."

When I suggested that Davoud join me on my visit to the Cyrus tomb, he agreed immediately. Like me, he had a fascination with Cyrus as a historical figure. Of equal importance, we both were interested in the historiography of Cyrus as a twentieth-century icon, a figure whose legacy has been alternately praised and condemned by Iranian leaders and thinkers in the highly contentious political and cultural battles of that century.

"The legacy of Cyrus the Great has been mixed up in twentieth-century Iranian politics," Davoud explained, when we discussed the trip. "The political discourse of this time created two prevailing views on Cyrus, both extremes. The first view is the part-royalist, part-nationalist caricature of the king as the unequaled founder of the Persian Empire, a king we should worship for achieving Iranian greatness, though this view rarely focuses on Cyrus's progressive views on religious tolerance. On the other side, the side of

---

2 Iranians have an unfortunate tendency to cultural arrogance, especially toward their Asian and Arab neighbors. Arabs come under particular scorn in the popular culture, resulting from a combination of twentieth-century Persian chauvinism propagated by the Pahlavi shahs, anti-Arab strains in a prominent eleventh-century epic, Iran's Aryan roots, and the political historiography surrounding the memory of the seventh-century Arab invasion of Iran.

the Cyrus-bashers—mainly leftist intellectuals and the group of Islamic clerics who supported the revolution—Cyrus is condemned as the first in the long line of absolute monarchs 'strangling Iran for twenty-five hundred years.' He is not a king to be loved and emulated, but just another tyrannical Shah."

The two Pahlavi shahs—Reza Shah (reigned 1925–41) and Mohammad Reza Shah (reigned 1941–79)—aggressively promoted Cyrus in the official nationalist propaganda as the founder of the golden age of Persia, the first in a great Persian kingly tradition, with the Pahlavi shahs merely the latest example. Reza Khan, a soldier and nationalist, enthroned himself in 1925 after leading a coup d'etat in 1921 against the weak and incompetent Ahmad Mirza, last of the Qajar shahs. He took the name Pahlavi from the name of the language used in Iran just before the seventh-century Arab invasion and became known simply as Reza Shah. An admirer of Turkey's secular nationalist leader Kemal Atatürk, he sought to uproot Islam from Iranian society, viewing the religion and Iran's clergy as regressive forces keeping his country down. By praising the era of Cyrus and the Achaemenian kings as the golden age to be emulated, he purposely ignored Iran's thirteen-hundred-year Islamic history, a fact of which Iran's clergy angrily reminded their compatriots after their victory in the 1979 revolution. His son, Mohammad Reza Shah, who took on the title King of Kings and Light of the Aryans, continued in the same tradition, though he showed less overt hostility to Islam. In 1971 he held a ceremony marking twenty-five hundred years of Persian monarchy, a lavish gathering that was widely criticized for its expense and opulence. In 1976, he sought to change Iran's Islamic calendar to an "imperial calendar" marking the birth of Cyrus as the first day, instead of the flight of the Prophet Muhammad from Mecca to Medina in the seventh century A.D. that marks the Muslim calendar. Overnight, Iranians were told that the year was no longer 1355, but 2535. The plan, however, fizzled when Iranians largely ignored the calendar change.

As a result of the official Cyrus worship, Cyrus became a derided historical symbol of monarchy among many anti-Shah revolutionaries in the 1970s. Leftist writers—and just about every prominent writer of the sixties and seventies was a leftist of some stripe—openly criticized what they saw as Cyrus worship, debunking the Achaemenian king's image as the first in the long line of tyrants that strangled Iran. Muslim clerics, for their part, disliked the Pahlavi praise of Cyrus because it glorified Persian history before Islam, an inferior history to them, called, according to Islamic law, *jahilliya,* the age of ignorance.

In the early years after the 1979 revolution, local revolutionary authorities took revenge. In several local districts, use of the name Cyrus (in Persian, it is Kurosh) or Darius, another celebrated Persian king, for newborns was banned. When parents insisted, officials simply wrote an Islamic name on the birth certificate: Ali, Mohammad, or Hossein. Today very few Iranian teenagers claim the name Kurosh or Darius (Dariush in Farsi).

Shortly after Iran's 1979 revolution, Ayatollah Khalkhali, the infamous "Hanging Judge," published a book branding Cyrus a tyrant, a liar, and a homosexual. He called for the destruction of the Cyrus tomb and the remains of a two-thousand-year-old Persian palace in southern Iran, known as Persepolis, built by Cyrus's successors. Fortunately, cooler heads prevailed, and Cyrus's tomb and the Persepolis palace remained standing. Davoud and I planned to visit both sites.

The attendant called our flight. We boarded the buses that would take us to the airplane. Seated next to me on the bus, a young man in jeans listened to a Walkman. From the faint sound emerging from his Walkman, I could make out the song, Celine Dion's "My Heart Will Go On," from the American hit movie *Titanic.* Iran still bans Western pop music, but like so many rules of the Islamic Republic, the people have learned ways to defy them quietly.

Currencies and Passports aboard Iran Air Flight 327 to Shiraz

Aboard the aging Boeing 737, one of several bought before the 1979 revolution and still used by Iran Air, Davoud and I wedged ourselves into our seats in the rear of the plane. A steward handed out candies. An Islamic prayer was whispered over the loudspeaker. After a smooth takeoff, we flew above Tehran, leaving the massive sprawl of the city of thirteen million behind us. A smiling stewardess with high cheekbones offered us spongy chicken sandwiches wrapped in plastic. A bearded steward, wearing a pilot's white shirt with black shoulder tassels, offered us tea.

"Ah, yes," Davoud said, sipping the tea, "this is exactly what I need now. I'm falling asleep. I was up late last night," he said, "reading a self-help book by an American nutritionist. You know, one of those best-selling books that offer seven or nine or twelve steps to a healthier life. I can't remember the number." He laughed.

"Anyway, as I read about the things I should not be eating, I realized that I should be dead by now!" He laughed again, slapping me on the shoulder. "It's a silly book," he added, shrugging his shoulders, "but I have to make a living."

Davoud, among other jobs, translated books for a leading publisher. The book by the American nutritionist was his latest assignment. A few years earlier he had translated Kundera, Günter Grass, and other noted writers to much critical acclaim, though small sales. His translations of doctors' self-help books and lyrics from Western rock bands sold better, so he had been spending more time on those lately.

"Iranians are no different from the rest of the world," Davoud once told me with a contemptuous intellectual sneer. "High literature cannot compete in sales with Leonardo DiCaprio or tips on how to reduce cholesterol levels." In the year I traveled in Iran, the second best-selling book in the country was a translation of lyrics from the vintage British rock band Pink Floyd.

Still, Davoud, in early middle age, harbored dreams of writing his own great novel, of becoming an Iranian Kundera. But life, children, and the need for money led him to put his dream on hold: to translate books by American nutritionists, to edit an industry magazine, and to write occasional advertising copy.

To my benefit, he had the novelist's eye for keen social observation and the comic's gift for wit.

"Did you find something strange about that stewardess?" he asked as the smiling stewardess handed out sweets.

"Not particularly," I said. She looked typical: A scarf covered her head, and a loosely fitting manteau covered any curves in her body. She was wearing the officially mandated women's uniform of the Islamic Republic.

"She was smiling," Davoud said. "Most women in service industries do not smile. It would be seen as too suggestive. Or perhaps they have little to smile about." Since he was ever the culture critic, I expected a disquisition on the history of smiling women in Iran, but he left it at that.

I told him that I had seen a fair number of smiling women working as travel agents and receptionists. "Those are service industries too," I said.

"Well, they smile at you because they know you have come from America." He laughed. "They want you to marry them and take them to the land of gold," he said, slapping me on the shoulder in his Davoud way. "You, my friend, are a walking green card!"

His smile suddenly turned serious, and he paused, gathering his thoughts, a signal that he was about to embark upon one of his customary cultural homilies.

"This fascination with going to America and the West is nothing new," he said. "Before the revolution, every high school student wanted to go to America and the West to study, but they all planned on returning home eventually to work in Iran. These days, if a student is lucky enough to study in the West, he will rarely come home. There are so few good jobs that everyone, from students to middle-aged engineers, is looking for a way out. For many, the West has turned from a distant dream to a daily obsession. People are always gossiping about the latest news on green card applications and foreign embassy visas. We have become a nation obsessed with leaving."

He was right. In record numbers, Iranian youth are heading for the exits, or at least trying to. European embassies are flooded with visa applications from Iranians. More than two hundred thousand left the country legally in 2001. Countless others left illegally, taking advantage of a smuggling route to the West that has become lucrative and sometimes dangerous, with stops including Bosnia for entry into Western Europe, and Cuba and Mexico for entry into the United States. In fact, in the early 1990s, several Havana hotels catered to young, economically strapped Iranians who plotted their boat journeys into Florida.

He fingered the tray table in front of him and continued in a soft whisper. "But in reality, can you blame us? Especially our youth. There are no jobs for them. Our economy is a mess. The middle class is decimated. Some young women have even turned to prostitution to help their parents with the bills or to support themselves."

"And what about you?" I asked.

His face widened in a smile. "Well, I don't think prostitution is my calling"—he laughed, slapping me on the shoulder—"but I'm willing to think about it!" He paused, his smile evaporating again. "No, no. I'm too old to emigrate. That is a young man's dream."

Traveling across Iran, one constantly hears of economic pain, and the subsequent talk is of emigration to a better place, a place with jobs. Government statistics put unemployment at 16 percent, though independent economists say it is closer to 25 percent. Prices of basic goods have risen steadily every year since 1988, as wages have fallen or stagnated. Massive underemployment adds to the struggle, with engineers working as taxi drivers, pharmacists selling T-shirts, professors becoming traders.

The state-dominated economy, mired in corruption, and excess bureaucracy, slows job-creating growth. Despite Iran's massive oil wealth (it has the world's fifth-largest oil reserves and second-largest gas reserves), the middle class is deeply wounded. Middle-class assets—carpets, gold, apartments—acquired in a four-year boom after the 1973 oil price rise, have largely been sold off to keep up with inflation and to offset low wages. Today, Iranians earn one-fourth of what they did before the revolution in real terms, according to economist Bijan Khajehpour. As a result, middle-class expectations have lowered. Sons no longer expect the economic security of their fathers. As for the poor, they have simply become poorer, while a different class of people (mainly merchants well connected with the government) have become rich. Periodically slums enflame in riot, like the one in 1995 in Islamshahr, a Tehran slum, but the authorities react swiftly: Police quell the unrest with force, then the authorities throw new money at the slum area, hoping to prevent future riots.

To be sure, Iran is not poor. Its natural resources ensure a middle-income status among developing countries. Indeed, several sub-Saharan African countries would long for the "economic problems" Iran has. Nor does Iran have the wretched swathes of poverty of, say, India and Egypt. Instead, Iranians have relatively high economic expectations, even among the urban working classes, owing to a prerevolution economic boom. The current state-dominated economy fails miserably to meet those expectations.

Davoud continued: "Before the revolution, the toman [Iran's currency] was strong. It was seven tomans to the dollar. Now it is eight hundred," he said, then paused again and repeated the figure: "eight hundred."[3]

Iranians constantly bring up this currency calculation, always reminiscing about the old days, when seven tomans equaled a dollar, when a middle-class man could take his family to Europe on a one-week holiday and a civil servant could afford a house. "What has come of us?" a frustrated but still haughty Iranian once

---

[3] The official currency is the rial, but the population largely uses the term "toman." One toman is equivalent to ten rials.

asked me. "Our currency is worthless. Those backward Arabs go to Europe with their rials, and we can barely visit Turkey with our worthless tomans!"

"And the Iranian passport," Davoud went on, "used to be welcomed all over the world. We held our heads high when we traveled. Today nobody wants to give us visas, and if we are lucky enough to get one, customs officials treat us like criminals when we arrive."

Davoud rarely complained, so his words rung with a particular force, as he continued. "There are people who say that the revolution reclaimed Iran's dignity because we are no longer beholden to the United States as we were under the Shah, because we can hold our head up high as an independent state. In that respect, I see their point. But sometimes I wonder: What dignity is there in unemployment? In nervously lining up outside foreign embassies hoping for visas? In having a passport that makes us unwelcome everywhere we go and a currency that impoverishes us as soon as we step outside our borders?"

We landed in Shiraz with a thud.

What Is the Name of This Street?

At the Shiraz airport, massive photos of Ayatollah Khomeini and the current Supreme Leader, Ayatollah Ali Khamenei, mingle with neon signs advertising detergents and hotels. Dense crowds, with bouquets and nervous smiles, wait in the arrivals lounge. Outside, at an official taxi stand, people line up (or, more accurately, crowd around) to pay the cashier, obtain a ticket, and step into a waiting car. Amid the crowds, free-lance taxi drivers, technically illegal, approach quietly, whispering, "Taxi, agha [Taxi, mister]?" These unofficial drivers usually hold other jobs, but in tough times every car can be converted into an unofficial taxi. Once I was driven from the airport by a man who had just finished his morning shift as an air traffic controller.

On the road to downtown Shiraz, toward our hotel, we passed rows of crumbling dirt-colored houses and billboards advertising soft drinks, soaps, and gray-bearded clerics. As we approached the city, we saw long rows of fabulous red roses and round, spouting fountains. We checked into our hotel, a three-star establishment with a garden full of dying roses and an empty dining room with bored waiters in ill-fitting red jackets. Davoud went up to the room for a rest. I set out into the streets for a look around.

On Towhid Street, just outside our hotel, fruit stalls overflowed with yellow apples and green oranges and fat limes and red, bruised pomegranates. Bread bakers roasted the flat, long strips of bread called *sangak* (little stone), named after the burning hot stones it is cooked on. A small crowd waited patiently for the next batch of the subsidized hot bread (the government sells the ingredients to bakers at low prices, making a long strip of bread a bargain even in Iranian terms and a virtual steal in dollars at about seven cents a strip). A black-mustachioed tea seller squatted by his massive pot, ringed by tiny plastic bags of sugar cubes. A sun-wrinkled village woman in colorful clothing sat on the sidewalk, selling fresh vegetables and greens. A pair of teenage boys with slicked, gelled hair and sunglasses swayed to the beat of a song playing from the speaker of a fruit juice stand. The singer was Shadmehr Aquili, one of many Iranian musicians who benefited from the Khatami cultural liberalization. Nearby a blind man whispered verses from the Quran. A young boy, in torn clothing, guided the blind man by the arm.

A nervous-looking thin middle-aged man walked slowly past me, whispering in Farsi, "*Varagh, veeskey, dolar* [Playing cards, whiskey, dollars]." All are officially illegal, but widely traded and used, sometimes openly by nervous-looking men on street corners.

I looked back at the bootleg trader; he stopped. "Do you want dollars?" he whispered. "Whiskey? What? Hurry up," he said, looking around. "Come with me to the alley. Come."

I declined. I already had a regular dollar-changer in Tehran, and I decided against the needless risk of changing money in an alley when I could do it easily over tea and biscuits in the currency trader's home. I continued walking, by T-shirt stores, bargain clothing and electronics stores, toy shops, booksellers, and as many posters of the handsome, blond-maned British soccer star David Beckham as there were pictures of Iran's revered, dark-bearded Imam Ali, first imam of the Shi'a Muslim faith.

I asked a tea vendor where I might buy some camera film.

"Keep walking down this street," he said. "Darius Street has everything you need."

"Darius Street?"

"Yes, you are now on Darius Street."

My map showed that I was on Towhid Street. *Towhid,* an Arabic theological term broadly defined as the "oneness of God," became a common street name in postrevolution Iran. Before the revolution, this had been Darius

Street, named after the ancient Persian king and Cyrus's most celebrated successor, the king whose reign consolidated the gains of the Persian Empire and laid the first stone for the fabulous Persian palace known in the West as Persepolis. Despite the postrevolution name change to Towhid, the tea vendor and most of Shiraz, I found out later, still called the street Darius.

Shortly after the 1979 revolution, any street name smelling of Iran's pre-Islamic golden age or linked to the royal family or the West was changed. Public squares bearing the Shah's name turned into Imam Square (Khomeini was widely called Imam, a reference that some of his supporters cunningly devised to equate him with the sacred Shi'a imams of the past). Streets honoring American presidents of course received the ax as well: Kennedy Square became Towhid Square, and Eisenhower Avenue was transformed to Azadi (Freedom) Avenue.

In Tehran the broad, tree-lined Pahlavi Avenue where cafés and clubs once drew people late into the night is now called Vali-Asr ("imam of the age," referring to the last imam, a Shi'a messiah figure who will one day return and bring justice to the world). In fact, the battle for this street name—one of the longest streets in the world, stretching twelve miles across the city—began shortly after the revolution. First, it was rechristened Mossadeq Avenue, in honor of the secular nationalist prime minister overthrown in a CIA-supported coup d'etat in 1953. The renaming of the street to Mossadeq took place early in the revolution, when Khomeini supporters were engaged in a postrevolution power struggle with other revolutionaries—nationalists, Marxist guerrillas, Communists, and democrats. Mossadeq's defiance of the British in nationalizing the Anglo-Iranian Oil Company, his chest-thumping nationalism, his avowed pursuit of democracy, and his opposition to the Shah proved appealing, in varying degrees, to all of Iran's revolutionaries. Hence the street name. But after the postrevolution power struggle had ended in victory for the Khomeinists, religious street names prevailed, and Mossadeq Avenue underwent further alteration: Mossadeq, the secular nationalist, was exchanged in favor of Vali-e-Asr, the promised messiah.

Many street names memorialize other "revolutionaries," creating juxtapositions that are sometimes downright cheeky: the street adjoining the British embassy is called Bobby Sands, named after the Irish nationalist who died of a hunger strike in a British prison. Other street names have caused international disputes, like the ongoing strain in Egyptian-Iranian relations over the street named in honor of Khaled Islambouli, the Egyptian Islamic militant who assassinated Anwar Sadat. Interestingly, the street names devoted to Iran's revered medieval poets remained unchanged. They weathered the storm of the revolution, signifying the importance Iranians attach to their poetry.

After a long walk on Darius/Towhid Street, I hailed a taxi driven by a Mr. Zari, a young man in his mid-twenties, a slightly pudgy fellow, with a quiet smile and a light brown beard. As he drove, we talked inevitably about jobs. Mr. Zari, a college graduate and an engineer, could find no work. "I don't like driving this taxi, but what can I do? There are no jobs. I knocked on the door of every company in this city," he said, "but no one will take me. Even if they do, I make much more money driving this taxi."

He drove purposefully and carefully, a welcome respite from his daredevil taxi driver colleagues who darted in and out of traffic as if playing a video game that allowed three crashes per coin. Feeling comfortable with Mr. Zari right away, I asked him if he would drive Davoud and me to the ruins of Persepolis and the Cyrus tomb the next day. He agreed, and we parted with the familiar Iranian display of ritualized hospitality, called *ta'rof.* It went like this:

"How much?" I asked.

"No, please, it is not necessary for you to pay," he said, repeating the familiar *ta'rof* line. "It was my pleasure to serve you. I am at your service."

"No, please." I persisted. "I must pay." I was going along with the familiar *ta'rof* routine, in which I, the customer, must absolutely insist on the need to pay and he, the seller, must refuse obstinately, saying what a pleasure it was to serve me.

"Be my guest, please. I am at your service," he repeated.

"Of course not," I replied, continuing to play my part in the drama well.

Often, at this stage, the driver will, with a great show of reluctance, charge the customer double the going rate. Mr. Zari, however, charged a reasonable rate. We shook hands and said good-bye.

Persepolis: Celebrations and Revolutions

The next morning, after a breakfast of tea, eggs, and hot flat bread with feta cheese, Davoud and I emerged outside our hotel to see Mr. Zari perched on the hood of his car.

"*Salam,* Afshin agha," he said, hopping off the hood and offering his hand and a quiet smile.

Iranians are exceedingly formal and usually say "Mr." (agha), even with the first name.

I introduced him to "Agha Davoud" and we engaged in the usual *ta'rof* pleasantries, hoping we had not troubled each other too much and pledging our service to each other throughout the trip.

A massive thermos of tea perfumed with orange petals filled the entire front seat, so Davoud and I slipped into the back. Mr. Zari's car, a worn and rusted white Paykan, chugged into first gear, and we sputtered out onto Towhid/Darius Street. The Paykan, the national car of Iran modeled after the British Hillman Hunter of the 1960s, has displayed an uncanny resilience over the years. All over Iran, twenty- and thirty-year-old Paykans still chug along the roads, defying their wheezing engines and rusted bodies. The Paykan inspires equal parts of love and hate in its drivers. "The Paykan is like an old, trusted servant," an Iranian once told me. "He doesn't look good, nor will he work very fast or do it the way you want it to be done, but in the end both he and the Paykan get the job done."

Leaving the crowded streets of downtown Shiraz, we drove past well-manicured rows of green trees, toward the coffee brown Zagros Mountains in the distance. Mr. Zari offered us biscuits and urged us to pour ourselves cups of tea from the thermos. We sipped tea redolent of orange petals. It tasted like a sweet, hot perfume.

Once on the highway, Mr. Zari asked us if he could play music. He popped in a tape. I recognized the voice: Ebi, an Iranian singer in exile, based in Los Angeles, California, home to most of the country's top pop singers of the 1960s and 1970s, now banned from singing in their homeland. Their tapes are banned too, but can be easily bought in major cities from an important player in Iran's economy, the underground trader.

"I listen to Ebi day and night," Mr. Zari said as we drove past cornfields and vast yellow and tan plains. In fact, Mr. Zari proved to be an expert on the Iranian pop music scene in Los Angeles (widely referred to as Tehrangeles), expounding at length on each singer's personal life and repertoire of songs. Interestingly, Mr. Zari, a religious young man from a traditionally conservative family of modest means, had no qualms about listening to the banned music. "There is nothing in Islam against music," he said when I asked him about the Islamic Republic's ban on Iran's pop singers. "That is just false." He turned up the volume, perhaps to prove his point.

The drive toward the Persepolis palace continued for about another hour on a two-lane highway flanked by dusty plains and sudden patches of green. Mr. Zari hummed along with the music as rumbling diesel trucks and speeding white Paykans rushed past us in the opposite direction. Ebi sang in Farsi, his deep voice soft and penetrating: "Your eyes are like the color of honey . . . your lips are oh so red."

As we got closer to Persepolis, I saw a collection of fraying purple and yellow tents in the distance.

"Those tents are from the Shah's big twenty-five-hundred-year monarchy celebration," Mr. Zari said. The 1971 Persepolis party, as it came to be known, featured delicacies from Maxim's in Paris and attracted more than sixty heads of state and royal houses, many of them housed in the once-luxurious tent suites with the marble bathrooms that I saw in the distance. The estimated cost of the event was between one and two hundred million dollars. The party proved ostentatious and shallow, as well as politically myopic. Just about everything for the event was imported from France. More critically, this was no party for Iranians; few but the elite received invitations.

Naturally, Iran's anti-Shah opposition widely criticized the party. The Persepolis celebration acted as a lightning rod for opposition forces that used the event to rally troops against what they viewed as an increasingly vainglorious and megalomaniacal king, unwilling to open up the political system to different voices. Today the tents still stand, worn and weather-beaten, flapping in the wind in the shadow of the Persepolis palace. The Islamic Republic, I was told, likes to keep the tents around as a reminder of the old, profligate ways.

Davoud asked Mr. Zari to make a detour to the tents, so we could see them up close. Mr. Zari stopped the car in a nearby park, where a jungle of green trees offered cool solace from the midday heat. Only a few of the tents remained in good shape. Age and weather had reduced most to domed skeletons of steel girders with patches of purple cloth hanging precariously to the metal. The once-splendid tents were described by a 1971 Iranian magazine as "a double bedroom apartment with bath, kitchen and sitting room laid out on five streets that came together to form a five-pointed star and were grouped according to geographical areas—Asia, Europe, Oceania, Africa, and America." Nowadays the tent suites that housed kings and prime ministers are strewn with rocks and marked with graffiti. In Farsi, one scribbler wrote: "In

Memory of Gholam Reza Nasr." I also spotted the ubiquitous "Death to America" graffiti competing for space with a sticker of Leonardo DiCaprio. In another tent, one scribbler had written simply, "I love Ricky Martin."

We sat down on a wooden board in one of the pockmarked tents. Davoud and Mr. Zari lit cigarettes, the smoke dancing and disappearing in the air.

I asked Davoud if he remembered the Persepolis celebrations.

"Of course, how can I forget? I was thirteen years old. My teachers organized contests for the students tied to the upcoming celebrations. I drew a picture of the Cyrus tomb from a magazine photo. I was excited about the celebrations. My father was a nationalist and a royalist, and he instilled some of that in me. The whole world would be looking at Iran and remembering one of our greatest kings."

Was Davoud aware of political unrest in Iran at the time?

"I was too young, but I do remember an older cousin of mine, a university student, arguing a lot with my father, saying the Shah and his family were corrupt and criticizing all the money that would be wasted on these 'silly celebrations' as thousands of people went hungry. He kept mentioning Karl Marx, no one I had heard of." He laughed.

"Later, after I got older, I realized what a public relations disaster the celebrations were. Chefs flown in from Paris while people suffered just a few miles away. Only elite Iranians and foreigners were invited. It was all so excessive and, ultimately, embarrassing for the Shah," he said.

"To be fair," he added, taking a deep puff on his cigarette "I believe that the Shah did many good things for Iran, things he should be given credit for, especially the economic modernization of the country, but sometimes he showed such poor judgment, like with this party".

"When I entered the university in 1976, I still did not understand Marxism, but I could see why my cousin fell for it. It was fashionable. All over the campus people talked politics, and just about everyone was an anti-Shah leftist of some variety. Marxism had a certain forbidden appeal to it, and many people quoted Marx without really knowing what they were saying. People had posters of Che Guevara in their dorm rooms, and they quoted Gramsci and just about any radical socialist they could think of."

What about you? I asked.

"I was very religious and also idealistic. I understood inequality and disparity, which I saw all over Iran. Like any emotional college student, I wanted to do something, something revolutionary, anything that would end the injustices I saw, the poverty of the poor and the corruption of the elite. Some of the older students told me I could find the answer to Iran's problems, its inequality and disparity, in Marx, in Mao, in Che Guevara. I read Mao, but it did not appeal to me. I thought there might be something wrong with me. Maybe I was not mature enough to understand Mao. Now I realize that I was the mature one.

"Personally, I was attracted to Ali Shariati," he said.

Shariati, a popular 1970s Tehran lecturer and essayist, mixed a revolutionary interpretation of Shi'a Islam with leftist and socialist rhetoric, capturing the imagination of a generation of Iranian youth like Davoud: middle-class, religious, and leftist. His message was simple and powerful: revolution and overthrow of the existing order. Imam Hossein, the sacred seventh-century Shi'a martyr, rose up against tyranny, he said: Why shouldn't we? Interestingly, Shariati also distrusted Iran's clerics, whom he viewed as reactionary forces, content to have the flock weep for Imam Hossein instead of emulating him.

What about Khomeini? I asked.

Davoud paused and squinted. The sun poured through a massive hole in the tent. "Well, to be honest, I knew nothing about him until just before the revolution. I had heard his name, of course, in political discussions on campus. But you see, for me as a young intellectual, I simply could not support a mullah." He used the term "mullah," a slightly derogatory term. Iran's clerics have taken to calling themselves *rouhanee,* translated as "cleric," as opposed to mullah or *akhoond,* which have slightly derogatory connotations. The word *akhoond* is derived from a Farsi verb meaning "to sing," and from some clerics' role as singers of mourning songs. The *akhoond* would, for a fee, sing songs of mourning for whoever wanted it, a task that cheapened the clerical class.

Davoud shifted his seat to avoid the sun. "I was very religious at the time, but I did not trust the mullahs. Many of us felt this way. The mullahs represented a reactionary Islam, not a revolutionary one, as Shariati argued. Of course, Khomeini proved to be different. He sounded more like Shariati than other mullahs, so I supported him too, though not as much as I backed Shariati."

Davoud went silent for a few minutes. I got the impression that he was gathering his thoughts, so I did not ask another question. Just outside our tent a family picnicked, a red-cheeked boy and giggling girl playing hide-and-seek in the tents once reserved for European royalty and heads of state. Mr. Zari had listened so intently to Davoud's words that he forgot to pull on his cigarette; a long, thin orange-and-black ash fell to the ground. This talk of revolution visibly fascinated Mr. Zari, who was five years old in 1979 and had probably had little idea what was happening in his country then. In Davoud's silence, Mr. Zari looked to me, almost imploring me to ask more questions.

"Shariati was very popular," Davoud suddenly continued, standing up as if to say that these would be his last words on this matter. "Of course there were Shariati supporters who did not understand his views," he said, as Mr. Zari and I stood up, following Davoud's cue. "There were even Shariati supporters who had never read a word of his or heard him speak. Shariati had become fashionable. But then again, thousands of Khomeini supporters were just like that too," he said, shaking his head in wonder. "It was not necessarily what these men said. It was how they said it. Khomeini managed to transcend some of my suspicion of mullahs because he was so brave. After the revolution, of course, my suspicions returned."

Davoud, like many young intellectuals, opposed the idea of a government run by Muslim clerics. He was also repulsed by the bloody postrevolution purges.

"Khomeini had all these Western-educated people around him. They assured us that Khomeini was interested in democracy. I'm not sure if they were lying or delusional."

Then he smiled. "I don't think they gave Khomeini and the clerics enough credit. They underestimated them. They thought they could push these 'simple mullahs' back to Qom [an Iranian holy city that is home to the most important religious seminary, the seminary where Khomeini and other leading clerics studied] and they would take over the government. But it didn't happen that way."

Mehdi Bazargan, a French-educated engineer and Iran's first postrevolution prime minister, resigned less than a year after taking office, frustrated by his inability to control the pro-Khomeini militia groups that ruled the streets of Iran. Bazargan, frustrated by his powerlessness, described himself as "a knife without a blade." Abol Hassan Bani-Sadr, the French-educated president of the Islamic Republic of Iran, fell out of favor with Khomeini over the power-hungry, shadow government of the Islamic Republic party, run by Khomeini disciples. He fled the country in 1981.

As for Shariati, he died just before the revolution's triumph, before an authoritarian king was replaced by an authoritarian cleric, and perhaps before his own views were tested—and possibly debunked—in the merciless and unforgiving light of the postrevolution reckoning.

The Zoroastrian Stamp

As we piled back into Mr. Zari's Paykan for the short drive to the Persepolis palace, the tall tan columns of the majestic Achaemenian structure came into view over a hilly, dust-colored horizon. Persepolis is a Greek term that translates as "the city of Persians," though, obviously, the Persians did not call their own city by that name. Today Iranians call the Persepolis palace Takht-e-Jamshid, from the mythical Iranian king Jamshid recorded in poetic epics as one of Iran's earliest and most celebrated kings, a just, wise, and semidivine ruler. Neither Persepolis nor Takht-e-Jamshid, however, find historical backing. The exact name of the palace has become lost in history, but early- and mid-twentieth-century Western archaelogists, whose work greatly resuscitated ancient Persian history, concluded that the Achaemenian kings probably called the palace Parsa.

In any case, the palace, even in its ruined state, provides one of the most stunning examples of pre-Islamic architecture in all Iran. Partially destroyed by Alexander the Great's invading armies, which torched the palace in 331 B.C., by seventh-century Arab Islamic invaders, who defiled it, and by kleptocratic nineteenth- and twentieth-century Western archaeologists, it remains a monumental and majestic testament to the architectural genius and splendor of Achaemenian Persia. Its size, scope, and attention to detail leave the visitor breathless. Only a few of its 550 columns are intact, though plenty remains to inspire awe. An American visitor wrote of his visit to Persepolis in 1942, "You cannot expect to come to Persepolis and remain as you were."

Approaching the palace, Mr. Zari parked the car in a rock-strewn dirt lot. The air was hot and yellow with sun. Nearby a tour bus disgorged a stream of elderly Japanese tourists, who moved in small steps amid much chatter and fanning toward the ancient palace. The palace, raised on a platform 50 feet above ground, occupies an area 325 by 487 yards, massive, the size of nearly five football fields. The palace has no ceiling now; its columns and staircases and bas-reliefs stand exposed to the daily sun. Quiet brown mountains paint the background.

Persepolis took a long time to build. First conceived by the king Darius in 518 B.C., the palace still needed refinement in 331 B.C., when Alexander set it on fire, though it was indubitably the greatest building of its time. The palace was intended to inspire awe, even fear, in visitors to the Persian kings, whose might knew no equal until they were humbled by Alexander.

The palace, however, stood for more than a symbol of Persia's might. It also signified, like so many of the world's most magnificent structures, a shrine to the Divine, and was intended for use primarily during the Now-Ruz (new year) spring festival. Arthur Pope, the late American historian of Persian art and architecture who helped rescue ancient Persia from obscurity, puts it this way: "Persepolis does proclaim boastfully, in traditional manner, the achievements of power of the Achaemenid kings, but it also emphasizes their divine investiture. . . . Persepolis was, in fact, a sacred national shrine dedicated to a specific purpose: to serve as a potent setting for the spring festival, Nawruz [sic]. By all the resources of symbolic representation, the Divine powers were implored to grant fertility and abundance."

The "divine powers" at this time were Zoroastrian gods. Long before the Prophet Muhammad emerged in Arabia, and Islam spread into Iran, the prophet Zoroaster preached what came to be for the one thousand years before Islam the Iranian faith.

It is a simple faith with a simple credo: good thoughts, good words, good deeds. Its Eastern origins lend it a softness akin to Hinduism's and Buddhism's. Unlike the Semitic faiths—Islam, Judaism, Christianity—the Zoroastrian god is not all-powerful or omniscient. There is no original sin, no fear-inspiring lord, no complex rules on how believers should live. The Zoroastrian god, Ahura Mazda, is the spiritual embodiment of truth and righteousness. The Zoroastrian holy book, the Avesta, praises truth and order and concludes that man is capable of discerning the right path. In the holy book, Ahura Mazda is set against a more evil god, Ahriman. The competition between the two, between truth and evil, reflects the internal struggle of man choosing between good and evil.

Scholars routinely date the life of Zoroaster, prophet of the faith, to the seventh century B.C., one generation before the rise of Cyrus the Great. More recent scholarship, however, has proved that timeline to be wildly wrong. Mary Boyce, the West's foremost authority on Zoroastrianism, dates the prophet Zoroaster's life to circa 1200 B.C. in eastern Iranian lands, today the steppes of Central Asia.

The Achaemenian kings were most probably adherents of the Zoroastrian faith. Throughout the Persepolis palace, carvings of Ahura Mazda as a winged angel appear above the carvings of kings. Kingly inscriptions—"I abhor the lie and pursue the truth"—reflect Zoroastrian teachings.

Zoroastrianism, today a minority religion in Iran, still influences Iranian life. The most prominent Iranian holiday remains the Now-Ruz of ancient Zoroastrianism. In other Muslim countries, Muslim holidays tend to dominate, but Now-Ruz reigns supreme in Iran. In a Christmas-like atmosphere, Iranian children receive gifts and play traditional games, and families pay regular visits to one anothers' homes. Shortly after the revolution a number of Iran's ruling clerics sought to downplay the importance of Now-Ruz; a few prominent voices even called for abolition of the pre-Islamic holiday altogether. Such a move would have been disastrous, however, and most of Iran's ruling clerics, many of whom have fond Now-Ruz memories of their own, knew that. Today, the traditional two-week Now-Ruz holiday still shuts down government offices.

Zoroastrianism has also influenced the course of Iranian Shi'ism. A mystical Shi'a school of thought, known as the Illuminationist or Eshraqi, owes its origins to the Zoroastrian worship of light. This school, which first emerged in the eleventh century, constitutes an important thread in the Shi'a seminary education. In both Zoroastrianism and Iranian Shi'ism, light constitutes a symbolic reminder of the spiritual in the material world. A visit to prominent Shi'a shrines and mosques in Iran reveals the importance of light, with their luminous rooms of cut mirror work and windows skillfully carved to spill light at all angles.

Zoroastrianism's influence did not stop in Iran. As the scholar Bernard Lewis notes, when Cyrus freed Jews from the Babylonian captivity, they took with them to Jerusalem some of the Zoroastrian ideas of good versus evil, which are reflected in the later books of the Hebrew Bible. These, in turn, contributed to the good/evil and heaven/hell dichotomy that plays such an important role in Christianity and, later, in Islam.

Colonial Markings

A wide staircase led up to the vast, exposed platform of the palace grounds. At the base of the stairs, I bought three tickets from a smiling, tea-sipping guard. Mr. Zari, according to the appropriate decorum of *ta'rof,* declined to join us. We insisted. He declined again. We insisted a third time, signaling that we were sincere. He relented, and we walked up the steps, each short enough in height, so the guidebooks told us, for visiting horse-backed dignitaries to ride up to the top. There, we entered the Gate of All Nations.

Once through the Gate of All Nations, Arthur Pope said, the ancient visitor would enter "a world of overwhelming splendor." We saw, instead, photo-clicking Japanese tourists, crowded around massive stone columns topped with figures of winged bulls. An Iranian tour guide described the scene in Japanese, not an unusual sight. In the 1980s and 1990s, poor economic times and the devastating 1980–88 war with Iraq sent thousands of young Iranians to Japan seeking jobs, many of them menial. While sweeping streets and washing dishes, some of these young Iranians saved money and learned the language. Several now make nice livings, talking about ancient Persian glories in broken Japanese to elderly pensioners from Tokyo.[4]

The faces of the winged bulls, partially destroyed, had the look of a boxer after a bad night in the ring, all smashed noses and cut eyes. The toll of successive invaders from Alexander's fourth-century B.C. arson to seventh-century A.D. Arab invaders to the thirteenth-century Mongol hordes was evident in the crumbling grandeur of the palace. Still, a modern defacement struck me more than the ancient ones. All along a wall of the Gate of All Nations, recent Western visitors had engraved their names neatly, in proper typeface, in the stone. The wall looked like this: "L Col Malcolm J Meade HBM Consul General 1898"; "1911–12 39th KGO Central India Horse"; "P Vanmali Bombay 1926"; "Capt John McDonald 1808–1810"; "Lt Col J McDonald Envoy 1826"; "FW Graf Schulenberg 1926–19 Gesandter-30–1931"; "Stanley New York Herald 1870."

Below the bull's belly, more captains and lieutenants had etched themselves in stone alongside a list of names written in Russian. This defacement, while unsettling, told the story of Iranian political life in the nineteenth and twentieth centuries. One meddling foreign power after another—most prominently Rus-

---

[4] Interestingly, the Shah used to pledge that Iran would become the next Japan.

sia, Britain, and the United States—saw Iran alternately as a critical piece on the Asian chessboard in the late nineteenth and early twentieth centuries or as a rich oil well and an important proxy state later, in the Cold War. Much has been said and written about American involvement in Iran in the twentieth century, especially the 1953 CIA-supported coup d'etat against the nationalist prime minister Mohammad Mossadeq, but before the United States entered the fray, the power game in Iran, chiefly between Britain and Russia, had played out for almost a hundred years. Russia annexed Iran's northern territories, parts of present-day Georgia, Armenia, and Azerbaijan, after a series of land wars between the two in the early nineteenth century. Britain, intent on protecting land routes to India, saw Iran as a vital buffer and began its gradual incursion into Iran in the mid-nineteenth century. Russia, interested in obtaining access to warm-water ports in the Persian Gulf and competing with Britain for Asian dominion, looked covetously at all Iran, not content with its northern territories. Inevitably, Iran entered the Great Game, that nineteenth-century battle for Asian imperial power played by Britain and Russia in Central Asia, the Caucasus, and Iran.

Throughout this Great Game period, especially in the late nineteenth century and early twentieth, a succession of weak Iranian monarchs sold concessions to British industrialists to pay for their luxurious lifestyles. The kings held little power beyond Tehran. In the countryside, feudal lords crushed the peasantry. In the early twentieth century, the British ambassador regularly lectured the Shah as if he were a naughty schoolboy.

In 1907, Britain and Russia put aside their rivalry and joined hands to carve the country into spheres of influence, Russia in the north and Britain in the oil-rich south. By 1918, shortly after Russia had fallen to Bolshevik revolutionaries, Britain thought Iran ripe for a takeover and made a bid to annex the country as a protectorate of the crown. To achieve this end, London bought off a few key Iranian politicians, whom it assumed could deliver the necessary parliamentary vote for British annexation. It failed. The Iranian Parliament voted against annexation, prompting one British observer to remark caustically: "Iranians will sell their country to the highest bidder. They just won't deliver it." Iranians, for their part, still harbor deep suspicions of all things British, seeing a devious, twisted British plot behind every ripple and flow in Iranian politics, including the fairly common popular view that a British and Muslim clergy alliance precipitated the 1979 revolution. (Britain funded several prominent members of the Muslim clergy beginning in the early twentieth century as either an insurance policy or simply an attempt to stay on its good side. Today there is a popular Iranian saying: "When you shave the beard of a mullah, you will see a 'Made in Britain' stamp on his cheek.")

After the British had failed to annex Iran, tribal unrest and widespread lawlessness still racked the country. Britain, realizing the danger of a chaotic Iran near the borders of its Indian crown jewel, decided to support a little-known but ambitious colonel in a palace coup. In 1921, Reza Khan, a tall, broad-shouldered soldier trained in the Russian Cossack brigade, led a small band of protesters into the king's palace, demanding control of the armed forces. The fearful king granted his wish. Naming himself minister of war, Reza Khan set about consolidating his power, and in 1925, in a somber ceremony, he had himself crowned the new king of Iran, beginning the short-lived Pahlavi dynasty.

Most infer British support in Reza Shah's rise. Even so, many Iranians revere the late king for his efforts to distance Iran from its foreign "backers," including Britain. Reza Shah also contributed immensely to the modernization of the Iranian state, boosting the country's roads, schools, and infrastructure, while helping create the first batch of technocrats that formed the modern state bureaucracy. Today books about Reza Shah, especially translated volumes less susceptible to the censor's pen, sell rapidly. During World War II, Reza Shah employed the old Middle Eastern idea that the enemy of my enemy is my friend and flirted with Hitler's Germany. The flirtation proved fatal. Britain's sun had not yet set on Persia. The Allied powers, who had occupied Iran as a resupply land link to Russia, quietly demanded Reza Shah's removal from power. His twenty-one-year-old son, Mohammad Reza, replaced him and ruled Iran until the 1979 revolution.

After World War II ended, British troops went home. Russian troops, however, stayed in northern Iran, prompting a 1946 confrontation with the United States. President Truman drew a line in the sand. He demanded a Russian retreat. Russia complied, giving the United States its first Cold War victory. As a result, American influence in Iran grew, and more ominously, American interests in Iran also grew. In 1953 the CIA helped foment a coup d'etat against Mossadeq, who threatened Western oil interests by dramatically nationalizing the Anglo-Iranian Oil Company. Iranians still complain of the CIA coup against Mossadeq, wondering what might have been had the popular prime minister remained in power.

Before moving on to the rest of the Persepolis palace, I looked back at the Western names etched on the wall of the Gate of All Nations. With such a tormented history of foreign meddling, it is not surprising that the names of British consuls, American journalists, Russian soldiers, and high Indian officials of the British Raj are etched in stone at Persepolis.

Ancient History and Green Cards

The crumbling stones and towering columns of the palace turned yellow-orange as the sun washed the plain. I walked amid the stone cuttings on the walls, of Persian soldiers doing battle with muscular lions, of processions of somber dignitaries waiting to see the king, of blank-eyed dignitaries in flowing robes, and of men in long beards, the beards a series of stone-cut circles like bunches of grapes.

Pulling out a copy of Donald Wilber's excellent volume on the history of the Persepolis palace, I showed it to Davoud.

"Donald Wilber? Isn't he . . ." He paused, searching for recognition of the name.

"Yes, he is," I said, explaining that he was the same Donald Wilber who had helped plan the 1953 CIA coup d'etat against Mossadeq.

Davoud laughed, saying: "And you wonder why we Iranians are so suspicious of foreigners!"

Donald Wilber will probably best be remembered in history for his part in the CIA manipulations, but he was also a great authority on Persia, with an obvious reverence for Persian civilization and culture. He long defended ancient Persia against modern scholarship that depicted the Persians as "barbarians" compared with the Greeks. He writes: "Greek writers such as Arrian employed the term 'barbarian' as interchangeable with Persian but in those years 'barbarian' meant only foreigner or alien. It has been only in modern times that the concept of Persians as barbarians, that is as uncivilized compared with the Greeks, has gained some currency. Actually, the Persians seem to have looked down on the commercially-minded Greeks, and it is clear that in such aspects of public life as administration, stable government, and tolerance of different races and creeds the Persian achievements outshone those of the Greek city states."

Wilber's view, defensive and pro-Persian, marks the tone of much Western scholarship on ancient Persia. The great University of Chicago Persianist A. T. Olmstead, who died in 1945, just as he wrapped up the seminal one-volume *History of the Persian Empire* (published in 1959), debunked Western admiration of Alexander, whom he treats roughly in his classic study. Describing Alexander's destruction of Persepolis, he writes: "The [Persian] men were all slain without mercy . . . and the Macedonians fought one another over the plunder. . . . To add to his evil reputation, Alexander even boasted in his letters how he had ordered the Persian captives to be massacred." Olmstead then depicts Alexander's arson of the Persepolis palace as "an act of sheer vandalism" and derides Alexander apologists who sought to lay blame on a Greek temptress, Thais, who allegedly urged Alexander to burn the palace in a drunken feast.

Interestingly, Alexander receives no hatred in Iran. Many Iranians see him as a relatively benign warrior-scholar, a notion planted by the eleventh-century Persian epic *Shahnameh*, or Book of Kings, an epic that includes Alexander (Eskandar) in the lineage of Persian kings. Alexander's attraction—against his initial instincts—to the Persian kingly way of pomp and grandeur fostered a widespread Iranian historical view that Alexander became Persianized. Because of that perception and Ferdowsi's depiction, little exists in the way of anti-Alexander historiography. Ironically, most criticism directed at Alexander comes from Western scholars of ancient Persia, scholars like Olmstead and Wilber, who bristle at the heroic tributes accorded to the Macedonian in the West.

Sitting on two-thousand-year-old stairs, the same ones used by nervous dignitaries preparing to meet the Persian king of kings, I flipped through Olmstead's book. Mr. Zari came to sit beside me. I showed him the book, and he seemed impressed as he flipped through the pages, stopping at the numerous diagrams and photographs. We heard the azan, the Islamic call to prayer, soft and lyrical and penetrating. I saw no minaret or mosque in sight. It was as if the call to prayer had come directly from the mountains behind us. The sun beat down on our heads, and we sipped tall cups of cold sweetened rose water, a Shiraz specialty. Not far away, a group of red-faced German women fanned themselves with Persian history pamphlets and loosened their head scarves, seemingly frustrated by the Islamic garb they were forced to don.

Mr. Zari knew little about ancient Persia, he told me. His school history lessons had focused more on Iran's Shi'a Muslim history, a millennium after the glories of ancient Persia.

"I think ancient Persia is a very important part of Iranian history," Mr. Zari said, gazing at the towering columns. "We should have learned more about it."

Davoud, who clicked photos a few feet away, had read widely of Cyrus and Darius and ancient Persia as a schoolboy before the revolution. His books and teachers, however, had concentrated little on Muslim history.

I tried to engage Mr. Zari in a conversation about these competing histories and the different textbooks, but he seemed more interested in another subject, green cards.

"I have been thinking about leaving Iran," he said. "There are no jobs for me here. Do you think I can get a green card to live and work in America?"

I told him that life was not so simple in America, that green cards required a long waiting period, that—

"I know all that," he interrupted, "but can you help me?" His eyes shone, as if he were about to burst into tears.

We exchanged phone numbers. I promised him I would ask around, do whatever I could.

He asked more questions about America: "What is the average salary for engineers?" "How much does a car cost?" "How about housing?" "Is it safe to walk around at night?" Finally, he said, "I'm sorry, you had asked me a question, and I did not answer it."

"Not a problem," I said, "we'll discuss it later."

Mr. Zari was not interested in of intellectual discussions on Iran's competing histories. He wanted to know about graduate study programs, the number of lanes on highways, what kind of car I drove, health-care plans, computer learning centers. His interests, like most young Iranians, spanned neither the exotic nor the ambitious: He wanted a job, a decent wage, a life, a chance to reclaim his dignity. A familiar story. Iran's population is one of the youngest in the world. Nearly two-thirds of its people are under the age of thirty and half under twenty-one, and many of them are frustrated, angry, and often looking for a way out of Iran. Emigration to the Far East for the less educated or to Canada and Australia for college graduates is on the rise. Iran has a high rate of brain drain; nearly one in four college-educated Iranians works outside the country.

"In America, I will have oportunities," Mr. Zari said. "Here, I have nothing."

Davoud returned from snapping photos, and we headed back to the car. Mr. Zari opened his trunk and pulled out a cooler that was filled with deep purple grapes packed in ice. Shiraz is renowned for its grapes, which produce an exquisite wine, though the postrevolution religious puritanism has all but killed the wine industry. Today traders manufacture an inferior Shiraz wine in low-quality conditions hidden from government view. We got back in the car and crunched the fat grapes, slurping the juice, and spitting the seeds out the window on our way to the Cyrus tomb.

Pilgrimage to the Tomb of Cyrus the Great

Cyrus's conquest in 539 B.C. of Babylonia, the premier power of the day, marked the first step in the rise of the Persian Empire; the way he conquered Babylonia ensured its subsequent success. Some weeks before arriving in Iran, I spent a few days in London's British Museum. There, in a glass display case in room 52, a small stone tablet called the Cyrus Cylinder tells the tale of the Babylonian victory in the king's own words: ". . . my great army entered this city without incident. The holy places of the city moved my heart. I accorded to all men the freedom to worship their own gods and ordered that no one had the right to bother them. I ordered that no house be destroyed, that no inhabitant be dispossessed. . . . I requested that the temples that had been closed be reopened. . . . I accorded peace and quiet to all men."

Such words radically departed from the kingly norm of Cyrus's era, which celebrated the death and destruction of the conquered city in declarations intended to inspire fear. Even if Cyrus exaggerated the peaceful nature of his invasion, the fact that he promoted tolerance came as something new. Consider the declaration of the Assyrian king Assurbanipal, the previous ruler of Babylonia, written just one hundred years earlier: "I conquered in a single attack the city of Ginabou. . . . I decapitated six hundred enemy soldiers on the spot and burned alive three thousand prisoners. . . . I carved up the governor with my own hands. . . . I grilled others on fire; I cut off the hands, fingers, ears, and noses of a large number of prisoners; ripped thousands of eyes from their sockets and tongues from their mouths. . . . I razed the temples to the ground and suppressed their gods. . . . I sowed salt and thorns."

In a time when the severed heads of enemies and the number of slaves captured measured political leadership, Cyrus's path represented a method of governance altogether new to the world. His praise of local gods, protection of ruling families, and encouragement of religious toleration had no precedent. As the great Persianist Richard Frye of Harvard University noted in his classic study *The Heritage of Persia,* "the victories of the Persians were not really greater or different from those of past conquerors . . . what was different was the new policy of conciliation."

That policy of conciliation is evident in the contrasting declarations of Cyrus and Assurbanipal. The difference between these two texts explains, in part, Cyrus's early success. A conquered people may be silent for a few years (especially if you grill their leaders over an open fire), but in the absence of firm, daily control, they will eventually become restive and rebellious. In the ancient Near East, no army in the world could manage a far-flung empire like Persia's through mere force. The respect and freedom of belief accorded to the conquered peoples contributed immensely to the initial success of the enterprise.

Shortly before his successful invasion of Babylon, Cyrus's troops won a decisive battle in the junction town of Sippor, on the Tigris River in modern-day Iraq. In a 1963 biography of Cyrus the Great, the author Harold Lamb describes the scene that followed: Cyrus proclaimed to the villagers: "Come forth, collect your herds, draw water for the animals, and give your families to eat. The disturbance is ended. The peace of the Achaemenian prevails. By command of Cyrus the King." The villagers then recounted all the hardships their Babylonian rulers had imposed on them. Cyrus reportedly responded: "It is the law—henceforth—that the strong shall not injure the weak."

Upon capturing Babylon, Cyrus proclaimed the slave trade illegal and reportedly said: "It is ordered that all the peoples who are captive in Babylon shall return to their homes. Are the Jews different from the others? My word covers you. Set out when you will and rebuild your temple [in Jerusalem]."

Still, the Cyrus legend cannot be taken altogether as fact. A great deal of romance has shrouded the memory of the Persian king, who has had no shortage of dazzled twentieth-century Western chroniclers, including Lamb and the late-nineteenth-century French Iranologist Comte de Gobineaur, who declared that "Cyrus towers over all other leaders of nations. There has never been one his equal." Many eminent Iran scholars have raised an important counterargument. For example, Elton Daniel, a highly respected Iranist and associate editor of the monumental *Encyclopaedia Iranica,* presents the counterpoint effectively in a passage that deserves to be quoted at length:

The personality and exploits of Cyrus have exerted a fascination upon writers down to the present day. Many of them, usually monarchists or apologists for one type of autocracy or another, have held him up as a paragon of the ideal ruler. Much recent scholarship has emphasized, rather anachronistically and just as tendentiously, his supposed "tolerance" of other cultures and his concern for "human rights." In reality, for every story about the virtue and justice of Cyrus, there is usually a contrary version that is much less flattering. . . . The favors he granted he probably bestowed to secure political tranquility, not out of any philosophical purity. The praise given him by Isaiah [in the Hebrew Bible] perhaps says as much about Jewish messianic expectations of deliverance from Babylonian oppression as about Cyrus. The gracious words of the 'Cyrus Cylinder' are formulaic repetitions of sentiments expressed by priests on behalf of Mesopotamian rulers at least as far back as the time of Hamurabi; they reflect not so much his convictions as the degree to which Cyrus was awed by Babylonian antiquity and deferred to the norms of a culture manifestly grander than his own. In summary, Cyrus was primarily a conqueror who dazzled his contemporaries and stirred their imagination with his rise from relative obscurity to mastery of an empire of unprecedented dimensions—but one with an enviable ability to do so without making unnecessary enemies and to come away with a remarkably unscathed historical reputation.

Seen in the cold reality of historical light, Cyrus was not the supremely dazzling monarch some of his chroniclers and boosters posited. Still, few will doubt his importance as an epochal figure in Iranian history. Indeed, a powerful argument can be made that Cyrus's policies of tolerance, whether motivated by purity or not, proved to be critical to the foundation of the Persian Empire and set a standard that Iranian kings sought, often unsuccessfully, to emulate. Cyrus was, indubitably, a trailblazer who could arguably be seen as one of the ancient world's most important leaders.

As we drove toward the Cyrus tomb on a two-lane highway flanked by dirt-colored emptiness, Davoud told me that he had once bought a replica of the Cyrus Cylinder. "This cylinder was very important. Too many Iranians just remember Cyrus for the empire he created, which brought power and glory to Iran. But this is not what I appreciate," he said as Mr. Zari lowered the Iranian pop music to listen. "After all, in one sense, Cyrus was an imperialist and conquered peoples much like the British imperialists we grew up hating. But it was a tolerant imperialism," Davoud continued. "By the standards of his age, Cyrus was extremely progressive. That is what we should appreciate."

Cyrus's successor, his son Cambyses II, contrasted sharply with his father. An intolerant brute, he died shortly after gaining power, though not before losing some of the sympathy that Cyrus had built up among the conquered peoples. The next ruler, Darius, combined some of Cyrus's tolerant vision with an administrative and military genius unparalleled for his era. Under his stewardship, Persia grew to the extraordinary power it became. Darius also "Persianized" the empire, since he no longer had to rely fully on the Babylonian bureaucrats who supported the empire that Cyrus had built. A tireless nation builder, Darius actively worked toward creating a uniform set of laws, which he called "the Ordinance of Good Regulations." He built roads, canals, and a new monetary system. The well-guarded roads allowed for the world's first effective postal service.[5] Perhaps most interestingly, given the corruption in today's Iranian courts, Darius harshly punished judges who took bribes.

Later Persian kings, the heirs to Cyrus and Darius, digressed, becoming traditional ancient Near Eastern autocrats, men who sought to inspire fear in their subjects, hungry for ever more land and power. To the west, the Greek city-states tempted these new Persian kings. Wars of conquest ensued, with the two sides battling intermittently for many years. The Greek wars (fifth and fourth centuries B.C.) drained Persia's resources. Back home, the rulers had become more aloof, interested more in the affairs of the harem than of state.

By the time Alexander the Great knocked on Persia's door, the empire and the state had lapsed into disrepair. With relative ease, Alexander's army felled the once-mighty Persian Empire, a feat that earned him his title. The Macedonian general deeply admired Cyrus and self-consciously sought to outdo his hero. After returning from India, he made a pilgrimage to the Cyrus tomb to pay his respects to the fallen king. When he saw the tomb's sad state, he personally ordered it cleaned and beautified, angrily dismissing the guards of the tomb.

Emerging from the monotony of the dry, hilly plateau on the two-lane highway, we approached a burst of green tall bushy trees lining the road, planted more than thirty years ago in preparation for the 1971 Persepolis cel-

---

[5] The unofficial U.S. Postal Service motto—"Neither snow nor rain nor heat nor gloom of night stays these couriers from the swift completion of their appointed rounds"— derives from Persia in the time of Darius.

ebrations, the part of the ceremony that took place at the Cyrus tomb. At the end of the trees, I saw the tomb in the distance: a white, ringed structure of seven levels set in the middle of a dramatically vast plain. We approached slowly, bumping on the tiny rocks that formed the road, the massive tombstone growing in height and size to its full thirty-six feet as we got closer.

A smiling potbellied guard sipping tea stepped in front of the car and signaled us to park further back. "But please, be my guest for tea and lunch," he said, showing the appropriate *ta'rof* hospitality, though I doubted he had lunch for three people ready in his tiny guardroom. Declining with thanks, we parked the car.

Bits of white, fluffy clouds hovered in a blue sky. Two German tourists snapped photos. An Iranian man leaned against one of the tomb's seven large blocks, his head cocked at the sky. According to historians, the tomb once boasted rings of imperial gardens. Today a vast, windswept plain has replaced the gardens.

The wind whooshed gently as it passed my ears. Up close, the light tan rocks sparkled with flashes of white and splotches of black. Blotches of brown fungus grew here and there. Two cucumber skins lay at the tomb's base, next to an empty Coke bottle.

Somewhere on the tomb, out of view, was written: "I am Cyrus, son of Cambyses, who founded the Empire of Persia, and was King of Asia. Grudge me not therefore this monument." The original inscription, historians believe, read simply: "I am Cyrus the Mede, the Persian king." Alexander the Great apparently decided to change it to its present elaboration, to befit the Persian king he admired so much.

The Iranian whose hands lay against the stone looked angry. He shook his head in disgust. "Look at this!" he said. "This is a travesty! Cyrus is the founder of our country, and look how dirty the tomb is. This is shameful. I come here all the time, and nobody cleans it." He reached down to pick up the Coke bottle.

"I once brought two Iranians who live in America to this tomb," he said. "They were doctors. When they saw the condition of the tomb, they began weeping. I felt so ashamed in front of the doctors," he said, obviously impressed by their profession.

Mr. Zari laughed and retorted: "Tell those doctors to weep for us young people. Cyrus had a good life. He does not need a clean tomb. We need jobs and a proper life." He walked away, toward Davoud, with whom he shared a cigarette.

I sat down in the dirt and stared at the tomb and the plain and listened to the wind. The vast plain and the hilly horizon and the somber lines of the tomb's structure had a calming effect. The simplicity of the tomb created a sense of restrained beauty. It left a powerful imprint on the mind, equaling the numerous elaborately designed shrines across Iran. After a few minutes Davoud sat down next to me. "It is a fine tomb," he said. Mr. Zari joined us. The three of us paused there together, quietly lost in our thoughts as hushed winds swirled by.

I flipped through my notes on Cyrus, the breeze flapping the pages of my pad. I came across a passage I had copied from J. M. Roberts, the eminent British historian, who argued that the Persian Empire gave rise to the first outlines of a world civilization. He says of the era: "We can mark an epoch. Right across the Old World, Persia suddenly pulled peoples into a common experience. Indians, Medes, Babylonians, Lydians, Greeks, Jews, Phoenicians, Egyptians were for the first time governed by one empire whose eclecticism showed how far civilization had already come. The era of civilization embodied in distinct historical entities was over in the Near East. Too much had been shared, too much diffused for the direct successors of the first civilizations to be any longer the building blocks of world history. . . . The base of a future world civilization was in the making."

The twenty-first century will probably be fairer to Cyrus's image in Iran. As the revolution's fire has tempered, the days of polemical battles over the meaning of Iranian history are on the wane. Recently, prominent leaders of the Islamic Republic have openly praised pre-Islamic Persia. During a visit to Persepolis, a powerful Muslim cleric and former president, Ali Akbar Hashemi Rafsanjani, said he was "humbled" by ancient Persia's achievements. President Khatami, for his part, regularly lauds the old Persian kings. Even Iran's conservative clerics, the men who stand in the way of reform, rarely engage in attacks on the country's pre-Islamic leaders. Ayatollah Khalkhali, the cleric who wanted to destroy Cyrus's tomb, is now a marginalized bit player.

As we sat in the dirt, the Cyrus tomb towering above us, I thought about my next pilgrimages, in the northeastern city of Mashhad, where I would reflect on the early Iranian encounter with Islam. The Arab defeat of Iran in the seventh century A.D., one thousand years after Alexander's defeat of the Persian Empire, would dramatically alter Iran's destiny, because the Arab invaders brought with them something Alexander did not: an enticing new faith, Islam. In Mashhad, I would reflect on how Iran, an old, sophisticated power, reacted to the arrival of the new invader and the new faith that would transform the Iranian landscape for the next thirteen hundred years.

Davoud and Mr. Zari smoked cigarettes while a small group of Iranian tourists approached the tomb, cameras clicking. A western wind coasted across the plain, scattering dust and swaying nearby weeds. Davoud and Mr. Zari shielded their cigarettes with their hands, covering the ash from the wind. As dusk fell, the orange sun softened. The sky grayed. The air cooled. We made our way to the car for the two-hour drive back to Shiraz. From the back seat, I watched the elegant white tomb disappear in the moonlit distance. An Iranian pop song scratched on the tape deck. Davoud ate grapes. Mr. Zari looked straight ahead, humming along with the music.

11

Cities: Mashhad, Tous

The Imam and the Poet: An Introduction

In Mashhad, six hundred miles northeast of the wind-swept Pasargad Plain that surrounds Cyrus the Great's tomb, two public spaces, just a few miles apart, frame the broad sweep of Iranian history: one a pilgrimage site for an eighth-century martyred Shi'a imam; the other, a park and a shrine for an eleventh-century epic poet. I went to Mashhad on pilgrimage to both sites.

The shrine of Imam Reza (d. 817), the eighth imam of the Shi'a Muslim faith, attracts millions of Iranian pilgrims every year, as well as Shi'a Muslims from South Asia and the Arab world. Imam Reza hails from the family of the Prophet Muhammad, Islam's holy messenger. Because of the imam's lineage and his designation as one of the twelve sacred imams of the Shi'a Muslim faith, the shrine is the most widely visited in Iran. Its splendor—aqua spires, flowing calligraphy, intricate wall designs, luminous chandeliers, glittering gold domes—effects an almost heavenly air. The British ambassador to Iran Roger Stevens, in his 1962 travel book *Land of the Great Sophy,* calls it "one of the most beautiful, if not the most beautiful, concentration of religious buildings in the world."

Just a few miles away, the marbled shrine of Ferdowsi, the tenth- and eleventh-century Iranian epic poet, shines as an oasis of pleasant gardens, tiled fountains, and large grassy areas in an otherwise desolate landscape. Ferdowsi's masterpiece, the *Shahnameh,* a monumental epic, part myth and part history, that required thirty-five years to complete, chronicles Iran's pre-

Islamic kings and glories in colorful and powerful verse. It ends with the seventh-century defeat of the Persians at the hands of Arab Islamic invaders. For Ferdowsi, writing 350 years after that event, the Iranian defeat presented an unmistakably tragic ending to a great empire, a moment when the universe shifted and "the good became unseemly and the unseemly became good."

In a sense, these two shrines, Imam Reza and Ferdowsi, frame the twenty-six-hundred-year Iranian odyssey: one shrine devoted to an Iranian poet who sang of Iran's pre-Islamic glories, the other to an Arab Muslim whose religion has profoundly altered the second half of Iranian history. In fact, the Arab defeat of Iran in 636–38 divides recorded Iranian history into roughly two thirteen-hundred-year slices, beginning with Cyrus the Great and ending with today's Islamic Republic.

Though the date of the Arab invasion makes for a neat divide in the sweep of the Iranian narrative, history rarely makes such distinctive breaks. Changes come gradually, slowly, sometimes grudgingly, over decades and centuries. The original force causing the break (in this case, Islam) undergoes change, transformation, and cross-pollination in the process as well. True, the arrival of Islam profoundly altered Iran, but Iran also influenced the course of Islamic history, and ultimately, Iran managed a feat that older civilizations, chiefly Egypt and Assyria, had been unable to do: It resisted Arabization.

My visit to these two shrines would recall the transition period in Iranian history when seventh-century invaders bearing an enticing new faith conquered the old and sophisticated Iranian civilization. Iran's reaction to that invasion, its accommodation of Islam, and its struggle to retain an Iranian identity in the new Arab-dominated order would define Iran's history in the ensuing three hundred years and would be the focal point of my pilgrimages.

But first, a funeral.

Mr. Ghassemi's Funeral

"**M**r. Molavi," the baritone-voiced caller said on the other line, "Mr. Ghassemi has gone to God's hands last week. I know he would have wanted you to attend the funeral ceremony."

The call surprised me. I had seen Mr. Ghassemi two months before in Tehran, where I lived when I was not traveling. I knew he had heart problems, but he had told me he felt "in great health and good spirits." At our last meeting, his silver hair was slicked back, curly tufts protruding on the sides. He wore a tie, "a sign of civilization," he always said. I assumed him to be in his mid-seventies. His cheeks sank into his face, his hands were liver-spotted, but he had bright eyes and a quick gait.

Mr. Ghassemi possessed an extraordinary ability to quote long passages of Ferdowsi's *Shahnameh*. Iranians deeply revere their old poets, often sprinkling their conversation with poetic verses, but Mr. Ghassemi took it much further. Strolling through a Tehran park, past gurgling fountains and underneath the green leaves of heavy brown trees, he quoted from the epic poet for hours, his voice moving to a fast, staccato beat as he described scenes of Persian warriors on the march and slowing into a melancholy-soaked drum when he described the Persian defeat.

I met Mr. Ghassemi through a friend, a journalist who knew of my interest in Ferdowsi. "You must meet Aghaye Ghassemi," he said. "Few people revere Ferdowsi as much as Mr. Ghassemi."

We met in a downtown Tehran park and sat across from each other on a freshly painted green picnic table. When I asked him about the tie he wore, he said: "I always wear a tie when I go out. It is my small act of defiance." Neckties are banned in government buildings in Iran (they are a sign of the "depraved" West, a view reflecting both the anti-Western Khomeinist interpretation of Islam and the anticapitalist leftism of the revolution). Ties are not banned in public spaces, however. As a result, the wearing of a tie makes more than a fashion statement. It also speaks a political language. It says to the Islamic Republic: "I'm not one of you; I do not support you."

Mr. Ghassemi described himself succinctly, in short, declarative sentences: "I am a nationalist. I revere Mossadeq. I despise our clergy, but I have religious faith in a Sufi [mystical] way. Reza Shah, our greatest king, was right to attack our clergy. Ferdowsi is our greatest poet. He rescued our Iranian identity when the Arabs tried to swallow us."

Mr. Ghassemi was born in "1921 or 1922," he told me. "We did not have birth certificates then, and my mother does not remember. She wrote the date in a Quran, but someone stole the Quran from our home. My God, how could anyone steal a Quran?"

He attended the university in the late 1930s, studying engineering. "In my university, we all hated the British. We knew their oil company exploited us," he said, referring to Anglo-Iranian Oil Company (AIOC), a British-operated company that paid more in profit taxes to its own government than it did in revenue sharing to Iran.

"We supported Reza Shah, and we wanted to support his efforts to create a modern nation-state, to lift us from our backwardness. At this time we talked of pan-Iranism, of reuniting Afghanistan with Iran. We also talked of nationalism. Ferdowsi became very popular, partly because of Reza Shah's support for him and partly because of the nationalist impulses the *Shahnameh* inspired."

Reza Shah used Ferdowsi the way he used the pre-Islamic Persian kings Cyrus and Darius: as a symbol of royalist, nationalist pride. He beautified the Ferdowsi shrine in 1935 and demanded that the poet be taught in the new secular schools he created, the schools that would send young men like Mr. Ghassemi to similarly secular universities to learn the physical sciences necessary to create an industrial modern state.

But it wasn't just the king who embraced Ferdowsi. Nationalists and secular intellectuals embraced the *Shahnameh* as a symbol of identity, Iran's version of the *Iliad* or the *Aeneid*. It helped that Ferdowsi lamented the Arab Muslim invasion, especially since several leading intellectuals and nationalists viewed Iran's Muslim clergy as a regressive force on society, errant weeds of "Arab backwardness" on pure Iranian soil. Ferdowsi, even more so than Cyrus the Great, was often interpreted by secular intellectuals, nationalists, and the royal family as a chest-thumping nationalist poet who displayed little regard for Islam. In fact, this characterization of Ferdowsi reveals more about the interpreters than it does about the poet's work, which is far more nuanced and subtle than the "nationalist interpreters" allow for. Indeed, there is no evidence of Ferdowsi's anti-Muslim stance in his work, though he does display a cultural pride in his Iranianness.

In one example of the extents these interpreters would go to present Ferdowsi as a nationalist, an early-twentieth-century Iranian nationalist and literary figure of some repute, Ibrahim Pourdavoud, even fabricated a Ferdowsi line to enhance the poet's nationalist image: "If Iran does not exist, then let me not exist!" The emotion-tugging verse became part of a martial anthem, and to this day, Iranians quote the line as Ferdowsi's own, though his epic contains no such phrase.

Motivated by the nationalism of his day, Mr. Ghassemi, the young engineering student, helped create what he called "a small informal association of nationalist students."

"We met weekly and we read aloud from Ferdowsi's *Shahnameh*. We drank whiskey. We wore ties. We talked of a new dawn in Iran, of a day when professionals like ourselves might help Iran rid itself of foreign control. Whether the Arabs or the Turks or the Mongols or the British, someone was always trying to control Iran."

When Mossadeq nationalized the British oil company in 1951, Mr. Ghassemi remembers it "like a dream, a blissful dream." He smiled, as if remembering that heady moment. "The British oil company was a slap in our face. They treated us like their servants. Besides, they did not give us an equitable arrangement, like the Americans did with the Saudis."

"I was working for a private company then. One of my colleagues came running into the hospital. He yelled out loud: 'Mossadeq nationalized the oil company! He did it! He really did it!' We hugged each other. We clapped our hands. I almost think that we would have begun dancing right then if there had been music," he said, laughing. "Our generation grew up fearing the British. Mossadeq defied them. It was extraordinary! Really extraordinary!"

Iran paid dearly for Mossadeq's defiance. A British-led Western oil embargo of Iranian crude choked the country's already tattered finances, leading to an economic slowdown that drew new recruits to Iran's growing Communist Tudeh party. The Tudeh party's support for Mossadeq in his battle with the British alarmed Washington and led to the subsequent unfair branding of Mossadeq as a Communist.

Mossadeq, unwilling to budge an inch in negotiations with the British, faced the prospect of social unrest. Meanwhile, an important ally in Mossadeq's coalition, the nationalist cleric Ayatollah Kashani, withdrew his support. This action inflicted a serious blow to the oil nationalization movement because Kashani could draw the masses to the streets through his use of the religious podium in far greater numbers than Mossadeq or any secular nationalist could.

By 1953, a combination of factors, most notably the defection of Kashani and the growing economic crisis, created fertile ground for an assault on Mossadeq's premiership. The Shah, who seemed powerless as Mossadeq dictated terms to the British, approved a CIA plan to overthrow the "pesky" prime minister. Working alongside royalist generals, CIA agents roused mobs to attack Mossadeq's supporters and display strength in numbers. When the plan seemed to go awry, the Shah immediately fled to Rome.

Still, the royalist generals were not done. In a classified report released in 2000 and printed by the *New York Times,* the CIA noted that Iranian supporters of the Shah managed to turn the situation around. Led by a local Tehran thug known as "Shaban the Brainless," they began to win the game of numbers on the street. Tehran residents, many of whom were frustrated by the economic and political chaos of the postnationalization years, were in little mood to fight, and critically, without the support of Kashani's religious card to rile the masses, Mossadeq's supporters were overwhelmed.

For Mr. Ghassemi and many Iranians, the overthrow of Mossadeq was a bitter pill to swallow and served as an anti-American rallying point for many of Iran's democratic-minded revolutionaries in 1979. Mossadeq, despite a political style that bordered on demagoguery, had made serious attempts to build a democracy in Iran, including his support for a free press that often excoriated the prime minister himself. Most of all, for Mr. Ghassemi and his generation of democratic-minded nationalists, Mossadeq represented a dream of a liberal and prosperous Iran, unencumbered by the weight of foreign interference and progressing toward a society based on laws and personal and political freedoms.

"When Mossadeq was overthrown in 1953, I was crushed," Mr. Ghassemi said. "I felt as if I was punched in the stomach. I heard the Americans were involved, but I did not believe it. I met many Americans in Iran through my work. They were different from the British. They were not arrogant. But it turned out to be true."

When the Shah returned from Rome and Mossadeq retreated into a quiet retirement, the royal court reasserted itself on the political scene. The free press of the Mossadeq era dried up under the royal censor's pen. The Parliament weakened, moving toward becoming a rubber stamp for the Shah.

On the cultural front, the Shah picked up where his father left off, embracing Ferdowsi as a symbol of royalist nationalist pride. The epic came to serve as not just a celebration of Iranianness but as a testament to Iran's affinity for monarchy. Passages and scenes that promoted kingship were read on state radio and television along with paeans to Iran's noble king, the King of Kings and Light of the Aryans, Mohammad Reza Shah.

In the 1960's, Mr. Ghassemi retreated from nationalist politics, still wounded by Mossadeq's fall. Throughout this period, the Shah's increasing authoritarianism disturbed Mr. Ghassemi. But he stayed away from politics. "SAVAK was no joke," he said, referring to the Shah's dreaded secret police. Quietly he supported the National Front, one of many organized groups opposed to the Shah, including Marxist guerrillas, the Communist Tudeh party, and the clergy. National Front supporters, heirs to Mossadeq, tended to be educated professionals, not the sort of people willing to go out and butt heads in the postrevolutionary free-for-all. They grew in stature in the 1970s, but they got pushed aside after the revolution.

"When the mullahs took over, I knew we were in trouble," Mr. Ghassemi said. "I admired Khomeini for his bravery in standing up to the Shah, but I didn't think the clergy should run our government."

Shortly after the revolution, Iran experienced war. "Throughout the war years I tried to do what I could to help, but I was too old to go to the war front. All I could do was help repair buildings hit by Iraqi missiles. I met many war veterans during this time. My brother was a doctor. He helped with their rehabilitation. Their pain and suffering hurt me like never before. I fell into a mild depression."

Around 1992, as he told it, Mr. Ghassemi—retired, restless, and recovered from his depression—picked up a dusty copy of the *Shahnameh* from his shelf. He began reading. He immersed himself in Ferdowsi's chivalrous world of great kings and deeds, of princes and maidens, of ogre-faced enemies and chest-thumping heroes, of grand battles and grand failures, of Iranian heroes and Arab or Roman or Turkic enemies. He also read of flawed heroes and human foibles and tales of morality.

"As I read more of the epic, I came to realize that the work was not just a nationalist tract, as some people tried to portray it. It was a work of great psychological depth, one that explores human nature in a universal way. It was an extraordinary piece of literature, and I thought it was a shame that the government banned it." Actually, the Islamic Republic never officially banned the *Shahnameh,* but its early attempts to promote Islamic over pre-Islamic history, as well as the stigma attached to the *Shahnameh* as the "favorite" of the deposed Shah, sent a clear message to people like Mr. Ghassemi: the *Shahnameh,* with its praise of Iran's pre-Islamic past, is not welcome in the Islamic Republic of Iran.

In 1992 the Islamic Republic made public peace with the *Shahnameh*. President Rafsanjani, a wily cleric who must have sensed the discontent with the ruling clergy seething in society, convened an international conference on Ferdowsi. He invited scholars from around the world to discuss the poet and praised Ferdowsi's work lavishly himself. A shrewd move, it said: "Look, people of Iran, we clergy also love Ferdowsi."

At about this time, Mr. Ghassemi decided to reconvene some of his old friends, the nationalist students, for weekly Ferdowsi readings. "Half of them had moved to America and Europe," he said, "but I managed to contact a few of the original members." He added two new members, and they convened the first meeting of "the new *Shahnameh* discussion group" in late 1992. They met about ten times a year until late 1999, when Mr. Ghassemi told his wife he felt a pinch in his heart and passed away before he made it to the hospital.

On the seventh day after his death a ceremony convened to remember him. In Iran's Shi'a tradition, friends and family mourn on the third, the seventh, and fortieth day after death and, once again, on the year anniversary. Mr. Ghassemi's wife, a devout woman, invited me to the *haftom,* the seventh. She, I found later, prompted the phone call from the baritone-voiced man.

When I reached their house in an upscale part of Tehran, the family was busily preparing for the ceremony. A pair of Afghan servants in black baggy pants and black shirts carried boxes inside the house. Mrs. Ghassemi's eyes watered when she greeted me. Nearby her thirty-five-year-old daughter labored feverishly, assembling trays of sweets and fruit, which were wrapped in plastic and tied together with black ribbons. These would be offered to guests at the memorial service, and the remainder given to the poor in the name of the deceased. I piled into a car with one of Mr. Ghassemi's three sons, and we headed out to the cemetery.

In front of a mid-size white tombstone, a crowd of about one hundred gathered to pay their respects. Most of the men in the crowd wore ties, like Mr. Ghassemi. A black-bearded cleric, young and muscular in a brown frock coat and white shirt, approached the group. Mr. Ghassemi's eldest son whispered in the cleric's ear. The crowd hushed.

"Mr. Ghassemi was truly an honorable man," the cleric said. "He has served his nation well. He has produced three sons and one daughter. He was a man who loved his country and loved his religion. Let us say the *fateheh* [the Muslim prayer for the deceased]." The crowd murmured the prayer under their breath. Mrs. Ghassemi's wife and daughter cradled each other, touching the tomb, sobbing.

The cleric then began a mourning song: "Oh, Father, oh, Father, oh, dear Father," he began in a melancholy voice. "Why have you left us, oh, Father? There is no more light in our home, dear Father . . . Ohhhh, Father, there is no more light, oh, Fatheerrrrrr."

As the cleric sang, Mr. Ghassemi's sons stood erect, their shoulders shaking; his daughter was reduced to a whimpering child. "My father!" she cried. "My father! My father!" The weeping spread, as more shoulders shook throughout the standing crowd, and several women joined the daughter and mother at the tombstone, touching it, crying, touching, and crying, in the typically emotional Iranian style of mourning.

As the cleric sang, the Afghani servants passed sweets around the crowd. Just then a group of ragtag children in torn clothing approached, their hands out, asking for the sweets. The Afghan lowered the sweet tray. They grabbed frantically, knocking the tray over, then picked the sweets off the dirt and grass, and dumped them in their shirts as they ran away. In Iran, poor children regularly go to cemeteries to be fed.

I thought of Mr. Ghassemi as the cleric sang. I had not got to know him well, just a few meetings in a park with discussions of poetry and politics. I looked around at the mourners, trying to find some meaning in their faces, something else I could remember about Mr. Ghassemi through them. I recognized one of the mourners, a tall, thin gray-haired man wearing a black tie, holding a black hat in his hand. We had met once before, by chance, as Mr. Ghassemi and I talked in the park. Walking with his grandson, who looked to be in his early twenties, he had joked with Mr. Ghassemi: "He is at the same age as you when you began chasing girls." Mr. Ghassemi, bright-eyed, responded: "Yes, but times have changed. Be careful, young man, don't get yourself into trouble. This *is* the Islamic Republic after all."

The man with the black hat nodded at me, as if to say, "Thank you for coming." It occured to me that the baritone voice on the other line belonged to him. The small crowd huddled around the tombstone. Mrs. Ghassemi wept. The cleric sang songs of mourning.

Islam and the Iranian Accommodation

When the Prophet Muhammad heard his call by Allah in A.D. 610, the Sassanids ruled Iran. The Sassanids, an Iranian dynasty that emerged in the third century A.D., returned Iran to superpower status after six hundred years of relatively unaccomplished rulers in the wake of Alexander's fourth-century B.C. invasion. The Sassanids created a unified imperial state that made them legitimate heirs to the Achaemenians of ancient Persia. Iran had risen once again to become a world power. As the Sassanid state grew in power and influence, Byzantine Rome looked on with concern. Inevitably, the two empires battled, their armies clashing for land and glory. Rome invested much time and energy into a strategy for a Persian defeat. As the historian of Byzantine Rome Garth Fowden describes it, [E]veryone knew that the worthy enemy, the enemy whose defeat would bring true glory was Iran. . . . The Iranians were not only a real state and a serious military power. They were a Kulturvolk too."

By the seventh century A.D., Sassanid rulers, once vigorous and dynamic, had fallen into the familiar pattern of Near East autocrats: ambitious and effective early kings gave way to later generations of decadent courts, wastrel kings, and oppressive policies. The splendors of Sassanid Persia had been squeezed by this time. The Sassanid rulers treated their soldiers and the general population with disdain, sending them off to ever more useless border wars with the Byzantine Empire. Meanwhile, a corrupt priestly class that perverted the original Zoroastrian faith into a rigid system of caste and ritual helped legitimize Sassanid rule, priest and king joining hands like never before.[1] So as the Prophet Muhammad preached the simple piety of Muslim faith in nearby Arabia, the Sassanids presided over a frustrated populace, disenchanted with the religion of the Zoroastrian priests and worn out by the heavy toll of the Byzantine wars on their treasury. The Sassanid realm tottered, ripe for attack.

Still, it required either extraordinary insight or large doses of hubris for the Islamic caliph Omar to believe four years after the Prophet Muhammad's death that his Arab tribes could defeat the soldiers of the still highly feared Persian Empire. But Persia's fabled riches and the prospect of plunder proved

---

[1] This Zoroastrian alliance between king and priest foreshadowed the later alliance between Muslim clergy and king beginning in the sixteenth century and unraveling in the twentieth, when the priest emerged as king.

irresistible to Omar, who also saw a Persian campaign as a way to unify the myriad squabbling Arab clans that made up the house of Islam. The climax came in 637, at the Battle of Qadissiya, when the Arab tribes defeated the once-mighty Persian army with relative ease and entered Iran as conquerors.[2]

When the Muslim wind blew across Iran, a religiously frustrated population must have appreciated the egalitarian nature of this new faith, which contrasted starkly with the rigid and hierarchical form of Sassanid Zoroastrianism in practice at the time. Still, Iranians were unlikely to accept the faith of an upstart invader right away, even in the spiritual vacuum created by the Zoroastrian priestly tyranny. Iranians remained characteristically proud of their heritage, wary of the "uncivilized" conquerors in their midst, and still adhered to the more positive aspects of the Zoroastrian faith.

The Arab defeat of Iran would have enormous influence on the future fate of the Islamic faith. By conquering Iran, the Bedouin tribes of Arabia inherited a bureaucratic class accustomed to ruling an empire. In much the same way that the early Achaemenian kings borrowed from Babylonian bureaucrats to help administer and spread the Persian Empire, the new Arab rulers of the Islamic realm tremendously benefited from the expertise of Sassanid administrators to consolidate their own empire.

The Iranian influence on the early Islamic empire gathered momentum in 750, more than one hundred years after the Iranian defeat, when the Abbasids, a competing Arab claimant, defeated the Arab Umayyad rulers of the Islamic caliphate. The Abbasids had close ties to the Iranian region of Khorasan, the province of present-day Mashhad. Under the Abbasids, Iranian influence on the caliphate grew dramatically. The Abbasids welcomed Iranian advisers and ministers, known as *vazirs*, into government. A Khorasani family, the Barmecides, became key *vazirs* to the Abbasids, in the crucial early years of rule. The Abbasid capital shifted from Arab Damascus to Persian Baghdad. The Abbasids had Sassanid texts translated into Arabic, Sassanid court traditions revived, and Sassanid administrative methods emulated. The new caliphs also followed the Persian model of establishing a large standing army beholden to the ruler (in this case, the caliph). In a move rich in symbolism,

---

[2] In one of history's strange ironies, the secular nationalist Arab Saddam Hussein called his 1980 attack against Iran that began an eight-year war "the second Qadissiya" and Ayatollah Khomeini called his Iranian troops "foot soldiers of Islam." Though Iranians represented Islam and the Arab invaders a secular leader, the old symbols remained.

an Abbasid leader ordered a rock from the destroyed Sassanid Persian palace in Ctesiphon fitted into one of the new palaces of the Muslim caliphate in Baghdad. As the Harvard Persianist Richard Frye writes, "A complete model of imperial rule was thus presented to the Arabs by the Persian realm, and the Arabs borrowed from Sassanian Iran more than from any other source."

The late-eighth-century Abbasid leader Haroun al-Rashid divided his caliphate upon his death into a western Arab empire and an eastern Persian one, giving each of his sons control of one region. The Persian region's ruler, Ma'moun, invited Imam Reza, an Arab Muslim and the eighth Shi'a imam, to visit him in Mashhad in 816. Shortly after Imam Reza's arrival, he died, the story goes, at the hands of Ma'moun (poisoned grapes the supposed culprit). Shi'a sources say Ma'moun worried about Imam Reza's growing popularity among Iranians after he named him his heir apparent and decided to kill him before he grew too powerful. This might explain why Imam Reza received burial with full honors by the king. Eventually the city took its name from this "martyrdom," Mashhad meaning "city of martyrdom."

Despite the growing number of Iranians in key administrative positions in the caliphate, Arab ascendancy dominated the house of Islam. Arab land remained fiscally privileged, the caliphate in the hands of an Arab ruler, Arabic the language of government, and the Arab garrison towns in Iran still treated the locals as mere sources of tax revenue or potential converts.

As a result, in Iranian Khorasan, a series of local dynasties rebelled against the Abbasids throughout the ninth century. The Khorasani rebellion centered on a bid to fight back the tax collector and have home rule but also included an effort to rescue an Iranian identity in the new Arab order.

For Iran's educated elites, the seventh-century Arab invasion dealt a crushing blow. Unlike the Byzantine elites in Rome's eastern territories who could flee to nearby Constantinople, Iranian elites had nowhere to go, no faraway capital to retreat to. The Arab invasion created in these elites what the Iranian scholar Shahrokh Meskoob calls "a sense of alienation and homelessness." Meskoob, in an essay on Iranian identity, written shortly after the 1979 revolution, puts it this way: "After the onslaught of the Arabs and the fall of the Sassanian Empire (224–651), we Iranians were in a state of consternation, numbness and psychological listlessness for two centuries."

The Khorasan rebellions spawned an Iranian nationalism of sorts. Successfully attaining virtual home rule status, these local rulers sponsored a series of scholarly works focusing on Iran's pre-Islamic identity. Khorasani scholars began writing volumes of history focusing on mythical and historical kings of the Persian pre-Islamic past, rescuing Iranian history from the Muslim view that all history before Islam is *jahilliya,* the age of ignorance. A proliferation of *Shahnameh*s (histories of kings) appeared in the ninth and tenth centuries, depicting a colorful collection of wise, humane, and just Persian kings who reigned before Islam. One noted scholar of this era, Tabari, wrote a book, titled *Annals of the Apostles and the Kings*, in 932 in an attempt to reconcile the pre-Islamic kings with the Muslim prophets.

During this period the Iranian language was also transformed. Iran accepted the Arabic alphabet because it proved to be manifestly superior to its own cuneiform. A new Persian emerged, using the new Arabic script but retaining an Iranianness through adherence to its Indo-European roots. This new Persian immensely benefited from the athletic nature of Arabic script to develop a new lyric Persian poetry, which has bloomed into a vibrant and rich garden of verse that Iranians revere to this day.

The imposition of a new alphabet on an old people was disorienting. The very real understanding that the new alphabet was far superior to their own must have been a blow to the psyche of elite Iranians of that era. Perhaps that is why Iranian elites sought to maintain the roots of their own language, at times fighting the infusion of Arabic words and ultimately resisting the full Arabization of their language.

Shahrokh Meskoob writes: "Only with respect to two things were we Iranians separate from other Muslims: history and language, the two factors on which we proceeded to build our own identity as a people or nation. History was our currency, the provisions for the way, and our refuge. Language was the foundation, floor, and refuge for the soul, a stronghold within which we stood."

By the middle of the tenth century, Khorasani elites openly expressed pride in their Iranianness, differentiating them from their Arab rulers, though testifying to devout Muslimness at the same time. For an educated late-tenth-century man like Ferdowsi, with ambitious poetic aspirations to go along with an Iranian cultural nationalism typical of the elite landed gentry of whom he was a member, writing a *Shahnameh* of his own seemed a logical idea. The poet spent the next thirty-five years writing the epic with the occasional financial support of local rulers. It represented a rescue of Iranian history and language.

Once Ferdowsi's work was completed, the energies of Iranian scholars turned away from histories of pre-Islamic Persia into an embrace of the subtleties of their new faith. Iranian-based scholars contributed immensely to early Muslim scholarship, and Iranian Muslim Sufi mystics and intellectuals proved instrumental to the spread of Islam eastward, especially into Asia. For nearly one thousand years after Ferdowsi, Iranian scholars revolved around the firmament of Islam. All education, even scientific, was conducted in a religious milieu, especially the *madreseh,* the Islamic seminary first introduced in the eleventh century. In fact, the next great scholar to emerge from Ferdowsi's hometown of Tous was the thirteenth-century Islamic mathematician of great repute known as Nasir al-Din Tusi.

By the twentieth century, the attempt by some secular intellectuals to "bypass" Islam in favor of pre-Islamic history faced the crushing weight of Iran's intellectual, scientific, and social traditions rooted in the faith. Still, the promotion of pre-Islamic Persia by the Pahlavi kings and by some leading twentieth-century intellectuals reminded Iranians of their rich heritage. This, combined with the influence of beloved works like Ferdowsi's *Shahnameh,* made it extremely difficult for the new Islamic revolutionary authorities to neglect Persia in favor Islam.

Mr. Ghassemi, a member of the educated modern middle class, came of age in an era when it had become fashionable among certain groups of intellectuals to downgrade the importance of Islam in Iranian history. Today, in Iran, it is not uncommon to find men of a certain class, education, and age, like Mr. Ghassemi, who do not know even the basic principles of Islam. Indeed, they would have a hard time reciting the traditional prayers whispered and spoken all over the Muslim world. Often, they hold their faith in barely concealed contempt, praising the Turkish secular leader Mustafa Kemal Ataturk, who sought to uproot Islam from society. Shortly after Mr. Ghassemi's funeral, I flew to Mashhad to visit the shrines of Ferdowsi and Imam Reza.

Mohammad's Melon Truck Tour

I arrived in Mashhad at midnight. The flight from Tehran, aboard a creaking Russian-made Tupolev, took an hour and a half. The air was cool and soft as I emerged into the noise of the airport taxi pit. A crowd of black mustaches and jangling key chains approached me, saying in Farsi: "Taxi, sir!" "Where to, sir?" "Please, sir, be my guest." I was tired and eager to sleep, so I accepted the offer of the first driver who addressed me, a thin man in a red shirt and black sandals.

On the way to the hotel, the driver, as most do, complained bitterly about the economy and the clergy. "We have nothing. Nothing! No jobs. No money. No means to make a better living! These mullahs are killing us! I have to work eighteen hours a day, driving this damn car just to make ends meet," he said, angrily. "I have a young boy! He is eight years old. I only hope he has a better life than I have."

As he complained about rising meat prices and the "corrupt fools" in government, I drifted in and out of sleep, waking every few minutes to the rising cadence of his diatribe: "worthless tomans," "idiot ministers," "wrecked economy." At some point I cannot recall, I shut my eyes and no longer heard his voice. When I awoke, the car was parked outside a red neon-lit hotel and the driver and my bags had disappeared.

Panicked, I rushed out of the car and into the hotel lobby, where I noticed the sign; it was the same hotel at which I had reserved a room. I saw the driver, sitting on a couch by the reception desk, smoking a cigarette. My bags were neatly arranged at his feet.

"You seemed to be having a good dream," he said. "I did not want to wake you."

Momentarily flustered about how to respond, I tried to give him an extra tip, but he refused. "It's not necessary," he said, handing the bills back to me. "You were asleep. I needed a cigarette. Very simple." Later that night I berated myself for cheapening his gesture of kindness with money.

The next day I breakfasted on hot flat bread, feta cheese, and sweet tea in the hotel lounge. It was a modest hotel. Middle-class Iranians as well as Pakistani and Indian Shi'a Muslims stayed there, within sight of the glittering gold domes of the Imam Reza shrine. I scanned an article in the conservative *Tehran Times* English daily on "Zionist Atrocities in the Muslim Land of Palestine." The article, like so many others of its kind in Iran's conservative press, dripped with animosity toward Israel and "Global Arrogance" (codeword for the United States, replacing the previously used "Great Satan"). Just then, as I read about "Zionist media conspiracies" with the "Global Arrogance," a thin middle-aged Iranian man with hollow cheeks and a bushy black mustache approached me, speaking in broken English. "Hello, my friend, are you from de Pakestan?"

Quickly, I responded in Farsi, hoping that it would send him a message that I was not a tourist to be hustled.

He jerked back. "You were reading an English newspaper," he said, apologizing. "Usually the Pakistanis and Indians read the English newspapers."

He began talking, telling me about his job: night desk work at a hotel popular among Pakistani visitors. "I have learned some Urdu," he said, referring to Pakistan's language. "The Pakistanis love Iran very much, especially the rich ones, the gold traders and the businessmen. They quote our poets Hafez and Saadi. Did you know that their own favorite national poet, Iqbal, I think his name is, wrote in Farsi?"

I nodded, remembering some of my own encounters with Hafez-quoting Pakistanis and the endless paeans to Mohammad Iqbal I heard in my Pakistan trips.

"They also think Iran is so wonderful because they say that Iran stands up to America and the West," he said. "Well, at least *somebody* loves these mullahs of ours." He laughed.

"Sometimes, I give tours to the rich Pakistanis from Dubai and Saudi Arabia. They want to see more of Mashhad than just the shrine," he said. "They make a lot of money in Saudi Arabia. For them, Iran is very cheap."

Iranian *ta'rof* dictated that I offer him a seat to join me for breakfast. The same *ta'rof* routine impelled him to say no, refusing to "trouble me."

"*Befarmah*," I said, pointing to a chair next to mine. "Be my guest."

"Thank you," he said, sitting down, failing to live up to his side of the unwritten *ta'rof* deal.

"My name is Mohammad. Just call me Mohammad," he said. The "just call me" part signaled that he was being purposely informal, unlike most Iranians who use their last names on first greeting.

"I once took two Italians on a tour. They asked me where they could get some wine. We went to the house of a friend who has some wine. They bought the wine, and we drank it together in the park. They thought it was very good wine! They went back and bought two more bottles!"

As he continued talking about his "special tours" and the Italian wine drinkers and the Pakistani pilgrims, I grew to like him. Something in his dancing eyes, mischievous smile, and breezy cynicism endeared him to me. Before I knew it, I found myself accepting his offer of a city tour.

We bade each other good-bye and agreed to meet later in the afternoon. Before he left, he said: "We will use my cousin's truck. I hope you like Mashhad melons."

I found out later that the two statements were linked. Mohammad's cousin, it turned out, drove a melon truck. Mashhad takes great pride in its melons, unique to the region for their tough yellow skins and beloved by Iranians for their sweet yellow middles. Iranians take their fruit seriously. At fruit stands across the country, Iranians poke, squeeze, shake, and smell the fruit, in search of the best ones. As Terence O'Donnell, the American writer who spent fourteen years in Iran living on a farm, noted, "Iranians love the fruit of a good season as much as the Frenchman a wine of good vintage."

A few hours later I waited for Mohammad just outside Malekabad Square. Mohammad had chosen the square as our meeting place, preferring the pre-revolution name, Malekabad, to the current name, Palestine Square.

"Why should I worry about the Palestinians?" he said when I asked about his use of the old name. "I have enough problems of my own."

Mohammad's views were typical of many middle- and working-class Iranians I met, to say nothing of the upper middle classes. Despite the Islamic Republic's vigorous propaganda efforts to promote the Palestinian cause, Iranian people, preoccupied with their own problems, lacking emotional and cultural ties to Palestinians, and unwilling to embrace a conservative clerical issue, have displayed little genuine support for the Palestinian cause. Nevertheless, Palestine squares and Palestine streets crisscross Iranian cities. The government regularly sends aid to various Palestinian causes, everything from transporting injured children to hospitals to supplying some of the more extremist groups with arms and funding. The television news routinely bemoans the atrocities of "the Zionist entity" against Palestinians. The Islamic Republic even placed a "Jerusalem Day," condemning Israeli occupation of the city, on the calendar. But Mohammad, like so many Iranians, cares little for the propaganda. Indeed, the very fact that it comes in the form of government propaganda turns off many Iranians, who might otherwise sympathize with the Palestinian plight.

By 3:30 P.M., half an hour later than our scheduled meeting time, I began to worry that Mohammad would not show up at all. Suddenly a rusty melon truck pulled up beside me. Mohammad leaped out of the truck with a big grin.

We greeted and embraced like old friends. Mohammad introduced me to Saeed, "the tour company's driver," his cousin and a local melon distributor. Saeed and I greeted each other in the Iranian way, one hand on the chest, a slight bow of the head, and a flurry of flowery pleasantries.

"I am very pleased to meet you," Saeed said, bowing slightly.

"The pleasure is mine," I responded, hand on my chest.

"I am your servant," he said.

"No, I am *your* servant," I replied, appropriately.

Saeed was a bulky fellow with big tufts of black hair waving across his head. He had sad eyes and a pleasant smile.

"OK, let's go, Mr. Afshin," Mohammad said. "This will be the best tour you have ever had. First, we will go to Doctors' Intersection. As a journalist, that area should interest you."

When we reached the four-way Doctors' Intersection, so named because of its proximity to a medical school, Saeed stopped the car and Mohammad stood up amid the melons, waving his arms in the air. "See this, Mr. Afshin. This is where the students demonstrated. May God bless them," he said.

In July 1999 student demonstrations rocked the country. In Tehran, Mashhad, and other major cities, Iranian students poured into the streets to protest a police attack on a Tehran University dormitory. During the demonstrations, students chanted slogans for freedom and democracy. Authorities badly beat many students, a few fatally. I remember the harrowing stories they told me of chain-wielding thugs working with the police to attack them. To this day Iranians talk about the summer of 1999's student revolts. Many wonder when the next big revolt will occur.

Had Mohammad seen the student revolts? I asked, standing up to survey the intersection.

"No." He laughed. "I was too scared to go near them. Revolt is for students, not for old men like me. Of course, I support the students," Mohammad added, standing up to face me. "They are the future of our country. It is so sad to think that some of them are in jail now. So very sad. I remember the student protests in 1978 and 1979. They took place near the same area. It is a shame. There is always something our students need to protest."

The car jerked back into motion, and the tour continued with Mohammad providing running gossip on the staff of each hotel we passed: "In that hotel a desk clerk was caught with a prostitute. He left in shame"; "The manager of that hotel is addicted to opium"; "The Italians stayed in that hotel. One night they drank wine with one of the hotel waiters. He still talks about that night with joy."

As we approached Martyrs' Square (formerly Shah Square), Mohammad asked if I would like to see the train station. "It was built by the Germans," he said, "more than fifty years ago. Those Germans really know how to build."

We pulled into the train station parking lot. I walked inside and saw a massive hall with high ceilings and wide, empty spaces where people shuffled, waited, and talked. There was something of 1930s Germany in the station's design, all towering columns and ornate ceilings and intricate white plasterwork on the walls: orderly, white, and cold.

Mohammad gazed at it, impressed. "Look at this," he said, as we walked in the station, staring at the ceilings. "It is beautiful. We Iranians could never do such a good job even if we built this today."

It was typical self-flagellating Iranian cynicism, the sort I heard all over the country. Remarkably, for a people with the capacity for so much cultural arrogance toward their neighbors, Iranians also beat themselves mercilessly as "inferior" to the West, unable to do anything right. In defense, I reminded him of some of Iran's extraordinary architectural achievements.

"That is all in the past, Mr. Afshin. We do not know how to build like that anymore," Mohammad said. Saeed nodded his head up and down, as if to show his glum agreement.

We drank a cup of tea at the station as Saeed and Mohammad talked about their family and children. "Life is hard," Saeed said. "The economy is bad. Prices rise every day." It was familiar talk, Iranian talk, of prices and inflation and economic pain.

Ayatollah Khomeini once angrily dismissed an aide who spoke too much on the matter of economics. "This revolution was not about the price of watermelons," he said. Today, however, the high price of watermelons, meat, cars, and housing seems to be all Iranians talk about.

After short stops at a park and a museum, Mohammad dropped me off in front of my hotel. We embraced and said good-bye. Saeed also emerged from the driver's seat to say good-bye. He bowed slightly, hand on his chest.

"It was very nice to meet you," he said. He reached into his car and pulled out a fat, yellow, heavy melon and extended it to me with two hands. "Enjoy it, Mr. Molavi. I am at your service. It is one of the finest."

I thanked him, slightly bowing, my hand on my chest. I put the melon on the roof of the truck and reached into my pocket, to pull out my wallet and pay for the thoroughly enjoyable tour.

"No!" Mohammad said.

"No! No!" Saeed said.

Here we go again, more *ta'rof* and a battle to pay them for their services.

"I inconvenienced both of you," I said, using the appropriate *ta'rof* language. "I just want to give you something for your children," I said, handing Mohammad a few bills. I had learned a few tricks of the *ta'rof* trade.

"No, please, it is not worthy of you to pay," they both said, almost in unison.

"For your children," I insisted. "Please buy them a nice toy."

Swayed by such a powerful argument, they agreed, reluctantly, though they gave it one last try, repeating the line about how I "embarrassed" them by paying for such a pleasurable afternoon.

"Tell your children that the gift is from me," I repeated.

We said good-bye with the traditional kiss on each cheek.

Before leaving, Mohammad said: "God willing, your pilgrimage to the Imam Reza shrine will be accepted."

Anyone can go on pilgrimage; only God can accept the pilgrimage as worthy.

Saeed agreed, saying, *"Inshallah."* God willing.

The Sunni/Shi'a Split

On Ayatollah Shirazi Avenue in Mashhad, the road leading to the Imam Reza shrine, an array of shrine-related shops caters to the pilgrim. Here one can buy mourning music on tape, prayer beads, rugs, plastic replicas of the shrine coated in a fake gold, and an assortment of electronics, cheap clothing, leather goods, and Chinese-made sneakers.

As I walked down the avenue, I saw the gold domes of the shrine and the towering blue faience minarets pasted against the gray-tinted blue sky. I stopped at a fruit juice seller for a cup of fresh melon juice.

"Are you on pilgrimage?" the fruit juice seller asked.

Yes.

"God willing, your pilgrimage will be accepted," he said. "You will need some biscuits," he added, pointing to his selection. "Just hide them in your bag. No food is allowed in the shrine."

As I approached the shrine, the crowd thickened. Tiny taxis darted past pilgrims. A woman beggar, in black chador, a sleeping child in one arm, an outstretched hand in the other, floated through the crowd, her eyes glazed in a hunger-induced haze. The weather was hot, but not oppressive. Outside the doors of the shrine, blankets were spread across the concrete as families picnicked in the shade of the minarets.

A guard casually frisked me at the entrance to the shrine. A 1995 terrorist attack on the shrine has prompted the extra security. After the frisking, I entered the first of a series of dazzling open-air courtyards. Arched doorways with intricate drawings of flowers and vines led to more splendid courtyards. Beautifully curved Islamic calligraphy flowed easily from courtyard to wall to minaret. Children dipped their toes in a massive tiled fountain in the middle of one courtyard. Inside the prayers rooms, red Persian carpets covered the floors. Pearl chandeliers dripped from the ceilings. On the ceilings, tiny bits of cut mirror refracted light in thousands of directions against the pink, blue, and gold designs on the walls, creating a luminous, almost heavenly air.

Light and illumination form an important part of Iranian Muslim Shi'a tradition, a remnant of the country's Zoroastrian religion. In the eleventh century, an Islamic philosopher, Suhrawardi, incorporated a theory of light into a mystical philosophy that occupies an important place in both popular and religious tradition as well as in the seminary education of a cleric. At the Imam Reza shrine, the intensity of light and color and refraction increases as you go deeper into the shrine complex, culminating in an intense glow just outside the room housing Imam Reza's tomb.

The current beauty of the Imam Reza shrine, the most elaborate Shi'a Muslim shrine in the world, has much to do with its location. Though Iran is the largest Shi'a Muslim country in the world, only one of the revered twelve imams lies buried on Iranian soil, Imam Reza. Hence the Imam Reza shrine has received the most attention of any other shrine in Iran, benefiting from centuries of Iranian artists, architects, and kingly patronage. The other ten imams (the twelfth is believed to be in hiding, to return as a messiah) of the Shi'a faith lie in Saudi Arabia, Iraq, and Syria, a reminder that the Shi'a-Sunni schism of the eighth century was chiefly an Arab versus Arab affair.

Iran came to the Shi'a way much later, beginning in the early sixteenth century, when a Turkish Sufi warrior with Shi'a sympathies, Ismail, took over Iran, established the Safavid dynasty, and secured the foundation of Shi'ism on Iranian soil. Before the Safavid emergence, Iran was a majority Sunni country, although its tradition of mysticism, distaste for Sunni puritanism, and nationalist desire to distinguish itself from Arab and Ottoman Turkish culture all created fertile soil for a new faith to take root. Shah Ismail and subsequent Safavi kings, with the help of imported Shi'a clerics from Arab lands, embarked on the massive (and successful) Shi'atization of Iran. Since then the shrine of Imam Reza, though it is not the most important Shi'a shrine, has benefited from its continuous location in Shi'a Iranian borders and the Iranian taste for lavish shrines. (The shrines of Imam Ali and Imam Hossein, currently in Iraq, benefited from Iranian patronage from the sixteenth century to the early twentieth century, but are now tightly controlled by Iraq.)

The differences between Shi'a and Sunni harken back to Islam's beginnings in the seventh century A.D. The Prophet Muhammad, who died A.D. 632, had no male heirs. After his death a dispute arose over his succession. According to the Shi'a view, Ali ibn Talib, the Prophet's cousin and son-in-law and widely respected believer, expected to be chosen. He was bypassed, however, in favor of three successive leaders: Abu Bakr, Omar, and Othman. Each decision progressively angered Ali's followers, particularly the Othman appointment.

While Abu Bakr and Omar were clearly pious men and confidants of the Prophet Muhammad, Ali's Arab supporters believed that Othman did not represent Islam. After all, Othman was of the Umayyad tribe, the group that originally opposed the Prophet Muhammad. Many Muslims thought the Umayyads had accepted Islam only as an act of political expediency. The Umayyads, to Ali's followers, had hijacked the caliphate.

Soon after, in 656, rebels unaffiliated with Ali murdered Othman at his home in Medina, 250 kilometers from Mecca. Not until then did Ali become caliph, but he ruled an increasingly factionalized community. Additionally, members of Othman's family grew angry that Ali did not vigorously seek retribution against Othman's killer. They forced Ali out of Medina, and he then retreated to Kufa in Iraq. Meanwhile, in Syria the late Othman's cousin Muawiya had begun to plot against Ali, proclaiming himself caliph in 660. Adherents took sides in the conflict between Muawiya and Ali. From this schism, Ali's followers came to be known as Shi'a Ali (the party of Ali), or simply the Shi'ites.

In 661, Ali himself was slain while entering a mosque in Kufa. Shi'a Muslims had their first in a long line of martyrs. The Syrian Muawiya became the de facto caliph of all Muslims. Muawiya, before his death, passed on the caliphate to his son Yazid, another Syrian Arab, who made the caliphate more worldly and less religious. This father-son succession marked the first hereditary handing over of the caliphate, which broke the Prophet Muhammad's expressed wish that the community of Muslims select its caliph (this idea is often used as the basis for the compatibility of democracy with Islam). The caliphate began to resemble a royal hereditary dynasty. Along the way a worldly caliphal court that cared more for empire and palace than for society and justice sidetracked the original mandate of social justice that the Prophet Muhammad preached.

The slain Ali's son Hossein, who lived in Medina, looked with dismay at the extravagance and worldliness of the Umayyad caliphs. He would, he decided, lead an army to defeat them and return the caliphate to the rightful hands of the family of the Prophet, Hossein's hands, as well as back to the goals of social justice that the Prophet Muhammad had preached. Armed with that resolve, Hossein embarked on a pilgrimage to Mecca in 680, stopping in Kufa, Iraq, to discuss battle plans with Kufan supporters. Before he could reach Mecca, however, word of Hossein's plans reached Yazid, and Yazid's powerful army cut off the pilgrimage caravan on the plains of Karbala in modern-day Iraq. There the army slaughtered Hossein and the seventy-one members of his camp, including women and children.

Today Shi'a Muslims ritually, and sometimes passionately, weep for Hossein's martyrdom. In the years before Iran's 1979 revolution, opposition groups of all stripes, even Communists, used the image of the revolutionary Hossein as a means to rile the masses to action, even to martyrdom, if necessary. Hossein's martyrdom forms such a central role in Shi'a history and ritual that Iranians traveling to the shrines of other Shi'a heroes and martyrs, like Imam Reza, call out to Hossein and mourn his death along with that of the martyr they have come to mourn.

On the road leading to the Imam Reza shrine, a hand painted sign carried by a pilgrim read: O HOSSEIN, O REZA, YOU ARE THE PRINCE OF MARTYRS.

Mourning and Miracles

At the Imam Reza shrine, all the color and pageantry and diversity of Iranian Islam parade on display. In front of me, a small crowd of young men in long-sleeve black shirts and green bandannas (green is the color of Islam) marched in tandem, singing a song of mourning for Imam Hussein and beating their chests in unison. "O Imam Hussein, why did they kill you?" the lead mourner sang in a melancholy-filled voice. The young men marching behind him then raised their arms and in unison brought them crashing to their chests with a loud thump, thump.

"Why did they deny you water?" the lead mourner wailed, recounting the events of the tragic martyrdom. The crowd responded: thump, thump, hands smacking chests. "We shall sacrifice ourselves for you, O Imam Hossein," Thump, thump. "O Imam Hossein." Thump, thump. "O Imam Hosseeyyyyyn." Thump, thump. "Hosseyyyn dear, Hosseyn dear!" Thump, thump.

The chest thumping has an entrancing effect. It is rhythmic and raw and powerful and potentially revolutionary. Revolutionary clerics whipped chest-thumping crowds into frenzies in the days leading up to the Shah's abdication. They turned him into the tyrant who had killed Imam Hossein and their supporters into thousands of Imam Hosseins willing to be martyred for their cause.

The Iranian Shi'a mourning ceremony bears a highly theatrical stamp. The young chest-beating men seemed well rehearsed, marching in tandem, their hands slapping their chests at just the right time. One boy in front carried a sign written in red, the color of blood, that said: O HOSSEIN THE MARTYR! Just behind him, another sign read: THE YOUTH OF [THE CITY OF] YAZD MOURN FOR IMAM HOSSEIN. Throughout the shrine, one regularly runs into groups of pilgrims singing or mourning together, with signs proclaiming their group affiliations or cities. In a sense, the religious songs and chest beatings are public performances, and the hand-painted signs tell the world that these particular performers come from Yazd or Tehran or the National Islamic Engineers Society in much the same way that a group of performers announce their city affiliation or university in American parades.

In major cities across Iran, prominent Shi'a holidays take on the air of an odd carnival: groups in black, singing songs of mourning, as crowds socialize and mingle and hand out sweets. In Tehran many young people take advantage of public mourning ceremonies as opportunities to mingle with members of the opposite sex and stay out late. Other young people take part in the mourning ceremonies, beating their chests with a thump, thump and singing the old songs of mourning for the fallen imams. On Ashura, the anniversary of Imam Hossein's martyrdom, street performers play out the events leading to his death in elaborate and colorful shows, Shi'a Muslim "passion plays," widely attended for both entertainment and religious purposes.

I recalled an Ashura play I had seen the year before in Tehran. The actors, in striking green and red costumes with mock swords and shields, played out the events of the tragedy before a large crowd of middle- and upper-middle-class Iranians. On the periphery of the crowd, young men and women flirted; two boys kicked a soccer ball; a vendor sold cotton candy; another vendor sold posters of Imam Ali and miniature Qu'rans; one precocious young boy fired a red beam from a laser gun (a hot toy at the time) at frustrated friends and family, who were trying to watch the play.

When the martyrdom scene of Imam Hossein approached, the crowd hushed, the soccer balls and laser guns and cotton candy were put away, and the previously flirtatious young men and women took their seats. Suddenly, a relatively jovial and distracted crowd had turned glum and attentive. A few people weeped quietly, anticipating the martyrdom scene. When the villain Yazid struck the actor playing Imam Hossein with his sword, cries and sobs peppered the audience. Several of the men put their heads in their hands, shoulders shaking gently. A few women in the front row weeped loudly, tapping their heads with their hands and crying out "Hossein! Hossein! Hossein dear!" In the end, an actor stood up and told the crowd: "And thus is the tragic story of Imam Hossein and his group, who were unjustly slain by the villain Yazid." A few minutes after the play finished, the crowd went back to normal, tears wiped away, eating sweets, and mingling with the actors.

Westerners who have witnessed the Iranian Shi'a passion play are often taken aback by the sight of suddenly crying Iranians, but they need not be: crying is an unwritten part of the play, and in fact, more people put their heads in their hands in a show of pity than actually shed tears. The audience knows its role: It knows when to cheer and when to cry. Regardless of whether the tears are genuine, the people have a part in the passion play just as much as the actors do.

So as I walked among the chest-beating crowd, I tapped my own chest, playing my own role. When I moved away from the crowd, I saw streams of pilgrims, mostly Iranians with a smattering of Arabs and South Asians, walking through the courtyards, moving toward the honeycomb of chandelier-lit rooms, smaller courtyards, and arched doorways that ultimately lead to the room housing the Imam Reza tomb. A big group crowded around the door, waiting their turn to enter.

"It's best not to go now," a young man said as I pushed behind a thick crowd to enter an inner courtyard. "It's too crowded. You will not be able to touch the tomb." He wore a black shirt and green scarf and had the curved eyes of a Central Asian, an Uzbek perhaps.

"Try to come back at night. After nine P.M. You might be able to touch the tomb then. Also, the miracles usually take place at night." He stroked his wispy beard as he spoke. "If you go now, you will only get frustrated."

It seemed a sensible idea, so I moved away from the jostling crowd and talked with the young man in the black shirt, wondering what miracles he might have seen.

"There was a woman with cancer," he said. "The doctor told her she had little hope. She came to the shrine. She slept all night here. A few months later her cancer was gone."

He nodded his head and widened his eyes as if hearing the story for the first time.

"And there was also a man with a bad cough. Every day he coughed. He coughed for hours. His lungs were clogged. As soon as he entered the shrine, his lungs cleared. He began screaming and crying and praying to Imam Reza. People tried to touch him, to benefit from his miracle, but I had to step in and help him get away. There were too many people around him."

He nodded again. "These miracles are true. We have proof. Doctors' notes and X-rays and everything. I work here at the shrine as a volunteer, so I see many of the miracles with my own eyes. When I am not here, I am a trader. I buy and sell goods. T-shirts. Cups. Socks. Anything. I buy goods from the Turkmen traders and also from Tehran traders, and I sell them in Mashhad. It is difficult to make a living. Times are tough. Thank God I am close to Imam Reza."

As we spoke, an elderly man, stooped, pink-skinned, and balding, approached. "My son," he said to the young man in the black shirt, "will you help me? I cannot get past the crowds. I want to touch Imam Reza's tomb."

"I am at your service," the young man responded, "but now is not a good time. Come back at nine P.M. The miracles usually take place at night."

Pilgrimage: Ferdowsi, the Poet

Leaving the Imam Reza shrine (to return after nine), I hired a taxi and headed toward the Ferdowsi tomb. My driver had a gray beard and meaty red cheeks. He looked to be in his early seventies, a few years younger than Mr. Ghassemi. He wore a white skullcap and fingered turquoise prayer beads as he drove. We headed to the city of Tous, just a fifteen-minute drive from Mashhad.

He had just returned from Mecca, he told me, apparently delighted with his experience in Islam's most sacred city. "Mecca is so beautiful," he said, "The sacred mosque is so big and so clean! The floor is all marble, and it stays cool even in the heat of the summer. It is marvelous. It is so clean and so big," he repeated, as he deftly downshifted to bypass a chugging moped in front of us.

The pilgrimage to Mecca, known as the hajj, stands as one of the five pillars of the Islamic faith, required of all able-bodied Muslims, both Shi'a and Sunni, who have the financial means to carry it out. Nearly two million Muslims descend on Mecca's twenty square miles to perform the sacred rites of this pilgrimage, unbroken for thirteen centuries. It is one of the most breathtaking human events in the world. Upon their return, the pilgrims acquire the title Haji, as an honorific. In Iran, returning male pilgrims are called Haji Agha (Mr. Haji) and females Haji Khanom (Mrs. Haji). In fact, the title Haji is often used in traditional Iranian settings, such as the bazaar, as a sign of respect, whether or not the person addressed has ever journeyed to Mecca.

Because the worldwide Muslim population is nearly one billion, each country has a haji quota. My driver had been on a fifteen-year waiting list. "I have no important friends in the government," he said, "and not enough money to buy my way to the top of the list, so I turned to Imam Reza. One day I went to the shrine, and I told Imam Reza that I wanted to go to Mecca. The next year my name appeared on the list. It was like a miracle."

Emerging from the clog of the downtown traffic near the shrine, we drove on a worn highway, past telephone lines and vast plains of tan shrubs punctuated by a series of sugar cube factories, some burned yellow bushes, and the Tus Hotel. The landscape greened as we approached the shrine's entrance.

Two red and green tour buses blocked the parking lot. Haji Agha beeped his horn loudly, repeatedly, angrily. The buses did not move. They were empty. He honked again, holding down the horn for about a minute, the steady noise ringing in my head. Still nothing. On the back of one tour bus, a sign read: GOD REMEMBER in English. On the other, it read O HOSSEIN in both English and Farsi.

Haji Agha beeped his horn for a few minutes, trying to honk and inch his way into a small opening between the buses. A line of cars formed behind us, all of them beeping and inching in a rough symphony of angry horns and slow-moving cars. In a few minutes, a smiling, round-bellied, bearded bus driver scurried toward the bus, waving at us in apology, and moved his vehicle out of the way.

We parked the car, and I asked Haji Agha to join me at the shrine. He declined, not wanting "to trouble me." I insisted. He accepted, smiling and saying, "But I will only trouble you." I bought two tickets, and we entered the shrine.

The courtyard of the shrine had all the symmetry, color, and tranquillity of a Persian garden on a vast scale. Two long, rectanglular fountains with shimmering green tile dominate the courtyard. Beds of tall yellow and red flowers ring the spouting fountains. Beyond the fountains and flowers, a massive white cube stands at the top of a series of stairs on all four sides. This was the monument to Ferdowsi, built in 1935 upon orders of Reza Shah, and refined by his son, Mohammad Reza. The massive shrine's ivory elegance includes verses from the *Shahnameh* on each of its four sides.

As we walked in the courtyard, a delicate scent of roses mingled with the smell of saffron-soaked chicken kabobs from nearby picnickers. I asked Haji Agha what he thought of Ferdowsi.

"He was a great man," Haji Agha said. "Ferdowsi truly loved Iran, and he was also a devout Muslim despite what some people will tell you. My wife's cousin is a scholar," he continued. "He reads many books. Many, many books. He told me that Ferdowsi was not opposed to Islam. He was opposed only to the Arabs." He said the last matter-of-factly, with a shrug of the shoulders, as if it were perfectly normal to be "opposed to the Arabs."

"Look at all these people who have come to see Ferdowsi," Haji Agha said, glancing around. "Did you know he was a poor man when he died?"

Popular legend has it that as Ferdowsi polished off his epic in 1010, a new invader appeared on Iran's doorstep, a Turkic dynasty, known as the Seljuks, that attacked Iran from the east. The new Seljuk ruler saw little reason to reward Ferdowsi for his work, which bristled with anti-Turkic sentiment and had been commissioned by the previous rulers. Just before Ferdowsi's death in 1020, however, the Seljuk ruler had a change of heart. Perhaps he realized the extraordinary achievement of the Iranian poet and did not want to be remembered as the king who failed to reward such prowess. Alas, it was too late. Just as mourners removed Ferdowsi's dead body from his home, a truck of gold appeared at his door.

Since then few Iranian rulers have ignored Ferdowsi. The Mongols, after their characteristically devastating and colossally murderous thirteenth-century attacks on Iran, embraced Ferdowsi, financing colorful and elegant *Shahnameh* volumes much as they supported artisans across their newly conquered lands. They saw their patronage of the *Shahnameh* as a means to add legitimacy to their rule by attaching themselves to Iran's revered poet. Mongol-era *Shahnamehs*, found in museums and expensive private collections, depict Iranian heroes with the high cheekbones and almond-shaped eyes of the artist's patrons. The Safavis, Iran's first Shi'a dynasty, continued in the Mongol tradition, producing some of the world's most exquisite Ferdowsi volumes, volumes that sell for seven figures in Sotheby's catalogs today.

Sitting on the steps of the shrine, I asked Haji Agha if he knew any of Ferdowsi's poetry by heart. He thought for a moment, stroked his gray beard, then began reciting a passage from the famous tragic scene when the hero of the epic, the warrior Rostam, mistakenly kills his own son, Sohrab, on the battlefield. He recited haltingly, stopping to correct himself, furrowing his brow in consternation. "I used to know this passage much better," he said, apologizing.

His choice of verse came as a surprise. Iranians rarely refer to these stanzas, though students of English literature know the scene well from Matthew Arnold's exquisite 1859 rendering of it, in his poem *Sohrab and Rustum*.

"My uncle used to read to us from the *Shahnameh* when I was growing up," Haji Agha said. I had guessed that he was about seventy years old, so the *Shahnameh* readings must have taken place in the 1930s. "He forced us to memorize a passage, and I did the one about Rostam and Sohrab. It was so long ago," he said.

Rostam, the mythical Iranian hero renowned for his unwavering devotion to Iran against all manner of foes, spent only one night in the three hundred years of his life with a woman. The woman, Tahmina, was "a creature lovely as the moon, radiant as the sun and fragrant in her beauty." She was also, ominously, the daughter of an enemy king. From that union came the birth of a boy, Sohrab, whom Rostam never knew by face because he lived in enemy territory. Even so, Sohrab learned of the glory of his father. By the age of twelve, Sohrab had become a Turanian warrior (*Turan* refers to the land of the Turks, in the east), determined to defeat the Iranian kings, subvert the Turanian king's throne, and place his father, Rostam, at the head of the united land. His dream, however, ended tragically.

In a major battle, Sohrab, who though young, already had the muscle and stamina of a seasoned warrior, challenged any Iranian hero who had the courage to face him in hand-to-hand combat. Rostam, ignorant of his opponent's identity, met the challenge. Sohrab sensed that the great Iranian warrior must be Rostam and questioned him as they prepared to engage in battle. Rostam angrily dismissed the question as impudent from such a young warrior, denying that he was the famous Rostam, much to Sohrab's sadness.

After two full days of fighting, Rostam overcame the younger warrior, piercing his heart with a sword. Shortly after victory, Rostam learned that he killed his own son. He fell to the ground, weeping and tearing at his hair.

Arnold's masterful poem captures accurately the spirit of this scene:

> He spoke; but Rustum gazed, and gazed, and stood
> Speechless; and then he uttered one sharp cry:
> O boy—thy father—and his voice choked there.
> And then a dark cloud passed before his eyes,
> And his head swam, and he sank down to earth. . . .
> And his sobs choked him; and he clutched his sword,
> To draw it, and forever let life out.

The dying Sohrab, however, restrains his father from committing suicide, blaming his death on fate and asking only that his father take Sohrab's dying head between his hands.

> ". . . But it was writ in Heaven that this should be."
> So said he, and his voice released the heart
> Of Rustum, and his tears broke forth; he cast
> His arm round his son's neck, and wept aloud,
> And kissed him. . . .

I told Haji Agha about the Matthew Arnold poem. I thought he might be impressed by the fact that a Ferdowsi story had so inspired an English poet.

Instead, he seemed mildly annoyed. "Those English even steal our poetry," he said, displaying the anti-British strain typical of his generation.

We walked around the grounds of the shrine some more. After about an hour Haji Agha looked tired, so we sat down on a bench in the shadow of a tree near the fountain. He was sweating, and I scolded myself for making him walk so much. I bought two orange sodas from a nearby vendor and sat down on the bench with him.

I overheard a man directing a group to the tomb of Mehdi Akhavan Salles, a prominent twentieth-century Iranian poet who, by request, had been buried near Ferdowsi's tomb. Akhavan Salles typified the secular nationalist poet who lamented Iran's fall from grace after the Islamic invasion. He, like many of Iran's secular-minded intellectuals, viewed the disastrous ending of the *Shahnameh,* the Iranian defeat at the hand of Arabs, as proof of the damage they believed Islam had wrought on Iran. In a 1957 poem titled "The Ending of the Shahnameh," Akhavan Salles used a harpist as the speaker, lamenting his instrument, "broken and out of tune," that once played in the glorious empires of pre-Islamic Persia.

Today the harp can only dream of its glorious past, unable to make music in the present:

> *This broken harp, heartsore and impossible dreamer,*
> *the singer of imagination's empty sanctuary. . . .*
> *We are conquerors of cities gone with the wind.*
> *In a voice too weak to come out of the chest,*
> *we are narrators of forgotten tales. . . . .*

The lament is typical of the secular intelligentsia of Akhavan Salles's generation, men and women whose hopes for a democratic Iran were quashed by Mossadeq's overthrow. Akhavan Salles viewed the Shah as a stifling force, a dark cloud hanging over the democratic and just Iran that he dreamed of. On another level, the lament can also be seen as a "cultural marker" noting where he stands on the pre-Islamic versus post-Islamic historical divide. In his opinion, 1957 Iran was no longer worthy of the harp that once played in pre-Islamic Iran. The Persian literature scholar Ahmad Karimi Hakkak notes,

"Akhavan's poem contrasts the ancient glory sang in Ferdowsi's heroic account to the degeneration and decadence that, in his view, mark the present [1957] age."

I thought about Mr. Ghassemi. He had mentioned Akhavan Salles once, calling him "one of our greatest twentieth-century poets." Haji Agha, a man who had come of age in the same era as Mr. Ghassemi, did not know any of Akhavan Salles's poetry.

"I have heard his name, but I don't know anything about him," Haji Agha said. Haji Agha had not attended the secular schools or joined the Ferdowsi reading societies, the kinds of places where he might have met people who wore ties and revered Akhavan Salles and heard laments for a pre-Islamic golden age. Haji Agha, whose associations revolved more around the mosque, did not think that the arrival of Islam somehow ruined Iran, as did several leading mid-twentieth-century intellectuals. Haji Agha prayed every day and made wishes at the Imam Reza shrine, as so many other Iranians.

But he had one thing in common with Mr. Ghassemi: a distaste for Iran's ruling clergy. "They are thieves," he said. "Just about all of them are thieves, except for a few maybe, Khatami and Khamenei and a few others. In general, I don't like them. Their religion is different from mine." It was a common viewpoint. In one Iranian village in the north, villagers told me of distinctions between "our religion"—a tolerant, if superstitious, one—and "the government's religion"—orthodox and rigid.

Haji Agha continued. "I supported Khomeini because he promised us a better economic life. I have been a working man all my life. My father struggled to make money, and I struggled to make money. I thought things would get better. But they didn't. I don't blame Khomeini, but I blame all the thieves around him."

Haji Agha's class—the laborers, the tillers—made the revolution work. They went out into the streets to protest the Shah and his tie-wearing technocrats who promised a rich bounty but offered little to the workingman.

"Now I say, God bless the Shah's soul. The economy was better then. I think it's time that we have the men with neckties running our government again," he said, using a common phrase I heard all over Iran: *cravat-poosha,* the men with neckties—the nonreligious technocrats.

"I go to Khomeini's tomb on pilgrimage every year in Tehran," Haji Agha said. "Khomeini was a great man. I would also like to visit the Shah's tomb [in Cairo] one day and say a *fateheh* for him."

I thought it odd, Haji Agha's professed allegiance to both Khomeini and the Shah, but it was not uncommon. Working-class Iranians all over the country said similar things: "We miss the Shah, but we also love Khomeini."

As we talked, an elderly man wearing a medieval helmet and carrying a sword and shield regaled a group of visitors with verses from the *Shahnameh*. He picked up a young boy from the crowd and cried out, in a poetic innovation of his own: "And then the great hero Rostam saw the new young hero and put him on his shoulders, as his family snapped a photo." The father dutifully snapped the photo. The crowd chuckled. The poetic chronicler gathered his tip.

Imam Ali or Rostam?

Nationalism is a modern phenomenon. It first arose in Europe at the beginning of the nineteenth century. European-style nationalism emerged in Iran in the late nineteenth and early twentieth centuries. At first, Iranian intellectuals embraced it as a tool of independence from foreign exploitation and tyrannical kings. It sparked talk of parliaments, a free press, and individual rights. It helped spawn a revolution of sorts for popular representation and a written European-style constitution. A civil war was fought for these principles, and a historical period was defined: the Constitutional Revolution of 1906–11. A potent longing for freedom mixed with new nationalism to produce an exhilarating, if short-lived, early victory for democratic rights. Of course, European nationalism has an ugly face too: ethnic chauvinism, fascism, war, genocide. This is the nationalism that produced Hitler, Mussolini, and Franco. Though Iran never plunged into depths of nationalist darkness and blood as many European nations did, its nationalism gradually took on a chauvinistic, exclusive, hollow tone. A state-sponsored nationalism emerged in the 1960s. The Persian kings Cyrus and Darius were adopted as golden age icons needed by a centralized nationalism. The country's Islamic heritage was largely ignored.

The late Shah fashioned himself as heir to the great old Persian kings. He presided over an age of massive industrial and economic modernization. The oil riches that poured into Iran with the dramatic 1973 oil price rise only boosted his confidence. In the old tradition, he called himself King of Kings and Light of the Aryans. He was proud of Iran's ancient Aryan roots, perhaps because it differentiated Iran from its Middle East neighbors, perceived to be inferior in the Shah's (and many Persian) eyes. The Shah draped his kingship in pre-Islamic symbols of the Persian past, particularly glorification of Cyrus and Darius. Though he paid lip service to prominent Muslim holidays, the message was clear to Iranians: The only history worthy of their attention was pre-Islamic.

For Ayatollah Ruhollah Khomeini, the unbending cleric turned authoritarian ruler who led the stunning 1979 revolution against the Shah, the golden age of Achaemenian Persia was anathema. He often spoke of the golden age of Imam Ali, a seventh century A.D. Muslim leader whose perceived piety and justice were revered by Iran's Shi'a faithful. Khomeini ignored Iran's pre-Islamic history of kings and empire. After the 1979 revolution, attacks on Cyrus and Darius as "imperialist tyrants" became commonplace. Khomeini, in describing Iranian kings of history, said that "even those who were reputed to be 'good' were cruel and vile." In the culture wars preceding and after the revolution, there was, in a sense, a battle of these dueling golden ages.

The British scholar Anthony Smith reminds us that "nations need heroes and golden ages." In his landmark book *Nationalism* Smith writes: "Heroes exemplify an age of gold, which embodies the ideals to which the present-day leader aspires and which matches the advanced civilizations of the West; and the golden age assures each generation of his distinctive heritage against the assimilative pressures and temptations of modernity, which might otherwise swamp them."

For the Shah, the Iranian hero was embodied in the kings Cyrus and Darius and the mythical hero Rostam from Iran's eleventh-century epic the *Shahnameh*. For Khomeini, the hero to be admired was the Shi'a Imam Hossein and Imam Ali. The Shah's aggressive nationalism and Khomeini's exclusivist Islam forced Iranians to choose, however, between Imam Ali and Rostam, between Cyrus and Hossein. Several prominent intellectuals in the Shah's era chose Hossein and Imam Ali. Jalal al-e-Ahmad, a prominent essayist and writer in the 1950s and 1960s, ridiculed what he called "a mania for honoring the ancient past . . . for competing and boasting vaingloriously and stupidly of Cyrus and Darius, and for basking proudly in Rostam's reflected glory."

The revolutionary and popular intellectual Ali Shariati said: "Our people remember nothing from this distant past and do not care to learn about the pre-Islamic civilizations. . . . Consequently, for us a return to our roots means not a rediscovery of pre-Islamic Iran, but a return to our Islamic, especially Shi'a roots." Today many Iranians are displaying a renewed interest in their pre-Islamic roots, repudiating Al-e-Ahmad and Shariati.

The revolution of course was only partially motivated by these competing golden ages. The rapid modernization initiated by the Shah brought Iran great prosperity—and equally great economic disparity. When the economy began to sputter in 1977 and the mass of rural migrants to the cities could no longer find jobs, they began to listen furtively to the tapes of Khomeini and his golden age of early Islam. Perhaps this ideal of early Islam might provide a chunk of bread, a job, and a decent wage, the rural migrant thought. Iranian students abroad, who benefited from government scholarships, returned home and turned against the undemocratic king who had sent them to the West for their education. The middle class, its rising expectations fueled by the 1973 oil boom, wanted more. Meanwhile, the Shah grew increasingly authoritarian and his secret police, SAVAK, increasingly intrusive. Protests mounted, the crowds swelling, everyone protesting for different reasons: democracy, Islam, Marx, a chunk of bread, economic mobility. The Shah loosened his authoritarian grip, leading to increased public space for protest. Then came the deluge. The government fell, overthrown by a coalition of nationalists and Marxists and Khomeinists and leftist students and middle-class democrats and the urban poor. In the aftermath of the revolution, the Khomeinists won. A new "golden age" was imposed from above. Once again Iranians were forced to choose between Rostam and Imam Ali.

Iranians, for their part, had long accommodated Iran's pre-Islamic history within its Islamic traditions notwithstanding the elite attempts to stoke the differences. A legend grew that the "Prince of Martyrs," Imam Hossein, had married the daughter of the last Sassanian king, Yazdegird, thus seamlessly linking pre-Islamic Iran with Shi'a Iran. In coffee shops across early-twentieth-century Iran, the celebrated storytellers wove tales celebrating both Imam Ali and Rostam. In the zurkhanehs (houses of strength), where traditional Iranian men gather to exercise with heavy wooden planks, the pictures on the walls include both Imam Ali and Rostam.

In an exquisite essay, Dr. Seyyed Hossein Nasr, the distinguished, Iranian-born scholar of Islamic philosophy, religion, and culture at George Washington University, describes the "exceptional synthesizing power of Persian culture, made necessary by its historical experience in being situated between various cultural worlds of East and West." He writes: "Persians have never viewed the more ancient past as something totally rejected by their present-day Islamic culture. They succeeded in absorbing the deepest elements of that past into their Islamic culture rather than rejecting it."

In one of these zurkhanehs in Tehran, I stumbled upon anecdotal evidence of Nasr's assertion. I asked a sweating, heaving mustachioed man what he thought of the duality between Imam Ali and Rostam.

"My friend," he said, "let me tell you a story I heard in my uncle's village. Imam Ali and Rostam took part in a friendly wrestling match. The two men were equally matched, and it was about to end in a draw. At the last moment, Imam Ali asked God for help. God helped him and Imam Ali won the match and the two heroes shook hands and embraced. Only God could have tipped the balance against Rostam. In all other respects, Rostam was equal to Imam Ali."

I had heard the story before. It represented a way for people like Haji Agha and the traditional wrestler to reconcile their pride in Ferdowsi and Iran's pre-Islamic past with their religion. Dr. R.K. Ramazani, the distinguished Iran scholar at the University of Virginia puts it this way: "There is no sense denying the Islamo-Iranic nature of our people. Both are important. One does not trump the other."

For most Iranians, Haji Agha included, these issues of cultural identity, the choice between Imam Ali and Rostam, matter little to their daily lives, which are filled with the normal things that occupy most people: jobs, money worries, friendships, marriages, hopes, dreams, traffic, children, death.

Before I left the Ferdowsi shrine with Haji Agha, I asked him who he thought more important to Iran: Imam Reza or Ferdowsi. Immediately after uttering the question, I wanted to retract it. It was stupid and arbitrary and somewhat manipulative, a question that would elicit different answers from different people. Mr. Ghassemi would probably have said Ferdowsi. Haji Agha said this: "I think they are both very important, but Imam Reza more so, because he can perform miracles."

Nearly one thousand years after Ferdowsi completed his masterpiece, Western and Iranian scholars, led by Ehsan Yarshater, the revered octogenarian professor of Iranian culture and history, are producing an epic of their own, the *Encyclopaedia Iranica*. The multivolume encyclopedia, more than twenty-five years in the making, will chronicle all aspects of Iranian history, culture, and heritage in dispassionate scholarship, neither glorifying Imam Ali over Rostam nor vice versa. For this important work, Yarshater might be seen as a contemporary Iranian Ferdowsi, using scholarship instead of poetry to record the Iranian odyssey. Perhaps most important, the encyclopedia, through its multiplicity of voices and subjectivities and its exhaustively comprehensive treatment of Iranian history and culture, will disarm Iran's numerous one-eyed historical interpreters who demand a choice between Imam Ali and Rostam.

"Global Arrogance" and Green Cards at the Nader Shah Museum

It was still early afternoon when we returned from the Ferdowsi shrine, so I asked Haji Agha to drop me off at the Nader Shah Museum, not far from my hotel. Nader Shah reigned from 1736 to 1747 and instigated a short Iranian revival after years of uncertainty following the fall of the Safavid dynasty in the early eighteenth century. Interestingly, Nader, a Sunni Muslim, believed Iranians were sufficiently Shi'atized that he took no steps to "reeducate" them. In fact, he even contributed to the embellishment of the Imam Reza shrine. His claim to fame rests chiefly on his sacking of Delhi and the magnificently jeweled Peacock Throne he brought back as booty.

A large portrait of Nader Shah, a man of reddish brown complexion, penetrating eyes, and a long, wavy black beard, stuck out most to me among the museum's exhibits. He wore a light brown conical cap bejeweled with green emeralds and red rubies and white pearls. Around his neck he wore a heavy gold medallion. By the looks of the jewelry he wore in this painting, the Peacock Throne was not his only booty.

At about 1:30 P.M., as I sat in the small, leafy courtyard of the museum, eating ice cream and enjoying a cool breeze, a voice boomed over a loudspeaker attached to a tree the radio rebroadcast of that week's local Friday prayer speech. The Islamic Republic uses Friday prayer speeches to broadcast its political views to the public.

Shortly after the revolution, Ayatollah Khomeini appointed Friday prayer leaders across the country. These prayers leaders were selected based on their loyalty to the Islamic Republic, not their knowledge of divine law. Their role is to preach the "party line" to the faithful. The institution of Friday prayer leaders may have had an unintended effect: it separated the "political" clergy from the "nonpolitical" clergy, those who refused to take part in the state apparatus of the Islamic Republic (and there were many). Before the revolution, Khomeini often noted that all Shi'a Muslim clerics are political, but his inability to attract leading Shi'a clerics to Friday prayer posts left him with a middle-ranking group of clerics who were more eager to please Tehran than to spread their religious message. As a result, Iranians widely acknowledge the Friday prayer sermon as a political tool rather than a mode of religious instruction, though a religious portion opens the sermon. The religious section generally illustrates a story that will later bolster the political point.

In 1981, the Friday prayer leader in Mashhad, Ayatollah Hasan Qomi, remained an anti-Islamic Republic voice. He criticized Khomeini and other clerics for being "un-Islamic," especially in the revolution's excesses. He differentiated himself and his traditionalist clerics from the newly resurgent middle-ranking political clerics. He said, "The real clergy does not want power . . . it does not approve of those clerics who govern us. The real task of the clergy is to advise and enlighten the people. Real Islam is the religion of forgiving and of compassion."

Ayatollah Qomi was not the only senior cleric who spoke out against the new clerical order, but his group of traditionalist clerics was gradually pushed aside by the Islamic Republic, which inserted its own voices in the Friday prayer posts of most major cities by the mid-1980s. Absence of the traditionalists in Friday prayer sermons became evident by the sermons' more political and strident tone.

The most important Friday prayer, held at Tehran University, gets aired in full on radio and television. The political portions of the sermons rarely change from typical fare that warns the flock of "foreign conspiracies" and the defense of Islam against Western cultural invasions. Sometimes they lay out a specific government view—that is, a conservative one—on a hot issue, such as border skirmishes with Afghanistan or economic reforms. On this day, the Mashhad prayer leader Ayatollah Ebadi, spoke of the recent student uprisings.

In his smoky, angry voice, the ayatollah reminded his congregation not to forget the "coup d'etat of 28 Mordad in the year 1332," referring to the 1953 CIA-backed coup against Mohammad Mossadeq. "They are trying to do such a thing again!" he railed. "They are attacking the dignity of our people! Their aim was another coup d'etat against us by manipulating our students!"

The "they" usually refers to the United States or Israel. It can also refer at times to the foreign media or the Western world in general. This "they" casts a wide net.

As the ayatollah's voice boomed from the tree, a group of young women at an adjoining table talked animatedly, largely ignoring the speech. I envisioned him stabbing the air with his finger as he pronounced the next line: "They failed in their plot. They should know that today is different from 1332. Today we are devoted to Islam and to Imam Hossein! Today, we have the *velayat-e-faqih!*" he said. "We are armed with Islam against any onslaught!"

At the next table, the women began whispering and looking at me. I kept writing, my head purposefully down, not sure why I had captured their attention but not eager to find out either. Conversations would have to wait, I thought, till I finished following the ayatollah's speech, jotting down notes.

I continued writing, trying to ignore the stares and whispers, as the ayatollah lectured. "They should know that Islam is a force more powerful than any of their arms," he said. "They should know we do not fear them. They should—" Suddenly one of the women, one with a yellow head scarf, stood just above me.

"Excuse me," she said in Farsi, "where did you get that bag?"

She pointed to my backpack, a Jansport with three zippers.

"In America," I said.

"That's what I told my friends," she replied. "Can I see it?"

"Sure."

She examined it closely, as if it were a fine diamond. "This is good quality," she said. "I have never seen that type here in Iran." A brief discussion of backpacks ensued, on the quality of the European versus the American, as the ayatollah's voice filled the courtyard: "We will not be defeated with such trickery!"

Her three friends joined us. They sat down at my table, all wearing their head scarves colorfully and reluctantly, their hair jutting out, their fingernails polished various shades of aqua and emerald. I looked around for any young men in beards, the morals police, who would frown upon such a meeting. Fortunately, none was around.

The ayatollah went on. "Oh, you revolutionary youth, our leaders are vigilant. No need to worry about these tricks!"

As his voice filled the courtyard, we talked. The young women were first-year university students in the arts, they told me, visiting the museum for a class assignment. They wanted to talk about America. One had a cousin in Los Angeles. Another had applied to an American university through the Internet, she said, and had yet to hear a response. Another, the one with the yellow head scarf, said she did not like America but wanted to live in Europe, somewhere like Italy or France, she said, somewhere "romanteek," she added, to the laughs of the other three. Another pulled out a sheet of paper from her bag, a one-page form with a passport photo affixed in the right corner, titled "Green Card Lottery." Every year the United States offers green cards to the world on a lottery basis, a lucky fifty-five thousand becoming eligible for instant residency in the United States. I had seen this form numerous times in Iran, carefully folded and reverentially treated by the green card hopefuls.

She asked if I would help her fill it out, handing me her identity card with all the essential information. As I wrote her name, date of birth, and other essentials, I could hear the ayatollah's voice in the background. "Global Arrogance will never defeat us!" he railed. "Our people are devoted to the memory of the imam and the Islamic Revolution!" I blocked his voice out with difficulty, trying to concentrate on the writing. The young ladies did it easily, it seemed, conversing about class assignments and art as I scribbled and Ayatollah Ebadi lectured. A few minutes later I handed her the finished form.

"Let's hope the luck of your handwriting will benefit me," she said. I wished her well, and the young women stood up, wishing me happy travels. As they walked toward the door, away from the semiprivate museum courtyard back into a more public space, they readjusted their head scarves, covering some of their exposed hair. Just then, the ayatollah cried over the loudspeaker: "Oh, you revolutionary youth, do not worry! We shall never be defeated! Never!"

Pilgrimage: Imam Reza Tomb

In the evening, I retruned to the Imam Reza shrine. The artificial white lights mingled with the moonlit sky and turquoise tile to give the entry courtyard a hazy blue glow. The crowds had thinned, but a steady stream of pilgrims still pushed toward the arched doorways leading to the inner courtyards and the chandelier-lit room of the Imam Reza tomb.

To get to the tomb, I headed toward Door 15, marked "Brothers." At this door men and women, or in Islamic Republic parlance "brothers" and "sisters," separated because there would be too much jostling near the tomb, too much physical contact among pilgrims. I handed my shoes to the shoekeeper, an elderly man who gave me a number and placed my shoes in a cubbyhole. Near the shoe rack, a young man sprayed the air with an aerosol can.

Clad in my socks, I turned into a luminous room with red Persian carpets and a yellow-white glow. Massive chandeliers dripped from the ceiling. Elegantly arched doorways with flowing calligraphy of Quranic verses led to a room with pearl and glass chandeliers, red carpets, and cut mirror work on the walls. Two boys chased each other across the floor, nearly knocking me over as I gazed at the ceiling, overwhelmed by the celestial glow. I was beginning to understand why Arthur Pope remarked that "no other group of buildings in the world gives such an effect of opulence."

The massive doors leading to the Imam Reza tomb, enclosed in glass and about fifteen feet high, towered over me, bright with gold and carved with Quranic verses. In the center of the gold door, a deep blue diamond-shaped canvas displayed more Quranic writings.

I waited amid a thick crowd of pilgrims, to get a chance to enter the room that houses the tomb. I waited my turn patiently for up to ten minutes behind a sea of people. Occasionally, sharp-elbowed pilgrims squirmed past the waiting crowd and surged into the tomb room. It became fairly obvious that patient waiting would not get me any closer to the tomb. With a firm push, some body twisting, and a few well-placed elbows, I managed to enter the edge of the room housing the tomb. Craning my neck above the surging pilgrims, I caught a glimpse of the gold grille enclosure surrounding the tomb. It was scattered with flowers and a few rial notes. Above the gold grille, a wide blue and white band of Quranic verses flowed. A bouquet of flowers perched atop the enclosure.

The crowd pushed and shoved and prayed and sobbed, reaching out to touch the tomb. One little boy simply crawled on top of packed shoulders toward the tomb, kissed it, and crawled back, to the delight of his father, who smothered the boy in kisses. Another man offered his toddler to the crowd, who handed him from shoulder to shoulder until he reached the tomb. After touching the tomb, the toddler, looking a bit shaken, was handed back shoulder to shoulder to his happy father.

On the other side of the tomb, behind a clear glass wall, I could see black-clad women praying and screaming and pushing to get closer to the tomb. Next to me, a young man, a laborer, it seemed, raised his calloused hands toward the tomb. Tears rolled down his stubbled face as he prayed. Nearby, a rail-thin old man with yellowing skin sat in a wheelchair, his hands raised, praying silently, oblivious of the crowds surging around him. An African man stood near the wheelchair, holding on to its back, observing the crowd, occasionally reading from a miniature Quran. In addition to the Iranian pilgrims, I saw Arab and Asian and even a couple of European-looking faces, many drenched in a wondrous light of religious piety, others blank and listless and visibly annoyed by the pushing and shoving.

I decided to move away from the tomb and pushed my way out of the crowd. I wandered back toward my favorite spot, the public performance area, and noticed a crowd assembling around a large wreath and the photograph of a young man, perhaps one of the many young Iranian soldiers who die on the country's eastern borders battling drug smugglers. The government calls them martyrs, and some are given elaborate burial ceremonies. However, a closer look, specifically at their clothes, raised doubts. The men wore well-cut black suits and cell phones strapped to their belts. Two young men wore black Ray-Ban sunglasses with three-day beard growths, effecting the look of mourning rock stars. The women wore chic black Chanel head scarves and lacy black veils. This family obviously had money. It was not the sort of family that would have a young man sent off to fight on a remote border. This family, it seemed, would have the money to pay off the right people, get its son out of military service or perhaps a cushy posting guarding a museum. By the look of their clothes, I might also have been able to guess their politics, not a difficult thing to do once your eye gets accustomed to Iran. The designer labels were a sign of the Westernized elite, the sort of Iranians who speak a bit of English, support reform or outright change of the system, and probably resent the social restrictions imposed on them by the government. Surely, this was not a group that supported the Islamic Republic.

My initial instincts turned out to be right. They had come to mourn the son of a wealthy businessman who had "connections in Europe," I was told.

He had been killed in a car accident, and they buried him in a tomb near the Imam Reza shrine reserved for the extremely pious or extremely rich. Later, I asked a friend who knew the Mashhad business community well about the businessman. I found out that he was a well-connected trader, a Westernized Iranian who moved in powerful circles before the revolution and who quickly adapted to postrevolution life. As my friend put it, "Before the revolution, he knew whose hands to line with cash, and after the revolution, he learned the new hands he had to pay. It made no difference to him, though he preferred the social freedoms of the Shah's era."

Interestingly, despite his Westernized exterior, the businessman still sought the most religiously important burial site for his son: a cemetery near the Imam Reza tomb. Though it might be argued that he chose the cemetery as a "a status symbol," much like rich Christians in the West might choose an affluent cemetery for their own loved ones, I saw numerous examples of Westernized, secular-minded Iranians suddenly becoming very religious in moments of crisis (not unlike secular Christians or Jews in the West).

I recalled another Westernized Iranian, an elderly doctor whom I had met a few weeks before my Mashhad trip. He had warned me to "not spend too much time with the mullahs and Islam. You must read Ferdowsi. He is a true Iranian hero!" I had told him that I planned to visit the Ferdowsi shrine and the Imam Reza tomb. "Spend more time at the Ferdowsi shrine. It will be more important for your writing," he had said, dismissing the Imam Reza shrine as "a place of superstition."

Shortly before my trip to Mashhad, I called him. He was feeling a bit anxious. His wife was in the hospital with flulike symptoms that would not go away.

"She is very old. I am worried. Are you still going to the Imam Reza shrine?" he asked.

"Yes."

"Please say a prayer for my wife."

I assured him I would.

As the mourning ceremony for the young man continued, I said a prayer for him. I also made good on my promise to say a prayer for the doctor's wife. In his name, I dropped a few bills in a charity box, saying the appropriate prayer as the bills fell. I walked away, into a small prayer room nearby. There, a group of sinewy laborers with sun-baked faces were stretched out on the carpet, sleeping. Tired from a long day of walking in the sun, I lay down with them, closed my eyes, and drifted to sleep, lulled by the quiet whisper of an African pilgrim reading from the Quran.

111

Cities: Tehran, Neishapour

The Politics of Personal Apearance

Ali Reza, like many sixteen-year-old boys, had a pimple problem. "Too much chocolate," he said, explaining it away at the time. So he stopped eating chocolate entirely, even scraping the chocolate sauce off his mother's special cream puffs. "But the pimples did not go away," he said glumly, "for two years!" By the time he turned eighteen, he grew seriously concerned and consulted a doctor. "I didn't like the pimples. I felt that many people laughed at me behind my back. I tried every medicine, but it did not work. Every morning, I woke up and prayed before looking in the mirror, but the pimples were still there."

One day he just stopped shaving. "I thought that a beard would hide the acne until it went away for good." University classes were to begin in a month. He would have a clean slate, a new group of people who did not know the old pimply Ali Reza. A few weeks before the university began, he had grown a relatively bushy beard.

At the university Ali Reza faced some unexpected opposition to his new look. A few of his high school chums teased him. "Have you become one of *them*?" A girl from his neighborhood saw him outside the university and exclaimed: "My God, Ali Reza, your beard! What will people think?" His fellow arts students either shunned him or looked at him with confusion.

He laughed, reflecting on the story as he told it to me two years later. "Many people thought I had become Hezbollahi," he said, using a term widely used by Iranians to denote a radical religious conservative who supports the conservative wing of the Islamic Republic. "That's why they reacted so negatively."

Ever since the Prophet Muhammad wore a beard in the seventh century, Islamic tradition held that pious men would do the same. In Afghanistan, where Islamic extremists known as the Taliban terrorized its citizens for five years from 1996 to 2001 in a twisted, thuggish version of Islam, the lack of a beard of a proper length was punishable by lashing. Iran has no rules on beards, nor do any other Muslim countries, but after the country's 1979 revolution, many of the religious-minded revolutionaries grew beards, and in many Muslim countries, the beard remains a symbol of piety.

Today none of Ali Reza's friends—liberal-minded arts students—wears a beard. They view it as a symbol of the hard-line students on campus, the "Hezbollahi" types that try to impose their social morality on others, the ones who lash out at female students who show too much hair from their head scarves or sneer at what they deem to be "Westoxicated," jeans-wearing students like Ali Reza.

The Hezbollahi types often are members of the college Basiji association. The Basijis, first created as a volunteer fighting force in the Iran-Iraq War, proved instrumental in Iran's war effort through the willingness of these mostly working-class urban and rural youths to "martyr" themselves for the cause. Key chains wrapped around their necks—the keys to heaven—some Basijis cleared minefields in acts of religious devotion, crying out to Imam Hossein, the Shi'a martyr, as explosions tore their bodies. Of course, not all Basijis fought in the name of Islam; many fought out of nationalist impulses. Morever, today not all Basijis are hard-line Hezbollahi types; in fact, the majority are not, including numerous Basijis whom I met who proved to be some of the most generous and noble people. Iranian journalists note that most Basijis support President Khatami and reform, though they tend to focus more on political reform and less on issues of social freedom.

Just about every Iranian city has a local Basiji organization, volunteers who act alternately as social service providers, public religious ceremony organizers, and—more ominously—morals police. It is this last role of the Basijis, as public purveyors of morality, that turns off Ali Reza and his friends and so many Iranians, tarnishing the reputation of all Basijis. The morals police punish youths for attending mixed sex parties, for listening to Western music, for walking in a park with unrelated members of the opposite sex. Enforcement of these "laws" varies from lax to severe. In the late summer of 2001 the morals police, backed by Iran's ruling conservatives, went on a rampage, publicly flogging youths for such offenses as drinking alcohol or going to parties, and demanded that restaurant owners refuse entry to women not wearing "proper" Islamic coverings.

In 1988 Iran's conservative ruling clergy decided to set up college Basiji organizations to fight a cultural and political war on campus against what they viewed as creeping "Westoxication" and potential student agitation against the government. Basijis gained easier acceptance to the university than before. Basiji groups, linked to conservative leaders, cropped up on college campuses. Though they represent a minority of students, they carry heavy weight because of their high-level connections up to the Supreme Leader, Ayatollah Khamenei, and their informal links with the security services and police. During the 1999 summer student protests, some members of the Basijis joined with police to quell the uprising.

Ali Reza continued. "I don't blame my friends' reactions," he said. "I would probably think the same. I do not like the young men with beards, the Basijis with the Hezbollahi look and attitude. They are too self-righteous, and they are confrontational."

The Hezbollahi look is familiar to Iranians. It consists of a simple, non-fashionable, collared shirt (Hezbollahis should not be interested in Western fashion), plain slacks (never jeans), and plain black shoes or slippers. The shirt must never be tucked into the pants. Also, a Hezbollahi might wear a black-and-white Palestinian-style scarf in the winter, a symbol of Iran's war with Iraq and solidarity with the Palestinian cause. He almost always has a beard or at least a three-day growth. Not all Basijis effect the Hezbollahi look, but those that do are often the ones who relish their role as morals police.

Ali Reza went on. "I think I confused people because I wore jeans and nice shirts and fashionable black shoes, yet I had this Hezbollahi beard," he said, laughing. "I knew some of my fellow arts students were uncomfortable with it. Many of us have had bad experiences with Hezbollahi types. I thought that maybe I could grow a Sufi beard, which is different from the Hezbollahi beard," he said. The Sufi (mystical) beard tends to curl at the mustache area and flow more freely, even recklessly. It is a beard favored by Sufi mystics as well as artists and writers.

"But I had grown tired of my bearded look anyway, so I decided to shave it," he said, today displaying his thin, acne-cleared cheeks. "One day the pimples just disappeared! Sometimes I get a few, but not like before."

Ali Reza's beard experience taught him an important lesson in Iran's politics of personal appearance. In Iran the clothes you wear and how you cut your hair or beard often define your politics. Even if they don't, as in Ali Reza's case, the perceptions remain.

In an authoritarian government that interferes in the personal lives of its citizens, as does the Islamic Republic, clothes become an important symbol of politics. Mr. Ghassemi's tie was a political statement, as are the clothes of a Hezbollahi.

Women are on the front line of this politics of personal appearance because of the *hijab,* the mandatory Islamic covering placed upon them. As a result, the woman draped in a black chador, the most severe form of *hijab,* has become the most visible symbol of the Islamic Republic to the outside world. After President Khatami's first election in 1997, when the veils started to slip and the makeup became more pronounced and colorful, diplomats and political observers saw it as defiance of the revolution. There seems to be an undefined "veil-o-meter" that gauges the mood of the country and its leaders by looking at the relative adherence to the veil. Bright toenail polish in open-toed sandals has also become part of the "veil-o-meter" gauge. In fact, I heard a mullah in a Tehran mosque rail for more than fifteen minutes against the temptations of brightly polished toenails. It was sad to me to hear this man of the cloth, one who represented an old and noble faith, reduced to worries about toenail polish.

Ayatollah Khomeini was a proud advocate of the *hijab.* He once remarked that if nothing else, the veiling of women was a great victory for the revolution. The issue of *hijab* is complicated. Some Iranian women adhere to it voluntarily and would do so even if it were not the law of the land. There are others, a significant number, who see forced *hijab* as a blatant violation of their most basic civil rights. The Quran, Islam's holy book, is ambiguous on the matter. It recommends only that women dress modestly, without clear specifications on what that means. The veil, some Islamic scholars point out, is an accretion from pre-Islamic Byzantine Rome or Sassanian Persia, societies that veiled their noblewomen. Others point out that the patriarchy of traditional societies has as much to do with veiling as does religion. Whatever the case may be, female veiling has come to be seen as an integral element of the faith, and early Islamic jurists, acting after the death of the Prophet Muhammad, wrote it into law. Women dressed in *hijab* are the most visible reminder that the Islamic Republic is still in power.

As a result of this politics of personal appearance, Iranians have come to refer to three types of woman, defining their politics by the clothes they wear: the chadory, the manteauy, and the *maghna'eh-poosh*. The chadory woman wears the most severe covering in layers of black that require a hand to hold the cloth from the inside, thus preventing the chadory woman from working. The chadory tends to be socially conservative and less inclined to support social reforms. The widespread Iranian view in the politics of personal appearance lumps chadory women with Iran's ruling conservatives, though I found several exceptions to this rule. Rarely, however, did I find a chadory who agitated for meaningful social reform.

In contrast, the manteauy woman wears the loose-fitting manteau, often fashionably with a colorful, loosely tied head scarf. She generally supports both political and social reform. The manteauy woman might speak foreign languages, is usually educated, and tends to hail from Iran's modern middle and upper classes. In Iran's politics of personal appearance, the manteauy woman is believed to be either opposed outright to the Islamic Republic or favoring the reform movement.

The *maghna'eh-poosh* lies somewhere between the two. She wears a loose-fitting manteau that frees her arms for work but a tight-fitting scarf that covers all her hair. She tends to be more liberal than the chadory but less than the manteauy. Often she hails from the more socially conservative traditional middle classes. She is an active participant in the workplace and generally favors the reforms of President Khatami.

Interestingly, the religious-minded manteauy woman (and there are many; one must not confuse opposition to the government with irreligion) often dons the chador when she visits the shrines of Shi'a saints. Iran's younger manteauy woman must wear the *maghna'eh,* the tighter head scarf, in the workplace and on the university campus. Many manteauy young women carry the *maghna'eh*s with them, in their bags, and reluctantly place them on their heads as they enter university grounds.

Regardless of whether a woman chooses to be a chadory, manteauy, or *maghna'eh-poosh,* she has no right to discard some form of veil altogether. Many Western scholars of Iran say the veil is not the issue. It is the laws that do not grant women equal rights or that do not grant them even the same protections they had before the revolution. The scholars have a point, but what more basic human right is there in the twenty-first century than choosing how you want to dress? If the law on *hijab* were lifted, who knows how many Iranian women would unveil entirely, but it seems to me they deserve the same right as women in other Muslim countries, excluding Saudi Arabia, who have the legal option to choose (of course, patriarchal societies and family pressures in many Islamic countries make that legal right meaningless).

By making the *hijab* such a critical part of the Islamic Republic's propaganda, however, there appears to me little way that it could be discarded entirely. The republic has boxed itself in. Lifting the *hijab* would signal a severe defeat for it, a repudiation of Ayatollah Khomeini. While the conservative ruling clergy has made room for talk of limited democracy, it is certainly not ready to give up its "God-given" right to veil its women.

A "Blasphemous" Play

While I was in Mashhad, a controversy had erupted in Tehran over a student play that allegedly insulted the Hidden Imam, Shi'a Islam's messiah-like figure who had gone into hiding 1,125 years ago and whom the faithful expect, like any messiah, to return and bring justice to the world. Hard-liners in the government attacked the play, blaming the newly liberalized press for creating "a climate of blasphemy." Reformists countered that Iran's hard-liners were recklessly creating a national crisis over a minor student publication. The controversy erupted into the latest row between the two sides, breathlessly reported in the newspapers.

The student's script—it had never made it to the stage—was actually a satire on Iran's tough college entrance examinations. In the play a young man meets the long-awaited Hidden Imam, who informs him that he has been selected to help bring justice and order to the world. The young man balks. He has college entrance exams the next day, he tells the imam. He has studied obsessively, he explains, and cannot afford to miss them. He then turns to the imam and asks: "Can't we save the world next week?"

Iran's yearly college entrance exams overwhelm Iranian teenagers and their families with anxiety. Of the 1,500,000 Iranians who sat for the exams in 2000, only 130,000 were accepted. The exam results not only designate those who gain or lose dear spots in the university but also determine a student's future course of study and therefore his life. The young man in the play, like most young Iranians, could think of nothing else—not even redemption and an opportunity to save the world.

I decided to head back to Tehran, to break away momentarily from my next pilgrimage—the tomb of the eleventh-century poet, astronomer, and mathematician Omar Khayyam in the nearby city of Neishapour—in order to look into the matter of the "blasphemous" play. The controversy seemed relevant to my next pilgrimage because Khayyam also angered religious puritans for poetry deemed "blasphemous." One contemporary critic called his poems "beautiful snakes, outwardly attractive, but inwardly poisonous and deadly to the Holy Law."

For the Iranian writer, whether a budding student playwright or a legendary eleventh-century poet, the religious puritan has been a frequent critic. Today in Iran journalists and writers routinely confront accusations of "insulting Islamic sanctities." Over so many Iranian writers throughout history, the religiously orthodox critic has cast a long shadow. It grew even longer after the 1979 revolution, when the cleric usurped the Shah, who himself had quashed free thought.

I booked a flight back to Tehran. During the one-and-a-half-hour flight, I caught up on news related to the controversy. The student playwright and the editor of the student publication that published the script languished in jail pending trial. Hard-liners stepped up their attacks on Iran's minister of culture and Islamic guidance, Ataollah Mohajerani, who vigorously supported free speech. Mohajerani fought back, telling one reformist newspaper: "These attempts to control information are futile. You cannot put the chick back in the egg."

The reformist and conservative power struggle heated up. The latest row reflected an important struggle taking place in Iran: the battle for free speech and, even more important, free will. I also thought it would make for a good newspaper story for the *Washington Post,* the paper I wrote for at the time. Hard-liners called the play blasphemous, "an insult to Islamic sanctities." Such harangues are aimed at writers, of course, but also at anyone who crosses a line that the hard-liners deem uncrossable. They assure Iran's youths, who are legally prohibited from dancing, mingling with members of the opposite sex, or listening to Western music, that these acts are "insults to Islamic sanctities." I once asked a clergyman in Qom, Iran's holy city, about this issue (one of the hard-line clergyman, mind you): "There is no free will," he said. "There are only laws of the Islamic Republic. The youth must obey them."

But most young people don't buy it and continue to do what the Islamic Republic tells them not to. Some have turned away from religion as a result of the strict prohibitions. Others, a large number, have turned to Sufism, a more mystical and personal path toward God and one with a long history in Muslim lands, especially Iran.

I decided to pay a visit to the leafy campus of Amir Kabir University, where the allegedly blasphemous playwright studied. I wanted to see how his friends and fellow students felt about his jailing, ask them what issues the play raised. I also wanted to learn more about the student, perhaps to find a motive in his play. All these questions intrigued me. The answers lay in Tehran.

But first the phone rang.

Dance Party

"**A**fshin, we are having a big party on Thursday! Everyone will be there! Music! Dancing! Even Mr. Johnnie Walker might show up! You must come!"

The excited voice on the other end of the line was Mehran, a twenty-five-year-old Tehran resident who always seemed to be throwing "a big party."

"We will have a DJ. Many girls! It will be great. You have been spending too much time with mullahs and politics and your books. You need to shake your hips a little bit! You need to party Tehran-style!"

Mehran lives in affluent North Tehran, scene of some of the most raucous youth parties. A North Tehran youth party is the Islamic Republic's worst nightmare: hip-shaking boys and girls, sometimes drunk, dancing to Western music blaring from sophisticated sound systems, snubbing their nose at the conservative values imposed from above.

I arrived late to Mehran's party. "Come in," he said, smiling, slightly buzzed. "Join the fun!"

The party was rocking. Boys in gelled hair and jeans, girls in trendy black pants and slinky dresses and red lipstick, moving and swaying on a large red Persian carpet-cum-dance floor, with Latin pop sensation Ricky Martin's voice booming.

Ricky Martin sang: "Go, go, go! *Allez, allez, allez!* Here we go! *Allez, allez, allez!*"

The DJ, a twenty-year-old named Keyvan, exhorted the people on the couches to get up and join the fun. "Everyone! I want to see everyone on the dance floor," he yelled. "C'mon. Go, go, go!"

The youth waved their hands in the air. *"Allez, allez, allez!"*

Keyvan responded: "Here we go!"

The group: *"Allez, allez, allez!"*

Ricky Martin's Latin pop hit preceded Madonna, a sampling of European dance hits ("just released in Paris," Keyvan proudly told me), and Iranian pop songs from Los Angeles. The dance floor thumped.

Leila, a twenty-one-year-old university student, exclaimed loudly: "I love you, Keyvan! You are the best DJ!"

Hamid, who was dancing with Leila, reached out to give Keyvan a high five.

Amid the noise and dancing, Mehran took me aside and offered me a beer. "Mr. Johnnie Walker could not make it," he said apologetically. "Maybe next time. This Turkish beer is not bad, though."

Mehran buys his alcohol, as do many Iranians, from Armenian Christians in Tehran. Armenians are allowed to have alcohol in their homes, so a few entrepreneurs have used this privilege to sell to their thirsty Muslim compatriots.

"The Armenian said he is out of Johnnie Walker," Mehran said.

Leila, a philosophical young lady, wondered what all the fuss was about Johnnie Walker. "I don't drink much, but I think wine is the best drink," she said, wiping away dance sweat from her brow. "Our great poets drank wine and wrote their beautiful lines with their brains soaked with wine. Wine makes me think deeply. Why is there no wine here?"

"The Armenian had only beer and *aragh*," Mehran said, referring to a vodka-like drink that was a favorite of an older generation of Iranian men. "Besides, you are already intoxicated with your love for Hamid." He laughed.

Leila reddened. Hamid, within earshot, smiled. Keyvan, the DJ, spun a rap song.

The party progressed, with more dancing and flirting, several requests to me for help to "get out of this country," and a special treat: DJ Keyvan singing one of his own songs, a heart-tugging love ballad. It was a relatively tame party: no drugs, no dirty dancing, not much drinking, no kissing, just a group of twentysomethings dancing and laughing.

"Are you having fun, Afshin?" Mehran asked, always the attentive host. "You see, we know how to have fun in Iran!"

Suddenly there was a buzzing sound. It was repetitive, agitated. Someone was at the door. The group hushed. Keyvan stopped in mid-ballad. A few young women scurried upstairs. "Oh, my God," Leila said. "I hope it's not them."

Yes, it was "them," the morals police.

Mehran and the other party host walked across the courtyard of their house. I followed. They opened the door. A young man with a beard, wearing a green jacket, his motorcycle leaned up against the wall, smiled.

"My friends, are you having a party?" he said.

Poker-faced, Mehran said: "No, we are not. My cousin is here from Germany. We put on a little music to celebrate her arrival. That's all."

The young police officer looked unconvinced.

"Here is a little something for you," Mehran said, handing him a few bills. "Thanks for your vigilance. We will lower the music."

"Yes, definitely lower it," the police officer said, "and give my regards to your cousin," he said sarcastically.

When they closed the door, they smiled, raised their hands for a high five.

They walked back into the house. Everyone was quiet, perhaps wondering if the vans awaited them outside, the vans that would take them to a detention cell for the night, charged with "insulting Islamic sanctities in a depraved party."

Mehran smiled. The room let out a sigh of relief. "Where is everyone? This is a party!"

He turned to Keyvan, nodding. The DJ inserted a CD. Ricky Martin's voice boomed: "Go, go, go!" The women came running downstairs, a few still wearing the head scarves they had placed on their heads in fear of a raid.

"C'mon, everyone!" DJ Keyvan said. "Dance!"

Campus Politics

ehran and his friends occupy the elite strata of Iranian youth. They grew up in wealthy North Tehran, watching MTV on their satellite dishes, playing the latest video games, listening to Western music. They have cousins who live in the United States and Europe. Their parents make sneering references to *akhoond-ha,* the ruling clerics. They speak fairly good English. They occasionally travel outside the country, to Europe, to America, to places where dancing is not a crime.

Abbas, the jailed student playwright, hails from a different background, the more socially conservative traditional middle class, which largely supported Khomeini in his efforts to topple the Shah. Abbas never went to mixed dance parties, did not drink, and prayed regularly. Yet he, like Mehran and his friends, voted for President Khatami and supports the idea of Iranian democracy.

Abbas joined an Islamic association when he entered the university. The group, Anjoman-e-Eslami, supported President Khatami's democratic reforms. It sponsored lectures by prominent reformists on campus, including the highly controversial and popular Islamic philosopher Abdol Karim Soroush, who argues, among other things, that clergy participation in politics has polluted the Islamic faith.

Hard-liners have attacked Soroush on numerous occasions when he tried to speak. One of those times, Amir, a friend of Abbas's, got caught up in the fighting. He described the scene this way: "They came in and started throwing chairs. They rushed toward the stage to attack Soroush. Several of us ran to the stage to protect him. We made a human chain around Soroush as they beat us with their fists and clubs. Thanks to Allah, Soroush made it out the door unscathed."

The group that attacked Soroush is known as the Ansar-e-Hezbollah (Helpers of the Party of God). It is a small fringe group, perhaps one hundred Tehran members at most, yet it skirts the normal rules of the law because of its shady links with police and security services and high-level conservative clerics. In fact, the Ansar's attack on a student dormitory in 1999 precipitated the nationwide summer student protests that rocked the country. In effect, the Ansar consists of hired hitmen, and its current patron is a small clique of extremely hard-line clerics, merchants, and officials, who view reform as a grave threat to their power and their access to Iran's oil wealth.[1] Many believe that even Iran's supreme leader, Ayatollah Khamenei, does not control the

---

[1] Reports surfaced that wily President Rasfanjani paid the Ansar to attack his own daughter's parliamentary campaign in 1996. Why? He knew an Ansar attack would make her more popular, given the distaste with which the Ansar is held in the population. It worked, propelling the already formidable Faezeh Hashemi to the top vote getter in 1996.

Ansar, one of the few areas he cannot flex his muscle. The Ansar is one piece of the security force that gives hard-liners the ability to act with relative impunity, the others being the military, the police, some elements of the Intelligence Ministry, and some of the Hezbollahi Basijis.[2]

"Abbas is a religious young man," Amir explained as we sat, cross-legged, on the floor in the campus offices of the Anjoman-e-Eslami. "He certainly did not mean blasphemy. The play was a satire on the pressure of the konkur," he said, referring to the college entrance examinations.

I looked around the small room: a computer, a printer, a teapot, and a telephone, all on the carpeted floor. Amir poured me a cup of tea and continued. "This is just a political move by the conservatives. They don't care about the play. They are just trying to create political crises so they can undermine Khatami and the reformists. If they create enough chaos, maybe Khatami will seem to be losing control and maybe they can step in with a coup d'etat," he said.

"Anjoman-e-Eslami will fight for the democratic reform of Iran. The Ansar-e-Hezbollah tries to intimidate us, but we are not afraid. We do not accept its interpretation of Islam. It is using Islam to maintain power. Islam is a peace-loving religion. It is democratic. The Prophet Muhammad always relied on consensus to solve disputes. We believe in Mr. Khatami. We believe in civil society, in dialogue. We do not believe in violence."

I reminded him gently that the Anjoman-e-Eslami did not always think this way.

Throughout the 1980s the Anjoman looked a bit like the hard-liners that oppose them today. Back then Anjoman members were hard-line revolutionaries, campus mouthpieces for Khomeini and conservative religious opinion. They beat students who disagreed with them and intimidated others into silence. Several Anjoman members took part in the American hostage taking.

"We have evolved since then," Amir smiled.

The early members of the Anjoman-e-Eslami formed part of the radical Islamic left that constituted Khomeini's inner circle. They competed for attention in that circle with the radical Islamic right, a group of clerics and merchants less interested in leftist rhetoric of anti-imperialism and more interested in conservative morality, economic privilege, and the preservation

[2] It is widely believed that rank-and-file soldiers in the military and rank-and-file Basijis support Khatami and reform. The leaders of these groups, however, are still on the conservative side.

of power, the group that largely runs Iran today. After Khomeini's death, in 1988, the Islamic right gradually took over the reins of power, pushing the Islamic left aside. Some Anjoman members went to jail on trumped-up charges.

In the early 1990s many of those disempowered Islamic leftists regrouped and formed into the core of the prodemocracy movement that emerged vocally in 1997. The Anjoman-e-Eslami, still leftist in its economic views, has become avowedly democratic in its political outlook.

"Most of us in the new generation of the Anjoman-e-Eslami began changing our views around 1994," Amir said. "The old Anjoman ideas were no longer relevant. The Islamic Republic was becoming too authoritarian, and we moved in the direction of democratic reform."

I asked him why so late, since the authoritarianism had shown itself early after the revolution.

He smiled. "Well, maybe some of the older members knew it before but were not willing to act on it."

He said he had a class to attend. We said good-bye. He wished me luck in my reporting, urged me to contact him if I needed anything. I strolled the campus. Black banners hung from trees, a sign of mourning. The banners, however, were mourning not the jailed student but the alleged insult against the Hidden Imam. WE MUST DEFEND ISLAM AGAINST ALL FOES, one banner read. THE LINE OF THE IMAM [KHOMEINI] IS THE ONLY WAY, another screamed in dramatic red letters. "The Line of the Imam" means the path of Khomeini, a term widely used by conservatives to denote a political and religious orthodoxy.

The college Basiji association, a group of religiously conservative students, had draped the campus with these banners. "We created the signs last night," one Basiji student with a peach fuzz beard and a black-and-white Palestinian-style scarf told me. "We did it to show our deep disgust with the student who wrote that blasphemous script. The Basijis of Amir Kabir are committed to protecting Islam," he said, "and we shall fight all those opposed," he added, rephrasing a line from the sign flapping above us.

The Basijis, however, held a minority opinion on campus. At Amir Kabir students walked the stone pathways to class, sipped orange sodas on benches, gathered to discuss class assignments, and generally ignored the black banners blanketing the campus and the Basijis who congregated around them.

"I think it is silly," said Ali, a nineteen-year-old jeans-clad student with wide eyes and a splash of premature gray hair, referring to the controversy over the play. "I consider myself a devout Muslim, but I do not fear the effects on our religion of a minor student play." A few nearby heads nodded in agreement.

Sudabeh, a twenty-two-year-old medical student with glasses and a white head scarf covering very little of her hair, interjected: "But it wasn't even a blasphemous play! It was a satire on the pressure of the konkur!" More heads nodded.

"This is just politics," she said, echoing a widespread view of most students who realized the real reason behind the conservative protest, political gamesmanship.

Iran's conservatives, besieged by the country's popular reformist movement, constantly searched for points of attack. A "blasphemous" student play, they thought, twisted easily into a general argument that President Khatami's press freedoms had opened the floodgates to vice and blasphemy. A concerted attack against this threat could possibly reenergize the committed troops, perhaps win a few new backers, and send a chilling message to all Iranian students who wrote plays, articles, and stories.

One of the Basiji students approached me. "There is a rally against the student playwrights at Tehran University. I can take you there if you like. It might be good for your report."

Yes, it would.

We walked across campus together, talking. I noticed glares from Ali, Sudabeh, and others I had spoken with earlier.

Inside the taxi the young hard-liner, whose name turned out to be Abdullah, talked about the student playwright controversy. "I don't know if he is guilty, but we must be vigilant. We must not allow such transgressions. If we do, a flood of vice will be unleashed. We are a traditional people. We are a religious people. We should not allow people to insult our faith."

I asked him what he thought about the prodemocracy students who flooded the streets in support of Khatami and reform and increased freedoms.

"I voted for Khatami too," he said. "I think we should reform our political system, but we must maintain our social system. We must fight vice. That is the only way."

Did he realize that some of those students had voted for Khatami because of the social freedoms they believed would be coming?

"Yes, I know that, but if those people want those kinds of freedom, they should move to Europe. That is not what the majority of Iranians want."

I asked if he had taken a poll, to see what the majority of Iranians wanted.

"What?"

A poll, field research, something.

"I don't need a poll. I know what we want," he said dismissively. "You have come from America. You do not understand these things."

I told him that I had spent a considerable amount of time traveling across Iran, talking to thousands of people along the way. I had no fixed conclusions, I said, but was willing to talk to everyone. I would be doing more travel in the future. Perhaps we could discuss some of my findings sometime.

"I know what you are finding," he snapped. "You are finding that everyone is complaining about jobs and complaining about the clerics and complaining about the economy and everything. I know that. I hear it too. But the revolution restored our dignity. My mother and sister now have dignity when they walk on the streets, wearing the chador. This is the dignity of our revolution."

But they were not forbidden from wearing the chador before the revolution, I said.

"I know, but they had to walk around near places that sold alcohol and underneath billboards advertising movies with women in bikinis. It was too much. Now there are no more billboards and no more stores selling alcohol. That is the victory of our revolution."

That was it?

"That's enough," he said.

We arrived at Tehran University. When I paid the taxi driver, I came to the realization that it was probably the first taxi ride I'd had in weeks in which the driver had not launched into a tirade against the government. He had remained quiet throughout the ride. When I handed him the money, Abdullah had already stepped out of the car. The driver turned back to me and said, "Your friend is a fool," and drove away.

Hard-Liners and Green Cards

The hard-liners' rally attracted a small audience, no more than one hundred people, trivial in comparison to the thousands of students who regularly agitated for freedom of the press and democracy. Several young bearded men in black shirts stood atop a stage, passing around a blue loudspeaker. A slim young man with a dark beard, sporting a green headband embroidered with "O Hussein," written in Farsi, yelled into the loudspeaker: "Reform means assault on our religion. The playwrights must die!"

The crowd cheered.

"Reform means blasphemy!"

They cheered loudly.

The speaker had soft eyes, but he did his best to summon ferocity by frowning and furrowing his eyebrows whenever he made a point.

"Death to the playwrights," he screamed.

The small, fist-pumping audience responded: "Death to the playwrights!"

"Death to the minister of culture who allows such blasphemy," he cried.

The audience: "Death to the minister of culture who allows such· blasphemy!"

"Death to America!" he yelled.

"Death to America!"

"Death to all those opposed to the *velayat-e-faqih* [rule by clerics]!"

"Death to all those opposed to the *velayat-e-faqih*!"

Suddenly a moment of silence broke his recital; perhaps he had run out of people to kill.

A stalky young man broke the silence after grabbing the microphone. "Death to Israel!"

Ah, yes, "Death to Israel!" the crowd chanted.

A number of foreign journalists stood in the crowd. Cameras rolled, zooming in on the angry and contorted faces of the chanters. A group of about twenty women, draped in severe black chadors, just their eyes showing, chanted loudly for the cameras, quieting down when the cameras left. Foreign reporters, their Iranian interpreters at hand, jotted notes. I wondered what they made of this. Looking down at my own notebook, I spotted the word "death" five times on a single page.

The foreign and domestic reporters on the scene, numbering about thirty, made for roughly one reporter per three hard-liners. Fifty or so students hung around the edge of the hard-line crowd, watching. They wore fashionable clothes, jeans, and sunglasses. The boys had shaved recently; their shirts were tucked in. The girls wore colorful, loosely tied head scarves. They openly smirked at the scene before them.

One student on the edge, a young man in sunglasses, approached me as I jotted notes. "Are you a journalist?" he asked.

Yes.

At first, he was friendly. He thought I worked for an Iranian reformist paper. When he found out I worked for a Western newspaper, he became agitated and angry. "You Western journalists record these fanatics on camera, and then you show them to the world and the world thinks we are all fanatics. It is not fair!" He walked away, huffing.

The demonstration slowed. The foreign television cameras had packed up and left. After the final death threat, the slim, soft-eyed leader stepped off the podium. I approached him. I told him my name and affiliation and asked if he would talk.

"You are from America?" he said, somewhat incredulously. "You write for an American newspaper?"

A crowd surrounded us. I nodded.

"You will not print what I say. All the foreign newspapers are in the hands of the Zionists," he said defiantly, with an upturn of his chin. The crowd nodded. He smiled. He did not look threatening, just arrogant.

I should not work with these papers, he said. He could connect me with a conservative daily. His admirers laughed and nodded.

I mumbled a polite response. Then I asked him if he really thought the young playwright should be killed.

"Well, these matters are complicated," he said. "If they are found guilty, then yes."

He already thought they were guilty, I said, judging by his slogans.

"These are slogans, just slogans," he said.

Slogans calling for someone's death?

"Yes," he said, "just slogans."

I had heard this argument before. Slogans make up an important part of Iranian politics, or so I was told. "Death to so-and-so" should not be taken literally. In fact, the "Death to America" signs in Farsi usually receive the translation of "Down with the USA." Still, the Persian word used, *marg,* means "death" in literal translation. Certainly, I can understand the importance of slogans in Iranian street politics, and I understand that the slogan is not literally a call to kill Americans, but when it is directed at one person, like the playwright in question, the slogan takes on a more ominous tone. Surely the United States of America need not worry about the petty sloganeering of a small band of basically harmless student hard-liners (the real threatening types, like the perpetrators of the World Trade Center killings, do not chant slogans in the streets—they plot destruction in whispers), but the young playwright, sitting alone in a jail cell, might have cause for worry.

"Look, why don't we discuss this later?" the hard-liner said. "Come to the university, and we can have a tea together. Maybe I can get these American ideas out of your head." He walked away, trailed by a group of young, bearded admirers.

I continued talking with young men in the crowd. None was interested in on-the-record interviews about the play controversy. They clamored for the information I had about America.

"How is life there?"

"How long have you lived there?"

As the crowd dwindled, one of the hard-line students approached me, a fellow whom I had noticed earlier as one of the more vigorous "Death to America" chanters. Glancing about furtively, he took my arm and asked, "How can I get a green card?"

Elites and Masses

Among Shi'a Muslim clerics, there is a distinction between *khawass* (elites) and *awwam* (masses). The *khawass* are religious scholars and clerics. Certain things may be said in front of the elites but not the masses. These things usually involve complex religious discourse, the sort of talk that might confuse "the simple believer." There are also some things that elites might have license to say in public, but the masses do not. For example, a cleric can question the mysteries of God, but a "simple believer" cannot.

Taken to a government level, it means this: President Rafsanjani can stand up in front of a crowd of reporters and say openly, "Ninety percent of what we do in the Islamic Republic is un-Islamic," and get away with it, as he did during his presidency. If someone else, not considered an elite, said the same words in front of reporters, there could be serious repercussions.

The Islamic Republic, true to this tradition, distinguishes between insiders and outsiders. The insider is a revolutionary who sided with Khomeini and the other religious revolutionaries, not the leftists or democrats or Marxists. President Khatami is an insider. That's why the other insiders allowed him to run for office in the first place. His conservative foes are also insiders. The current struggle between reformists and conservatives remains, thus far, an insider-only struggle. Few outsiders—secular nationalists or liberal democrats or opponents of the Islamic Republic—have a public voice in the debate. A conservative election supervisory body stymies outsider attempts to run for Parliament by denying them insiderness.

But President Khatami and other insider reformists have found a breach in the line, or so their conservative opponents often complain. Khatami talks too directly to the people, "the simple believers." He "confuses" them with these ideas of democracy and civil society. Some conservatives whisper that Khatami may not even be a true insider, that his ideas on democracy seem to go too far. Several former insiders, like the revolutionary turned investigative journalist Akbar Ganji, have been booted out of the circle. Ganji is currently in jail on charges of "insulting Islamic sanctities" and "defaming public officials" for his book and articles criticizing what he deems as the "religious fascism" of conservatives. In today's Iran the circle of insiders shrinks as opposition grows. As more reformists speak out vigorously and boldly, conservatives cry "betrayal," and yet another insider becomes an outsider. As the circle shrinks, it will become increasingly untenable for the insiders to silence the outsider voices crying for change.

The ultimate public proponent of this *awwam/khawass* idea is the hard-line and powerful cleric Ayatollah Mesbah Yazdi. He once said: "It doesn't matter what the people think. The people are ignorant sheep." This viewpoint was reflected in the young hard-liner's assertion that he does not need a poll to gauge people's opinions. The hard-liner did not care about people's opinions. Vice should be stopped. That is the way it should be. The opinions of "simple believers" do not matter. They are sheep.

This *awwam/khawass* distinction, on a more subtle level, refracts the complex lines between private and public space in Iranian society. High walls separate traditional Iranian homes. Some of what goes on inside the home should not occur outside. Across social classes, Iranians constantly assert, in effect, "Not in front of the guests." Of course, most traditional societies erect these walls of secrecy around their private lives. They are necessary. The Islamic Republic, however, sought to disrupt this age-old system. By knocking on people's doors, to check for dancing couples or alcoholic drinks, the new system knocked down private walls fortified by centuries of use.

I wondered what Omar Khayyam, the eleventh-century poet, might think of today's Iran. He might have seen some familiarity to his own era. In Neishapour, where Khayyam was born in 1044, the Turkish Seljuks ruled. A powerful and alien tribe from Central Asia, they needed legitimacy to bolster their rule in newly conquered Iran. They sought this legitimacy in traditional Sunni Muslim orthodoxy, which had risen as a counter to Shi'a victories across the Muslim world in the tenth century. The orthodox Sunni cleric became a court fixture. Sunni clerics derided and often killed philosophers. The Seljuk era vexed speculative men like Khayyam, who reached beyond the simple truths provided by rulers or orthodox clerics.

Still, Khayyam was a member of the *khawass*, an elite. He garnered great respect as a court astronomer and mathematician. His calendar, based on the sun's movement and his interpretation of the weather through the movement of the stars, demanded attention. What's more, he could engage with other members of the religious *khawass* on deep issues concerning the faith. Thanks to such exploits, the ruling elites granted Khayyam his private space to philosophize, criticize, and even display skepticism toward religion. The Persian literature expert Ahmad Karimi Hakkak puts it this way: "Khayyam was allowed to say things a normal man could be hanged for. He had a certain license that most men do not. He was told, however, to keep his poetry and philosophizing to himself and close associates. It should not invade the public space."

For nearly eight centuries, Khayyam's poetry remained in the world's private space until a minor Victorian poet, Edward FitzGerald, translated in free verse the Khayyam quatrains, winning for himself—and Khayyam—a place in the pantheon of world literary masterpieces. FitzGerald's translations also renewed interest in Khayyam among Iranians. Today intellectuals and free spirits flock to Khayyam's tomb, largely ignored just a century ago. I flew back to Mashhad to resume my pilgrimage journey with Omar Khayyam.

The Road to Neishapour

Upon my return to Mashhad, I contacted Haji Agha, my driver to the Ferdowsi shrine, to ask if he would drive me to Neishapour. The next day, at the appointed hour of our meeting, his white Paykan sputtered toward me. He had a load of passengers inside. Three children and a black chador-clad woman smiled at me from the back seat. "This is my family," Haji Agha said as I sat down in the front. "I hope you don't mind that I brought them too."

Haji Agha's wife, a pink-cheeked, plump woman who had prepared pantries of food for the trip, offered me biscuits and tea from a thermos as the car jerked to a start. Shortly thereafter a plate of sliced juicy pears, tart oranges, and crunchy grapes came forward from the back seat, along with the requisite apologies for such "humble hospitality." The children, two girls and a boy, smiled and giggled as I exchanged pleasantries with their mother. Even before I ate the last grape, Haji Agha's son, a seven-year-old sporting the red, green, and white shirt of the Iranian national soccer team, proffered a plate of sunflower seeds (a seventy-year-old man with a seven year-old son. What virility! Perhaps there was something in the seeds). The girls, eleven and thirteen, wore black head scarves and had red painted fingernails. When I spoke to their mother, they looked away and giggled.

Mercedes diesel trucks, colorful buses, and speeding Paykans choked the narrow, one-lane highway from Mashhad to Neishapour. Cars swerved in and out, passing slow-moving trucks and buses. Haji Agha, not much of a risk taker, rested in the slow lane, content to amble along behind a bus with a sign saying GOD REMEMBER pasted on the back window.

"First, we shall go to Qadamgah," Haji Agha said as he drove and munched on grapes and spit sunflower seed shells out the window, "and take our lunch there, and then we can pray at the mosque there." Qadamgah was a shrine dedicated to Imam Reza. In fact, Qadamgah means "the place of footprint." Legend has it that when Imam Reza traveled to Khorasan in the eighth century, he dismounted from his horse and stopped for water at the site of the shrine. Since it was the first spot Imam Reza's holy foot touched, the locals preserved the soil. Today pilgrims to the shrine kiss a clay tablet with a huge footprint believed to belong to Imam Reza. Built in 1643 by the Safavid Shah Suleiman, this familiar shrine greets most religious pilgrimage tours in the northeast.

On the road to Neishapour, the tan and dry and rocky landscape occasionally burst into patches of green and yellow trees. Every so often a dust-colored village appeared on a hillside in the distance. As the rolling brown hills in the distance turned clay red, we drove by a field of tall, long yellow sunflowers. Iranians consume their black sunflower seeds almost obsessively at picnics and at home. The sunflowers we passed all drooped downward, as if tired from providing Iranians their source of pleasure.

We arrived at Qadamgah, a small, elegant blue-domed mosque at the top of a hill surrounded by tall, thick trees. Up the stairs leading to the shrine, a group of shirtless boys splashed inside the green-tiled fountains. At the top of the stairs a smattering of Iranian, Arab, Indian, and Pakistani pilgrims crowded around the door to the shrine. Its blue dome sparkled in the sun.

Inside, a lighthearted crowd surrounded Imam Reza's footprint, jostling to touch and kiss it. A few boys marveled at the size of the footprint, spreading their hands across it. The arched foot with gigantic toes enveloped their tiny hands: perhaps a size fourteen or sixteen by American standards, a Shaquille O'Neal-sized foot.

Outside the shrine I chatted with a young Arab Shi'a Muslim cleric from Bahrain. He had a short, well-trimmed black beard and wore a flowing brown frock coat and shiny black shoes. After we had exchanged greetings in Arabic, I asked him about the legend of the footprint. He responded in Arabic, but my comprehension creaked with rust, so I asked him if he spoke Farsi. He did, in an Arabic accent, somewhat difficult to follow. A small crowd gathered as he explained the story.

"Imam Reza was on his way to Khorasan," he said. "He came to this spot to do *namaz* [prayers]. He stepped off his horse here. After he stepped off his horse, someone told him that there was no water for *wuzu* [preprayer ritual washing]. Imam Reza then created water from the ground. That's the story." He smiled. The crowd nodded.

I thought this miracle of water a more saintly act than merely stepping off a horse. "Why," I asked the cleric, "was the creation of water not celebrated in the name of the shrine?" Looking amused, he shrugged his shoulder and repeated an Arabic phrase loosely translated as "It is best not to question mysteries. It will only mystify you." He looked around at the gathered crowd, who did not understand his Arabic response.

Later, after the crowd had dispersed, he turned to me and said: "It is best not to ask uncomfortable questions in front of simple pilgrims. Such matters are best left to *khawass*. Your question could disrupt the faith of a pilgrim," the cleric told me. "Still, it is a valid question, one that can be discussed among scholars of Islam." He gave me his telephone number in Bahrain.

"You are most welcome at my home if you visit Bahrain," he said. "I will take you to our mosque. We can debate issues with other Shi'a scholars. I also want to show you the plight of Shi'a Muslims in Bahrain. We are not respected there. Here, in Iran, I feel free."

He then excused himself to wash his hands before leading his group of pilgrims in prayer. Haji Agha called me over to a spot underneath a large tree. His wife and three children sat cross-legged in front of a mat decked out with bread and yogurt and fruit. Once we'd enjoyed the fruit and yogurt, Haji's family uncovered a pot with steaming saffron-soaked chicken. Haji Khanom filled my plate with rice and chicken and bread.

"You have embarrassed me," I said sincerely.

"What embarrassment? You have honored us," she said.

We ate in the cool shade of the shrine's blue dome and thick green trees. After we had finished eating, Haji Khanom offered the remainder of the fruit to fellow pilgrims, and we got back in the car. We drove for about one more hour. The heavy meal made me doze off. When I awoke, I heard giggling from the back seat. The boy had begun a game of poking my ear with a feather. Even Haji Agha was amused, laughing when I grumbled awake.

When we arrived at my hotel in Neishapour, the whole family emerged from the car to bid me good-bye. I embraced Haji Agha's little boy. According to the custom of a traditional religious family, I did not reach out my hand to the women. Instead I put my hand on my chest and bowed slightly in good-bye to his wife and her two daughters. They smiled and did the same. I asked Haji Agha to walk with me to the hotel reception desk since it might have been in poor taste to exchange money in front of his wife and children.

Handing him a few bills beyond our agreed price, I thanked him immensely.

He refused, vowing to accept only the agreed price.

I tried the line about buying gifts for his children, but he refused to budge. This was not simple *ta'rof*. He seemed determined to stick to our deal.

He pushed the extra money back in my pocket. "You will need it when you get married," he said. It amounted to five thousand tomans, the equivalent of about eight dollars. I wobbled, not sure whether to push harder. Being a younger man, perhaps I would wound Haji Agha's pride. *Ta'rof* matters are complex.

Finally, I urged him to take the money and give "some of it" to the Imam Reza shrine and pray for me. He agreed reluctantly, and we embraced and said good-bye.

Notes on a Pilgrimage: Omar Khayyam, the Poet

FitzGerald's translations of Khayyam's quatrains stand as a singular achievement in the rendering of the poet's spirit in free verse. Though critics may argue that FitzGerald's *Rubaiyat of Omar Khayyam* exaggerated, romanticized, and Westernized Khayyam's philosophy, other specialists argue that FitzGerald captured the essence of the Khayyam spirit in his poems. The Iranian critic Masud Farzad puts it this way: "A century ago a ray of inspiration from the poems of Khayyam fell on the white pages of FitzGerald's mind, and from this contact sprang one of the great literary masterpieces of the English language."

FitzGerald's Khayyam, as portrayed in the *Rubaiyat* free verse translations, comes across as a "seize the day" agnostic philosopher, burdened by worries about the shortness of life and the insignificance of the human in the grand cosmos and retreating to the Epicurean pleasures of wine and beautiful women in response. Some religious Iranians argue that Khayyam's moments of "intoxication" in the original poems were a Sufi conceit, the intoxication of the religious worshiper with the Divine Beloved. Other Iranian critics dismiss the Sufi argument as bunk and proclaim Khayyam a freethinker in an age of orthodoxy (admittedly, most Iranians side with the freethinker view).

Whatever the case may be, as with all significant Iranian poets, debates will always rage about the true meaning of the work: Was Khayyam a Sufi intoxicated with love of God or a freethinker merely intoxicated? Many ask the same question of the fourteenth-century poet Hafez, perhaps the greatest in Iran's chest of poetic marvels.

Regardless, FitzGerald's Khayyam met with a tepid response when first published in 1859. Shortly after FitzGerald's death, in 1883, a group of admiring English critics resurrected his translations. There followed a minor Khayyam craze among the Western literary set. FitzGerald's Khayyam captivated a generation of young Western poets and freethinkers, with verses like the following:

> *Why, all the Saints and Sages who discuss'd*
> *Of the Two Worlds so learnedly, are thrust*
> *Like foolish Prophets forth; their Words to Scorn*
> *Are scatter'd, and their Mouths are stopt with Dust.*

Oh, come with old Khayyam, and leave the Wise
to Talk; one thing is certain, that Life flies;
One thing is certain, and the Rest is Lies;
The Flower that once has blown for ever dies.

While FitzGerald's rendition of the Khayyamic quatrains introduced the poet to the world, ironically, it also reintroduced him to Iranians, who had long ignored the Neishapouri poet. As a result of FitzGerald's work, Iranian intellectuals took a closer look at Khayyam. In 1934 one of Iran's most prominent writers, Sadeq Hedayat, wrote a book titled *Songs of Khayyam,* which shaped the way a generation of Iranians viewed the Neishapouri poet. The Hedayat picture of Khayyam differs from FitzGerald's: Hedayat's poet is less the "seize the day," wine-drinking, agnostic philosopher and more an anti-Arab nationalist freethinker who deeply resents the seventh-century A.D. Arab invasion that brought Islam to Iran. Hedayat notes that Khayyam "from the bottom of his heart despises the Arab highwaymen [Islamic invaders] and their base thought." He goes on to say that Khayyam's "sympathy lies with Iran which had been trapped in the mouth of this seventy-headed dragon and which flayed its arms and legs convulsively."

In many respects, FitzGerald's Khayyam resembles the original more than Hedayat's politicized "anti-Arab" Khayyam. Hedayat was himself a nationaist who resented the seventh-century Arab invasion. He attributed some of his own views to Khayyam. Still, Hedayat's Khayyam held a special importance for me because it shaped the historiography of the poet, the way Iranians perceive him today. Hedayat's work led to other explorations of Khayyam's perceived character: his religious indecision, his defiance of conventional orthodoxy, and his attempts to speak freely in a repressive environment. A picture of Khayyam emerged in the popular mind: a freethinker, unconventional, a questioner of eternal mysteries. The Persian literary scholar Michael Hillman expresses it nicely: "In twentieth century Iran, Khayyam has been mythologized into a figure quite different from what the known facts about his biography imply. But no matter, the view is that he bucked the tide of religious orthodoxy and dared to say what many Iranians feel in the heart of their hearts: that answers which governments give about human and social progress buttressed with technology and science and the answers offered by religion neglect to account for that occasional or perhaps frequent flash of insight to the effect that the only meaning to human life lies in the individual lives of human beings."

Though Khayyam rarely rates as high as the four great poets of Iran's classical period—Ferdowsi, Saadi, Hafez, and Rumi—he still occupies an important place in Iranian literature and the Iranian psyche. More important to my mind, Khayyam represents a struggle Iranians continue today: free expression and free will in the face of orthodoxy.

The Spice Men of the Bazaar

Before visiting the Khayyam tomb, I decided to look around Neishapour, to get lost in the crowds and not think about the pilgrimage ahead. It was my first visit, and like any traveler at a new destination, my heart quickened. I was eager to see what my journey would bring. As in most provincial Iranian cities, the main road took Khomeini's name, Imam Street. Along it, I saw news vendors, bookshops, neon-lit clothing stores, bread bakers, tea houses, and vegetable sellers, of the sort seen on every provincial Iranian Imam Street.

Turning off Imam Street, I wandered into the spice bazaar situated next to the communal Friday mosque. There the gap-toothed old men of the spice bazaar smiled as I browsed in their stores, overflowing with massive straw bales of red and yellow and green spices. In one of the stores, a group of gray-haired men in tattered sweaters sat cross-legged on a Persian carpet, leaning up against bags of spices, drinking tea. Inevitably they offered me a cup. Thirsty and needing a caffeine jolt, I accepted.

Sitting on the floor with them, I told them I sought a bottle of rose water syrup. Two of the spice men disagreed vigorously on which one I should buy.

"The best rose water syrup is from Kashan," one said, referring to a central Iranian city.

"Ridiculous! The best rose water is from Shiraz," the other countered, finger jabbing the air. A heated debate about the best rose water ensued.

Not wanting to offend either side, I bought two bottles—one from Kashan, the other from Shiraz—and promised to offer my own verdict later. One of the older men, who wore a blue sweater and had blue eyes, suddenly piped in: "Why do you want to drink rose water anyway? Our own *sharbat-e-rivas* is much better," he said, referring to a drink popular among

Neishapouris. The comment was met with vigorous head nodding and appreciative smiles. The blue-sweatered, blue-eyed man looked satisfied, as he kept repeating his line: "Our *sharbat-e-rivas* is much better."

Sharbat is essentially a purified syrup form of plants, flowers, fruits, or vegetables that are mixed with cold water to produce refreshing drinks. Sour cherry syrup, *sharbat-e-albaloo* (*sharbat* meaning "syrup" and *albaloo* meaning "sour cherry"), is a particular favorite in Iran, but I was not familiar with *rivas*.

When I told them of my unfamiliarity, the older men dispatched a young clerk to fetch some cold water. He placed the water in front of me, and the shop's proprietor poured the brown syrup essence of the *sharbat-e-rivas* into the cold water, stirring vigorously, the spoon making a clinking sound against the glass.

"Now, try this," he said.

The men of the spice shop gathered around. How would the Iranian from America, the reporter full of questions and always writing in his notebook, like their drink? I drank with a small gulp. The taste, slightly metallic and less sweet than the rose water, couldn't match *sharbat-e-albaloo*.

"Very good," I said, politely.

They seemed pleased, particularly the man with the blue eyes in the blue sweater. "I told you our *sharbat-e-rivas* is the best." Later, looking in my Farsi-English dictionary, I found out that *rivas* means "rhubarb."

"Take this," the proprietor said, handing me the bottle of the *sharbat* he had poured for me. "It is a gift. Go and write in your newspaper that the best *sharbat* is from Neishapour." He poured me another cup of tea.

All through tea, the men debated spices and sweets. No one argued where the best greens came from: Neishapour, of course. For saffron, Mashhad had an edge. The best *nabat*, crystallized sugar, also happened to hail from Neishapour. "Go next door and try the *nabat*," the blue-eyed man said, "you will see what I mean about its excellent taste."

Next door, at the *nabat* shop, I watched as a large man with thick forearms and a curling black mustache cooked massive bowls of gooey sugar over an open fire by stirring it with a baseball bat-size mixer. The blue-eyed man had followed me into the *nabat* shop. He approached the store clerk and said: "Our friend here is a journalist. He thinks our *sharbat-e-rivas* is the best. Take care of our friend."

The usual pleasantries passed back and forth. I had "honored" the storeowner, he was "at my service" in his "humble" store. For my part, I was "troubling" the storeowner and hoped that he was "not too tired" from his long day at work.

His shop produced the traditional rock candy of yellow crystallized sugar, which when boiled in hot water helps settle stomachs or warm chilled Iranians in the winter. Another product, hail-size sugar balls, attracted children especially. They liked to eat them with their morning tea. This *nabat* shop, I learned from the clerk, belonged to Central Asian immigrants, who had migrated to Neishapour in the 1930s, when the Soviet system had ruined their business.

"People did not have money to buy *nabat,*" the shop's clerk said, "and sugar was given away for free. So the owners of the shop left and settled in Neishapour, where they could make a better living. Business has been good in Iran, "he said," but it was much better before the revolution. Before the revolution, everything was better," he said glumly. "We had more money, more jobs, everything."

The phrase "before the revolution" peppers so much of Iranian talk. *Ghabl az enghelab,* "before the revolution," the toman was strong, seven to the dollar; *ghabl az enghelab,* beef was cheap, apartments were affordable, and Frank Sinatra gave a concert in Tehran.

"Come with me," the clerk said, leading me to a back office. He opened a drawer and pulled out a receipt dated 1356 (1977), a year before the revolution. Carefully unfolding the twenty-three-year-old receipt, he showed it to me. It said in Farsi: "one kilo of nabat = 235 rials."

"The same kilo costs four thousand rials today. There has been inflation," he said, "and you may think that the higher prices are good for us, the shop owners. But it is not," he said.

He seemed defensive, perhaps hoping to eradicate a view that shop owners in the bazaar laughed all the way to the bank as prices rose. "That same four thousand rials is not even nearly worth the two hundred and thirty-five rials of goods we could buy in the Shah's time," he said. In economic terms, he tried to explain that the real, inflation-adjusted price of *nabat* had fallen, so the shop owner actually suffered just as much as, if not more than, the consumer. "All the tools and materials we buy have gone up in price."

He talked more of his economic troubles. In Iran, complaining about the economy has become a national pastime. For small and medium-size businesses, not to mention common wage earners, such complaints are well justified.

The clerk then turned to me and said: "Did you know that in the time of the Shah one dollar could be bought with seven tomans? God rest the Shah's soul."

I bought a few bags of *nabat* as dusk approached. I heard the muezzin, the Islamic call to prayer, emanating from the nearby mosque. I walked back to my hotel, stopping in a few bookstores along the way. I bought a lavishly illustrated coffee table book with Omar Khayyam's poems written in English, French, and Farsi. The pictures included sensuous women, their curves well defined, eyebrows arched, the sort of picture that conservatives struck out of magazines or newspapers. Somehow, Iran's censors never bothered to use their red pens on illustrated poetry books, many of which include idealized, cleavage-busting maidens surrounding an older, gray-bearded, dreamy-eyed man relishing fruits and wine. As I leafed through the book, I thought of my friend Ahmad, an artist chastised for drawing "lewd" portraits of fashion models. Perhaps he might be able to use his skills to illustrate Khayyam books.

The Pilgrimage: Omar Khayyam Tomb

The next morning I hitched a ride to the Khayyam tomb with a thirty-two-year-old veteran of the Iran-Iraq war, Hassan, a new acquaintance. Soon to be a groom, Hassan, like many Neishapouris, would seal the wedding vows with a visit to the Khayyam tomb for good fortune and—if no one looked and he had paid off the right people ahead of time—a bit of mixed-couples dancing. I think Khayyam would have reveled in this dancing tradition, given his stated penchant for pleasurable pursuits. I think he would also have taken pleasure in knowing that residents of Neishapour remembered him, after he had been largely ignored for centuries after his death.

In a fine late-nineteenth-century travel narrative titled *Khorasan and Seistan,* an English colonel relates his visit to the Khayyam tomb in the 1890s, and notes his considerable distress that few Neishapouris even knew who Khayyam was. He scoffed to hear his Iranian guide "gravely turn and ask if

Omar Khayyam was a Christian, as every *Farangi* (Westerner), and especially every Englishman, he said, who came to Neishapur, went on pilgrimage to his tomb."

The *Farangis* and the Englishmen, dazzled by FitzGerald's Khayyam, wanted to pay their respects to the Persian poet that sent them daydreaming of the exotic East from their Cambridge dormitories or their rain-soaked Welsh homes. Colonel Yates, one of that breed, chafed at the Iranian treatment of Khayyam's tomb. He wrote, with some measure of anger, that "the tomb is utterly neglected by the Persians and is in fact treated with disdain."

When Khayyam died, in 1123, court philosophers mourned his passing as the loss of a kindred spirit. But most orthodox theologians must have thanked God that the questioning poet had ceased troubling them. Since Khayyam kept his poetry to court elites, his name meant little among the largely illiterate masses, which transmitted poetry orally. The people probably knew him only as a man of science. Most Neishapouris who knew Khayyam's verse aurally died in either an earthquake in 1145 or the Turkoman invasion of Neishapour in 1155. The devastating Mongol invasion of the thirteenth century destroyed Neishapour and added another layer to the hazy memory of the quatrains. As a result, scholars spend a considerable amount of time grappling with the veracity of poems attributed to Khayyam.

Today Neishapouris keep Khayyam's tomb well tended and surrounded by fertile gardens. The tomb had annexed the gardens, built four centuries after his death, from a local Shi'ite saint's tomb. In the twentieth century, Reza Shah, the first Pahlavi king, ordered the restoration of all the tombs of Iran's great poets, including Khayyam. Today a tall narrow oval blue-and-white structure, sprinkled with Khayyam's verses, covers the tomb. Like so many of Iran's shrines, the blue denotes an otherworldly quality.

Leaving me alone to approach the tomb, Hassan slipped away to the tea-house adjoining the gift shop in the far corner of the shrine. Off to one side of the tomb, a small crowd gathered around a squat coffee-skinned old man who wore the simple clothes of an agricultural worker. He animatedly related the great legends of Khayyam in a heavy Neishapouri accent: "The Great Khayyam was learned in all fields!" he boomed like a vaudeville actor. "Science! Philosophy! Religion! Law! And, of course, poetry!" Suddenly turning silent, he closed his eyes and put his hand on his ear, as religious men do when reciting verses from the Quran. He began reciting popular Khayyam poems. The crowd, nodding in appreciation, was rapt with attention as he sang.

After he finished, the crowd dwindled, handing him small bills, while a few stayed on to talk. He claimed day laborer as his profession, whenever he could find a job. Working or not, every day he rode a moped from his village to the nearby tomb. He said he had learned Khayyam's poetry from his father, a cleric.

"He was the cleric of our village. He read a lot of poetry, and he taught all of us, his children, to read poetry too."

Why hadn't he gone into the religious seminary to study? someone asked.

"I am not good at lying," he deadpanned, cracking a smile as the smattering of listeners chuckled.

I handed him a few bills and walked toward the tomb, where a young man wrote in a small notebook. I struck up a conversation. His name was Mohsen, and he was a student in optometry, his "forty-fifth choice," he said ruefully. On the university entrance exams, a prospective student is expected to name his or her preferred choice of study and location. Only the top students nationwide gain their first or second choices. Mohsen had marked medicine in fifteen different cities, chemistry in fifteen more, and so on. He'd ended up getting optometry at a university in a northern Iranian city, hundreds of miles from his family in Tehran.

"When I read Khayyam, I feel an almost religious inspiration," he said, "almost the same feeling as when I read Kafka." I wasn't sure how Kafka inspired religious inspiration, but I let him go on. "So I decided to make a pilgrimage to Khayyam's tomb and reflect on his poetry. My mother argued with me. She said a visit to a poet's tomb does not count as a proper pilgrimage. She is so full of traditions in her head that she can't see beyond them. Khayyam has meant so much to Iranian intellectuals. He deserves our reverence and our prayers and our pilgrimage. Almost a thousand years ago he was fighting the same fight for freedom of expression that we fight today. I wanted to come to the tomb and tell him that we carry on his legacy. This is my life and these are my pilgrimages and nobody can tell me otherwise."

His real passion was literature, though he did not think it a "practical" field of study. "There are barely enough jobs in the sciences, let alone in literature," he said. He flew from his university to meet his family in Mashhad, where they visited the Imam Reza shrine. The Imam Reza shrine bored him, however, so he had boarded a bus for a visit to Khayyam's tomb. Twenty years old, born one year after Iran's revolution, he fondly quoted the numerous Persian and Western authors he read.

I asked Mohsen what he thought about the current battle for freedom of expression.

"We are fighting, but I am not so optimistic. Our people are *bee-farhang* [without culture]", he said. "Look around you," he said, sneering. "Look and see how many people are at this Khayyam tomb." I counted about thirty people. "How many people go to the tombs of unknown Shi'a saints every day? Millions. This is not a country ready for democracy and freedom of expression. We are still full of superstitions."

I had heard this argument before, often from disaffected youths like Mohsen. Sometimes, it sounded artificial, as if they were repeating something they had read in the books of Sadeq Hedayat, a gifted mid-twentieth-century writer whose works often lamented his compatriots' tendency toward what he viewed as religious superstition, and regularly excoriated Iran's clerics.

"Hedayat is a great writer, one of our best ever," Mohsen told me. "I have a collection of all of his works."

I asked Mohsen to focus less on what he sees is wrong with Iran and tell me what he hoped for Iran.

"I want our country to wake up. I want us to enter the twenty-first century as the great people we are. But everywhere I look, I see problems. I see corruption and I see ill-educated professors at universities and I see these backward clerics running us and I see the world passing us by. Every day newspapers are being closed and journalists are being jailed simply for writing their beliefs. I just hope my grandson can come to this tomb one day and tell Khayyam that we have won the fight for free expression."

He leaned down, placed two fingers on the tomb, and said the *fateheh,* the Muslim prayer for the dead. Just then, a crowd of Iranian women in heavy black chadors approached the tomb. Part of a tour group of families of "war martyrs," they visited Neishapour as part of a pilgrimage tour. They crowded around the tomb, a sea of black robes. The tour leader, a woman in large glasses that overlapped with her tightly bound head scarf, covering all her hair and chin, gave the group a quick sketch of Khayyam's life.

"Omar Khayyam," she said "was a great Sufi poet who loved God and his religion. Many of you know his poetry already. Let us say a *fateheh* for Omar Khayyam."

The women knelt around the tomb, whispering verses from the Quran.

Mohsen seethed in the background—on the grass near the rose garden—barely able to contain his disgust. "Khayyam was not a Sufi," he said, kicking the grass. We walked toward the tea shop, to find Hassan.

Mohsen, the Student, and Hassan, the War Veteran

"Are you ready to go?" Hassan said to me, after I briefly introduced him to Mohsen. Hassan had promised to take me to the martyrs' cemetery of Neishapour. The "martyrs" buried in these cemeteries are not poets or saints, philosophers or clerics but are mostly young men who died in Iran's devastating 1980–88 war with Iraq, which took 300,000 Iranian lives. The Iran-Iraq war haunts the land, having left orphaned children, widowed women, and the deaths of a generation of Iranian youth in its wake. Iran's government has sought to portray these young men who died as martyrs in a holy war. The war is used in the current government struggle. "The martyrs fought for Islam and the revolution," the conservatives often say, "not for democracy."

"Will you join us for a visit to the martyrs' cemetery?" Hassan asked.

"I'm not interested," Mohsen said brusquely, barely making eye contact with Hassan and then resuming his conversation with me.

For many young people like Mohsen, the war is a distant memory, a moment in their childhood when bad things were taking place, but they know not what. Today Mohsen and many young people like him—prodemocracy, liberal, secular—resent the war. They oppose the use of its memory in current politics and don't much care for the veterans they see on TV who talk of martyrdom and religious zeal. People like Mohsen especially resent the easier university placement for war veterans and the families of martyrs. They also associate the war negatively with the hard-line Basijis who stifle them on campus.

Hassan, however, was not the sort of veteran who fitted the official conservative line depicted on television and in newspapers, the young man fueled by religious fervor. When I asked him about the war, he said: "I went to war to protect the honor of our Iranian soil. I never believed in the religious paradise stuff and the talk of defending Islam. I am a religious man, but I believed that Iran was sacred and that Iraqi dogs should not occupy a single inch of it!" He stressed the word "dogs."

Mohsen did not know this, and when he met Hassan, he turned cold. I got the impression that in about a minute Mohsen had sized up Hassan—a war veteran, a beard, wants to visit the martyrs' cemetery—and decided he did not like him. Traces of arrogance crept into his tone when he spoke to Hassan. A guy like Mohsen does not mix with many war veterans. President Khatami often talks about "dialogue of civilizations," but from my experience, Iranians needed some coaching in "dialogue of Iranians." It seemed, at times, as if Western journalists were the only ones talking to all sides.

Hassan seemed to sense the chill and moved away from us to wrap up his talk with a friend in the tea shop.

Mohsen turned to me, laughing. "Why do you want to go to the martyrs' cemetery? Don't you have anything better to do?"

I told him that I made a point of walking through martyrs' cemeteries in every city I visited. It was an important part of my travels. I left it at that. I did not elaborate. I did not tell him that the war somehow haunted me, that I placed flowers on the tombs of those fresh-faced young men I never knew, who, had they lived, would be just about my age now. I did not tell him that the rows of tombs and flowers and photos of young men in their prime produced a numbing melancholy in me. I did not tell him that sometimes I spent whole afternoons in martyrs' cemeteries watching weeping mothers wash the tombs of their sons as Shi'a Muslim songs of mourning echoed in the air.

When Hassan returned, he turned to Mohsen and said: "Well, if you are not interested in the martyrs' cemetery, maybe you would like to join us to visit the ruins of an eight-hundred-year-old village?"

Mohsen looked at me. It was the first I had heard of this change in plans. "OK," he said, with a shrug of the shoulders. "I'll join you."

As Hassan drove, I sat in the front and Mohsen in the back, saying little. When Mohsen did talk, he addressed only me, asking questions about Western writers, a subject that Hassan, who had never gone to college, might not know much about.

Hassan drove the car off the road amid the craggy rocks and shrubbery, toward the dust-colored ruins. He stopped the car and leaped out. He had jumped out to show us a field of melons.

"Come with me, Afshin," he said excitedly, "and you too, Mohsen," he added less enthusiastically. He leaped into tall weeds that came to our chests, and we followed slowly behind him. We lost sight of him amid some taller weeds. He came back carrying what looked like three baby melons.

"We call these *sofcheh*," he said. "Only found in Neishapour. They are small melons. We eat them like cucumbers. Please, be my guest."

Amid the tall plants we munched on the *sofcheh*. Mohsen declined, opting to smoke a cigarette instead. Suddenly Hassan jumped back into action, hurrying us along. Mohsen, cigarette dangling from his mouth, jogged behind us.

We got back in the car, which bumped along a rocky dirt road toward the ruined village. Once there Hassan leaped out of the car again and scurried up to a squat tan house. We walked on the rooftops of the ruined houses, jumped from house to crumbling house. Atop one house, we sat down. Mohsen lit another cigarette. Hassan threw a rock at an approaching lizard, sending it hurrying away.

"See over there." Hassan pointed to what looked like a small cave in one of the ruins. "Many people gather there at night and do heroin," he said glumly. "There are many war veterans among them too."

"Mohsen is of course too young to know," he said, looking at Mohsen, "but the war was so awful. We saw our friends get shot up and bleed to death and fall on mines that just blew them apart. Can you imagine your friend screaming as he dies and you can do nothing about it? After the war, the government helped us, but the money it gave us was small. Some of us, who had good connections, got university slots, as Mohsen knows. But I did not have such connections." He threw a glance at Mohsen, who continued smoking, not looking at Hassan as he spoke. "You cannot explain war," Hassan said. "Some people could not get the war out of their heads. They turned to heroin to forget the war."

Mohsen looked up from his cigarette and asked: "Does the government help the war veteran heroin addicts?" He asked the question in a normal tone, politely.

"Nothing the government can do can cure an addict," Hassan said.

Mohsen nodded and offered Hassan a cigarette, perhaps a gesture of peace.

Hassan refused, saying: "I'm getting married in two weeks. I promised my fiancée I would not smoke. She is already controlling me!" He laughed.

"Congratulations on your marriage," Mohsen said, showing the first signs of warming to Hassan.

"Congratulations?" Hassan laughed, "I told you I'm getting married, not that I found a new job!"

Mohsen smiled.

"Enjoy your freedom, young Mohsen. You too will one day fall!"

Mohsen informed us that he had to catch the last bus to Mashhad, so we got back in the car and dropped him in the city center.

Mohsen and Hassan exchanged phone numbers and said good-bye. Hassan told Mohsen to give him a call next time he was in Neishapour. They had come to an uneasy truce, though I doubted Mohsen would call.

Martyrs' Cemetery

At the martyrs' cemetery Hassan and I walked amid tombstones of his dead friends. Their faces stared out from photographs, boys with barely grown mustaches and earnest eyes. We read each name as we passed it: Gholam Reza Borgi, Mehdi Bourhani, Ahmad Taheri, Mohammad Haghighi. We leaned down and ran two fingers down the tombs and said the *fateheh*.

Nearby a funeral ceremony took place. A young Neishapouri man, an army conscript, had died recently in a shoot-out with drug smugglers on the Afghan border, a drug-fighting "martyr." Black-clad women wept and beat their chests. A group of working-class men and boys bowed their heads, fighting back tears.

A heavy man with a shaggy black beard began preaching. He lacked clerical garb. Hassan and I sat down nearby to listen, and I scribbled furiously as he spoke.

"This boy is a martyr," the man said, "just like our great martyrs in the sacred defense [the Iran-Iraq war], and that is why he is being buried here." The women, a collection of ten heavy black chadors, squatted near the tomb and wailed as the preacher continued.

"Oh, you weeping women, do not cry. Say your prayers and read the Quran. That is what every martyr wants his mother to do." They continued weeping.

"Allow me now, dear brothers and sisters, to talk of an important subject," the preacher said as the women wept quietly. "Many of us today complain of hard economic times. Yes, the price of cooking oil and rice and meat has gone up! Yes, there are not enough jobs! Yes, many of us are dissatisfied! But we must always remember our martyrs and not fall into the trap of being baited by our foreign enemies! We may be discontented with our economic situation, but let's not forget that our martyrs are discontented with us!" The women wept still more.

The eulogy turned political, a not uncommon path. I remember a eulogy for an older man in Tabriz at which the cleric spoke for five minutes about the man's good qualities and twenty minutes about the need for women to wear the Islamic dress.

"The martyrs are discontented with us," he continued, his voice rising. Turning to the tombstones of the martyrs, as if addressing them directly, he said: "Oh, you martyrs, you did not die in vain. You fought for Islam and the *velayat-e-faqib,* and we shall always preserve that. Your mothers did not weep for you because they were happy to have a martyr in the family." The women wailed on.

"People say we want freedom," the Neishapour preacher went on. "You know what these foreign-inspired people want? They want the freedom to gamble and drink and bring vice to our Muslim land! This is the kind of freedom they want!"

The women wailed on, and the men bowed their heads, an older man weeping in uncontrollable, shoulder-shaking sobs.

"We shall not allow this freedom. No! Not on our Muslim land," he said. The women wept.

"We shall not sacrifice the blood of our martyrs for these foreign-inspired reforms," he said. "There is no need to cry. Islam will emerge victorious." The women sobbed, the men looked down, and Hassan drew circles in the dirt with a stick.

IV

Cities: Tehran, Shiraz

The Silenced Satirist

There is an Iranian short story/parable that tells of a man cheated of his wealth and possessions by a powerful local dignitary. The newly impoverished man, Gholam Ali, responds by spreading loudly the tale of the dignitary's treachery in the bazaar, the public marketplace. The dignitary, incensed when he hears of Gholam Ali's public accusations, uses his connections to have him arrested. The next day local authorities publicly flog Gholam Ali.

The following day Gholam Ali presents himself in the bazaar. This time he wears the guise of "a village madman" who has gone "mad" because of the terrible injustices he has suffered. To make his point, the "village madman" relates the tale of his woe in the form of a melancholy song and dance. Everyone in the bazaar knows this "village madman" is Gholam Ali. They also know who has caused his woes, the local dignitary. This time the police are powerless to intervene: The local bazaaris will defend Gholam Ali, citing the lack of a prohibition against song and dance shows.

So the dignitary turns to the local mullah, and urges him to issue a religious edict banning song and dance performances. The mullah complies, and Gholam Ali is forced out of the bazaar again.

A few days later Gholam Ali turns up at the bazaar a third time, now wearing the disguise of a religious mourner. In a public square near the bazaar, he beats his chest in the fashion of a Shi'a religious mourner, crying out against the evil actions of Yazid and Shemr, notorious Shi'a villains universally despised by religious Iranians. Everyone in the bazaar knows the identity of the religious mourner and thus understands the subtext: The local dignitary is Yazid and Shemr, the epitome of evil.

Again the dignitary turns to the mullah. This time, for a fee, the mullah issues a religious edict that bans anyone from implicating pious Muslims (i.e, the local dignitary) with notorious Shi'a villains. Gholam Ali is forced out of the bazaar again.

Undaunted, he appears once more, a cat perched on his shoulder. In front of the assembled crowd, Gholam Ali berates his pet cat for all the injustices it has committed against him and demands justice from the hands of such a dishonorable cat.

The parable, published in 1988 by the satirist and writer Ali Akbar Sa'id Sirjani, elicits chuckles of understanding from many a literary Iranian. Most twentieth-century Iranian writers of some repute have experienced either government repression, represented by the police and the dignitary, or clerical-inspired repression, depicted by the local mullah. As a result, all Iranian writers have a bit of Gholam Ali in them: the ability to tell the truth in disguise, to write between the lines. Allegory, symbolism, satire: all are tools especially indispensable for the Iranian writer. As the prominent, recently exiled Iranian writer Faraj Sarkuhi puts it, "I have learned to write between the lines for people who have learned to read between them."

Sirjani, Sarkuhi, and many other writers saw great promise in Iran's 1979 revolution. After all, the Shah had made few friends in the literary set. The censor's red pen slashed out offensive lines, and the threat of prison always loomed. Just before the revolution, leading poets gathered for nights of antigovernment poetry in a Tehran institute. As word spread of the defiant poets, the crowds swelled to the thousands. A few days after the revolution, the mood among writers exceeded jubilant; one pamphlet, distributed widely, noted that "2,500 years of censorship have finally been lifted."

However, the revolution proved a false dawn. When an authoritarian government ruled by clerics formed from the debris of the postrevolution power struggle, the two traditional oppressors of free thought—clergyman and king—became one. The new revolutionary order set a low ceiling on criticism of the government. What's more, the offending writer, by his mere political dissent, suddenly became an unbeliever, a blasphemer, "an enemy of Islam." Several prominent writers fled to the West, where they wrote wrenching poems of exile separation in small apartments in Europe. The government killed a few on broad, grandiose charges, like "spreading corruption on earth." Others, who stayed behind and survived, like Sirjani, told their tales of woe in different guises, like Gholam Ali.

Sirjani himself managed to play the Gholam Ali role well for several years after the revolution. Through satire and allegory, he daringly criticized the Islamic Republic for what he saw as its authoritarianism, religious hypocrisy, and obtrusive meddling in people's personal lives. His essays, framed loosely as stories but resembling personal episodes and remembrances, often targeted Iran's clerics, depicting them as power-hungry and devious. In one of his "remembrances," he tells the story of a local cleric and a landowner who conspire to sell a batch of watermelons at double the usual price. The cleric tells all the villagers of a dream he has had that their local shrine was blessed by Imam Reza, the eighth Shi`a imam. The next day thousands of villagers descend on the shrine, where the watermelon seller, winking at the cleric, waits for them. All the watermelons sell at double the price.

Eventually, inevitably, Sirjani began to run afoul of authorities. The first open confrontation arose following a book he published in 1989, a collection of his satirical essays, stories, and parables, titled *You of Shortened Sleeves*. The title of the book emanates from a prominent poem by the revered fourteenth-century poet Hafez that chides Iran's Muslim clergy for meddling in the personal lives of fellow Muslims. The theme was particularly salient to Sirjani's contemporaries because of government attempts to restrict the public and personal lives of Iranians. In the collection of essays, which became a national best seller, Sirjani employed all his satirical skill in the service of his one aim: a vigorous questioning of the political and social repression of the Islamic Republic.

The first printing sold out in days. Alarmed by the book's popularity, Iran's Ministry of Culture and Islamic Guidance, the government agency that carries the red pens of censorship, banned its second printing. It also placed a blanket ban on other Sirjani books. Not surprisingly, Sirjani's popularity exploded to previously unimagined heights. Mimeographed copies of the first printing circulated among university students and intellectuals.

In response to the ban, Sirjani initiated a letter-writing campaign, demanding that a second printing be released. Iran's Supreme Leader, Ayatollah Ali Khamenei, let it be known to the writer through intermediaries that he would have to halt his writings and his protestations. Sirjani's next step proved fatal: He uncloaked his protest and directly assailed the Islamic Republic in an open letter. Shortly thereafter authorities incarcerated him despite numerous appeals from international human rights groups. Ahmad Karimi Hakkak, the Iranian scholar, notes that "the letter sealed the author's fate in a way that no previous writing of his—be it anecdotal essay, political allegory, or open appeal—had done." A few months later a letter supposedly written by Sirjani himself admitted to a range of crimes against the state. He died under mysterious circumstances in his prison cell.

Iranians watching the Sirjani case saw an example of art reflecting reality. In one of his most memorable essays in the banned book, Sirjani describes a fictionalized episode of mistaken identity that leads the writer/narrator to an office inside Iran's notorious Evin Prison in order to clear his name. Before the narrator of the story goes to the prison, he tells his wife not to worry, that he will be back shortly, but he notes:

If for any reason—God forbid—tomorrow evening you decide to turn on this abandoned TV set of ours, and happen, instead of such extremely edifying shows of pious preachers and illuminating lamentations [for the fallen Shi'a imams], to see my image on your screen, sitting erect upon a stool, in the presence of the grand mufti [cleric] . . . engaged in the act of what our zealous youth have termed "revealing secrets" of my own treachery and crimes, recounting all the lies I have been delivering to the God-fearing Muslims, confessing the secret contacts I have had with [foreign diplomats], and detailing all the money I have received in return for my spying, . . . you must promise me here and now that you will not turn against me, saying such things as: you hypocrite hack! You were receiving all these pounds and dollars, and still made us live life in such abject misery.

Though Sirjani himself never made the sort of "public" television confession he detailed in his essay, the satirist's pen never crossed the Islamic Republic again. Beyond the obvious and self-evident injustice of his jailing, Sirjani, it might be said, made a tactical error. He strayed from the accepted rules of the game, which grudgingly allowed allegorical criticism read by an educated elite (the popularity of his book might have been his first "crime"). The rules do not allow for direct opposition and open letters to newspapers questioning the Supreme Leader. When Sirjani crossed that line, he moved from writer and thinker to rebel. He had become a political activist, a freedom seeker, joining the ranks of other twentieth-century activists who openly defied authoritarian governments and who, for the most part, paid a dear price for it in the end.

When Sirjani chose the title of his book, *You of Shortened Sleeves,* he knew his readers would see the immediate relevance of that phrase from Hafez's fourteenth-century poem. Hafez's warning to falsely pious clerics in "shortened sleeves" who sought to impose a narrow social code on others similarly commented on his times. When Sirjani published his essays, he believed that his readers would see the theme of "false piety" and "religious orthodoxy" as not an abstraction, but as one that affected their lives directly as they struggled under the weight of a government much concerned with the personal lives of its subjects.

By invoking Hafez, Iran's most revered poet, Sirjani drew a powerful sword. Hafez casts an enormous shadow over Iranian literature and culture. Iranians widely regard him as the greatest Persian poet. Not surprisingly, he is also the most popular. In Farsi, Iranians say: "In every Iranian home, you will find at least two books: the Quran, Islam's holy book, and the *Divan* of Hafez."

My next pilgrimage, to the tomb of Hafez, was to take me back to Shiraz, the poet's birthplace and beloved city, which serves as a backdrop to so much of his poetry. In a sense, Sirjani and other Iranian writers and poets all are children of Hafez. Like them, Hafez faced the dual censors, king and clergy. What's more, just about every prominent twentieth-century Iranian literary figure has expressed admiration for Hafez's immense literary talents.

Of course, writers alone do not solely appreciate the gifts of Hafez. Average Iranians, including the less educated, sprinkle Hafez's poetry liberally into their conversations. A well-timed Hafez quotation in a conversation serves a similar purpose as a biblical proverb or a line from Shakespeare in the West. Additionally, a popular Iranian pastime, known as *fal-e-Hafez,* involves fortune-telling by one's randomly opening to a page in the *Divan* and then interpreting the verse. A rendition of this pastime is played out in streets across Iran: A caged bird, perched on the finger of its trainer, for a small fee selects a Hafez verse from a basket of bits of paper. The ensuing verse is ment to be prophetic. Hafez statues and Hafez streets mark every Iranian city. Politicians quote Hafez. Writers quote him. Television personalities quote him. Hafez surpasses the title of mere poet: He is a cultural icon.

Yet Hafez, unlike Khayyam and, lately, Jalaladin Rumi (the thirteenth-century Iranian mystic poet who has numerous Western followers, from Christian mystics to the pop singer Madonna), has never developed a Western following. He remains primarily an Iranian phenomenon. Despite some good translations of his poems in English and French, somehow, Hafez does not speak to the Western reader. To the Iranian, however, Hafez comes as close as possible to distilling a common experience, and he does it—at least most Iranians would agree—with an extraordinary aesthetic flourish.

Red Lines

My visit to Shiraz was to reunite me with Davoud. Being a writer, an essayist, and a translator faced with the sorts of problems Hafez might have faced if he were alive today, Davoud seemed an appropriate companion for my visit to the Hafez tomb. Each time Davoud completed one of his translations, a mixture of satisfaction and anxiety set in. The more complex Western novelists required long periods of sustained concentration. He read each book twice, seeking to understand both the practical essence and the spirit. Then he methodically translated, groping for the right word or phrase. "When I am done, my brain is exhausted," he said. "I feel an enormous relief. I am proud the work is done."

Then came the anxiety. When the work was completed, he handed in the manuscript to the Ministry of Culture and Islamic Guidance. There it fell under the pens of Iran's censorship board, which rules the fate of every Iranian writer or translator. "When the book goes to Ershad [the Ministry of Culture], I feel a terrible uncertainty," Davoud told me. "I wonder what they might object to. I hope that all my labor has not been done in vain. I hope I managed to avoid the red lines."

Every generation of Iranian writers has unwritten red lines beyond which the writer goes at his peril. Sirjani leaped past the red lines and paid a price for it. For the prerevolution writer, the obvious red lines tended to be the questioning of SAVAK, the Shah's dreaded secret police, and direct attacks on the Shah. Today the red lines are the questioning of rule by clerics and direct attacks on the Supreme Leader, Ayatollah Ali Khamenei. Red lines can also be more arbitrary, decided upon by a single cleric or a group of government officials in reaction to a work. They may range from passages that "insult" Islam to sexually explicit material to "politically subversive" writings or even to the oft-used charge "confusing public opinion."

Sometimes the review process of a single book could take years. The longer the process, the higher the tension for Davoud. He began to second-guess his word choice. "Should I have used different, more ambiguous words? Was I thorough enough in my own self-censorship? What about the kissing scene or the passage that criticized Christian priests? Every possibility goes through my mind."

In 1997 a new minister of culture, Ataollah Mohajerani, shook up the organization, injecting a breath of free speech into the halls of the ministry. He demanded the book review process be sped up. He licensed hundreds of reformist newspapers. He regularly spoke out against censorship. Soon political books proliferated; they included some promoting democracy and others exposing corruption in Iran's government. Translations of Western novels that had become musty and worn from years sitting on the censor's desk suddenly surged into the public, away from the tyranny of the censor. Many banned writers (the Farsi phrase is translated as "a prohibited pen") published new works. Mohajerani had seemingly erased the red lines.

This era of openness, which spawned a three-year Iranian newspaper and publishing renaissance, eventually came to a crashing end. Iran's hard-liners rallied their bureaucratic power to outmuscle the liberal culture minister. They closed newspapers, jailed journalists, and pressed writers back into allegory and symbolism. Mohajerani resigned his post in frustration, though he continued to support a free press. Still, when Davoud heard of the culture minister's resignation, he decided to stop work on his latest project, a translation of a Spanish author. He did not want to face the pain of the censorship process again.

One can almost draw a continuous line of censorship from the time of Khayyam and Hafez to Sirjani and Davoud. In fact, only rarely has Iran been free of censorship. Early in the twentieth century, for several years, the progressive political movement for a liberal constitution, known as the Constitutional Revolution of 1906–11, spawned a flurry of liberal newspapers, but the movement sputtered after the Constitutional Revolution failed, and it died when Reza Shah took power in 1925 and crushed most press freedoms. During the confused climate of World War II, when the British deposed Reza Shah in favor of his son, Mohammad Reza, writers breathed relatively freely once again—that is, until 1953, when the CIA helped overthrow Mossadeq amid the paranoia of the Cold War. The uncertain young Shah, his throne regained after the Mossadeq affair, decided that he would tolerate no opposition, and journalists and writers relapsed into the old fears.

In the summer of 1966 a small group of Iranian writers gathered at a popular literary café in Tehran to discuss creation of a writers' union. "Above all, to defend freedom of expression," the constitution of the fledgling organization proclaimed. Of course, this fledgling union ran afoul of the authorities. Police prohibited meetings in public halls; internal security agents conspicuously followed prominent members and arrested several for works deemed "treasonous." The death of the union's founder and leading light, novelist and essayist Jalal Al-e-Ahmad in 1969, led to competing factions—chiefly Communist versus non-Communist—and squabbling over power, leadership, and the direction of the union. By 1970 the union had ceased to function, dying under the weight of factionalism and government repression.

In 1998 the new climate of openness initiated by President Khatami's reforms led a few writers to discuss reviving the defunct union. The poets Mohammad Mokhtari and Mohammad Jafar Pouyandeh were tired of "writing between the lines" and self-censorship. Writers needed protection, solidarity. A union would be the perfect vehicle. They talked about the idea with friends.

In December 1998, however, these hopes died once again. Acting at the behest of a shadowy group of hard-line clerics, a small group of Intelligence Ministry agents killed both Mokhtari and Pouyandeh. Three more assassinations followed, including those of the secular nationalists Dariush and Parvaneh Forouhar, as well as the disappearance of the poet Majid Sharif.

"Even before the talk of the union, we were marked men," a prominent Iranian writer told me. "Perhaps the union talk just sped up matters." He described a bus ride in 1997, when twenty-one Iranian writers were en route to a conference in Armenia. The bus driver, in a clear attempt to kill the writers, nearly steered off a cliff, diving out of the vehicle just as it careened toward the edge of the thousand-foot free fall. Fortunately, the bus hit a boulder and stopped. The driver ran away. If the plan had been successful, twenty-one of Iran's "pesky writers" would have met the same fate as many of their counterparts over the years: an early death under mysterious circumstances.

Narges and the Censoring of Milan Kundera

N arges, a thirty-year-old literature teacher, always knew that censorship was a fact of life in Iran. When she studied literature at Shiraz University, she took it for granted that certain books were not available, others were not written, and a few were banned. This was not new. Her older professors told her the same rules applied during the Shah's era, just with different red lines.

Her favorite poet was Forough Farrokhzad, the 1960's Iranian female poet whose work represented both extraordinary artistic achievement and a brave feminist consciousness. Narges also read Persian translations of Western novels. She particularly admired the work of Milan Kundera.

Narges visited the United States for the first time in 1998. She attended a few conferences on Iran that were sponsored by Washington think tanks. She did not like what she heard, especially what she described as "America's love affair with Khatami." She argued vehemently with journalists and scholars at the conferences. "They all think that Iran is a democracy now," she said. "They do not realize that we are far from it. They go to Iran for two weeks and meet a few journalists and politicians and think they know everything about the country. They do not understand the indignities we face as women. They do not know the indignities we have faced over the years." There was more than a trace of bitterness in her tone, but it was a tone that I had been accustomed to in Iran. Deep wells of anger, borne of daily humiliations and psychological wounds, bubbled at the surface of the Iranian psyche, an anger and pain that Narges says are too easily dismissed by Western visitors who spend too much time with reformist politicians and too little time with the people.

"When I was in college in the late 1980's, my friends wanted to give me a birthday party. They surprised me in my dorm room with gifts, but because we were not allowed to play any music, we used a Walkman and passed it around the room. Everyone listened to the Walkman for a few minutes, as the others talked. Sometimes, two of us would push our heads together to listen at the same time. When I think back on it, I get very angry. I mean, how dare they tell me I can't have music at my own birthday party! What a pathetic scene it was, five girls sharing one Walkman, all of us afraid to pull the plug on the headset that would have made the music broadcast louder! It is fine to make nice-sounding phrases about democracy and civil society, but you journalists who come here for a few weeks don't understand the indignities we face. You just don't get it!"

While in America, Narges picked up an English-language copy of Milan Kundera's novel *Identity*. She had already read the Persian translation and considered it one of her favorite books. When she began reading the English version, she realized that several key passages had been omitted in the Persian translation. An entire section had been totally deleted. "I felt cheated and violated when I read the English version. It seemed so unfair. I felt like I could never read a novel in Persian again."

Her reaction was intriguing. She said she felt "cheated." What she thought was a faithful Persian translation in reality was a gutted version of the original. In a sense, the censorship was sophisticated since it "fooled" Narges, who held a master's degree in literature. Perhaps the fact that she was deceived angered her just as much as the censorship itself. Perhaps this sort of censorship is even more damaging than the open and blatant censorship of totalitarian states.

Conservative Iranian clerics often say that they are not opposed to Western ideas. They simply want to pick and choose from among those they believe should be allowed to enter the arena. That's why they fear satellite dishes; after all, one cannot block the air waves. In the case of Kundera's novel, someone from the Ministry of Culture (or perhaps the translator himself in an act of self-censorship) decided that certain passages were not suitable for the arena. This "clever censorship" creates a deception of freedom.

But does it work? No. Though Narges and thousands of other literary Iranians who read the book were fooled by the clever censorship, Narges eventually found out and has spoken often about it to her other literary friends. In fact, many literary Iranians play a game of "matching" the translation to the original.

The Islamic Republic of Iran does not often ban books, but those it does decide to ban become instant hits on the underground book circuit. In fact, it has become a truism that banned ideas and books become more popular than they might otherwise be. The Shah's repression of Communism in the

1970s gave the ideology a certain modish panache. The conservative clerical repression of democratic ideas has done the same. In the end, neither type of censorship works. It only gives the repressed ideas an aura of mystical power.

Perhaps that's why Iranians revere their great poets so much. Their poets, particularly Hafez, have often been able to tell truths that others have feared to discuss. Narges puts it this way: "Hafez speaks to all Iranian poets and to all Iranians with such a subtle and beautiful voice that he has managed to transcend politics. I, as a poet myself, and Iranians, as a people, are all indebted to Hafez."

Narges's sentiment was fairly common. Somehow, Hafez remained—perhaps—Iran's most widely respected cultural figure. My next pilgrimage, to the shrine of Hafez in Shiraz, would explore both Hafez the poet and the Iranian reaction to his work. Any nation's cultural icons reveal something about the people. The almost universal praise of Hafez says something important about Iranians. I went to Shriaz to explore what that might be.

Why a Fourteenth-Century Poet Speaks So Eloquently to Contemporary Iranians

In Shiraz, I checked into the Park Hotel, a pleasant establishment with clean rooms, hearty soups, and a decaying garden veranda in the front. In the morning I waited for Davoud in its courtyard. A small, algae-ridden fountain in white marble gurgled quietly nearby. Long and worn red roses swayed gently in the morning breeze. I sat in a white plastic chair, flipping through a morning newspaper. I spotted an article describing an upcoming international conference on Hafez's poetry to be held in Shiraz. UNESCO, the United Nations' cultural arm, was sponsoring the conference. Iran's minister of culture was expected to open the event. "International scholars will discuss the multifaceted layers of our greatest poet," the newspaper said.

Davoud approached, carrying a long strip of the hot flat bread known as barbari. He wore a collared tan shirt rolled up to his elbows and tight-fitting black jeans, along with a wide smile.

"Salaaaaaam," he said, rolling his a's in a sarcastic tone, then mockingly adding in English, "Are you the great sir Dr. Afshin Molavi, the great Orientalist scholar of Persian literature, from the great land of America? I am your humble servant." He laughed, slapping me on the back, looking at me, moving his head up and down, as if he were sizing me up for a suit. "You have gotten fat, my friend. Your aunties in Tehran are feeding you well, eh?" I laughed, self-consciously pulling in my stomach. Noticing my vanity, he smacked my stomach with an open palm. "Relax," he said, "it is a sign of success. Eat more." He tore off a piece of the barbari and handed it to me.

We hailed a taxi outside the hotel. A heaving, spitting hunk of white metal stopped at the curb, and the driver invited us in. The driver, an elderly man with neatly combed white hair, looked in much better shape than his car.

The driver made small talk, the rising price of meat, the recent press crackdown, the weather. He asked us if we needed a driver for the whole day. There were many sights to see besides the Hafez tomb, he said, and he would be "most pleased" to show us. We politely declined.

"There is a cave in Shiraz where a small candle has been burning for hundreds of years," he said, trying to pique our interest. "I can take you there."

I thought of the old Zoroastrian fire temples and their eternal flames. "Where is it?" I asked.

He paused for a moment as his car wheezed into a left turn. "Well, you see, the candle is no longer burning. They extinguished it a few years ago."

"Extinguished? They? Who?"

He turned around, showing us his profile. Long gray hairs poked out from his ear. "It must have been the British," he said matter-of-factly, narrowly missing an oncoming truck as he turned back (to our relief) to look at the road. Davoud smiled and poked me in the ribs with his elbow. We both marveled at the extraordinary crimes attributed to the British all across Iran.

"And why would the British do that?" Davoud said.

"How do I know? I am just a workingman. They are so cunning that they probably had a reason to do it. They must have had a plan." Yes, the British always had a *naqsheh,* a plan, and this plan was often too cunning and devious for the average man to understand.

"Yes." Davoud said, winking at me and addressing the driver, "it must have been a very devious plan." The driver nodded.

We turned onto Golestan (Rose Garden) Street, and the car's engine, whirring loudly, reached a crescendo as the driver downshifted. It sounded as if every metal piece under the hood had dislodged and begun dancing and clanking and smashing into one another as we made left turns.

"There it is," the driver said, "our greatest poet."

We got out of the car and bade him good-bye as he stroked his dashboard, like a mother caressing a crying baby. The car seemed to respond, its high-pitched whir slowing to a dull whimper.

We had to cross an avenue of high-speed cars. A green, coal-stained Mercedes truck rumbled by, emitting black smoke clouds into the air. Two children in bright orange backpacks raced across the street, narrowly avoiding the oncoming truck.

On the other side, white metal gates announced the entrance to the shrine and, behind them, a splendid garden with tall, elegant, slim cypress trees. The English traveler John Fryer called the Shiraz trees "the loftiest cypresses in the universe." The cypress tree regularly shows up in medieval Persian poetry as a symbol of freedom. Davoud told me a popular story about the cypress tree: The cypress was once asked why it did not bear any fruit. "The truly free are poor," the tree responds.

"This might be your most important pilgrimage," Davoud said as we approached the shrine, "because so many Iranians revere Hafez. He is so universal. There is actually little debate on his greatness. A few have stepped forward to criticize medieval Persian poetry, but it has never stuck. Hafez remains an icon."

Over the past few weeks I had been engaged in a fever of Hafez reading and Hafez discussions. I met with specialists, talked to Iranians, read and reread his work. One question burned in my mind: Why would a fourteenth-century poet speak so eloquently to Iranians?

Here's a possible answer.

Hafez, né Shemsuddin Mohammad, was born in Shiraz in 1320. He lived in agitated times. By the time he was born, the Mongol hordes had just swept across Iran, leaving charred homes and pyramids of heads in their wake. Embers remained where libraries had once stood; whole villages were massacred, local rulers impaled; the earth itself was scorched. An Iranian who worked with the Mongol government, Hamdallah Mustawfi Qazwini, put it this way: "There is no doubt that the destruction that happened on the emergence of the Mongol state and the general massacre that occurred at that time will not be repaired in a thousand years, even if no other calamity happens."

Shiraz, more fortunate than most Iranian cities, bore less pain from the Mongol invasion because of a local ruler who was quick to compromise with the Mongol chieftain Genghis Khan. Later, after the Mongol armies had returned to western China, Shiraz, with its meandering and pretty Ruknabad River and its splendid gardens, became a coveted prize in the family feuds among the sons of Genghis Khan. As a result, often a pawn in the internal wars of the Mongol heirs, Shiraz experienced few periods of peace, in Hafez's day. By the time Hafez reached middle age, he had seen a succession of foreign rulers rise and die by the sword. Gertrude Bell, the most able translator of Hafez's poems into the English language, puts it nicely: "His delicate love songs were chanted to the rude accompaniment of the clash of arms, and his dreams must have been interrupted often enough by the nip of famine in a beleaguered town, the inrush of conquerors, and the flight of the defeated."

The Mongols had converted to Islam, and once the initial destruction ended, several Mongol leaders served as great patrons of the arts. The eastern Iranian cities—Bukhara, Samarkand, and Balkh (in present-day Uzbekistan), Herat (in present-day Afghanistan), Mashhad, and Neishapour—had become flourishing cultural centers. Traditional Persian art forms incorporated Eastern techniques from China to produce some of the most extraordinary mosques and shrines. Shiraz, Hafez's birth city, had also emerged as a cultural center by the time of his birth.

Hafez came of age amid a growing Sufi movement. Sufi adherents sought the truth of God in personal experience and Divine love. Sufism, originally a reaction against the worldly faith of the early Islamic rulers, takes its name from the word *suf,* meaning "wool," or the coarse woolen garments worn by the early, self-denying Muslim mystics. Some contemporary scholars think that Sufism got a boost in Iran after the Mongol invasion because of the inevitable questionings that follow massive calamities; people seek alternatives to a belief system that has led only to death and destruction. Others argue that the increasing religious puritanism and literalism of Seljuk rulers in the tenth to twelfth centuries repelled the more philosophical Iranians and planted seeds of the Sufi way, a striving to see beyond daily lives and laws into a higher spiritual realm.

Legend has it that Hafez first took to verse in order to complete a Sufi poem that his uncle grappled with unsuccessfully. The Sufis used poetry to express their love of God. Hafez not only completed his uncle's poem but began to write his own. In a short time he mastered the Persian lyric poem, a genre that often elevates style over substance. The young Hafez clearly possessed a gift. After much practice, he emerged as a stylistic genius, a Mozart of the Persian language. Just as important, he quickly moved beyond style to become a profound thinker and scholar as well.

He memorized the Quran by heart at a young age (a sign of education in medieval Persia), hence his poetic title Hafez (memorizer). His poems explore the human condition, philosophy, God, love, and religion with an advanced insight and timeless depth. In one memorable poem, "Wine Worship," Hafez reminds his readers of the shortness of our time on this earth in a work reminiscent of the Khayyamic worldview. He writes:

> Saki, the dawn is breaking;
> Fill up the glass with wine.
> Heaven's wheel no delay is making—
> Haste, haste, while the day is thine!
>
> Ere to our final ruin
> Space and the world speed by,
> Let wine be our great undoing,
> Red wine, let us drink and die!
>
> When Fate on his wheel is molding
> Jars from this clay of mine,
> Let this be the cup thou'rt holding
> And fill up my head with wine!
>
> Never was I a shrinker,
> No hypocrite monk am I;
> Let wine, the pure wine of the drinker,
> Be the talk men address me by.

The third verse particularly jumps off the page. Hafez reminds his reader that we all shall return to the ground someday, our remains molded into clay jars. If so, he says, "fill up my head with wine." It is a startling image, a normal clay jar used for wine drinking that could be made from the remains of anyone, even a celebrated dead poet's head. In the fourth verse, he takes a jab at the "hypocrite monk," the overtly religious ascetic who might transgress laws when no one is looking. Hafez regularly disparaged falsely pious clerics, as in "You of Shortened Sleeves," the Hafez poem that Sirjani used as a title for his own work. In Hafez's contemporaries, who struggled under the weight of such falsely pious clerics, his words must have struck a chord.

Like Khayyam before him, Hafez expresses in some poems a "seize the day" nihilism: We all shall die one day, we are insignificant bits in the cosmos, the mysteries of life are beyond our reach, so bring on the wine and the pleasures. This is an oft-quoted verse:

> *The wheel of fortune's sphere is a marvelous thing:*
> *What next proud head to the lowly dust will it bring?*
> *Tumult and bloody battle rage in the plain:*
> *Bring blood-red wine and fill the goblet again!*

Beyond its *carpe diem* nature, the verse also appeals to Iranians on another level. For a people who lived in almost constant fear and awe of their kings, it is startling—and perhaps quietly satisfying—to read a poem reminding them that the wheel of fate knows no distinction between the "proud head" of the shah or the peasant.

Hafez, however, was not immune to flattering kings or wealthy benefactors. Still, he wrote the minimum of panegyrics required of a poet of his stature. Iranians rarely quote those poems. More likely, an Iranian will quote a verse in which Hafez criticized rulers who displeased him. One ruler who particularly rankled Hafez was the prince Mubarizu'd-Din Muhammad, who reigned from 1353 to 1357. Unlike his liberal, laissez-faire predecessor, Mubarizu'd-Din Muhammad ruled as a harsh, stern ascetic who expected the same of his subjects and poets. A strict Sunni Muslim uneducated in the subtleties of Sufi wisdom, he closed all of Shiraz's wine taverns and demanded a strict religious orthodoxy from the population. In a poem that earned the ruler's wrath, Hafez wrote bitterly of those days:

> *Drink not wine to the strains of the harp, for the constable is alert.*
> *Hide the goblet in the sleeve of the patchwork cloak,*
> *For the time, like the eye of the decanter, pours forth blood.*
> *Wash your dervish cloak from the wine stain with tears,*
> *For it is the season of piety and the time of abstinence.*

They have closed the doors of the wine taverns; O God, suffer not
That they should open the doors of the house of deceit and hypocrisy!
If they have closed them for the sake of the heart of the self-righteous zealot,
Be of good heart, for they will reopen them for God's sake!

All of Hafez's contemporaries who read or heard the poem knew his target, including the target himself. But Hafez, like Gholam Ali, played by the rules. He did not directly implicate the king; he named no names.

Clearly, Hafez's perceived ability to tell the truth, and get away with it, under harsh circumstances has tickled the fancy of Iranians across the centuries. So has his open contempt for false piety. Hafez's occasional Khayyamic "seize the day" stance also appeals to Iranians, who generally must hide epicureanism from the government in today's Iran and from "the nosy neighbors" in traditional Iranian society. His philosophical frustration at understanding some of the mysteries of life, the cruel wheel of fate, speaks to a broader audience, to anyone who believes the wheel has given him a particularly bad turn.

Still, one cannot reduce Hafez's popularity to such social and political issues emanating from his poetry. Many of his poems do not fall so neatly into categories like attacks on false piety, ruminations on fate, subtle jabs at rulers, or "seize the day" songs of pleasure. These other poems have spawned numerous debates on the poet's worldview.

As with any poet so revered, interpretations abound. For example, when Hafez writes of wine and intoxication and the beloved, the devout Muslim interprets the verses as the drunken state experienced by coming close to the Divine Beloved (God), a common conceit used in Sufi poetry. Still, other readers smile and say that the wine Hafez spoke of was all too real, as was the beloved he wrote about.

In this fashion, Hafez interpretations abound. The religious man finds verses to support his view of Hafez the Devout. The antireligious can find verses to support his claim of Hafez the Agnostic. Some see Hafez the Free-Thinker and Hafez the Sufi and Hafez the Liberal. Indeed, a liberal opponent of Hafez would even could construct a case against Hafez the Reactionary.

Hafez offered Iranians poetry in a beautiful package that alternately appears anti-authoritarian, religiously devout, or hedonistically defiant depending on the perspective of the reader or, indeed, of the poem itself. With

The tomb of Cyrus the Great. Pasargad, Iran. Photo credit: Afshin Molavi

View of Persepolis. Photo credit: Sasan Afsoosi

The author and Haji Agha in front of the Ferdowsi shrine. Tous, Iran.

Workers unloading Saeed's melon truck. Mashad, Iran. Photo credit: Afshin Molavi

The farmer who recites Omar Khayyam poetry standing in front of the Omar Khayyam shrine. Neishapour, Iran. Photo credit: Afshin Molavi

The tomb of the poet Hafez. Shiraz, Iran. Photo credit: Afshin Molavi

The breathtaking grand square of Isfahan. Photo credit: Sasan Afsoosi

Wall painting in the palace of Ali Qapu. Isfahan, Iran. Photo credit: Afshin Molavi

Tehran coffee shop gathering where young boys and girls mingle, flirt, and furtively exchange phone numbers. Photo credit: Ulla Kimmig

Tehran aerobics class. Photo credit: Ulla Kimmig

The Tabriz Constitution House. Tabriz, Iran. Photo credit: Afshin Molavi

Interview with conservative Muslim cleric Haji Agha Abu Torabi, former prisoner of war in Iraq. Tehran, Iran.

A woman and young boy playing a hand drum duet. Tehran. Photo credit: Nahid Afsoosi

A young woman in thought after a boating trip. Karaj, Iran. Photo credit: Nahid Afsoosi

Village girl holding her brother. Mahabad, Iran. Kurdish region. Photo credit: Afshin Molavi

The author with village boys in Ardebil, northwest Iran. Photo credit: Afshin Molavi

Tehran's sleepy carpet bazaar, where merchants regularly complain about government competition in the carpet market. Photo credit: Sasan Afsoosi

Fruit market merchant. Tehran. Photo credit: Sasan Afsoosi

Paying respects at the martyrs' cemetery in Shiraz, one of hundreds of government-funded cemeteries that commemorate Iran's approximately 300,000 dead from the 1980–88 war with Iraq.

A young man studying for the hotly contested college entrance examinations. Photo credit: Sasan Afsoosi

Iranians crowding around newsstands. From 1997 to 2000, the newstand became the most crowded place in Iran as Iranians gathered to read the latest from newly freed press. A conservative crackdown on the press in April 2000 has slowed sales at the newsstands. Photo credit: Ulla Kimmig

Young men dancing to the latest music from Los Angeles–based Iranian pop singers. Cassettes and CDs of popular "Tehrangeles" singers—though technically illegal—are widely sold on the Iranian black market. The "morals police" periodically crack down on the black market cassette sellers. Photo credit: Ulla Kimmig

harsh foreign rulers and tyrants at the helm for centuries, Iranian poets had to develop a language rich in ambiguity. No one developed this more gracefully than Hafez. This ambiguity of language, according to Harvard University scholar Roy Mottahedeh, "allowed them to keep a distance from the generations of rapacious and parasitical rulers, Iranian as well as non-Iranian, who had held power by standing on the necks of their Iranian subjects."

In fact, Hafez reveled in the ambiguity, openly proclaiming "I am a reciter of the Quran in one gathering and a wine drinker in another." Iranians can immediately sympathize with that sentiment. It recalls the complex lines and different faces between public and private space, tradition and desire, the law and justice that many Iranians traverse daily. Herein lies an important reason for Hafez's popularity. The poet does not demand of his readers a single worldview. He acknowledges that different faces correspond to a world of complex social interactions and meddlesome clerics and political leaders. You can shamelessly be a wine drinker in one gathering and a Quran reader in another.

Perhaps the Hafez line goes deeper than that. The Persian literary scholar Ahmad Karimi Hakkak argues that Hafez did not just play a cat-and-mouse game with his principles to avoid scrutiny from authorities. "He may have genuinely felt the heavy weight of philosophical ambiguity that confronts most men who think deeply," he remarked to me in an extensive interview. Much like the tormented seventeenth-century Muslim artists in Isfahan who drew beautiful portraits during the day and washed their hands in their tears at night for transgressing the Muslim rule of portraying the human image, Hafez may have suffered from deep internal conflict as one who believed in his faith but who also struggled to come to terms with some of its exoteric rules.

Karimi Hakkak puts it this way: "When Hafez says that he recites the Quran in one gathering and drinks wine in another, it is often seen by many Iranians as the various faces that one must don in order to survive. We can all relate to that. In my opinion, however, Hafez might also be saying that he is just as confused as the next guy. If we look at the whole of Hafez's oeuvre, we can make a valid argument that the verse may reflect his own inner torment, his own struggle about right and wrong. This is a struggle that we all—Iranians or not—have experienced."

This act of donning different faces seems often to Westerners as the height of the hypocrisy that Hafez so criticizes. It also leads to an unfortunate Iranian character trait, a remarkable ability to be evasive, tell half-truths, and lie outright. Iranians rarely discuss this issue, but numerous Western travel writers and journalists have remarked on it. The early twentieth-century British foreign minister and lifelong Persianist Lord Curzon—a colonialist and racist, mind you—once wrote: " [s]plendide mendax [mendacity] might be taken as the motto for the Persian character." A more contemporary Western observer, the astute journalist and far more sympathetic Iran watcher Elaine Sciolino, concurs, writing in her book *Persian Mirrors*: "A number of Iranians I have met over the years know how to be splendidly deceptive." A conservative Parliament member revealingly told Sciolino: "If you don't speak of everything so openly, it's better. Being able to keep a secret even if you have to mislead is considered a sign of maturity. It's Persian wisdom. We don't have to be ideal people. Everybody lies. Let's be good liars."

A Western businessman friend, exasperated by a tough set of negotiations, once launched into an angry tirade against Iranians at a Tehran party. "You are all liars," he said, slightly drunk from the bootlegged whiskey. "I think it starts with your poetry, which you interpret in five different ways! And there is your *ta'rof,* all that fluffy talk you Iranians say but don't really mean! What bullocks! Saying you are each other's 'servant' or pledging to serve each other, when you are really stabbing each other in the back!"

A few Iranians, listening to the tirade, smiled and nodded appropriately, giving him a "yes, how unfortunate" look. After he walked away, one Iranian turned to me and said: "What a fool that man is. He is just upset because we don't believe his own lies. His own country, England, is full of the smoothest liars I've ever seen."

When the drunk Brit returned, he apologized, saying that maybe he had spoken out of line. The Iranians nodded, assuring him that his comments were fine.

The businessman's remarks hold an unfortunate degree of truth, but perhaps the real reason that Iranians have developed a facility in lying has, I think, less to do with *ta'rof* or the tradition of ambiguity in poetry than with a history of authoritarianism and foreign invasion. The authoritarian leader forces you to lie in order to survive. The foreign invader forces you to lie in order to adapt or refrain from adapting. As the revered thirteenth-century poet Saadi notes, "If you cannot cut the hand of the king, then it is best to kiss it."

Throughout history, Iranians have developed a remarkable ability to adapt to new circumstances. In some respects, Iran has weathered the storms of invasion and entrapped its invaders with its culture, kissing the king's right hand while guiding his left hand toward what it really wants. Examples abound. Alexander and some of his generals took on attributes of Persian kings. Iran accepted the Arab faith but not the Arab culture, while significantly contributing to the cultural development of the early Muslim world. From the tenth through the thirteenth century, both the Central Asian Turk invader and the eastern Mongol invader were caught in the attractive web of Iranian culture, organizing their courts in the Persian manner, building Persian-style cities atop those they destroyed, and embracing Ferdowsi, the poet, as their own. Persian became the court language in both dynasties, and the Persian poet emerged as the favored courtier. The Iranian Safavi dynasty, though Turkic in origin, protected Iran's borders like devoted nationalists, while battling the Ottoman Turks. Persian influence even spread beyond Iran. By the seventeenth century the three dynasties of significance in the Muslim world (the Ottomans in Turkey, the Mughals in India [Persians of origin], and the Safavis in Iran) all used Persian at their courts (though, ironically, it took a hundred years for the Safavis to do so). The Iranian architectural stamp on Mughal India clearly shines in the Taj Mahal, built by an Indian king of Iranian ancestry.

Iranians developed a pattern in dealing with foreign invaders: accept them reluctantly, take the best from their culture, continue a quiet (kissing hands) resistance, and ultimately, Iranize them. Certain aspects of ancient Iran have continued to this day despite numerous invasions: the absolute power of the king (today's king wears a turban) and the associated patriarchy, the idealized sense of justice, and the worship of beauty. The latter two remain strong cultural characteristics, while the first, absolute power, wavers. Iranians often take pride in other aspects of the nation's cultural continuity, especially the survival of the Persian language after the Arab invasion.

Despite these examples of cultural continuity, twentieth-century Iranians displayed a marked cultural disorientation. Throughout the century Iranians alternately condemned Islam as the source of all their problems and praised Islam as the solution to all their problems; they pledged to imitate all things Western and to defy all things Western; they stepped forward toward modernity and pulled back in the face of tradition.

The reason for each of these steps usually had something to do with "identity" issues. The Iranian who argued for defiance of all things Western often did so in the name of preserving Iranian identity. The Iranian who stepped forward to condemn Islam also did so often in the name of Iranian identity, arguing that Islam came from Arabs who forced it on them. In the early twentieth century one prominent Iranian thinker called for a drastic change in the Iranian identity. "We need to become Europeanized to our very bone marrow," he said.

This question of an Iranian identity elicits much discussion even in this century. The issue supports a small book industry. One recent best seller was a political science book by an Iranian professor titled *Who We are and What We Have Become*. Another briskly sold book was titled simply *Iranian Identity*. State-run (conservative) television regularly produces programs on Iranian identity. In the minds of TV programmers, the ideal Iranian gentleman is a pious, hardworking, bearded man who respects his elders, reveres Khomeini, obeys his government, and eats his dinners on the floor in the old manner.

Much revolutionary discourse of the 1960s and 1970s revolved around identity issues. Leading intellectuals, alarmed by the growing Westernization in Iran, urged a return to tradition, to religion. Ali Shariati called on Iranians to emulate the example of Imam Hossein, presenting the martyred imam as the pillar of Shi'a Iranian identity. Jalal Al-e-Ahmad, a leading writer and essayist, wrote often on the subject of return, criticizing the "Westoxication" of Iranians and urging a return to the traditions of Shi'a Islam, to simple, rural values. In many ways, Al-e-Ahmad's own life typified Iran's cultural disorientation. Even while he counseled a vague return to Shi'a Islam, his own religious faith was weak; he decried "Westoxication" but preferred quoting Western philosophers; he joined the Communist Tudeh party, only to retreat into the embrace of religion. Ultimately he came to question if he could possess any real religious faith at all.

A psychologist friend once told me that his compatriots suffered from a case of cultural schizophrenia in the twentieth century. "We are not sure who we are, and every few years someone steps forward to define us. Half the country agrees with that person and waves pamphlets about the real Iranian identity, and the other half disagrees and writes its own pamphlets."

I view the Iranian cultural schizophrenia as an inevitable reaction to a succession of political leaders who sought to define an Iranian identity on their own arbitrary terms. Twentieth-century Iran saw two extremes: the Shah's relegation of religion and embrace of a chauvinistic Persian nationalism, and shortly thereafter, the Islamic Republic's proclamation of a "real" Iranian identity—revolutionary, anti-imperialist, socially conservative, and overtly Islamically pious. Both sides had their pamphlets, and the other half of the population quietly wrote its own.

Amid these shifting winds of cultural identity, Hafez stands apart. His poetry does not draw clear, unbreakable lines about identity and culture. He allows for the ambiguities that ripple through Iranian culture. In that respect, Hafez did what so many Persian poets have done. He expressed, according to Mottahedeh, that "the ambiguity that was at the heart of Iranian culture lived most freely and openly . . . was not an enigma to be solved but an enigma that was unsolvable."

Hafezian ambiguity allows for shades of gray in a world where authority figures constantly demand black or white. Hafez's poetry, it seems to me, also might serve the private mind of the thinking Iranian who, faced with so many competing truths from different worlds and different rulers, has somehow lost faith in the power of absolute truth and settled only on the certainty of enigma and faith in the aesthetic.

Pilgrimage: The Tomb of Hafez, the Poet

Along the stone walkway to the tomb flanked by tall red roses, people packed the green park benches. A girl in a light blue manteau and gray head scarf sketched the Hafez tomb in pencil. A family of four drank bottles of Zam Zam, a sweet Coca-Cola substitute made in Iran. Straight ahead, the white stairs led to a multicolumned portal where the tomb of Hafez rested. Davoud and I walked toward the tomb, past two long blue reflecting pools and beds of yellow and red roses. The tombstone, a deep white and cream marble, sang with Hafez verses etched on the stone. The tomb itself took shelter under an unadorned black dome. On the inside of the dome, a profusion of color—gold rims, celestial blue background, and red and black diamonds and stars—surrounded poetic verses from Hafez.

Davoud approached the tomb reverentially. A small crowd stood by the tombstone. Following tradition, each person placed two fingers on the marble and said a prayer for the deceased. One young man with long black hair and a soft, curly black beard closed his eyes, gently rocking back and forth, seemingly in a Sufi-like trance. Later I found out he was a war veteran. "The world is ugly," he told me, "I am at peace only when I read Hafez." Nearby a father read verses from Hafez to his son. The female sketch artist from the bench had approached for a closer look.

After moving away from the tomb, we walked amid the lemon and orange trees in the courtyard. I asked Davoud why he thought Iranians revere Hafez so much.

"Every Iranian sees in the *Divan* of Hafez like seeing in a mirror," he said. "He writes about so many aspects of the human condition that you can find your own plight or sadness or joy squeezed between two lush and beautiful lines of verse. He also labored under sometimes harsh rulers, and it shows in his poetry. Every Iranian knows the difficulties of living under absolute and sometimes harsh rulers and empathizes with Hafez's own plight," he said.

We sat down on a bench in the shade of a bandari orange tree. The oranges—green, ripe, and heavy—pulled the branches toward the ground. I retrieved my notebook and asked Davoud some more questions.

How would he compare Hafez to the other great classical poets of Persia?

"I think Hafez is exceptional," he said. "There is both depth and beauty in his poems. He is also quintessentially Iranian, and I think that is why he does not have the same number of admirers outside Iran as does Omar Khayyam or Saadi or even Rumi. He does not translate well, both literally and culturally."

I pressed him on that point.

"His poems are more complex in meaning than the others. Khayyam, as popularly known, is an agnostic skeptic struggling with the mysteries of life who urges people to drink wine and make love. Of course, some might argue against that depiction. Still, the view that has come to be attributed to Khayyam is easily understood by all. Saadi, for his part, has simple moral tales that anyone can understand, though he was also a stylistic genius like Hafez. Rumi is more complicated, but his mystical poems of love for God can be understood by many. Hafez, however, works on so many different levels and seems to speak a private language that only an Iranian can understand. Hafez is also the most gifted with the Persian language. I have read some Hafez translations in English. They are stilted. They do not move me at all, but when I read the original Farsi, sometimes I feel a stirring in my stomach at the beauty of the verse."

He continued. "There are so many different views of Hafez: as mystic, as epicurean, as rebel against authority. I sometimes like to view him as an intellectual. It is important for Iranian intellectuals to continue to think and write and express their views. These contributions will serve the Iranian people," he said.

I pointed out that some might argue that Iran's late-twentieth-century intellectual "contributions" added up to little more than a jumble of Marxist and Communist and leftist utopianism, which ultimately did not serve Iranians very well.

He smiled. "Yes, there are some who think that way," he said quietly, almost sadly.

He took a breath, seemingly pained by my statement. "You know, Afshin, I have been struggling with this question myself, but you have to understand the perspective of a writer in the 1970s. We lived under a military dictatorship supported by the West, especially the United States. We saw great disparity in wealth, tremendous corruption among the elite. In those days we did not understand the failures of the Soviet system, and those among us who did blamed not the system but the practitioners of the system. We wanted to create an ideal, classless egalitarian society. We were idealistic, and I do not think there is anything wrong with that."

He spoke more in resignation than in defense. He looked down as he spoke. His voice lowered as he went on. "Most of the writers that I grew up reading had leftist views. Many were Marxists, and many were sincere in their desire to improve Iran," he said. "Perhaps literature should not have been used in this way, but since we had no newspapers, it was our only way of expressing our views."

Marxist and leftist ideas suffused Iranian novels and short stories of the 1960s and 1970s. For many, the quality of a book rose with its commitment to Marxist revolution. One writer at a Tehran conference in 1977 put it this way: "The philosophical perspective of an artist is derived from socialism, Marxism, and existentialism." Many thought that literature must be revolutionary to be great.

"I do not think we can blame that generation's intellectuals," Davoud said. "They saw the problems while the rest of Iran ignored them. Perhaps their solutions were not ideal, but at least they saw that all was not well and tried to do something." He continued. "I think if we look at our intellectuals today, however, they seem to have a better perspective on things. The younger generation of intellectuals and writers, whether religious or secular, is less dogmatic and more open to dialogue. They are not interested in the Marxist and utopian clichés of the past," he said. "I think that this is a good sign." He breathed in heavily, as if he were trying to gulp the air. I expected him to go on, but he stopped and looked away. We lingered for a while on the bench, watching the crowds.

A group of bearded young men, black-and-white Palestinian-style scarves wrapped around their necks, walked into the shrine area. The scarves were a dead giveaway. They were Basijis. As they walked toward the shrine, I noticed a few young women tighten their head scarves and walk away from them.

Notebook in hand, I approached them. They had been on a pilgrimage tour of martyrs of the Iran-Iraq war. They had visited important battlefields in the south and paid their respects to martyrs' families and cemeteries across the region.

"Why have you come to the Hafez tomb?" I asked one of them, a thin boy of no more than twenty, with soft eyes and a wispy beard.

"Hafez was a great poet and a devout Muslim," he said. "We should pay our respects to this great Muslim poet. When I read his poetry, I feel great religious inspiration."

Soon enough a small crowd of Basijis had gathered. Typically, the interview turned around, and the questions started coming at me: "What do you think of Iran? How is life in America? Why do the Western media hate Iran?"

One young man stepped to the front of the boys. He stood tall and slim with brown eyes and a hawklike nose and a black, scraggly beard. He leaned forward and asked me: "What do the American people think about the Basijis?"

"Most Americans do not know what a Basiji is," I responded candidly. "Frankly, most Americans do not know much about Iranians."

He seemed confused by the answer. After all, most Iranians spend a lot of time thinking about America and Americans. Why wouldn't Americans do the same? "Many Americans still have a negative image of Iran," I explained. "They remember the hostages and all of the 'Death to America' slogans and the flag burning."

A few more Basijis strolled over. I stood on the steps of the Hafez shrine, leaning against a column. "But after Iran's reform movement and the influx of Iranian films in the United States, the American perception of Iran has softened," I said. A few more young Basijis straggled in, creating a small circle as I spoke. By now my lecture had twenty people in the audience. "People around the world are watching closely Iran's struggle for freedom," I said. "Almost every day there are articles in Western newspapers about Iran."

The young man with the hawklike nose interrupted me. He seemed like a group leader. The others deferred to him. "We support freedom and reform too," he said, "as long as it is within the line of the Imam."

Several young men nodded. One added, "Yes, and as long as the reform is supported by Agha." The line of the Imam (*khat-e-Emam*), the path of Khomeini, was the phrase used by conservatives to denote a conservative political and religious orthodoxy. *Agha,* in this case, was an honorific term used to mean Iran's Supreme Leader, Ayatollah Khamenei.

I took a breath and continued. "Perhaps the revolutionary age might be winding down into new realities," I suggested, though I think I garbled the Farsi, making it sound harsher than I intended, something like "The revolution has ended." I knew it was a bad mistake (even I practiced the art of self-censorship), but I plodded on. "Perhaps this is a new age, and Iran needs new ideas. You have just spent the past few days visiting shrines of Iran's war martyrs. They deserve to be respected," I said, sincerely. "I have visited Shalamcheh myself," I said, referring to a prominent war veterans' shrine.

I began to sweat. My voice cracked. How had I got myself involved in this political sermon on the steps of the Hafez shrine? Forty eyes fixed intently on me, awaiting my next statement, as I stumbled on. "There is no longer any need for war. I know that some of you might be involved in campus politics. Some of you might even be opposed to the students who support democracy, but perhaps—"

The young man with the hawklike nose, the group leader, interrupted me again. "We are not involved in politics. We believe in the line of the Imam and in the *velayat-e-faqih*. This is what all Iranians believe in. This not just a political view. It is our religion." A few boys nodded in agreement.

At the back of the crowd, I spotted Davoud. He looked worried. He nodded slightly, indicating that I should halt my impromptu discourse. I trailed off, wishing all the young men well on their next pilgrimage. They shook my hand and wished me well on my journeys. "We are at your service," a few of them said perfunctorily.

The tall one with the hawk nose smiled and shook my hand and told everyone to meet by the bus in ten minutes. "I hope you enjoy the rest of your stay in Iran," he said, staring at me for longer than was appropriate. He turned and walked away.

After they left, Davoud laughed and slapped me on the back. "You are going to get us into trouble one day." He walked away and lit a cigarette. I snapped a few photos of the shrine and watched a young sketch artist trace the outlines of a long-stemmed red rose. Suddenly, I noticed four of the college Basijis rushing toward me. I tensed up and instinctively clenched my fists. They stopped, panting. "Mr. Molavi," one of them said, handing me a black-and-white scarf, "please accept this as a gift from our Basiji association to you as a fellow Iranian who has returned to his homeland and who cares about our martyrs." The scarf was the Basiji symbol of war. He spoke rapidly, breathlessly. "We appreciated your taking the time to talk with us, and we understood your words well." He paused. I felt as if he had paused for dramatic effect, so I might find some meaning in his last sentence: "we understood your words well."

"We hope you have a safe and happy journey. Please take this also," he said, handing me a tan prayer stone, "as a personal gift. Remember the martyrs, and remember Iran when you pray with this stone." Deeply touched, I shook their hands. A message underlay this hurried gesture. They ran back out to the bus, perhaps hoping that the tall young man with the hawk nose had not seen what they had just done.

Mrs. Teimouri's Wedding

Later that afternoon, Davoud returned to Tehran. Before he left, he suggested that I meet with Mrs. Teimouri, a woman whose love of Hafez matched his own. Mrs. Teirouri, however, was more interested in recalling her wedding day. "Let me tell you about my wedding night," Mrs. Teimouri said. "It may interest you." We sat in the living room of her large apartment in Shiraz with her husband. We had just finished dinner, saffron and lemon chicken with white rice and cooked cherries. There was a small glass beaker of hot cherry juice extract, which we poured on the rice and the chicken, adding a sweet tang to the buttered and salted rice. "Do not pour too much," Mrs. Teimouri warned. "Your rice will become runny." Her paintings, showing gray-haired Sufi men surrounded by apricot-eyed maidens, dotted the walls.

Mrs. Teimouri had olive skin and black eyes and dusty rose cheeks. The skin on her face was smooth, unblemished except for small circles under her eyes. Just below one of the circles, she had a small brown mole. It looked like a permanent tear.

"My wedding will tell you a little about our condition," she said, her face a picture of gloom. She was a melancholy woman. Smiles did not come easily to her. Her face seemed to rebel when she smiled, two lines appearing in the middle of her cheeks, pushing the smile back down.

A tall and lanky twelve-year-old boy, Mrs. Teimouri's son, entered the room, carrying a tray of honey-glazed sweets. He placed them on the chipped wood coffee table. He wore white Nike sneakers with a blue swoosh sign. The sneakers looked real, not like the Chinese-made fakes that flooded the country. The Shiraz apartment was tastefully decorated. In the kitchen there was a state-of-the-art refrigerator. The Nike sneakers, very expensive by Iranian standards, and the refrigerator were the only overt sign that the Teimouris had a bit of money. Mrs. Teimouri looked at her son and tilted her head slightly, almost imperceptibly, but the message was clear: Sit down, my son; listen to this.

He sat down, offering me sweets. Mr. Teimouri looked on, shifting in his chair, as if still upset by the thought of his wedding night. He had a black mustache and wavy black hair, with traces of gray emerging at his temples. He was slim and fit and quiet and mostly deferred to his wife to lead the conversation.

"We decided to get married in the fall of 1987," she said. "It was a bad time. We were living in Tehran. The Iraqis had begun bombing Tehran. Every night for two weeks we heard missiles and sirens. We were so scared. Have you heard the sound of air sirens? It is a terrible sound.

"We all agreed that we should postpone the wedding. I prayed that there would be no more bombing of the cities. I wanted a peaceful wedding. You may think it sounds selfish to pray for such things when our boys were dying by the thousands against the Iraqis on the borders, but what could we do? Should we stop living?"

Her husband interrupted, pointing a finger in the air angrily as he spoke. "Anyway, the war should have ended in 1983! The Iraqis were ready for a cease-fire! We had regained our lost territory! The Saudis were ready to give us billions of dollars in reparations on behalf of Iraq! There was no reason to continue fighting, but all we heard on the damn TV and radio was '*Jang, jang ta piruzi*' [War, war, until victory]!"

He did not seem comfortable speaking, though he looked as if he wanted to go on, to cite more facts about why the war should have ended, but he trailed off, mumbling about the Saudis and billions of dollars. History will write the legacy of Iran's postrevolution leaders, but perhaps the most devastating indictment might be that they needlessly killed thousands of their own young men by refusing to accept what would have been an honorable cease-fire.

"Yes,"—Mrs. Teimouri picked up the story—"my father always said that we must continue to live. He always gathered the whole family together every Friday for a bit of food and music and poetry. Sometimes he served wine. He would not accept any excuses. The kids would play in the garden of his house, behind the walls, and we would spend a few hours in escape, pretending that a war and a revolution were not destroying our lives."

Mrs. Teimouri, like many upper-middle-class Iranian women, turned against the revolution on the day that Khomeini mandated the use of the *hijab*. She took part in the Tehran protests denouncing the *hijab*. Only a few weeks after the announcement, Mrs. Teimouri remembers the grocery stores and the plastic head scarves that appeared at the front of the store, with the sign: PLEASE OBSERVE ISLAMIC DRESS WHILE SHOPPING. She refused to use the disposable plastic head scarves.

"It was the same plastic used in trash bags!" she said. "One day, while I was shopping, a bearded young man approached me. He said he would throw acid on my face if I did not comply with the rules. Of course I did.

"At my father's gatherings,"—Mrs. Teimouri continued—"we would walk in his courtyard unveiled. He had tall walls to protect us. It felt good to feel my hair blowing in the wind. I had forgotten what that felt like. Sometimes we would sit by the fountain and listen to him recite poetry after lunch. His favorite was Hafez. He would recite lines of Hafez, and strangely, they would have meaning for our own lives today.

"My father insisted that we have a proper wedding, with music and dancing. He invited a singer who was charging double his going rate because of the risk of getting caught. In those days the *Komiteh* raids on homes that were having parties were common. It's not like today, where you can just pay the police off so easily," she said.

The neighborhood *Komiteh* was Iran's version of the local Communist commissar. It had the power to intervene in the personal lives of Iranians if they broke the *Komiteh* rules: No mixed parties, no alcohol, no gambling, no public displays of affection, no antigovernment speech, and respect for the conservative dress code. Today the *Komiteh* has been disbanded, melded into the police force. Many of its members now work as police patrols, advance squads on motorbikes, ready and eager to take bribes, like the one who knocked on the door at Mehran's party.

Mrs. Teimouri went on, "Everyone had gathered in my father's house. We had completed the wedding ceremony earlier in the day. The house was full of white flowers, lilies. When I walked in wearing my wedding dress, everyone clapped for me. I was amazed to see all the walls draped in white blankets. Later I found out that my father had done that in order to muffle the sound of the music. He bought twenty white blankets at the bazaar. The sad thing is that the merchant knew why he needed them.

"My friends and family all were there, though a few made excuses and did not come. I did not blame them. It was a bad time to throw a party. The singer was singing a popular song, you know the one that calls for the groom to kiss the bride. Vali [her husband] leaned in and kissed me, and everyone laughed and clapped. It was a typical wedding, you know what I mean," she said. Middle-and upper-middle-class Iranian weddings are usually vibrant and loud with dancing and, often, drinking.

"My father wanted to offer alcohol to the guests, but we convinced him not to. It was too risky in those days. He agreed, only reluctantly. A few guests left early, before ten p.m. They were perhaps happy that they had not got caught. They could go home and sleep easily."

As she spoke, her son stared intently at her, leaning forward in his chair, rocking back, his bright white Nike sneakers pushing down on the ground, as if he were about to leap up from his chair any minute. He seemed to know the ending of this story. So did I. I had been in Iran long enough to sense an unhappy ending.

"My father stayed for only one dance. He stood outside the door, on the street, constantly checking to see if the *Komiteh* was coming. He had a pocket full of rials in case they came, though it was much riskier to try a bribe in those days. I kept looking for him, but everyone said that he was outside waiting for the *Komiteh*. Eventually they did come. He tried handing the leader a few bills. The leader refused and told my father that everyone must leave the house immediately. I shall never forget the look on my father's face when he entered the room amid all of the singing and dancing. I had never seen him afraid, but that night I saw a frightened man.

"He whispered to the singer. The music stopped. Immediately people assumed the worst, and women ran upstairs in search of their head scarves. My father went to the microphone. He told everyone that there was no need to worry, though his face showed a lot of concern. If they all went home now, the *Komiteh* would not take them to the station. A few people cursed the *Komiteh* quietly, but most just nervously gathered their coats. They didn't even protest. The women wrapped their head scarves tighter than usual. They walked out into the street, got in their cars, and drove away. The singer asked if there was a back door.

"My father told me that he had to fill out some paper work at the station. He would be home soon. He did not come home that night. He was charged with attempted bribery and sponsoring a "depraved gathering." My father stayed overnight in jail. On my wedding night, the most special night of my life, I cried all night. We wondered if one of the early departing guests had informed the police. Perhaps it was an old business feud or family feud or just an attempt to get on the good side of the *Komiteh*. People did strange and bad things in those days. The next morning we bailed my father out of jail."

Her son kept staring intently at his mother. Mr. Teimouri shifted in his chair, sighing and occasionally rubbing his temples.

"You see, Mr. Afshin, I am not saying that this was a terrible tragedy and that everyone should weep for us. Thank God we have our health and we are comfortable economically. Still, sometimes you journalists forget to chronicle these little but important things. In your rush to interview politicians and journalists, you forget the rest of us. One of the sweetest nights of my life, my wedding, was taken away from me. Surely, you can find some tragedy in that."

The Case of Akbar Ganji: Journalist, Prodemocracy Advocate, Prisoner

Back in Tehran, I received a telephone call from a colleague in the Iranian press. "Ganji has been jailed," he said. "This is the beginning of a crackdown. Be careful what you write." He bade me a hurried good-bye and hung up the phone.

Akbar Ganji, a wildly popular prodemocracy journalist, had grown legendary for his scathing attacks on Iran's powerful conservatives and hardliners. Most who followed his case expected his imprisonment. No one could speak out so boldly with impunity and go free. Still, news of the jailing sent a chill through Iran's reformist journalists and the prodemocracy movement. Ganji's bravery lifted the movement to a higher level. Where would it go now?

I knew Ganji only slightly, having interviewed him a few weeks before. We had met in the newspaper-lined basement of an apartment building in Tehran. Yellowing copies of the weekly *Rah-e-Now* (New Path)—Ganji's newspaper prior to its being shut down by Iran's hard-line judiciary—formed neat stacks along the white concrete walls. When I entered, he sat alone, reading a book in the carpeted room. He turned away from his book and sprang to his feet, a small man with a light brown beard and brown, dancing eyes. I concealed a tinge of surprise. I suppose one expects national heroes to be tall.

He greeted me warmly, embracing me as if I were an old friend. "Welcome," he said, smiling. "It is nice to meet you."

A small stack of his best-selling book *Darkroom of the Ghosts* leaned against some newspapers. In the book he brands Iran's conservative clerics "religious fascists" and links a small clique of hard-line clerics and intelligence agents to assassinations of up to eighty dissidents and writers since 1988. The chilling book also contains brave passages defending free speech and democracy.

Ganji pioneered a new journalism in Iran: brash, aggressive, intellectual, fearless. He crossed red lines routinely. He received death threats from government-affiliated thugs almost daily. When we met, I found to my surprise that none of the usual hangers-on or security types surrounded him. He tarried alone in a basement office, reading a book, despite the fact that a few months earlier his friend and colleague Saeed Hajjarian had taken a bullet in the head. He offered me a seat at a long, rectangular brown table. "I am not looking to become a martyr," he said. "I have a family, and I enjoy life. However, I realize that sometimes in life one must be prepared to fight and pay the consequences, if necessary. If we really want democracy in Iran, we must be willing to fight for it. There has been a great deal of talk in this country. It is time to act."

He then talked at length about the revolution. He said it was a fine example of a vigorous and determined act by the Iranian people, but it ultimately failed. "Our revolution was an act for freedom, but we did not follow through properly. We ended up with tyranny and fascism. We Iranians have been fighting for freedom in one form or another since the beginning of the twentieth century. Today, as we enter the twenty-first century, we still have not tasted long periods of freedom. We still see a free press as a privilege, rather than a right. We still see a popular government as a privilege, rather than a right. I hope to see Iranians one day come to expect these things."

Ganji, like many of today's reformists, came to these views after the revolution. In the early days of the revolution he would have turned his nose up at the title of democrat. He then belonged to a radical Islamic leftist faction, the sort of people who took Americans hostage. A vehement anti-imperialist and vigorous pamphleteer, he wrote often of foreign exploitation in Iran. He saw solutions in Islam, in a return to a native identity, even though he acknowledged, then and now, that Iran has several identities. He fought in the war with Iraq. Later he joined Iran's intelligence service.

"Around 1984 or 1985 I was becoming disillusioned," he said. "I saw a pseudofascism and political tyranny emerging in Iran. Anyone who asked questions was branded 'antirevolutionary' and 'against Islam.' In my opinion, Islam was being abused by a fascist system."

He harped on this theme often. A personally religious man, he found the abuse of his faith in the service of tyranny unacceptable. "A certain faction in Iran," he said, referring to conservatives, "has turned religion into ideology, faith into fascism. It promised us heaven, but it created a hell on earth." The last line was a Ganji trademark, one that was often quoted. "Every religion has had its dark moments with inquisitions and narrow-minded prejudice," Ganji said, "but this moment we have had in Iran goes against the spirit of Islam and all major faiths."

Did he agree with the Islamic philosopher Soroush that politics pollutes religion? As a corollary to this thought, did he believe in the need for the separation of mosque and state?

"Most of today's religious intellectuals," he said, "greatly admire Soroush, but he is a philosopher, and we must deal with practical political realities. We believe that Iran must embrace the principles of political modernity: civil society, free press, democracy, rule of law. These are principles of secularization." He used the English word with a Persian accent: "sekularee-zaseeon."

He did not answer the questions outright, and I did not press him. They were red line questions, and at a first meeting, he may have felt uncomfortable addressing them.

He continued. "Most of us, the religious intellectuals, believe in a Popper-ian view of the world."

The Austrian philosopher Karl Popper, author of the landmark political study *Open Society and Its Enemies,* was a favorite of Iran's reformists. Popper makes a powerful defense of democratic liberalism and a devastating critique of the philosophic underpinnings of totalitarian systems. Like many Iranian intellectuals of Ganji's generation, Popper in his youth was a Marxist. By 1945, when he published *Open Society,* describing how Marxism as a theory soon failed on the weight of empirical evidence and degenerated into pseu-doscientific dogma in the defense of totalitarianism, he had abandoned Marx-ism. Ganji saw parallels in Popper's view of Marxist history and the evolution of Iran's Islamic government.

"In a sense that is what happened with our Islamic revolution," he said. "We had a theory—that Islamic government could provide us with just rule—but then there was a great deal of pseudo-Islamic dogma added in defense of totalitarianism."

His voice paused, as if to go on, but the phone interrupted us. The German embassy waited at the other end. One of Ganji's aides handled the call. Ganji's visa was ready, he was told. He could pick it up when he wanted.

"There is a conference in Berlin on our reform movement," Ganji explained to me. "I'm not sure what it's about, but I shall make my points," he said, smiling. "Why don't you drink some tea?" He leaped up from his chair, catlike, but I insisted that he not trouble himself. We wound up our conver-sation with talk of my travels in Iran. "Have you been taking pictures? We have some beautiful sites, don't we?"

The following week Ganji went to Germany. The conference turned into political dynamite for those Iranians who attended. Iranian opposition figures in Europe came to the event, where they openly ridiculed the rulers of the Islamic Republic and attacked Ganji and other reformists as lackeys of the Islamic Republic, trying to preserve the system through reform instead of trying to defeat it through revolution. At times the conference degenerated into a circus. One woman, protesting the veil, took off all her clothes and stood naked in front of the Iranian delegates. A man, also moved to unclothe, joined her. Another woman got up and started dancing in protest against the prohi-bition on the public display of dancing in Iran.

When Ganji returned from Berlin, conservative newspapers slammed him for attending a conference side by side with opposition figures that sought to overthrow the government and "morally lax" ladies who ridiculed Islamic traditions. Undaunted, Ganji continued his open onslaught against Iran's hard-liners and his vigorous advocacy of democracy. He pulled few punches. Throughout his rise to legendary journalist, Ganji amazed Iranians with his bravery. He did not smile, kiss the leader's hand, and say things behind his back. He said them openly, brazenly, defiantly. He felt no need to hide his views behind ambiguous language, allegory, symbolism, or satire. He did not want to be Gholam Ali.

Eventually hard-liners had heard enough. One of the charges leveled against him was his attendance at the Berlin conference. After a show trial that Ganji dismissed openly as "illegitimate," the judge handed him a sentence of fifteen years on January 12, 2001.

V

Cities: Tehran, Isfahan

Islam and Democracy

Akbar Ganji's sentence came from an Islamic judge in clerical robes, an orthodox figure of the sort that first became familiar in Iran a thousand years ago with the invasion of the Seljuks, the Sunni Turkish tribe that took over the country until the Mongols devastated it in the thirteenth century. Iran's 1979 revolution elevated religious judges to positions of power unseen in history. Not only did they rule the pulpit, but for the first time in Iranian history, they ruled the state. In both the era of the eleventh-century Khayyam and the fourteenth-century Hafez, the orthodox religious judge was a Sunni Muslim, whose relative power depended on the king's relative religiosity. After the sixteenth- to the eighteenth-century Safavid dynasty successfully implanted Shi'ism on the Iranian soil, Shi'a judges replaced Sunni ones, but as in the past, they derived their power from the kings, who often gave them broad leeway to form social laws. Though the Shi'a tradition allowed for a more vibrant debate over interpretations of the Quran than the Sunni did, the orthodox literalist judge much concerned with detections of heresy still retained a prominent place in the seminary.

The story of Shi'a Muslim clerical power that climaxed in 1981, when an Islamic Republic ruled by Shi'a Muslim clerics rose from the ashes of the revolution, begins five centuries ago in the Safavid era. My next pilgrimage, to the shrine of a seventeenth-century Safavid-era cleric, Mullah Mohammad Bagher Majlesi, would take me to Isfahan, the splendid seat of the Safavid Empire. Majlesi represented to me the first supremely powerful Shi'a cleric, and in that sense he was a precursor to Khomeini and Iran's other ruler clerics, including the judge who sentenced Akbar Ganji.

Ever since the sixteenth-century rise of the Safavid dynasty, Iran's Shi'a Muslim clerics (who traveled to Iran from Shi'a communities in Arab lands) have wielded tremendous influence in national affairs, often acting as the most potent opposition force to the all-powerful king. Shi'a clerics often criticized kings as unfit to rule and, starting in the late seventeenth century, occasionally stood in open defiance of the king on social and sometimes political issues. In the nineteenth and early twentieth centuries, under an alliance of convenience between king and priest, the Shi'a clerics granted legitimacy to the king and the king granted the clergy sway over primary education and the courts, though the alliance sometimes frayed as the clergy became more assertive in their denunciations and defiance of Iranian kings in the late nineteenth century. Both institutions—primary education and the courts—later became targets of Reza Shah, who sought to wrest them from the clergy in the early twentieth century. During his reign the traditional alliance between the orthodox cleric and king weakened.

Even before Reza Shah became Iran's king in 1925, a growing group of nationalist clerics found fault with Iran's kings, whose misrule frustrated all segments of society. In 1890, a Qajar king had granted a foreign company a wide-ranging tobacco concession that was widely protested by Iranian merchants and nationalists as an affront to Iranian economic sovereignty. In response, a leading Tehran cleric announced a religious declaration banning the use of tobacco. He led a revolt against the concession, which later was retracted. During the first twenty-two years of the reign of Mohammad Reza Shah (1941–63), the leading clerics, the grand ayatollahs, restored the old king-clergy alliance, though it began to fray after the death of Ayatollah Borujerdi, a powerful cleric who advocated a retreat from politics. In the 1960s and 1970s, clerical opposition to government peaked. Shi'a clerics, located in every city and village across Iran, were instrumental in attracting the masses to the streets. No intellectual Marxist or democratic nationalist (also key revolutionary strains of thought) could whip the masses of urban working classes and rural residents into a frenzy as the clerics could—and did.

Though Muslim clerics in Iran have exerted significant social and political influence on leaders for up to a thousand years, the notion of clerical rule of the state espoused by the late Ayatollah Khomeini in fact departed radically from the traditional Shi'a Muslim thinking that held all governments to be profane. In the absence of the messianic Hidden Imam, the argument went, participation in government was tantamount to blasphemy. To this day most senior Shi'a clerics in Iran hold that view, albeit quietly. Of the fourteen grand ayatollahs living in Iran, only one has publicly advocated clerical rule (and that one, Ayatollah Montazeri, today leads a dissident faction). Of the five thousand recognized ayatollahs in Iran, a mere eighty work in government. The nongovernmental clerics are the ones left stranded on the side of road for hours by taxis that refuse to pick them up; the government clerics have chauffeurs.

So the question arises: Was Khomeini an aberration? Historically, yes, but a close look at the trajectory of Iranian Shi'a clerical history reveals an almost ticking inevitability to a clerical bid for political leadership. If not for Khomeini, someone else might have done it.

During Khomeini's rise to power, he regularly spoke of Imam Hossein, the seventh-century martyred Shi'a imam. In one of Khomeini's most memorable slogans, he popularized and politicized an old Shi'a saying: "Every day is Ashura and every place is Karbala." Ashura marks the day Imam Hossein was martyred in the Iraqi city of Karbala. The statement implies that Iranians should become millions of Imam Hosseins, rising up and ready to martyr themselves against the Shah, who by implication should be seen as the villain Yazid, Imam Hossein's murderer.

Hossein's "martyrdom," a watershed event in Shi'a Muslim historiography, gave the previously political Shi'a movement a decidedly religious tone. As German scholar Heinz Halm notes, politics motivated the original support for Imam Ali, Hossein's father. The martyrdom of Hossein, however, spawned an opposition movement that took on a religious tone. No longer could supporters of Ali accept the faith of the people who killed Hossein, the grandson of the Prophet Muhammad. The death of Hossein, Halm says, "marked the big bang that created the rapidly expanding cosmos of Shi'ism and brought it into motion." In other words, two peoples separated by the death of Hossein developed two different cosmos, with the Shi'a cosmos the smaller one that remained in opposition to the larger Sunni cosmos of the wider Muslim world. The cosmos image fits well with what happened in sixteenth-century Iran. A major planetary realignment occurred in the sixteenth century with the rise of the Safavid dynasty, planting the seeds for Khomeini's meteoric rise and the establishment of the Islamic Republic.

I went to Isfahan to look into the Safavid legacy, the Shi'atization of Iran, and the rise of the Iranian Muslim cleric. But first, I paid a visit to the presidential palace in Tehran, where sitting on a Louis XIV chair, I met with a reform-minded Muslim cleric in an ornate, chandelier-lit room. We spoke of democracy, Islam, and the rising tide of anticlericalism.

In a different age Mohammad Ali Abtahi, the smiling reformist chief of staff to President Khatami (now vice president), might have led a quiet life of religious instruction and personal piety. He might have presided at weddings, offered religious guidance to the faithful, and studied the finer points of Islamic law. Instead, the stout Muslim cleric in white turban and closely trimmed black beard works in plush offices in a palace built by the late Shah. He confers with visiting ministers and ambassadors. He entertains foreign journalists. He has a cell phone and a fax machine. When we first met, he toiled in the midst of arrangements to leave for Paris to accompany his boss, Mohammad Khatami, also a Muslim cleric, on a state visit.

I waited for him in an ornate, gilded room in the presidential palace, munching on pistachios laid out on expensive white bone china plates. The exquisitely designed ceilings flowed into an upper wall decorated with white flower moldings, effecting a faintly French, fin-de-siècle air. This plush room with its big windows, delicate antiques, and fine silk carpets housed meetings with dignitaries. I felt uncomfortable with the formality of the room.

"I am sorry to be late," Abtahi said, whisking into the room, breathless. "There is so much to do," he said, explaining his half hour delay, "and so little time." He wore a brown frock coat and elegant black shoes. He had a round, pleasant face and soft black eyes. He sat down on cream-colored Louis XIV sofa and rearranged his cloak, folding it over his girth. He tapped his foot as he spoke, with that hurried air displayed by aides to important men around the world.

"I understand that you have come from America," he said. "Is anyone else coming?" he asked.

"I don't think so," I said, hoping I hadn't lost my exclusive interview.

"Fine. Then we can begin," he said.

His businesslike manner startled me. In my interviews I had come to expect some *ta'rof* small talk, the exchange of pleasantries, the wishes for each other's family's health. Caught off guard, I asked a rambling question about the future of Iran's reform movement.

He launched into a well-rehearsed lecture. "There are several angles to this matter. Firstly, we must remember that the vote for Khatami was a loud vote for democracy and civil society. Secondly, it was an affirmation of the revolution, though a call for reform within the revolution. Thirdly, Mr. Khatami has come to the conclusion that democracy is our only possible next step, and the people seem to agree."

Iran's clerics have a habit of answering questions in lists: firstly, secondly, thirdly. For the most part, they are skilled and unflappable public speakers, an art taught in the seminary, where they debate finer points of Islamic law for hours during the day and often turn to politics in informal courtyard discussions at night.

Still, I hoped a "fourthly" and "fifthly" dissertation would not keep us for too long away from the question I itched to ask: his view of Iran's clerical class. All over Iran, anticlericalism percolated and grew while frustrated and economically strapped citizens grumbled loudly about their quality of life and Iran's social and political repression. At crowded prodemocracy demonstrations, I regularly heard people chanting: "The clerics live like kings while we live in poverty!" Working-class Iranians lamented clerical wealth in the face of their own poverty. Stories about the Swiss bank accounts of leading clerics circulated on Tehran's rumor mill. Former President Rafsanjani had acknowledged his own Swiss account publicly, noting that he would be "pleased" to use it for the country if necessary. Cleric jokes, usually referring to greed, were widely told.

Seeing an opening in between "thirdly" and "fourthly," I raised the subject of anticlericalism.

"In one respect, it is natural," Abtahi said, not pausing to think, as if he had heard this question many times. "A group of clerics have not properly interpreted Islam. They have interpreted it as oppression and limiting freedom, and this has naturally frustrated the Iranian people, who then blame all the clerics. This is not our interpretation from the reformist side. We believe that Islam allows for freedom and democracy. Let's not forget that Mr.

Khatami is a cleric and Mr. [Abdollah] Nouri [the popular prodemocracy leader] is a cleric. Still, I think it is our duty as clerics approaching the twenty-first century and twenty years after our revolution, to approach matters more sensibly. We must lead the reforms."

I asked him if he believed the mingling of religion and politics was unhealthy, that it might have damaged both religion and political life.

"Yes, it may have damaged some people's perceptions of Islam, but that does not mean that religion has no role in politics. What is often claimed as Islam by the right wing is merely a form of oppression. Again, we do not regard this as a proper interpretation of Islam," he said. "This is a very important point and lies at the heart of the current struggle. We promote an Islam that is compatible with democracy. The right wing supports an oppressive interpretation. Anyone who says that Islam is not compatible with democracy does not understand the essence of the faith. Democracy is a human need, and Islam addresses human needs. The West should understand this."

I told him that we might want to look at it another way. The question often posed by respected Western newsmagazines and scholarly journals—are Islam and democracy compatible?—seemed to me unfair, depicting the Muslim world as a strange monolithic other that might or might not be fit for "our great democracy." A hollow understanding underlies the question. The fact that most Muslim countries have failed to embrace democracy has nothing to do with the faith; it is chiefly because their traditional or secular-minded leaders make up a class of petty tyrants and traditional monarchs. Their societies retain patriarchal and, in some senses, tribal airs. Most Muslim countries have not had their Age of Enlightenment, the critical period that separated religion from the state in most of Europe, the moment when religion settled into a private home, removing its obstructions from the path of public growth through democratic systems. In Iran's case, I told Abtahi delicately, the cleric simply replaced the king after the revolution. For democracy to work, it seemed to me, religion needed to retreat into the private space.

He smiled, folded over his robe, and seemingly ignoring my long editorial insertion, went on with his statement. "Yes, our view is that democracy is compatible with Islam. There is no doubt about that. Unfortunately, there have been many extremists in Iran who say that Islam is incompatible with democracy. Some conservative clerics say that democracy would somehow corrupt the faith. This is just wrong. Others, on the liberal side, especially during the Constitutional Revolution [1906–11], made an argument similar to the one you just made: that we needed an Age of Enlightenment, to separate religion from the state."

In the early twentieth century, a small group of Iranian intellectuals sought to create an Enlightenment type of atmosphere in Iran. Borrowing heavily from French Enlightenment thinkers (especially their anticlericalism), this group of political activists, poets, and journalists sought to create a Parliament and curb the powers of the king and interference by the foreign powers.

However, the liberal intellectuals were not the only ones interested in a constitution. Several leading clerics lined up to support the idea, though for different reasons. After some initial success, the Constitutional Revolution was beaten back by a collusion of royalist and foreign (chiefly Russian and British) forces. The Parliament building was attacked, and Constitutionalist newspapers were shut down. As a result, many of the Enlightenment thinkers fled abroad or were killed.

Abtahi spoke bluntly, "The other side [the conservatives] fear true democracy because it would mean a loss of power for them. The elections have proved that. That's why they are using all the other formidable tools at their disposal to fight our reforms."

What about the reformists? I asked. In a truly democratic system everyone should have the right to run for office. Voters would not choose from only a limited group of clerics. In that scenario, did he think the reformists could lose power as well to, say, a secular nationalist?

"Our president is very popular." He smiled. He had a point, given the overwhelming nature of Khatami's elections in 1997 and 2001. I also met thousands of Iranians in my travels who genuinely liked Khatami, even the ones who expressed frustration at his inability to defeat his conservative foes. Still, it must be said that Khatami mostly ran against already disgraced conservative candidates, I told Abtahi.

"I think our people want democracy, but they also want to preserve the honor of our religion from extremists. That's why they trust President Khatami. I think there is a role for religion in democracy, and there is no reason a cleric cannot ensure a democratic system.

"This is an exciting moment in our history," Abtahi said, folding over his cloak. "In fact, it is an exciting moment in the history of the world. So many peoples across the world are embracing the ideas of civil society and freedom and democracy. We, and President Khatami, are just doing our humble part to help Iran achieve those goals. It will be an uphill struggle, but we shall continue to say the things we believe, and we hope, with God's help, we shall be successful."

He leaned forward, a gesture that the interview should end on that note. "We are at your service, Mr. Molavi," he said, standing up in a quick jerk.

We bade each other good-bye with the traditional three kisses on the cheek. Waiting for the escort delegated to see me out of the building, I stayed behind after Abtahi walked out. I watched him through the window, his clerical robes flowing, walking across the beautiful palace courtyard. To an outside observer, it is slightly disorienting to see a cleric working in a palace, chatting with an ambassador over a cell phone or running off in a black stretch Mercedes-Benz limousine. Around the world, the conditioned human eye expects to see men of religion in a certain light, humble, quietist, pious. Even men of religion who reject poverty and silence, the ones who wield political influence—rabbis in Israel, Hindu preachers in India, Catholic priests in Rome, Muslim scholars in Egypt—must contend with secular governments that try to dilute their influence. It takes awhile for the eye to adjust to Iran's Shi'a clerics in turbans stepping out of limousines for meetings with dapper European ministers in their silk ties or simply strolling across a palace courtyard to their plush corner offices near the president.

Ayatollah Khomeini, though never one for the creature comforts of power, wanted it exactly this way. He believed that the Western notion of separation of religion and state, pushed by "foreign imperialists" and their "native lackeys," intended to divide the Muslim world and plunder Iran's resources. Khomeini had been clear in his prerevolution writings:

This slogan of the separation of religion and politics and the demand that Islamic scholars not intervene in social and political affairs have been formulated and propagated by the imperialists; it is only the irreligious who repeat them. These slogans and claims have been advanced by the imperialists and their political agents in order to prevent religion from ordering the affairs of this world and shaping Muslim society, and at the same time to create a rift between the scholars of Islam, on the one hand, and the masses and those struggling for freedom and independence, on the other. They have thus been able to gain dominance over our people and plunder our resources, for such has always been their ultimate goal.

My escort arrived, a smiling man with a dark black beard and rumpled gray suit with red pinstripes. After a firm, almost painful handshake, he said good-bye, apparently feeling no need to walk me out, as he was assigned to do. I walked across the palace grounds alone toward the front door. "How was your interview?" the guard asked. "Write good things," he said. "There have been too many bad things written about Iran in the West."

Just outside the presidential palace, I hailed a taxi. The driver wasted no time. "These mullahs are killing us," he said. "We are poor, they are rich. They are killing us."

The Shi'atization of Iran

I n the northwestern city of Ardabil, a thirteenth- to fourteenth-century mystical Sunni Muslim religious leader with deep reverence for Imam Ali, Shi'a Islam's first martyr, attracted a large following of Iranians as well as Turks from eastern Anatolia. Known as Sheikh Safi of Ardabil, he emerged as the leader of a Sufi mystical order with devoted adherents who viewed him as a semi-Divine figure. The order came to be known as the Safavis, from its founder's name. After his death, Sheikh Safi's sons continued in his footsteps, leading the Safavi Sufi order as it attracted more followers from nearby lands. In 1501, Ismail, the Safavi leader who added a loyal following of Turkish warriors to his circle of believers, burst out of Ardabil to conquer the northwestern Iranian city of Tabriz.

Ismail differed markedly from his Safavi predecessors. He despised Sunni Muslims and fancied himself a messiah figure, cultivating an image of himself as an unconquerable military leader protected in battle by a halo of God. Many of his followers rushed into battle with the phrase "There is no God but Allah, and Ismail is the vice-regent of Allah."

Having conquered large parts of Iran, Ismail set about converting the population to Shi'ism by a mix of persuasion and force. In Tabriz he forced residents to chant slogans denouncing the three early Muslim caliphs who had "usurped" Imam Ali's rightful caliphate. Resistance popped up here and there to Ismail's call, but on the whole, Iran provided relatively fertile ground for a Shi'a conversion. Several old Iranian cities had harbored large Shi'a populations. In the tenth century an Iranian dynasty, the Buyids, had briefly tried to accomplish Ismail's feat of Shi'a conversion. One powerful Mongol ruler of Iran, the fourteenth-century Uljaitu Khudabanda, had converted to

Shi'ism. Throughout the Mongol era, wandering Sufis had introduced an element of Imam Ali worship into Iranian religious tradition. No doubt some Iranians even saw Shi'ism as a way to set themselves apart from their Arab neighbors, whom they still viewed with a mingling of scorn and distrust. When Ismail sensed resistance, he used the sword, killing "nonbelievers."

As for Ismail, perhaps he had geopolitical aspirations in his Shi'a call, seeing it as a way of challenging Sunni Ottoman Turkey and the Sunni Uzbeks of the northeast, or perhaps he truly regarded himself as a messiah. Whatever his motivation, he needed clerics to spread the Shi'a message. When he first arrived in Tabriz, a search of all Islamic libraries unearthed only one book on Shi'ism. Ismail and his Safavi successors imported Arab Shi'a clerics from Bahrain, Iraq, Syria, and Lebanon in order to preach the Shi'a faith. These clerics arrived in an Iran with an avowed Shi'a king, to be sure, but also with a population (and king) that little understood the basic tenets of the orthodox Shi'a faith. Thus far Ismail's Shi'ism involved little more than cursing the three early caliphs; praising Imam Ali, the fourth caliph, and Imam Hossein, the great Shi'a martyr; and administering heavy doses of Ismail worship to followers. Ismail's agents led people to believe that he descended from the infallible seventh Shi'a imam, a claim never substantiated.

The newly arrived Shi'a clerics must have sensed the delicacy of their task: to teach Iranians the principles of their new faith, while holding their noses at some of the unorthodox Shi'a ideas of the Safavi King. An uneasy alliance formed between a state that needed the religious legitimacy accorded by Muslim scholars and the scholars who desired the protection and patronage of a powerful king.

Meanwhile, Iran's neighbors grew restless. Ismail's aggressive Shi'a propagation in eastern Anatolia alarmed Ottoman, and staunchly Sunni, Turkey. Soon the two Muslim powers came to blows. While Ismail's soldiers relied on the heavenly powers of their leader, the Ottomans relied on a more potent weapon, European gunpowder. Ismail's faithful turned beneath the cannon, an embarrassing defeat for the "infallible" king. He spent the rest of his life in bouts of depression and pitched battles with Uzbeks in the northeast until his death, in 1524.

Ismail's successor, Shah Tahmasp, who ruled from 1524 to 1576, opted not to portray himself as a semi-Divine figure. He sought, in fact, to suppress this view among his followers. Shah Tahmasp instructed his Shi'a clerics to teach the orthodox faith, known as Twelver Shi'ism because of its reverence for the twelve imams. By the time Shah Abbas I, Safavid Iran's most celebrated king, came to power in 1587, Shi'a clerics held great influence in society and the court. Court clerics advised kings and wrote laws. Abbas, well known for his patronage of the arts and architecture in Isfahan, also established a network of religious colleges. Today's most powerful Iranian leaders, including President Khatami and the Supreme Leader, Ayatollah Ali Khamenei, underwent their education in religious seminaries not unlike the first one built in Isfahan under the direction of Shah Abbas.

Shah Abbas will always be remembered for one major thing, his architectural legacy in Isfahan. Few Muslim cities boast such exquisite mosques, bridges, gardens, and palaces. The Zayandeh Rud River, which cuts across the heart of the city like the Thames or the Seine, adds another element of romance to the city of aqua blue spires. Its seventeenth-century residents often said Isfahan was *nesf-e-jahan* (half the world).

History will also remember Shah Abbas for policies that endeared Shi'ism to Iran's population. Though Ismail and Tahmasp laid the groundwork, it was not until a leader of Shah Abbas's ability and vision that Shi'ism could truly find its home in Iran. Shah Abbas, for instance, established the aforementioned religious colleges that produced generations of clerical leaders. In addition, he had a somewhat laissez-faire policy toward Sufi and mystical views. Under his reign, a major intellectual development in Shi'ism began that challenged the dry and legalistic orthodox Shi'ism. This new philosophy would combine Greek rationalism with soul-searching mysticism. This mysticism allowed each individual believer to take his own path toward God, attracting many followers who originally disliked the orthodox Twelver Shi'ism of the law. This movement of divine theosophy, later called the Isfahan or Illuminationist school because of its mystical view of the world of light, grew after the death of Shah Abbas and often came into conflict with the more orthodox clerics, who dismissed the Sufi path to God as semiblasphemous. The legacy of this divine theosophy has had a profound impact on Shi'a scholarship and has led to disagreements with many of the scholars who espouse a more orthodox view. Interestingly, the Illuminationist school also served to link some of Iran's pre-Islamic traditions of Zoroastrianism and light with the new faith.

Still, despite Shah Abbas's considerable efforts to promote Shi'ism among elites, only after his death and the rise of Mullah Mohammad Bagher Majlesi did Shi'ism truly overcome the masses.

Majlesi was a leading court cleric in Isfahan from about 1680 until his death in 1698. Appointed by a weak king to the position of chief mullah in 1695, he successfully exploited his position to propagate his message broadly to Iranians. His message lacked "confusing" complexity; it was socially conservative, anti-Sunni, and anti-Sufi (mystic), as well as an orthodox and unbending interpretation of Twelver Shi'ism. At the time other viewpoints existed, but Majlesi fought against these views, especially that of Mullah Sadra, who argued for a more esoteric, mystical Islam of the Spirit, as opposed to Majlesi's Islam of the Law. Today's Islamic seminary student still gropes to combine these two viewpoints—the Sadraian and Majlesian. Even Ayatollah Khomeini, whose public actions reflected a harsh "Majlesian" Islam of the Law stance, pursued mystical studies in the seminary, winning renown among his own students for his teaching of the subject.

I suppose the Iranian seminary student will never reconcile the two viewpoints. Indeed, as in so many aspects of Iranian culture, many a seminary student has generally retreated into the embrace of multishaded ambiguity on this subject, acknowledging the importance, and truth, of both strains of thought.

For most Iranians, however, religious seminary disagreements matter only peripherally to their faith. Majlesi's most significant achievement remains his successful propagation of Shi'ism to an Iranian population little aware of the faith. He is credited with propagating numerous Shi'a rituals that Iranians regularly practice, including mourning ceremonies for the fallen imams and pilgrimages to shrines of imams and their families. Shi'ism, somehow, worked in Iran. Today Shi'ism is not only the majority faith, it also forms an important part of the Iranian cultural identity. With a few books of Majlesi's writings and some essays that described his life and philosophy in my rucksack, I flew from Tehran to Isfahan to make a pilgrimage to the Majlesi shrine.

Sensual Isfahan

In the grand square of Isfahan, I sat on a bench at dusk and listened to a young Isfahani play the tar, an ancient Persian instrument with an intoxicatingly sweet sound, like the sugary, soft center of *gaz*, a popular Isfahan candy. A crowd gathered as he caressed the tar strings. The last defiant rays of the orange sun lingered in the gray-pink dusk sky. The shining blue-domed mosques sparkled. The waters of the central fountains shimmered. The whole maidan, the public square rimmed by the blue and gold of exquisite mosques and four-hundred-year-old buildings, seemed aglow. There was a softness in the air, the kind of softness that might be scooped with a spoon and spread on the hot hard flat bread sold by Hossein, the baker down the street.

Isfahan's grand maidan, the monumental public square five times the size of Piazza San Marco in Venice with equal amounts of charm and romance and history as that legendary Italian square, shines as a monument to Shah Abbas's vision of his splendid late-seventeenth-century capital. Shah Abbas ranks as one of Iran's most able leaders for resuscitating the faltering nation, recapturing lost territory, and reclaiming Iran's place as a world power at a moment when the Safavid dynasty had faced the specter of kingly decadence and neglect.

Today the grand maidan built by Shah Abbas and his architects attracts tourists from around the world. On this night I saw groups of Italians, Germans, French, and Arabs, as well as a young American photographer from Wyoming, who seemed to relish the attention he was getting as a novelty, an American tourist. "I love it here," he said. "The Iranians are so nice," he told me, somewhat incredulously. "I never expected this. They all want to go to America! I have been invited into three homes already. I traveled in Asia for months, and nobody invited me in. It's amazing."

Later that night I walked back to my hotel, on a busy street in the middle of the city. My room had not been ready when I arrived earlier, so a plump, pleasant cleaning woman showed me to my room, chattering in a lilting, singsong Isfahani accent. "Your towels are over there," she sang. "In the morning we have breakfast," she crooned. "I'm so sorry your room was not ready earlier. We have terribly troubled you!"

A small, modest, clean hotel with worn Persian rugs in the lobby and tasty breakfasts of eggs, flat bread, and sweet tea, the Hotel Aria attracted middle-class Iranians and European budget travelers. It stood across the street from Isfahan's most famous hotel, the Abbasi (known before the revolution as the Shah Abbas). The Hotel Shah Abbas once provided Iran's elite with nights of singing, dancing, and drinking in a lavish and lovely setting. The revolution abruptly ended the party, much to the chagrin of a few of the older waiters, who told me that they fondly remembered the "good times," especially the whiskey-induced large tips.

In my room at the Aria, the bare and yellowing walls had little decoration except for one painting above the bed, a picture of a striking woman in a red scarf and blue headband, carrying a flower in one hand and a massive clay jug on her shoulder. Her eyes were big and brown and curved. She also had big red lips and tufts of hair jutting out from the scarf.

Above the bed, a small, intricately designed copper lamp enclosed a red light bulb. I turned off the ceiling light and switched on the lamp to do some reading. Hundreds of tiny red light spots splashed and danced across the room, giving it the faintly seedy air of a European red-light district. I landed on a page in Moojan Momen's excellent study of Shi'ism that included drawings of both Shah Abbas and Mullah Mohammad Bagher Majlesi. In the picture, Shah Abbas wears a plumed and bejeweled turban. His mustache juts out from his face, extending far beyond his ears but not curled toward them. He has thin eyebrows and a wrinkled forehead. He wears a delicately embroidered cape that rests on his buttoned and jeweled shirt. Shah Abbas looks every bit the Persian royal in the picture. Majlesi, for his part, looks no less regal, his only affectation of modesty being the position he sits in, knees to the ground, as if in prayer. He wears a large checkered turban and has swarthy eyes that contrast with his white beard. His clerical robe, finely cut, well fitted, and elaborately designed, is draped across one shoulder. Majlesi reflects a traditional look, one of a pious and serious man who once proclaimed dancing the height of irrationality. Shah Abbas, no less religiously devoted than Majlesi, has the air of a man with a taste for beauty, a man for whom dancing would be part of court life.

The next morning, in the hotel restaurant, as I ate breakfast, I noticed on the back wall a seductive painting of a dancing woman wearing bright red and blue and yellow form-fitting robes, carrying a wine jug and offering a cup to an old dervish with a gray beard sitting by the river. Not the sort of painting that Mullah Majlesi would have approved of.

All over Iran, especially in private homes and restaurants and hotels, I saw these paintings of subtly sensual women dancing or carrying wine jugs. The magnificent Hotel Abbasi provided a home to a virtual shrine of these murals of subtle and sometimes not-so-subtle female sensuality. At the beginning of the revolution the new Islamic revolutionary authorities in Isfahan deemed all such murals offensive and ordered them destroyed. Dancing women, they said, echoing Majlesi, are not Islamic. The hotel management, however, found the thought of destruction abhorrent. The artist, after all, had worked on the art for more than ten years. A compromise was reached. The artist would return to the hotel and paint long sleeves on some of the women and cover the cleavage of others. The artist did a masterful job, with no traces of change. A waiter in the Hotel Abbasi, however, told me that the artist had left his work incomplete. "The artist made one mistake," he said. "He should have drawn frowns on the men in the paintings."

As I ruminated on the issue of Iran's seemingly contradictory faces of public modesty and private sensuality, I had an appropriate visitor at my table, Ali, a young Pakistani I had met the night before in the lobby. He had an urgent question for me. Looking around, he took a sip of tea and whispered: "Mr. Afshin, yesterday a taxi driver asked me if I want woman. He said that he can get me woman for ten thousand tomans (fifteen dollars). He said she is a very pretty and young woman. What should I do?"

I knew that prostitution had become fairly common in Tehran, but in Isfahan? I was surprised. What could I say?

"I mean, is it dangerous?" he asked.

I told him he would be better off visiting Isfahan's great sites.

He looked deflated. "So, it is too dangerous, yes?"

I was not sure what to say. "It is better to avoid these things," I advised him.

Suddenly he perked up. "Yes, maybe you are right. Why should I risk it? Besides, we have good women in Karachi. There are Bosnians and Russians and Afghani women. Oh, the Afghani women," he said, smiling. "The Afghani women are very beautiful, Mr. Afshin. You must come and visit me. I shall take you to an Afghani woman."

He paused for a moment, perhaps waiting for me to thank him for the promised Afghani woman. I sipped my tea and reflected on the unhappy prospect of sitting through breakfast as Ali described various types of prostitutes he had been with. Just then his father walked into the restaurant. Ali looked at me nervously, giving me a "please don't say anything" look. His father, a tall and exceedingly formal man with gray hair, conducted business with Isfahan traders. He walked into the room with the air of a high-ranking official on a state visit. He wore the traditional Pakistani *shalwar* and *khamees,* the long cotton shirt and baggy pants. I rose to greet him and offered him a chair. "Please," he said, "we shall not disturb you, Mr. Molavi." They sat down at a nearby table to talk about the sites they planned to visit that day.

A group of four Frenchmen in jeans and colorful sweaters sat down, talking animatedly about the veiling of Iranian women.

"*C'est tragique*," three of them agreed, especially since they knew so many bright and intelligent Iranian women in Paris.

The fourth disagreed. "*Ca c'est culture iranienne*," he said, explaining how the chador intertwined with Iranian culture.

"Maybe you are right," one of the others said, wavering for a moment.

The other two disagreed vigorously. "Iranians are not fanatical," one of them said. "I mean, look around you," he said, pointing at the dancing woman on the wall. "That is the real Iran!"

The wavering tourist nodded, saying, "The women on the walls have more fun than the real women!" They all laughed, dipped their bread in their eggs, and mapped out their plans for the day.

I gathered my rucksack of books and headed to the old Isfahan bazaar, where I would visit the Majlesi shrine.

The Bazaar and the Mosque

The Majlesi shrine and mosque stand at the end of the Majlesi bazaar, a typical mid-size outdoor bazaar jammed with bartering crowds, colorful textiles, fruit juice stalls, clothing and toy stores, tea-sipping merchants, and old men carrying heavy loads on their straining backs.

When I arrived, crowds had begun to stream in for their morning shopping. At a stall selling bright fabrics, a heated argument took place between a female customer and the merchant. "In the name of God," the angry woman said, "when will you stop raising your prices?"

The merchant rubbed his bushy mustache, raised his arms, and widened his eyes, displaying appropriate offense at the comment. "This is the best price you will find, madam. You will not find such quality at this price."

An old man with a wide load on his back came barreling toward me, a popping green vein running across his red forehead. "Out of the way!" he yelled. "In the name of God, out of the way!"

A few stalls sold fake Western designer clothes, badly misspelled—

"Adeedas" and "Kalvin Kline" the most notable—and a fruit juice vendor sang the praises of his oranges and melons. "The finest oranges in Isfahan!" he cried. "There are none finer, except for my melons, which are even finer than the oranges!"

A group of old men with wizened brown faces and black glasses sipped tea and stared at the passing crowds.

Many of Iran's most important mosques make the bazaar their home, testifying to the traditionally close links between men of religion and men of commerce. The bazaar has always played a critical political role, particularly in twentieth-century Iran. The closing of the bazaar to protest a government policy dotted twentieth-century Iranian political life. In fact, powerful bazaar merchants bankrolled Iran's clerics in opposing the Shah.

The links between the bazaar and the clergy are social, economic, and political. The bazaari and the cleric often hail from the same traditional middle class and intermarry. Economically, the clerics look to the bazaar for money in the form of an Islamic tax that bazaaris scrupulously pay to clerics and mosques. Bazaaris in turn look to clerics for religious cover and, indeed, perhaps for salvation. One veteran bazaari jokingly explained: "When you spend your days cheating your neighbor out of ten tomans, it makes you feel better to give one of those tomans to the mosque."

It did not stop there. In the nineteenth and early twentieth centuries, the clergy also served as judges and public notarizers, so the men of commerce went to the men of the cloth to solve a dispute or stamp a bill of sale. In fact, even when the Pahlavi kings created civil courts and civil notarizers, many traditional men of the bazaar preferred using trusted bazaar clerics for their transactional matters, instead of the white-collared, necktied government men in air-conditioned offices.

It is therefore not surprising that Iran's economy has grown to resemble a vast bazaar with its distorted mix of fantastically wealthy merchants, dirt-poor laborers, and struggling petty traders, with very little in the middle, Iran's struggling middle class. Like the bazaar, Iran's economy benefits well-connected risk-taking speculators, such as real estate developers and, for a while, currency traders. Insider dealings between bazaar bigwigs and senior officials also grease the wheels of commerce. If a businessman wants to import Toyota cars, he needs a license. The appropriate government office, for a fee, might provide that license to a "friendly" businessman, one of the family.

The license would have been sanctioned by a conservative cleric. The Toyotas enter the country, and all three parties get their cut.

It is the bazaari background of many clerics that has contributed to the Iranian folk culture criticism of clerics as greedy, a common caricature even before the revolution. After the revolution a number of bazaaris gained incredible wealth from their newfound access to power. Several bazaar merchants became ministers in the new government, especially in posts dealing with commerce and economics.

Just below the bazaari in the hierarchy of traditional Iranian commerce is the *maydani,* who makes a living trading and selling in public squares. One *maydani* trader, Mohsen Rafiqdoost, rose to the most powerful economic post in Iran, chairman of the multibillion-dollar Bonyad-e-Mostazefan va Janbazan, a "charitable" foundation that owns banks, hotels, shipping lines, and manufacturing companies, hundreds of semiprivate companies that are unaccountable to the technocratic Central Bank governor. Created from confiscated assets of leading members of the prerevolution elite as well as the Pahlavi "charitable" foundation, the *bonyads,* estimated to control up to 20 percent of Iran's GDP, jealously guard their books from prying eyes. They answer only to the conservative Supreme Leader, Ayatollah Khamenei. Rafiqdoost's close ties to senior clerics replicated the old bazaar system, this time with much higher stakes. Rafiqdoost left his post in 1999 amid serious corruption charges by reformist newspapers.

Still, the Iranian bazaar, no different from other public arenas in Iranian life, should not be seen as a monolithic force in collusion with the government. In many respects, bazaaris are just as frustrated as other Iranians. Many note that only a small minority of bazaaris entered the state apparatus and benefited from their newfound access to power. Indeed, within the bazaar, the state-affiliated merchants are no longer considered "one of us." They are "one of them." Researchers and anthropologists who have spent considerable time in the bazaar note that the traditional bazaar-clergy alliance has been strained since the 1979 revolution. Many bazaaris complain that the government's heavy involvement in trade and business crowds them out. Iran's carpet traders are particularly incensed at the government practice of making machine-made carpets and selling them around the world, undercutting their own handcrafted items. As one carpet trader in the Tehran carpet bazaar told me, "How can I compete with a government official in some ministry who can make a phone call, get a free export license, and send his inferior carpets to European markets at lower prices?"

An important battle is taking place today between a group of technocrats and a small group of state-affiliated bazaaris. Technocrats in the Central Bank and surrounding President Khatami have called for a breakup of the *bonyads*, but powerful bazaar merchants and senior conservative clergy resist. The current closed economic system, with its convoluted, corrupt avenues of horse trading, benefit the merchant with state connections and the official willing to take a cut of the deal. Iranian officials have taken note, making the combatting of corruption a centerpiece of their political discourse, though few meaningful steps have been taken to change the system. The outcome of this battle may be as important to the future of Iran as the raging political battle over reform, because it could mean a spark of life to Iran's stagnant economy. The Iranian bazaar after all works wonders as a clearinghouse of goods that supplies cities with tires, socks, and linens, making a few tire and sock sellers rich along the way. It struggles when it acts as the model for an entire nation's economy.

I moved on, toward the shrine of Mullah Mohammad Bagher Majlesi.

Pilgrimage: Mullah Mohammad Bagher Majlesi and the Rise of the Shi'a Cleric

As I walked amid the clutter of color and commerce, I saw a dust-colored dome in the distance and a cracked sign, written in Farsi, that read MAJLESI STREET and led into the mosque courtyard. There a small pool of green, brackish water flanked by simple, low arches led me into the shrine, where I removed my shoes. Three large, coarse red Persian carpets with white flower designs covered the floor, and four chandeliers hung from the ceiling. Safavi-style artistry covered the walls: flowers and vines in blue and gold. A thin crowd gathered around Majlesi's tomb. A man leaned toward the metal grillwork surrounding the tomb and kissed it. Most pilgrims to the shrine probably had little understanding of Majlesi's role in Iranian history beyond the fact that he was an important cleric in the Safavi era. Actually most Iranian pilgrims know few facts about any of the saints they honor. It is simply enough to honor the saint by pilgrimage, not to know the saint's history.

Inside the metal grille, three tombs lay together: Majlesi, his father, and his brother. A green spotlight shone on the tombs and the crumpled pieces of money strewn about; pilgrims' donations accompanied by a prayer, perhaps for the health of an ailing relative or for admission into a university. On the outer rim of the shrine, luminous white Quranic calligraphy spelled out the names of the twelve Shi'a imams.

A cold, persistent wind blew in from the courtyard. I moved away from the shrine and sat down next to an electric heater against the back wall of the shrine. All around me creaked the tombs of prominent Isfahan clerics. The shrine felt cozy, warm, small, and bright. Opening Moojan Momen's work again, I turned to the passages in which he describes Majlesi: "It is necessary to take a close look at the activity of Muhammad Baqer Majlisi since he was one of the most powerful and influential Shi'a ulama of all time and since his policies and actions reoriented Twelver Shi'ism in the direction that it was to develop from his day on. Majlisi was an important scholar in his own right. . . . It is, however, in the social and political role that he played rather than his scholarly work that his importance lies." Majlesi, one of the most prolific writers in Iran's history, produced more than sixty works. More important, he wrote mostly in Persian in a time when Iranian clerics still relied on Arabic. Like the Reformation priests of Europe who first wrote in the vernacular, Majlesi chose Persian because he wanted to reach the people with his broad message. Again, Momen writes: "Up to [Majlesi's] time, it would be true to say that Shi'ism had sat lightly on the population of Iran, consisting mostly of mere expressions of love for Ali and hatred of the first three caliphs. Majlisi sought to establish Shi'ism firmly in the minds and hearts of the people. . . . Although the writing of books of Shi'a doctrine and law in Persian was begun as early as the reign of Shah Ismail. . . . Majlisi was the first to write in Persian so much, on such a wide range of subjects and in a manner that could be understood by the ordinary people."

Majlesi's pen ranged far and wide. He wrote on everything from complex theological matters to the proper way for a believer to sneeze or spit. Nothing was too abstract, and nothing too personal, including long disquisitions on Islamically proscribed sexual intercourse. Majlesi's thoughts on sex in fact are a subject of prurient interest and much humor among young seminarians and a point of ridicule for his secular critics. In reading his writings, one realizes that this man believed in the absolute righteousness of his cause. No Hafezian ambiguity in Majlesi. In his world, Sufis were heretics, and a stomach ailment required the exact Islamically prescribed cure.

After the 1979 revolution, some clerics followed directly in Majlesi's footseps. They not only helped engineer a political revolution (something that Majlesi never thought of) but also pursued a massive social revolution. They wanted, like Majlesi, to control every aspect of the believer's life. A massive propaganda campaign pushing a socially conservative and revolutionary way of life targeted everything from children's books to television programs, from what to read to what to wear. Ruling clerics mandated the veil. Alcohol, dancing, and mixed gathering parties were prohibited. "Dancing is forbidden by religious law," Majlesi once wrote, "and reason leads every person to the judgment that it is an abomination." Iran's postrevolution clerics seemed to agree, despite the fact that Iranians of all classes include dancing as part of their wedding ceremonies.

Shortly after the revolution, clerics appeared daily on television, reminding believers to pray, to give alms, to pay allegiance to Khomeini. Not even hygiene and sexual relations escaped their notice. Tehranis still joke about a prominent TV cleric who, in the early years after the revolution, obsessively discussed proper ways to use the bathroom.

If Majlesi lived today, I believe he would work for Iranian television and radio. Though orthodox religious programming of the early eighties has moderated, religious content—especially instructive comment on what a believer must do—remains a fixture. Even nonreligious programs have an unsettling tendency to preach. Nighttime dramas tell sappy, moralistic tales. Even comedies preach an underlying moral message. For the most part, these moral messages stay simple, even laudable: Be good to your parents; respect your elders; keep your temper in check. Still, Iranians grow weary of the preaching. One woman's comments, off the air, to a TV reporter demonstrate the point. She took the reporter aside and began a small tirade: "I turn on the TV for entertainment and news. Instead I get lectures on how to act, when to pray, and whom to praise! A program I saw the other day was deeply insulting. It was a program aimed at women, and it was telling me how I should raise my children. I have six children in their twenties and thirties, and they have been raised very well so far without the help of your television station!"

Watching Iranian TV, one recalls Majlesi's voluminous works preaching the proper way to perform daily functions of life. In fact, this all-encompassing morality became typical of Iranian clerical writings following Majlesi's example. In order to achieve the highest stage of the Shi'a clerical hierarchy, to become an ayatollah, one must write a major work that touches on both theology and the proper way to perform daily functions. In Khomeini's writings, one finds both analyses of Plato's *Republic* and instructions on the proper way to use the bathroom. Iranian television merely extended Majlesi's style of pervasive preaching, using satellites and airwaves instead of books and sermons.

The scholar Ahmad Karimi Hakkak notes that the Majlesi approach to theological inquiry, emulated by many other leading ayatollahs, contained a fatal flaw that came to haunt Shi'ism: "By addressing all of the hypothetical situations a true believer could or might face, leaving little to individual common sense, they opened themselves to harsh ridicule from their opponents, especially secular and agnostic intellectuals of the 20th century."

One of those critics was the secular intellectual Shahrokh Meskoob. In my rucksack, I carried a work by Meskoob, *Iranian National Identity*. In a section on Majlesi, Meskoob writes plainly for his audience, with no need for satirical asides, though they are implied: "[Majlesi's] book called *Countenance of the Pure* states as its subject 'the exposition of virtues of proper behavior,' from wearing clothes to sexual intercourse and association with females, clipping fingernails, sleeping, waking, urination and defecation, enemas, sneezing, entering and leaving a domicile, and treatments and cures for many illnesses and diseases. The seventh chapter of the fifth section is 'on plucking nasal hairs and playing with one's beard.' The sixth chapter of the eleventh section treats 'proper ways of sneezing, belching and spitting.'" Meskoob also quotes extensively Majlesi's views on science, defined as "knowledge of the clear, secure *ayeh*s [divine signs, verses in the Quran]; of the religious duties and obligations which God has fixed in his Justice; and of the Prophetic Traditions, which are valid until the day of Resurrection." Majlesi's contradictory picture of the Prophet Muhammad, the messenger of Islam, struck me, since the Prophet consistently counseled his followers to "seek knowledge, even as far as China." Majlesi, on the other hand, writes that studies of sciences beyond his own narrow definition "are a waste of one's life . . . which generally lead to apostasy and heresy, in which case the likelihood of salvation is remote."

Meskoob has support in his criticism of Iranian clerics. Leading religious intellectuals have also been harsh critics. One of the twentieth century's most prominent critics of clerical views, Ali Shariati, was the son of a prominent cleric himself. Shariati, educated in the religious seminary, also radically opposed the Shah. In his writings and lectures, he attacked the Safavi-era clerics, noting that they infused too much superstition and ritual into Iran's Shi'a faith. He decried Safavi clerics like Majlesi for creating what he called Black Shi'ism, characterized by endless mourning and weeping for the fallen imams. Instead he promoted a Red Shi'ism, which counseled believers to emulate Imam Hossein and fight against injustice. Shariati dreamed of an Islam without clerics. He once wrote that Iran's clerical class "seeks refuge in times long past and outdated ceremonies and is satisfied to be the gatekeeper at the graveyard." Of course, Shariati angered traditional mullahs, though the more radical clerics like Khomeini sweetened to his revolutionary and anti-Shah views.

Perhaps the twentieth century's most vociferous clerical critic was Ahmad Kasravi, a fiery essayist and orator, also educated in a religious seminary. He condemned Iran's clerics for failing to support the liberal principles of the Constitutional Revolution of 1906–11, the moment when Iranians stood up and demanded an elected parliament and the rule of law. Kasravi criticized the clergy for creating what he called a false Islam, one that sought to protect the clergy's power and veered from principles of the faith. He vigorously criticized what he viewed as their hypocrisy, their obsessive reliance on tradition, and their hostility to representative government. In one of his articles, he set out his objections to the Islam created by Iran's clerics: "This religion is incompatible with reason; it is incompatible with the sciences; it is incompatible with history; it is incompatible with Islam itself; it is incompatible with life. Finally, it is incompatible with representative government." Kasravi's seminal work, *On Islam and Shi'ism*, published in 1944, bristles with the literary energy of a devoted revolutionary. The chapter titles are revealing: "The Detrimental Consequences of Islam," "God Is Weary of This Islam," "Criticisms That Can Be Made of Shi'ism," "The Bullying of the Clerics." Kasravi makes no attempt to conceal his contempt for clerics. In the chapter titled "The Bullying of Clerics," he writes: "They [clerics] are ignorant people who do not know as much about the world and its affairs as a ten year old child. And since their minds are filled with religious jurisprudence, reported sayings and long, involved fabrications of principles and philosophy, there is no room left for knowledge or information. So much has happened in the world, sciences have appeared and changes have occurred, which they have either not known or understood or have understood but not paid any attention to. They live in the present, but cannot look at the world except from the perspective

of thirteen hundred years ago." Later in that chapter, he says: "In their ignorance, in trying to preserve their own organization, they are content with the
misery of twenty million people."

Of course, Kasravi's book caused a storm of protest among Iran's clergy,
the more so since he wrote it in their style, being one of their own. Here was
no mere Europeanized secular protester who could be easily dismissed. Here
was a man who studied in the seminary and spoke the language of the clergy
and confronted clerics with harsh negations of their most sacred truths. Kasravi shocked the clerics, who found themselves at a loss on what to do with
this angry former seminary student. As Roy Mottahedeh points out, "Iran had
a long tradition of the quiet skeptic, but Kasravi was entirely different. . . . He
was a noisy unbeliever, a preacher whose texts were secularism, the triumph
of science, and the superiority of constitutional democracy."

Alas, Kasravi came too early, and his voice was too loud for his time
(indeed, perhaps even for this time). An Islamic extremist assassinated him in
1946. This assassin belonged to the group founded by a religious seminary
student who called himself Navab-e-Safavi, a name linked with the Safavi
state where Majlesi once reigned supreme as head mullah.

Kasravi thought little of the clerics he came into contact with, even though
Iran, and Safavid-era Isfahan in particular, produced some of the Muslim
world's most profoundly important scholars, whose interests and skills ranged
from Sufi poetry to architecture. Sheikh Baha al-Din (1546–1622), the leading
scholar of Islam in his day, served as the key architect for one of Iran's most
breathtaking monuments: the Shah Mosque of Isfahan. Today's architecture
student still marvels at the sophisticated design of this extraordinary structure.
Sheikh Baha al-Din was also the greatest mathematician and astronomer of
this period. Surely, here was a man of religion whose mind was filled with
more than just "long, involved fabrications of principles and philosophy." In
Kasravi's era, however, Western science far exceeded anything produced from
the religious seminary, and his impatience with the seminary, and indeed anything that did not imply progress, including Persia's beloved medieval Persian
poets, was legendary. In fact, Kasravi encouraged the burning of books by
Persian poets, even the revered Hafez, whom he felt was not progressive
enough for Iranian needs. Kasravi was, in a sense, just as righteous about his
cause as Majlesi was in the late seventeenth century.

How might Kasravi view Iran today? As a fervent believer in representative government he might speak for Iran's democracy movement, and surely, he would condemn conservative clerical attempts to quash the movement. In gloomy fact, if he were alive today, he would probably be in a jail cell, if he had not met the same fate as he did in 1946.

Zipping my backpack, I stood up, stretched my legs, and watched the crowd mill into the shrine, on the edge of the Majlesi bazaar in Isfahan. A young boy, barefoot and bright-eyed, followed his father. They leaned into the metal grille and kissed it, then stood together, bowing and praying. Inside the golden grille enclosure, Mullah Mohammad Bagher Majlesi's father also is laid to rest. Ironically, Majlesi's father was a follower of the Sufi way. Inside the enclosure, father and son represented two strains of Shi'a Islamic thought. In this case, the son triumphed over the father. Still, the Sufi way has not died in Iran and has only grown stronger as the government of the Islamic Republic acts more like Majlesi the son than Majlesi the father. On the other side of the shrine—the women's section, which I could not see—I heard weeping. Perhaps a mourning ceremony for Hossein, the martyred Shi'a imam. Later I learned that a woman who had recently lost her husband had visited the shrine every day for the past two months, bewailing her loss. Her husband was buried far away, so she used the shrine for her daily weeping, visiting her husband's tomb on weekends.

I looked at my watch. I had spent nearly two hours in the shrine, reading, thinking, and observing. I wanted to stay longer, into the night in my warm spot by the electric heater with my books. I was tired, my legs were sore, and I wanted to sit back down and doze off on the floor, joining a few nappers. But there was no time. I was running late for my next appointment. I walked toward the door, handed a few bills to the shrine's caretaker, and walked back out into the courtyard, where two little girls in white head scarves chased each other around the reflecting pool.

When I emerged from the Majlesi shrine at dusk, back into the bazaar's light, a blind man chanted mourning songs for Imam Hossein. Next to him lay a hat filled with small bills and coins. A slight chill hung in the air. Nearby a man roasted corn on an open fire. I stood next to the fire and listened to the blind man sing. "O Imam Hossein, why did they kill you? Why did they refuse you water? O, O, O Imam Hossein, you are the prince of martyrs." The mourning song the old man sang formed part of the seventeenth-century Majlesian rituals prescribed for believers.

Several men of the bazaar in crisp shirts and beards, perhaps rich whole-salers, made their way home. They wore turquoise rings on their small fingers, as do many clerics. As they walked by the Majlesi shrine, they stopped, whispered a prayer, and moved on. A few dropped bills in the blind man's hat. As each bill landed in the hat, a young boy nudged the blind man, causing him to cry louder: "O Imam Hossein." I hurried off to my next appointment, the mourning songs of the blind man filling my head.

Mr. Mohseni, the Young Cleric

A friend in Tehran had suggested that I meet Mr. Mohseni. "He is a young cleric with interesting ideas," he said at the time. A final-year student in one of Isfahan's *madresehs*, religious colleges, Mr. Mohseni said he would be glad to meet when I arrived in Isfahan. Emerging from the Majlesi bazaar, I hailed a cab and handed the driver the directions Mr. Mohseni had read to me over the phone. My driver, however, paid more attention to his carefully crafted rant on high fruit and meat prices than he did to my directions to the cleric's house. We got lost several times.

"Yesterday I went to the market and bought watermelon. You will not believe what that crook charged me," he said as we drove past one of the marked streets. I pointed out our misdirection, and he promptly backed up into oncoming traffic, horns blaring, all the while lamenting the fact that the price of onions, a domestic good, was only slightly less than the price of bananas, an imported good.

At our destination, a small dust-brick house in a clutter of side streets, I rang the buzzer. A young, well-built man with a sharply defined jaw and thin black beard greeted me, Mr. Mohseni. He wore a white skullcap on his head, the sort of cap worn underneath a turban. The fact that he answered the door himself and wore a skullcap instead of the turban indicated that he meant our meeting to be casual. I was pleased.

"Hello, Mr. Molavi," he said, smiling and offering the traditional cheek-to-cheek greeting. I apologized for my delay, handed him a box of sweets purchased at the bazaar, and offered greetings from our mutual friend.

"You have embarrassed me," he said, taking the sweets. He gestured for me to enter the small courtyard of the house. We walked across the courtyard toward the door, where a variety of men's and women's shoes lay neatly outside. I slipped off my own shoes and entered, a common ritual in many traditional middle-class Iranian homes, but not so among the modern middle and upper middle classes. Inside, a middle-aged man in a crisp, collared shirt and a closely cropped black beard greeted me. He wore a cell phone strapped to his waist. He was a bazaari, I found out later, a well-connected trader of light fixtures bought by government offices. Behind him, a teenager with a crooked-toothed smile approached, bowing slightly, one hand on his chest. He took my jacket.

Mr. Mohseni turned to the man in the collared shirt. "This is my uncle," he said. "My brother and I are often putting him to trouble." Mr. Mohseni's younger brother, he of the crooked teeth, smiled.

His uncle predictably protested. "What trouble? It is always a pleasure to see both of you." Suddenly I realized that my visit might have caused this latest "trouble." After all, a seminary student who lives in a dormitory does not have the means to host a foreign guest in the properly generous Iranian way. Mr. Mohseni's own parents live in a nearby city, so Mr. Mohseni must have put his uncle to this "trouble" on my behalf. I felt a rush of embarrassment.

His uncle guided us into a large, carpeted sitting room, where we sat on the floor and leaned up against soft cushions. Mr. Mohseni's younger brother soon brought us tiny glasses of tea and sugar cubes. He sat in the corner, staring at me as the conversation drifted from talk of my travels to Isfahani sweets to gemstones.

"Mr. Molavi," the uncle said, "if you want to buy some gemstones for your family, let me know. It is important that you buy them with somebody who knows these things. I wouldn't want anyone to fool you.

"Don't bother buying *feeroozeh* here," he said, referring to a turquoise stone. "Buy it in Mashhad or even Neishapour."

Mr. Mohseni interrupted, saying: "Mr. Molavi, my brother wanted to meet you very much. He reads all of these reformist newspapers, and now he wants to become a journalist and be famous like Akbar Ganji!" His brother's face reddened.

"Iran needs more good journalists," I said, wishing him well. Mr. Mohseni laughed and asked me if I had met the reformist reporters. I described some of my meetings. The teenager leaned forward, listening intently.

As I offered my impressions of each reporter, an elderly man with a brown, wrinkled face approached Mr. Mohseni's uncle and whispered in his ear. Mr. Mohseni's uncle stood up. "Mr. Molavi, we have prepared a very humble meal. Will you do the honor of joining us?" We moved to another room where a tablecloth was set out on the floor.

There was nothing "humble" about the meal. There were three different meat stews, alternately spiced with saffron, turmeric, herbs, sour plums, and other spices. A mound of saffron-flecked rice occupied the center of the cloth, and each spot—there were four of us—had a bowl of steaming hot soup. Mr. Mohseni's uncle's wife could not join us, I was told. She had a prior engagement, though she sent her greetings. After dinner, more tea and honey-soaked sweets arrived, and we retired back to the sitting room.

Gently stuffed, we sat back on the cushions. Mr. Mohseni's uncle bade us good-bye. He had to go pick up his wife from her mother's house, he told us. Mr. Mohseni's brother walked out with him, leaving me alone with the young cleric I had come to interview.

Mr. Mohseni, a fifth-year clerical student, looked to be in his early thirties. He studied Islamic jurisprudence and philosophy, having worked through the first level, known as the *muqaddamat* (introduction), which involves rigorous Arabic grammar, basic logic, and rhetoric classes, in addition to the countless readings of Quranic commentaries by Shi'a scholars. He also read and discussed Western philosophers, particularly Kant and Hegel.

What did his fellow seminarians think about the ideas of reform and democracy?

"You know, I can safely say that about seventy percent of seminary students support these ideas of democratic reform. They are rational, and they are based on philosophy and a sound interpretation of the Quran and current conditions," he said.

I asked him how he came up with that number? Did he conduct a survey?

"It is a general estimation," he said. "I think you will see that I am right as you spend more time with young seminarians. Of course, there are still those who do not believe in these ideas. They say that these ideas are Western perversions. Among the students, we have some heated debates."

He popped a sugar cube in his mouth, urged me to help myself to the fruit bowl, sipped his tea, and continued. "For all of us, the debate is far deeper than a simple one about democracy. There is also a debate about what role religion should play in politics. In this respect, Abdol Karim Soroush has played a profoundly influential role in my own thinking and that of many young clerics."

Iran's reformist clerics and religious intellectuals consider Soroush, a lay Islamic philosopher, a master. In his writings and lectures, he argues that the mingling of religion and government reduces religion to ideology, endangering the faith by exposing it to the pollution of politics. While neither new nor profound, the idea is highly charged, for it contradicts a core principle of the Islamic Republic: the fusion of religion and the state. As a result, hard-liners often target Soroush, inadvertently broadening his popularity on college campuses.

Though Soroush has earned some measure of international recognition for his views on religion and state, young seminarians like Mr. Mohseni consentrate more on his views on the rights of the individual. "Few Islamic philosophers have written so widely and argued so persuasively, in an Islamic context, on the rights of the individual. In this respect, Soroush is really changing opinions," Mr. Mohseni said. "By doing this, expressing the rights of the individual in Islamic terms, he is setting new precedents."

And helping build the philosophical foundation for democracy in Iran?

"In a way, yes," Mr. Mohseni said. "Individual rights are very important in a democracy. This is an argument that we have a lot in the seminary."

Mr. Mohseni also said that he follows closely the writings of Mohsen Kadivar, the reformist cleric jailed by the Islamic Republic for his works denouncing the country's ruling clergy as "religious despots." In a public letter from prison, Kadivar wrote that "the holiness of religion should not authorize the religious leaders to force others to obey their own way of thinking and to denounce any objection or criticism as blasphemy." He went on to say that "the irresponsible lifelong ruler who thinks himself above the law, with unlimited authority, should not exist in this country."

I asked Mr. Monseni what he liked about Kadivar's philosophy.

He smiled, saying, "I would rather not go into specifics. He is in jail after all."

In our conversation, Mr. Mohseni regularly used the Farsi word *bahs,* which can be alternately translated as "debate" or "argument." He and his fellow seminarians seemed to be in constant *bahs.* Iran's Shi'a clerics, unlike their Sunni counterparts, have broad leeway to interpret the Quran through a legal process called *ijtihad.* This can lead to numerous interpretations of

Islamic law. Though Mr. Mohseni would need a minimum of five more years of study before he could be considered a mujtahid, an interpreter of the Quran, he already seemed willing to interpret a myriad of Quranic matters. He was, in a sense, a mujtahid in training, and he seemed to enjoy answering my questions about aspects of Islamic law, employing history and anecdotes and passages from the Quran in his responses.

It might not have been this way for Shi'a clerics were it not for an eighteenth-century mullah, Mohammad Baqir Vahid Behbehani. The Shi'a tradition of *ijtihad* came under fire in the mid-eighteenth century from a powerful array of critics who thought that Iran's Shi'a clerics abused their right of interpretation, thereby disregarding the basic tenets of the faith. Behbehani, an Isfahan-born cleric at the center of the debate, vigorously backed the clerical right of *ijtihad*. Behbehani, like Majlesi before him, had the absolute righteousness of cause and single-minded determination to defeat his opponents. Also like Majlesi, he vigorously sought to root out "heretical" innovations from the orthodox Twelver Shi'a faith. For his efforts, he earned the title Sufi killer.

Behbehani's largest achievement, however, was his defeat of the Akhbaris, a clerical movement that sought to limit a cleric's power to interpret the Quran and principles of Shi'ism. The Akhbaris argued that the cleric should simply follow the words of the Quran and the sayings of the Prophet. Behbehani led the counter charge, labeling all Akhbaris "unbelievers" and promoting thuggish attacks on these "infidels." Without clerical interpretation, the believers would be lost, Behbehani argued. In truth, without clerical interpretation, the clerics might have been the ultimate losers, stripping them of an important power.

The proponents of *ijtihad* won this battle easily. That's why, in the late twentieth century, Khomeini could so radically interpret Shi'a history and the Quran as to come up with the idea of rule by clerics. Conversely, Khatami and Nouri fall well within their clerical rights to advocate a limited form of democracy with legitimacy in the Quran. This tradition of interpretation makes the seminary a lively forum for debate, notwithstanding the regular attempts by conservative clerics to stifle that debate.

Young seminarians like Mr. Mohseni, as a consequence, aspire to be future interpreters of the Shi'a way. In a government ruled by clerics, the endless seminary debates mean much more than mere academic exercises. They

offer clues to the political future of Iran. "We are a new generation, a generation that has access to all of the world's information through television and
the Internet," Mr. Mohseni said. "It is inevitable that we shall bring new ideas.
In today's seminary, we do not concern ourselves only with ancient religious
tracts or superstitious rituals as some people on the outside might think. Our
debates are highly sophisticated. We discuss Hegel and Habermas [the post
modernist philosopher] and Popper and Nietzsche. Even the hard-line faction, which I disagree with, bases its arguments on reason and often quotes
Plato's *Republic*."

It struck me that in his mind, "sophisticated" meant "Western." The seminary discussions he described reminded me of meetings I had with secular
Iranian intellectuals, in which many of the same philosophers were discussed
and some of the old leftist ideas were proffered. Perhaps, I ventured, the average Iranian was less interested in philosophical theories and more in an effectively governed state that provided them with security, prosperity, freedom,
and personal dignity.

"Yes." He smiled. "Yes, perhaps, but there must always be a theory behind
it. Without theory to back up a state, there will be chaos." I remembered a
leftist intellecual saying essentially the same thing.

Has the theory of *velayat-e-faqih,* rule by clerics, stood the test?

He sipped his tea and continued, answering my question from a different
angle: "I think it is a shame that many people have developed a distaste for
clerics. Most of my generation of seminary students are different from the
ruling clergy that people are upset with. We believe in the reform of the system, in democracy, in civil society, and dialogue, many of the same things the
Iranian people believe in. We are not all elitists. We mingle with the people. I
stand in the same bread lines. I wait for the same taxis. Sometimes, the taxis
won't even stop to pick me up."

But he had power, I said, and that was the difference, no?

"Yes, of course. The price of political power is high."

Which brought us back to the question of *velayat-e-faqih,* I ventured, trying again.

Just then his younger brother walked back into the room, carrying a clear
glass bowl of freshly cut watermelon. Mr. Mosheni smiled, perhaps relieved
that our interview was interrupted. "Aha, on this all Iranians can agree. We
have the finest fruit in the world." He reached over, picked up a fork, and

placed three slices of watermelon on a plate for me. His younger brother sat down to join us. Tentatively, quietly, he asked if I had seen the American movie *Titanic*. Mr. Mohseni smiled. "I must see this movie," he said. "This is all my brother talks about."

VI

❖ Winds of Reform ❖ A Murder in Kashan ❖ Tabriz Student Protests, 1999
❖ The Case of Ahmad Batebi ❖ Iran's Fight for a Constitution: 1906–11
❖ An American Constitutionalist in Tabriz ❖
❖ "The Strangling of Persia": A Constitutional Ending ❖
The Parliament of the Islamic Republic of Iran ❖

Cities: Tehran, Kashan, Tabriz

Winds of Reform

When the Safavid state fell in the early eighteenth century, Iran fell into a period of chaotic rule marked by foreign incursions, tribal and feudal division, and stifled economic development. The Qajar dynasty (1798–1921) restored some stability but presided over a period of relative stagnation in comparison to other regional powers, notably Turkey and Egypt, which made significant strides in building and modernizing their institutions. In Iran, piecemeal, court-inspired initiatives in the mid-nineteenth century modernized the state to some degree, but, as esteemed Iran scholar Nikkie Keddie noted, the modernization attempts were "slight and abortive." The Qajar rulers styled themselves in the Persian kingly tradition of absolute power, though they lacked the magnanimity and effectiveness required of this stance. With elaborate titles such as Shadow of God on Earth, King of Kings, Supreme Arbitrator, Guardian of the Flock, and Asylum of the Universe, the Qajar kings represented, in the eyes of nineteenth-century Western travelers to Iran, a caricature of "Oriental Despotism." Sir John Malcolm, the early-nineteenth-century British envoy to Persia, called it "one of the most absolute monarchies in the world," unencumbered by laws, institutions, or checks and balances.

The Qajar kings built few significant institutions of lasting value, contributed little to the economic development of the country, granted outrageous concessions to foreign countries, and further polarized the country's communal and feudal politics by playing tribes and feudal lords against one another in a delicate balancing act of power preservation. As a result, turn-of-the-twentieth-century Iran had become a chaotic place, prey to both foreign and domestic bandits, a country that princes, foreign customs officials, and feudal landlords looted, where rival tribes ignored the central government, kings tended more to palace intrigue than affairs of state, and British and Russian legations dictated Iranian policies most favorable to them, often lecturing the king like a naughty schoolboy.

Late-nineteenth-century Iranian intellectuals viewed the "backwardness" of the Iranian state with serious concern. Most notably, they worried about the arbitrary nature of the nation's laws and the continuing encroachment of foreign powers, notably Britain and Russia, on Iranian sovereignty. Mirza Malkum Khan, a late-nineteenth- and early-twentieth-century liberal reformist newspaper editor, captured the mood of his generation of Iranian intellectuals in the first issue of his newspaper (*Qanun*): "God has blessed Iran. His blessing has been negated by lack of laws." In the early twentieth century, men like Malkum Khan (an Armenian Christian who converted to Islam), frustrated by royal privilege and foreign interference in Iranian affairs, set forth a powerful idea: A written constitution with a body of fair and just laws would free Iran from its current condition and embark the state toward modernization. Intellectuals, merchants, and nationalist clerics began agitating for a constitution. In response to the movement, in late 1906, Mozaffar-ed-Din Shah, the Qajar king, reluctantly signed two laws that provided the country with a European-style constitution and a parliament, known as the House of Justice. The Constitutionalists had won an early, albeit short-lived, victory.

Standing high above a major Tehran highway, a billboard honors the early-twentieth-century cleric Sheikh Fazlollah Nouri, an important player in the era known as the Constitutional Revolution of 1906–11. The billboard commemorating his death depicts the cleric as a noble martyr. Nouri heartily opposed Iran's constitutional movement. He called it "un-Islamic" despite the fact that several leading clerics supported it. He roused mobs to attack Constitutionalists. He wrote breathless pamphlets warning of the dangers a parliament posed to Islam. He colluded with royalist opponents of the constitution. While Mr. Mohseni does not care much for Sheikh Fazlollah

Nouri, today's conservative clerics owe allegiance to him as a forefather. Ayatollah Khomeini, in particular, offered high praise for Nouri.

Iran's struggle for a constitution and the creation of the "House of Justice"
ebbed and flowed from 1906 to 1911. In one of the moments of Constitutionalist ascendancy, Nouri was executed as "a traitor to the constitution." He
was hanged outside the Parliament building he so ferociously opposed.

Democratic-minded Iranians do not mourn Nouri's execution. To them,
Nouri, represents traditional reaction to liberal reforms. Democratic-minded
Iranians rue his efforts to crush Iran's adolescent movement for freedom and
representative government.

The Tehran billboard of Nouri, erected shortly after the revolution by the
Islamic Republic of Iran, presents a different story, one of martyrdom. Nouri's
face dominates the ad: oval, dark, with small eyes, and an enormous
salt-and-pepper beard. Just below his face, a dying red rose dangles from a
noose. The message is not subtle: The unjustly hanged Sheikh Fazlollah
Nouri, "the rose of Iran's clergy," was martyred for his defense of Islam
against democracy and representative government.

The Islamic Republic uses billboards as another vehicle for its propaganda machine. All across the country, even in remote hinterlands, billboards
showcase the faces of important clerics and righteous doctrines. Traveling
across Iran, one becomes accustomed to seeing the oversize visage of a
gray-bearded cleric staring down from a square in the sky. The Nouri billboard
towers, appropriately, over the Sheikh Fazlollah Nouri Highway. I passed it
often, on my way to appointments, gatherings, or the airport. It always eerily
reminded me of Iran's Constitutional Revolution of 1906–11, a moment in
Iranian history that seems to be repeating itself today, at least in broad brush-
strokes. Then, as now, Iranians fought for freedom against powerful reactionary
forces. Again, intellectuals and journalists lead the charge while the population
simmers with anger at the current order, longing for an undefined new one.

I had spent a considerable amount of time covering Iran's reform movement:
the crowded student rallies, the reformist president Mohammad Khatami's rock
star–like public appearances, the growing disillusion with the president as his
opponents outmuscled him, the trials and jailings of leading prodemocracy journalists, the public debates between conservative and reform-minded clerics on
Islam and democracy, the student deaths, the rise of new intellectual journals. In
my reading of Iranian history, I had come to the conclusion that every democratic

movement in Iran, in one way or another, must contend with the ghosts of the Constitutional Revolution. I headed to Tabriz, the northwestern Iranian city home to key Constitutionalist struggles, to revisit some of those ghosts.

Tabriz was at the forefront of the Constitutional Revolution; many of its sons and daughters died in those chaotic days. From June 1908 to April 1909, when Tehran's Constitutionalists were silenced and defeated by a collusion of conservative clergy, royalist forces, and Russian troops, Tabriz stood alone in resistance. The scholar Janet Afary writes: "When the Majlis [the Parliament, in Tehran] was bombarded [by Russian and royalist soldiers] and the leading intellectuals of the movement were forced into exile in June 1908, the revolutionary center moved from Tehran to Tabriz." She calls the ensuing Tabriz resistance "one of the most moving chapters of twentieth-century Iranian history." I wanted to look back on the chapter in Iranian history.

To do that, I chose an unorthodox site as my choice of pilgrimage, an old, elegant Tabriz house that served as the backdrop to some of the Constitutionalist struggles. Today a museum occupies the house that once sheltered the first reformers. The Tabriz Constitution House, its current name, offered the Constitutionalists a place to discuss strategies, reload their weapons, and lick their wounds.

I also wanted to look into the Tabriz student protests of the summer of 1999. Rumors circulated around Tehran that the police and student clashes in Tabriz rivaled any in Iran for brutality. Four students allegedly died, dozens were injured, and hundreds jailed. The students fought for some of the same freedoms their great-grandfathers and -grandmothers had died for in the Tabriz resistance at the start of the century.

Before visiting Tabriz, however, I bade good-bye to Mr. Mohseni in Isfahan and boarded a bus to Kashan, a three-hour drive away. There I would recall a mid-nineteenth-century murder, one inspired by the classic Iranian conflict between tradition and modernity, a conflict that colored the debates of the Constitutional era and, indeed, influences the Iranian debate today.

A Murder in Kashan

The Isfahan bus terminal, a dust-colored brick building, jangled with colorful buses lined up outside the doors. Competing bus operators shouted out destinations: "Tehran! Shiraz! Rasht! Kashan!" One touted the seats on his bus. "Comfortable chairs!" he yelled. "The most comfortable chairs around!" I bought a ticket for Kashan and walked over to a government-run bookstand, similar to the Islamic books library at Tehran Mehrabad Airport. I saw the usual books: the writings of leading clerics, panegyrics to Ayatollah Khomeini, and a few books praising Iran's "Islamic Revolution." Amid the Islamic Republic books, I also saw Farsi translations of *Oliver Twist* and *Robinson Crusoe*, as well as sticker decals of Iranian war veterans, martyrs of the Iran-Iraq War. The decals looked much like the billboards around the country commemorating the youths who had died in the war. A collage of red tulips surrounded one young man with green eyes and a black beard. Another picture showed a young man, dead on the ground, his head surrounded by fresh tulips. Iran's war propaganda department often wrote of the miraculous growth of tulips from soil watered by the blood of martyrs.

I bought a few stickers and walked toward my bus, past abundant stores selling fruits, nuts, sweets, newspapers, and handicrafts. Back outside, I located the bus amidst the collection of Mercedes diesel buses with colorful signs on their back mirrors. The Farsi signs cried: O HOSSEIN, O MOHAMMAD, and O ALI. On the back of two buses, English signs read: GOD REMEMBER and GOOD TRAVEL OUR WISH. A couple of European backpackers boarded the Good Travel Our Wish bus, while I boarded the O Hossein bus to Kashan, headed to the Bagh-e-Fin Gardens, built by the late Shah Abbas and scene of the murder of the mid-nineteenth-century modernizing prime minister Mirza Taqi Khan Farahani, better known as Amir Kabir.

When Nasiruddin Shah, the nineteenth-century Qajar king, sent an assassin to kill Amir Kabir in 1851, it may have seemed to contemporaries like simply another case of a *vazir* who had lost favor with his king. But the murder has grown far beyond that in the Iranian popular mind. It has come to represent a tale of a reformer unjustly struck down. Amir Kabir believed in the need to reform Iran's traditional state structure, to modernize the backward country along the lines of the European nation-state, with organized finances, a well-trained army, universities that taught the sciences, and a bureaucracy of technocrats. He also sought to curtail the social influence of Iran's clergy, viewing them as a regressive force in society. For his efforts at reforming the Iranian state, many dub Amir Kabir "Iran's first reformer," the grandfather of other reformers who, like him, paid heavy prices for their efforts.

Nasiruddin Shah appointed his former guardian and tutor, Amir Kabir, to the post of prime minister when he ascended the throne in 1848. Amir Kabir immediately set about modernizing the Iranian state. He organized the nation's finances, cut the salaries of freeloading court members, devised a tax system, and wrote new guidelines for army divisions, strengthening Iran's tattered defenses. He appointed trustworthy governors to border areas, people he believed would protect Iran, displacing the corrupt, money-hungry governors of the past. He also began Iran's foreign policy of playing off Britain and Russia against each other, an effort to stem the encroachment of both covetous nations.

Perhaps Amir Kabir's most immediate success was his effort to vaccinate Iranians from smallpox, which cut the death rate significantly and represented a tangible contribution to the daily lives of Iranians. He also built in 1848 an upper-level high school, Dar al Fonoun, that would teach the modern sciences and languages that would undergird his modernization efforts. Built on the outskirts of Tehran, it symbolized his belief that Iran needed to enter the modern world of science and information in order to emerge from its current state of backwardness, marked by rampant disease, feudal exploitation, minimal central government control, and literacy rates below 5 percent.

By 1851, however, Amir Kabir's reforms and his growing power had begun to rankle some members of the court elite, whose privileges he threatened. Nasiruddin Shah began to hear complaints, including some from his mother, Mahd ol Olia, and a powerful former official named Mirza Agha Khan Nouri. One night they convinced the intoxicated Shah of the "treachery" of Amir Kabir. Despite the fact that Amir Kabir was married to the Shah's sister, Nasiruddin promptly signed an execution order for the reformist prime minister and sent a notorious executioner on the kingly mission to the Bagh-e-Fin Gardens in Kashan, where Amir Kabir vacationed.

Our bus rumbled past acres of yellow fields, telephone lines, rolling hills, bursts of flowers, and spots of brown mountains on the three-hour drive to Kashan. The mountains over the horizon looked like undulating ocean waves. I sat next to a young man with a shaved head who had just completed his military service in Isfahan. He was now headed back home to Kashan. The trajectory of the conversation followed a familiar route: He worried about his future; there were no jobs; the government was corrupt; the university exams were prohibitively difficult.

When I told him that I planned to visit the site of Amir Kabir's murder in Kashan, his eyes brightened. "Ah, yes, Amir Kabir was one of our greatest leaders. We need more men like him today. The trouble is that all of our reformers are overthrown or killed."

Shortly after the bus turned out of the station, I saw an extraordinary piece of government propaganda neatly typed in big, bold Farsi letters against a brick wall. It said: OUR GOVERNMENT IS THE SAME GOVERNMENT AS THE ONE OF THE PROPHET MUHAMMAD, MAY HE REST IN PEACE. The propaganda writers had equated the current era with the most sacred moment in Muslim history, the time of the Prophet Muhammad—an extraordinarily bold assertion.

Of course, the analogy is silly: how can one compare the seventh-century government run by a small group of devoted religious followers of a Divinely inspired prophet in Medina to a modern, resource-rich, postrevolution state of nearly seventy million people in Iran? In fact, I doubt most officials of the Islamic Republic would bother trying to make an argument supporting that statement. But the literal interpretation of the statement mattered less than its reflection of a way of thinking among a powerful segment of Iran's rulers, a view that held Western ideologies in contempt, a view held by Khomeini and some of today's hard-line clerical rulers. Harkening back to the "ideal time" of the Prophet Muhammad effectively repudiates those who call for progress along modern, and Western, lines. It is a powerful argument and one that soothed many traditional Iranians in the 1970s who were disoriented by the Shah's headlong rush to modernization following a Western model. After all, was not the Prophet Muhammad's community a peaceful and successful one? Did it not achieve great things without Western ideologies?

This tension between traditionalists, who saw modernization as "Westernization," and the modernizers, some of whom groped for a middle ground and others who pushed for total Westernization, animated much of Iran's political discourse from the mid-nineteenth-century period of Amir Kabir onward. He fell into the camp of the modernizer groping for the middle ground. Unlike later intellectuals, some of whom called for the total "Europeanization" of Iranian institutions, Amir Kabir attempted gradual reform that would import Western science and administrative methods without importing Western ideas of political modernity.

Today, Amir Kabir is widely respected by liberal nationalist Iranians as a reformer ahead of his time. In fact, he has come to represent a certain type of farsighted nationalism, an image that President Khatami has used in some of his own campaign literature, in which he refers to the late modernizing prime minister in flattering tones, thus equating himself with a respected historical figure who tried to reform a state structure that seemed resistant to change.

The bus stopped in Kashan station at midday. On Taleghani Street, named after a prominent revolutionary ayatollah, I saw apple carts and tree-shaded shops and a square named 15 Khordad, an Iranian date corresponding to June 15, when Khomeini supporters, in 1963, first protested openly against the Shah in the holy city of Qom.[1] Amid the square, an enormous clock rose to the sky. It read 1:20 P.M.

A young boy, Najibullah, in a torn sweater, asked me if I wanted to buy gum. He carried a small box of Chiclets. "It is very good gum," he said. "Really, very good." I bought a few packs and asked him how to get to the Bagh-e-Fin.

"You will need a taxi," he said. "It is far from here."

I asked him if he knew who Amir Kabir was.

"No."

I asked him where he lived, if he had a home (most of the Chiclets sellers in Tehran are street kids).

"Yes, I live near here, but my father went to God [died], so I help my mother."

We stood in front of a fruit seller. I bought the rest of the Chiclets from him and asked him to hail a cab for me. He scurried away. When he came back with the taxi, I handed him two bags of fruit. "When will you be back?" he asked, wide-eyed. "I can bring more gum."

The taxi driver, an elderly man driving a worn Paykan, talked like most Tehran drivers, lambasting the clerics and lamenting the state of the economy and marveling at the days *ghabl az enghelab,* before the revolution, when he had bought a car for thirty-six thousand tomans. "Today," he said, "I must pay five million tomans for the car. I went out on the streets to demonstrate during the revolution," he said. "What for? We have nothing now."

We drove on Ayatollah Kashani Street, where children played on the periphery and motorcycles buzzed by us. We passed Imam Hossein Square

---

[1] A conservative foundation known as the 15 Khordad Foundation continues to promote the execution of Salman Rushdie, despite the fact that Iran's Foreign Ministry has sought to distance itself from Khomeini's notorious fatwa against him.

and Navab-e-Safavi Street[2] before reaching Bagh-e-Fin. The gardens mean-
dered around flowing water canals and stone walkways. The canals were tiled
with light blue ceramic. Tall trees shaded the green benches and low-spouting
fountains dotting the area.

My driver and I walked toward a squat brick building that housed the
public bath where Amir Kabir met his demise. The marbled bathroom floor
sparkled. "See this wall," my driver said, pointing to the tiled wall of the
hamam, the large area where dignitaries like Amir Kabir bathed with the help
of servants who scrubbed the week's dirt off their bodies. "I heard that it took
two weeks to fully scrub away the bloody hand marks on that wall."

I tried to imagine the scene. Sources say that Amir Kabir saw his executioner and stoically accepted his fate when he learned of the Shah's order for
his execution. He had only one request: to choose his own form of death. The
executioner agreed but broke his word, slitting the prime minister's wrists
and shoving a towel down his throat, as his bloodied hands pushed against
the wall.

"Amir Kabir was a great man," my sixtyish driver said, echoing the words
of the twenty-year-old returning army conscript aboard the bus. "It is a shame
he was killed. He could have done great things for Iran."

I heard the tinkle of the canals just outside the *hamam.*

"But in Iran we always kill our reformers. Have you read Rezagoli's book?"

Yes, I had. In a recent best-selling book titled *The Killing of Iran's Elites,* the
Iranian sociologist Ali Rezagoli lamented Iran's tendency to kill its reformers
either physically or politically. He named Amir Kabir as one of three examples. Apparently, the book sold well in Kashan too, according to my driver.

"I am a former army colonel," he said. "I read many books about our history these days. There are many things that we Iranians should be ashamed
of. Many of us are always blaming foreigners for our problems. Yes, the British
were bad, and so were the Russians and even the Americans, but we also need
to look in the mirror. Men like Amir Kabir looked in the mirror, saw the problems, and tried to change them. What happened? He was killed by Iranians."

The former colonel turned taxi driver raised his arms in disgust. "President
Khatami has already been killed, politically speaking. It is a familiar pattern."

---

2 Navab-e-Safavi, as you may recall, is the name of the man who killed Ahmed Kasravi,
the noisy secular nationalist, in 1946.

We walked back to the car, a light rain sending the streams of water rushing down the blue-tiled canals.

The death of Amir Kabir did not quench the educated elite's thirst for modernization of the Iranian state. In the late nineteenth century, a new generation of intellectuals emerged with ideas far more progressive than Amir Kabir's, whose court affiliations and personal outlook made him a more conservative modernizer, albeit an important one for his time. These new intellectuals sought not to grope for a middle ground between tradition and modernity but instead embraced European ideas wholly.[3] As Ervand Abrahamian notes in his classic book *Iran between Two Revolutions,* the new generation of intellectuals believed in the principles of liberalism, nationalism, and even socialism and were influenced by the French Enlightenment, which led them to venerate "not the Shadow of God on Earth (i.e., Iran's Qajar kings), but the triumvirate of Equality, Liberty, and Fraternity."

These intellectuals would play a critical role in the events leading up to the early-twentieth-century Constitutional Revolution (1906–11). I flew from Kashan to Tabriz to recall an important episode in that revolution: the Tabriz resistance. But first, I followed the trail of a more contemporary resistance, the student protests in Tabriz in 1999. During those protests, which rocked that city as well as several other major Iranian cities, students took to the streets to call for an end to authoritarian rule, for greater political freedoms, for an open press—ideas rooted in the thinking of the Constitutionalists in the early twentieth century.

Tabriz Student Protests, 1999

I arrived in Tabriz on a chilly afternoon just before winter. A few months had passed since the summer student protests of 1999, the ones that included student chants for "democracy," "the rule of law," and "civil society." The city had returned to its normal rhythms of life. The vast, winding, underground bazaar, the biggest in all the Middle East, buzzed with the sound of shuffling feet and brisk business. On Vali-e-Asr Street, young, sharply dressed boys and girls flirted and furtively exchanged phone numbers. The *maidan-e*-ShahGoli, a public park with a huge man-made lake and

---

[3] This new generation coined the modern Iranian term for intellectual, *rushanfekr*. Literally, it means "enlightened thinker."

tall hills, in the evenings attracted large crowds of families who strolled underneath the blue-gray dusk sky and the swarming blackbirds above. Young people kicked a soccer ball, bantering in Azeri, the language spoken in Tabriz and its larger province, Azerbaijan.[4]

Tabriz University remained relatively quiet, with students turning their minds to upcoming exams. Khomeini billboards, including one with a celestial-looking Khomeini transposed over Noah's Ark, dotted the roads. The crisp, chilly air marked a prelude to the cold and snowy winter ahead.

I spent the afternoon with two Tabriz University students: Behrooz, a slim, gregarious and loquacious student in the sciences, and his friend, Yadollah, a squat, reserved young man with an air of quiet dignity. We sat cross-legged on elaborately designed burgundy carpets, in a small room with white, bare walls and plastic flowers on brown tables, in Yadollah's parents' house. A large silver samovar full of hot tea steamed in a corner of the room as we recalled the student protests in the summer of 1999.

The summer student protests had begun, as do most important political events, in Tehran. A small group of politically active students protested the closure of a pro-Khatami daily newspaper, *Salam,* by Iran's conservative judiciary. During the protests, the hard-line Ansar-e-Hezbollah confronted the students. Both sides taunted each other, and a few blows flurried from each side. Police ordered the students to disperse, and the Ansar-e-Hezbollah, whose shady links with senior conservative clerics give it inordinate power, went unpunished.

Later that evening the situation turned for the worse. Several students continued their protests from their dormitory, chanting slogans for freedom of the press and democracy. Their opponents lurked outside, then entered the dormitory with police officials, intent on cracking down hard on the protesters. Ansar-e-Hezbollah thugs beat, punched, kicked, and threw students against concrete walls. According to one student eyewitness, one of the attackers shoved a club into a student's back, saying, "Where is your Mr. Khatami now?" Another attacker went even further, forcing a student out the window. He fell to his death. Another student had an eye gouged out in the melee.

Predictably, Tehran University erupted after the dormitory raid. The next

---

[4] Iranian Azeris, who make up nearly one-fourth of the country's population, are fully integrated and often intensely nationalist, despite their preferred use of their local language. The majority of Azeris also speak, read, and write Persian.

day thousands of students and their supporters spilled onto the nearby streets. The Basijis fanned out across campus and nearby hot spots, hoping to maintain order. The Ansar-e-Hezbollah hit the streets again, looking to knock some heads in. Angry, disaffected, unemployed youths joined the students in their protests. Tempers inevitably flared, and clashes ensued. Ansar thugs, carrying knives and chains, attacked protesters. The Basijis, ostensibly dispatched to maintain order, lacked discipline, and some even took part in the student beatings. A few Basijis disguised themselves as students—jeans, T-shirts, clean-shaved—and threw bricks into shopwindows to prove that the students were anarchists. Prodemocracy chants were soon transformed into personal attacks on Iran's conservative clerics. Even the normally off-limits Supreme Leader, Ayatollah Ali Khamenei, felt the sting of student slogans.

Back in Tabriz, Behrooz and Yadollah, moved by the courage of Tehran's students, decided to show their solidarity with a protest of their own. "When we heard about the Tehran student protests," Behrooz said, "many of us decided to have our own protest in Tabriz. We gathered at the university and began chanting slogans against the conservatives. Across the street from the university, the headquarters for the Basijis was buzzing with activity. A rumor had spread that the Basijis had Kalashnikovs and were going to fire on the students. I did not believe it, so I stayed. The next thing I knew, I was hit and knocked down."

As Yadollah began pouring tea, Behrooz stood up, and lifted his sweater to his chin. He turned his back to me. Two long pink scars crisscrossed his back. "This is my souvenir from the student uprising," he said. "I still don't know what hit me. One minute I was chanting slogans—'We want freedom, not fascism!'—and the next minute I was on the ground, and something lashed at my back. I think it was a chain."

He lowered his shirt and faced me. An unmistakable hint of pride tinted his eyes. "After I was knocked down," he said, "I put my hands on my head and yelled. I was waiting for another blow to hit me. I felt a kick in my ribs. And then another kick." He touched his ribs. "Then I felt an arm on my shoulder, lifting me up. It was Yadollah," he said, pointing to his friend, who sat across the room, pouring tea from the samovar into tiny glasses.

Yadollah smiled in acknowledgment, and Behrooz continued: "Yadollah lifted me up, and we began running! I felt a sharp pain when I ran because as I moved my arms, I was stretching the wounds on my back. I tried to run without moving my arms, but that slowed me down, so I just bore the pain and ran at full speed. We wanted to get out of there," he said.

Yadollah placed a teacup and saucer in front of me, with two jagged white sugar cubes leaning against the cup.

"Yadollah brought me right here to his own house, and they laid me down on the floor as they washed my wounds. His aunt could not stop screaming! His older brother was very angry. It was good that we had got out of there because I heard later that the police vans began rounding up students," he said, "and the Hezbollahis kept beating them."

As in the Tehran student uprising, hard-line Ansar-e-Hezbollah thugs and the police worked together to crush the student protests in Tabriz. Police and intelligence services questioned many students detained after the riots. A number of students received beatings while in custody, not to mention the four students who died in the Tabriz unrest.

Were any of the students fighting back? I asked. I looked at Yadollah. I wanted to get him involved in the conversation, but Behrooz responded instead. "Some of the students gathered bricks. There was a new mosque being built on campus. There were many bricks lying around. Some students picked up those bricks to defend themselves against the attacking Basijis."

I took a moment to conjure the image: a group of young men using bricks from an unconstructed mosque as their weapons against a band of religious hard-liners. Behrooz smiled. He knew I had caught the irony.

Yadollah furrowed his brow, as if he were thinking deeply, then entered the conversation. "I want you to know something, Mr. Afshin," he said haltingly. "Not all the Basijis are bad. My brother is a Basiji. He fought in the war with Iraq. He does not think it is right for Basijis to beat up students. The ones who attacked us are a minority." He breathed deeply after his statement, as if a weight had been lifted from his shoulders. I assured Yadollah that many of my friends are Basijis. Behrooz simply rolled his eyes.

As they provided more details about the student protests, I reflected on the friendship of these two young men. They hailed from two different middle-class backgrounds. Behrooz belongs to Iran's "modern middle class," the class of civil servants, technocrats, and professionals built up during the Pahlavi years, who tend to be more open to the West and less socially conservative than the traditional middle class of bazaar merchants, clergy, and more religious-minded civil servants. Iranian scholars and historians have pointed out the distinction between these two classes in the years preceding the revolution. They have noted that both groups generally favored the overthrow of the Shah, though for different reasons. The modern middle-class man might have been frustrated by a world in which his education granted him a certain mobility, while his lack of important connections created a glass ceiling. He might also have supported political liberalism but wanted more freedom of the press and a greater say in his government. The traditional middle-class man might have felt his religious faith and values under assault in a world where modernization came laced with Westernization. He might also have seen his livelihood in danger as the country filled with cheap manufactured goods, the traditional bazaar system being encroached upon by supermarket chains and modern middle-class merchants who spoke English and French.

Behrooz's father works as a university-educated engineer for a private-sector firm. His mother speaks a little English and wears the loose-fitting manteau and head scarf typical of her class, as opposed to the more severe chador. His teenage sister plays the guitar and wants to become a classical musician. Family gatherings occasionally involve a bit of whiskey. They eat dinner sitting in chairs around a table, as opposed to the traditional middle-class family, which usually eats on the floor, a tablecloth spread out on the carpet. Behrooz's family ignores most Islamic holidays, except for the major ones, much like Christians in the West. They proudly back nationalists as well as more social and political freedoms. They have a satellite dish on their apartment balcony aimed at Istanbul. In the evenings they watch Turkish television game shows with scantily clad women.

Yadollah hails from the traditional middle class. His father is a moderately successful merchant in the bazaar. His mother wears the *chador*. His parents expect his seventeen-year-old sister to marry soon. The family eats dinner on the floor, cross-legged, seated around a tablecloth spread on the burgundy carpet we now sat on. It celebrates virtually every Islamic holiday. In family gatherings, people lean up against cushions on the floor—no chairs—and alcohol is never served. Yadollah's family also has a small satellite dish on the balcony. When his grandmother is not around, the family also watches Turkish television game shows with scantily clad women. Obviously, the satellite dish knows no distinction between the traditional and modern middle classes.

In the 1970s men like Yadollah's father began listening to the clandestinely distributed tapes of Ayatollah Khomeini. The brave and unbending cleric in exile tapped into seething class-based resentments as well as into chest-thumping nationalist pride. He spoke for the have-nots in a world where the haves callously disregarded them. When Khomeini talked of economic exploitation, Yadollah's father knew what he meant because he saw his own profits fall while Iran's petro elite with Western connections grew fabulously rich. When Khomeini talked of an assault on the faith by Westernization, Yadollah's father remembered sadly the bikini-clad women on the billboards advertising movies, the government promoting pre-Islamic history, and a local mosque illuminated by the neon lights of a tavern billboard.

Behrooz's father, on the other hand, knew little about Khomeini until one year before the revolution. According to Behrooz, his father had eagerly followed Iran's National Front, a democratic and nationalist opposition party that vehemently opposed the Shah. He spoke fondly of Shahpoor Bakhtiar, the National Front leader, whom he had met once at a seminar in Tabriz. Bakhtiar called for a secular, democratic parliament and massive curbs on the power of the Shah. Nothing in his rhetoric mentioned the veiling of women or strident anti-Westernism, though he espoused populist and nationalist themes similar to those of Khomeini.

After the revolution and the victory of the Khomeinists, an extreme version of the values of the traditional middle class, of Yadollah's family, became the "official" values of the government, promoted aggressively by a government with an unwavering righteousness of its cause. An assault on modern middle-class values ensued. Seemingly harmless acts, such as dancing, listening to pop music, and men and women holding hands in public, came under harsh scrutiny. Women's dress proved a key issue of the assault. The modern middle class found the thought of forced veiling abhorrent. When Khomeini mandated the veiling of Iranian women one year after the revolution, massive street protests ensued in Tehran, especially peopled by modern middle-class women and men.

In the end, Khomeini's view prevailed publicly, but privately, modern middle-class women resisted, wearing the latest European-cut dresses under their veils, dancing at closed-door parties among other modern middle-class friends. The modern middle-class woman resented the new structures and all that it implied. As one woman put it to me, "Just because I don't want to drape myself in a black chador, *those people* assume that I am somehow immoral! That is so deeply insulting!" But she and most of Iran's modern upper middle class learned to live dual lives. Publicly, they conformed to the new orthodox ways. Privately, behind closed doors, they sat in their chairs and listened to their music and drank their whiskey and cursed these traditional men who changed their lives. They had no choice: The government belonged to men more comfortable sitting on the floor than in chairs.

Behrooz's father found the postrevolution intolerable. "We have known something different," he told me later when I met him. "We have lived in freer days socially. It is difficult for us to accept the current ways, to go backward. It's not just the social conservatism that they have imposed on us. But people of my class also had a dream of democracy and social progress. It seems that the clergy are not the right people to lead us in social progress." Yadollah's father, on the other hand, approved of the new order of things but gradually grew disillusioned as the economy slowed and corruption increased. "Still," he told me, "female veiling was an important victory for the revolution."

The sons of these two men have forged a close bond. They study together every night. On Fridays, their day off, they sometimes go hiking in nearby hills. They watch European soccer games broadcast from Germany. They eagerly read the latest newspapers and discuss political events in Tehran. Both support President Khatami and reform, but Behrooz's patience has worn thin. "If Khatami can't do it, he should step aside," Behrooz says these days. Occasionally they visit each other's homes, Behrooz sitting on the floor in Yadollah's house and Yadollah using a chair in Behrooz's. Their friendship strengthened on that chaotic day in June, when Yadollah saved Behrooz from the chains of an angry thug.

The Case of Ahmad Batebi

A hmad Batebi, a striking young man with long, flowing black hair, a chiseled jaw, piercing eyes, and a closely cropped black beard, is perhaps Iran's most famoust student protestor. Behrooz and Yadollah both spoke of him fondly. During the Tehran student protests Batebi carried with him the bloodied shirt of a student who had been beaten a few days before. In a moving and daring act, he raised the bloodied shirt above his head and marched with the protesters. In that heady moment of rebellion, he looked like a young Che Guevara—wavy black hair flowing around a green bandanna—and symbolized the anger and frustration of student protesters. A

Reuters photographer snapped his photo. The next day Batebi's face and the bloodied shirt graced the front pages of every major newspaper in the world. He was doomed.

I inquired about Batebi's prison conditions and pending trial from the sort of people who might know these things. Rumors circulated that he was in solitary confinement. I had heard tales of severe beatings. There was talk of a death sentence. My sources, however, were tight-lipped. Finally, I came across a politically active student who knew something about Batebi's case. He handed me a letter. "It's all there," he said, "the whole sad story."

It was a chilling letter from Batebi addressed to Iran's judiciary. In it, he presented some of the details of his incarceration, which included beatings and death threats. It was covertly distributed from hand to hand on the Tehran University campus, where I got a copy.

The letter begins: "On the first day of my arrest by plain clothes security officials, I was brought inside the university where they confiscated all my documents and possessions. While taunting me with insults, they beat me in my testicles, my legs, and abdominal area. When I protested, they answered that this is the land of the 'Velayat' and that I should be blinded and not live here."

He was then taken to prison. There, he writes, "The soldiers bound my hands and secured them to plumbing pipes. They beat my head and abdominal area with soldier's shoes. They insisted I sign a confession of the accusations made against me. Next, they threw me on the floor, stood on my neck and cut off not only all of my hair, but also parts of my scalp, causing it to bleed. They beat me so severely with their heavy shoes that I lost consciousness."

After outlining more humiliations and beatings, he describes a harrowing bathroom scene: "I said I needed to have the [bathroom] door closed, but they refused. Not wanting to expose my bodily functions to others, I told them I no longer wanted to go to the bathroom. They insisted I must go and the door must be open. Then they began lashing at me. I resisted and punched one of them in the face. At this point, they took me and ducked my head into a closed drain full of excrement. They held me under for so long, I was unable to hold my breath any longer, and excrement was inhaled through my nose and seeped into my mouth.

"During the investigations, they threatened several times to execute me and to torture and rape my family members as well as imprison them for long terms."

At one point, in a particularly cruel act of psychological torture, his inter-rogators wrapped a noose around his neck while he sat in a chair for two hours. Eventually he broke down and signed a confession. A trial ensued. The judge branded his courageous lawyers "spies." Batebi was given the death sentence. The charges against him were "creating street unrest" and "agitat-ing people to create unrest." Later, after an outcry from Iranians and interna-tional human rights groups, the death sentence was commuted to a fifteen-year prison term.

Because of his high profile from the photograph, Batebi had entered the international media and foreign activist radar, an exclusive club with impor-tant privileges for Third World political activists. Shortly after the jailing, there were protests from human rights groups, the world's news agencies filed dis-patches, petitions were signed on the Internet, and foreign governments "expressed alarm." When he was placed in solitary confinement, the news rip-pled out through the news agencies, causing more international protest.

Authoritarian governments regularly dismiss the work of human rights groups as biased and politically inspired. Though human rights organizations are not without fault and their researchers are not without bias, people like Batebi and thousands of other prisoners of conscience around the world are certainly pleased to be on their watch lists.

During the uproar over the trial I met a student, Hamid, who had been briefly detained after the student protests. He had been, by his own admis-sion, a bit player in the demonstrations, merely joining the crowd for a bit of fun and to let off steam. He told me: "When I was in jail, I wished that I were a well-known figure and that Amnesty International knew where I was. I felt so alone. When Ganji or Shams [Iranian journalist Mashallah Shamsolvaezin] goes to jail, the whole world knows about it. I could have died, and only my family and friends would mourn me. This made me sad. If I were to die, I wanted to have some impact. At least I would not have died in vain."

Hamid , twenty years old, he was talking about dying for a cause. Just one generation ago there was also talk among politically active young men and women of dying for a cause. Thoughts of revolution gripped the young and idealistic of the 1970s. The guerrilla culture of sacrifice for a cause was "in." As the literary historian Kamran Talatoff writes, "Death became a theme that modern committed writers praised. Death for one's principles was accepted without hesitation." The Iranian intellectual and Marxist writer Samad

Behrangi encapsulated the mood in a highly political "children's book" titled *The Little Black Fish*. Behrangi describes the effort by a little black fish to break away from his group, to explore the world, to move fearlessly away from tradition. It was widely seen as an allegory for modern times. Most Iranian intellectuals, Behrangi included, opposed to the Shah and agitating for change, were eager to swim, like the little black fish, away from the status quo. It was important to swim against the current, even if it meant death, because the act of swimming against the tide, the act of defiance, would have an impact on society. In Behrangi's book, the little black fish says: "Of course, if someday I should be forced to face death—and I shall—it doesn't matter. What does matter is the influence my life or death will have on the lives of others." Talatoff notes that "this sentence became the axiom for a whole generation that went out to meet death—first in small groups and later in masses during the course of the 1979 Revolution." The idea of secular martyrdom coincided with the religious martyrdom that plays a critical role in the Shi'a Muslim faith. As Talatoff notes, "both secular leftists and religious activists died in their fights with what was a common enemy."

Ironically, the author of *The Little Black Fish* died while swimming in a river. He drowned. Iranian writers of the day depicted the death as a murder by agents of the Shah's secret police, though it has not been proved to be so. The most prominent intellectual of the 1960s, the writer and essayist Jalal Al-e-Ahmad, wrote a panegyrical essay on Behrangi. He took Behrangi's life and made it a paragon of the committed writer dying for a cause. Behrangi became a hero among young writers. His example of life and death was seen as a model to be emulated.

When Hamid talked about dying for a cause, I remembered Samad Behrangi and all the young Iranians who "died for a cause" in the 1970s. Who remembers them today? Did their deaths truly have the kind of impact they wanted?

Iran's Fight for a Constitution, 1906–11

Iran's early-twentieth-century Constitutional movement gained ground in Tehran as a result of the twin evils of a badly managed autocracy and efficiently run foreign domination. On these two points, all sides generally agreed, including the secular liberals, the reformist clergy, the more orthodox clergy, and the conservative bazaar merchants. Still, while the movement agreed on what it did *not* want, it differed on what ultimately it did want. Sandra Mackey, the author of *The Iranians,* sums it up nicely: "For the secular intellectuals, [the Constitutional Revolution] translated into the adoption of some form of Western liberalism. For the merchants, it equaled economic redress. For the reformist clerics, it converted into strength for the Shia state. For the traditionalist mullahs and their followers, it stood for reestablishing the Koran as the legal, political, social, and cultural model for society."

The liberal wing of the Constitutionalists won an initial victory in late 1906, when a dying Shah signed the papers allowing for the Parliament and a written constitution. This constitution replicated, for the most part, the Belgian Constitution of 1831 with foreign words simply inserted into the Farsi text. As a result, many of Iran's conservative clerics, who originally favored the constitution, opposed the final document. They demanded oversight of the Parliament to make sure laws conformed with Islam.

Sheikh Fazlollah Nouri, who led the conservative onslaught against the constitution, continued a drumbeat of criticism. The constitution would bring all sorts of vice to Iran, he proclaimed. It would tear at society and ruin the morals of the nation, he cried. He worked feverishly against it. As a result of Nouri's persistent attacks, the liberal wing inserted language in the constitution that would allow a committee of five clerics to oversee all legislation. Nouri was momentarily appeased, but the Constitutionalists ignored the clause, ensuring that Nouri's attacks would begin again.

Nouri found an ally in the new Shah, who adamantly opposed the Constitutionalists and a representative parliament. He once said: "I have nothing against the Parliament, as long as they do not interfere in politics and matters of state." He schemed constantly to crush the parliamentarians and the ideas associated with them. To that end, he allied himself with conservative clerics like Nouri as well as with Russia. Tsarist Russia had recently defeated a group of pesky Constitutionalists of its own. To ensure that this constitutional contagion did not spread to Iran, Russia joined with the Shah and conservative clerics to defeat the movement.

Britain, at first, found the anti-Russian strain in the early constitutional movement useful and originally supported the Constitutionalists. However, when Britain and Russia effectively partitioned Iran into respective spheres of influence, in 1907, Britain's support waned. The door opened for Russian troops to bombard the Parliament. In June 1908, less than two years after the constitution had become law and Iranian Parliament members had debated the issues of the day from the "House of Justice" in Tehran, Russian and Iranian royalist soldiers attacked the Parliament building in Tehran and violently evicted its members. Tehran intellectuals and writers who supported the constitution met a similar fate. The dream of representative government vanished for the time being, momentarily crushed.

The action moved to Tabriz, a city that stood on a crossroads of sorts in the late nineteenth century. The vast Ottoman Empire to Iran's west prevented a fluid transmission of European ideas to Iran. Iranian students who traveled to Europe usually used a northern route to Tabriz, then went on to Baku and Moscow, where they boarded a long train to Paris. European ideas traveled along a similar route back to Iran, often filtered through Transcaucasian intellectuals to the north down to Tabriz and then to Tehran and elsewhere. Tabriz became the transit point for some of the most progressive ideas of the early twentieth century, the most powerful of which were the rule of law, representative government, and a written constitution. As Nikkie Keddie notes, "[T]he profundity and radicalism of the Iranian [Constitutional] Revolution in the North can largely be attributed to contacts and influence from the very revolutionary Russian Transcaucasus."

Many of Iran's leading intellectuals and even some liberal clerics had come to believe in the almost magical powers of the written constitution and establishment of the rule of law. These two progressive institutions would solve hundreds of years of Iranian problems, they believed, including unlimited royal autocracy, draconian landowners, an increasingly corrupt clerical class, and wide disparities in wealth. The 1905 victory of Japan, an Asian nation with a written constitution, over Russia, an imperialist European power, only confirmed what many Iranian intellectuals believed: A written constitution would produce a prosperous Iran governed by just rule and freedom from foreign exploitation.

In the late nineteenth and early twentieth centuries, Tabriz had small but significant pockets of intellectuals who formed debating and politically active societies known as *anjumans*, where they talked of writing an Iranian constitution. In the early twentieth century, Tabriz emerged as a key intellectual center of the liberal/secular wing of the Constitutional Revolution. E. G. Browne, British Persianist, described the Tabriz Palimentarians as a cut above the rest, more progressive and more insistent on democratic rule. Tehran of course also stirred with its own proconstitution *anjuman*s. They all avidly kept up with Iranian exile newspapers in Baku, Tiflis, London, and Calcutta that agi-tated for a constitution and the rule of law, including Mirza Malkum Khan's London-based newspaper *Qanun*.

Just as Tehran's Parliament lay tattered from Russian bullets, Tabriz fought back. For nine months after Tehran Constitutionalists had fallen, the city resisted a massive bombardment by royalist troops, a Russian invasion, and an economic and agricultural blockade that left thousands starving. In central downtown Tabriz there stands a living reminder to the resistance: the *Khaneh-ye Mashrutiat* (Constitution House), an elegant residence with a stone courtyard, vaulted arches, intricate moldings, and hardwood floors. Through-out the five years that Tabrizis agitated for a constitution, this home of a wealthy merchant often was at the center of events. Constitutionalists regu-larly gathered there to debate strategies, nurse the wounded, and revive their spirits. Today a museum reminds visitors of the sacrifices made during the Tabriz resistance. The museum has been tolerated by both Shahs and the Islamic Republic for different reasons: The Shahs saw the Tabriz resistance as a repudiation of conservative clerics, as it was, in part; the clerics see it as a repudiation of kings, also true. I visited the museum with Behrooz and Yadol-lah. I wanted to see how they viewed the events of 1908 in Tabriz. I wanted to see if they thought it relevant to their struggle today.

Near the entrance to the museum, a massive bust of Sattar Khan, the folk hero of the Tabriz resistance, greets visitors. Sattar Khan, a semiliterate former bandit, somehow emerged as the most brave and forceful advocate for the rein-stitution of the constitution. He did it through sheer determination, great phys-ical courage, and an unbending promotion of freedom and the rule of law.

As we entered, Behrooz touched the bust, running his fingers across the sharp nose, down the bushy mustache and thin lower lip. I opened my bag and pulled out Janet Afary's social analysis of Iran's Constitutional Revolu-tion. I found a quote attributed to Sattar Khan: "What we want is an end to this regime of oppression: laws, freedom, a constitution. This is the only way to assure the salvation of the country. We are ready to die for this. I have four thousand men under arms, and I can have ten thousand if I want to, and I can hold out for ten years. God is with us! They say we are rebels. No, we do not want any harm to come to the Shah. But he should give us what we want! Or we will proclaim a republic!"

I made a rough translation on the spot for Behrooz and Yadollah.

"Sounds a lot like the things we are asking for now," Behrooz said. Yadollah nodded in agreement, and Behrooz added: "The difference is that we do not have any armed men the way Sattar Khan did."

We moved upstairs, our shoes clicking on the hardwood stairs. We walked among the museum display cases. We looked at black-and-white photos of Tabriz constitutional revolutionaries, including a photo of several hanging from the gallows, killed by Russian soldiers in 1912, when Russian troops invaded Iran's north and exterminated all remaining Constitutionalist sympathizers. We saw the pen case and eyeglasses of one of those revolutionaries, Sighat-ol Islam, several of whose descendants now enjoy successful lives in the United States. We also saw a forty-year-old letter from Iran's Parliament posthumously thanking Sattar Khan and the people of Azerbaijan for their efforts. On the wall, a painting of Sattar Khan's ragged band of Constitutionalists depict them with wide mustaches, long coats, and rifles slung on their shoulders.

After besieging Tehran's Parliament in June 1908, royalist forces descended on Tabriz, where Sattar Khan and Bagher Khan, a lesser folk hero with a similar background to Sattar's, had taken control of key sectors of the city in defiance of the royalist countercoup. Royalist forces, working in conjunction with conservative clerics and hired thugs, easily overran most of Tabriz, except for a few districts where Sattar Khan and Bagher Khan still remained entrenched. Members of the Tabriz *anjuman*s found themselves targeted by angry and well-paid mobs. The Shah so desired to crush the Tabriz opposition that he freed a notorious bandit from jail with orders to rally a band of criminals into an army and kill all resisters. The bandit, known as Rahim Khan (*Khan,* in all three last names, roughly translates as "sir" or "mister"), began a frightening campaign of rape and robbery in Tabriz that cowed many residents. The Russian consul, who had supported hard-line Islamic groups that opposed the constitution, urged all residents who wished to be spared to raise white flags on their houses.

The situation looked grim. Few residents saw much hope in resistance anymore. Then, suddenly, in one of those rare moments that combine grand political defiance with grand gesture, Sattar Khan rode through the streets of Tabriz, dramatically removing the white flags of surrender from the people's houses. Hundreds of Tabrizis, excited by Sattar Khan's move, offered to join his army of resisters on the spot, and a vigorous recruiting campaign began. Next, Sattar Khan did what few Iranian politicians had ever been able to do: He resisted a bribe from a foreign embassy. The Russian consul offered him more money than he could ever imagine, but he staunchly refused. The Tabriz resistance had begun.

"You know, I really admire Sattar Khan," Behrooz said. "He was a man of action. We need more men like him. We need people like him today, people who are willing to back up their talk with action."

Yadollah, nodding in agreement, said, "When we were out there demonstrating during the protests, I got the sense that so many of us were waiting to be guided. We were waiting for a leader. We wanted someone to take charge."

Someone like Sattar Khan?

"Yes, why not?" Behrooz said. "I know he was not an intellectual," he added apologetically, "but our intellectuals are always too busy debating each other. While the debate goes on, the strongmen step in."

I looked at Yadollah. He nodded. Behrooz continued. "Sattar Khan also knew something that the prerevolution intellectuals like Shariati and Al-e-Ahmad did not know. He knew that no mullah will ever support freedom." Though Shariati and Al-e-Ahmad were deeply suspicious of Iran's clerics, at least Behrooz judged Sattar Khan's view on Iran's clerical class correctly. Sattar Khan, in all his pronouncements, reflected the general view of Tabriz intellectuals of the day—that is, that Iran's clerics were backward-thinking and reactionary. They were members of the wealthy elite who owned large swaths of land. Iran's conservative clerics in conjunction with the wealthy landowners, kings, and foreign embassies conspired against the common man. For that reason, they felt, Iran's clerics despised the constitution. Though several prominent clerics, in fact, supported the constitution in Tehran, few felt the same way in Tabriz. In the early days of the Constitutional Revolution in 1906, Tabriz *anjuman*s forced several leading anti-Constitutionalist Tabriz clerics out of the city. In response, the Russians helped construct an anti-Constitutionalist Islamic *anjuman* to replace those turned out of Tabriz.

"My father thinks that mullahs will always be enemies of freedom and democracy," Behrooz said. "I agree with him. Even Mr. Khatami is just another mullah."

I knew Behrooz's comment would result in a clenched-teeth debate with Yadollah. It did. Yadollah looked pained. He said: "Yes, there are clerics who are opposed to freedom and democracy. But we must not forget that there are others who think differently. Let us also not forget that there are many clerics in jail because of their prodemocracy beliefs." I nodded. He was right.

After spending a few days with these young men, I had become familiar with the routine. Behrooz would dismiss clerics as "all corrupt" or Islam as "antifreedom," and Yadollah would seek to moderate his statements. "Not all clerics are bad," Yadollah would say, or "The religion must be interpreted properly."

For young men like Yadollah, who grew up in traditionally religious homes, Iran's Islamic Republic created a predicament. At home they learned the basic virtues of honesty and piety that constitute the Muslim faith. They learned to pray and revere the twelve imams of the Shi'a faith. They went on pilgrimages to Shi'a shrines, where they gave alms to the poor and prayed for the health of their families. Yet many of Yadollah's university friends and peers largely distrusted the very people who guarded their faith, the clerics. For Yadollah, these two poles tugged at him. It resulted in an almost perpetually defensive stance. "Real Islam is different from the conservative interpretation," Yadollah said regularly. "Not all clerics are bad," he would retort. "Khatami is a cleric, and he believes in democracy."

Normally, neither boy seemed to take offense in these frequent duels over religion, though they came up with regularity when we discussed the issues of the day. This time, however, I noticed sharp glares on both sides. An icy silence ensued as we walked amid the glass display cases. I decided to leave them alone. I told them I needed some fresh air. In front of me, I felt, their young men's pride would prevent them from saying the things that needed to be said to mend fences. I left, having agreed to meet them half an hour later.

An American Constitutionalist in Tabriz

Later we met up again in the courtyard of the house. They had returned to good spirits. Apparently they had made peace. We sat down together on one of the steps of the house.

Yadollah spoke: "My grandfather often told me stories about the Constitutional Revolution. I think he was only a baby during the Tabriz resistance, but he often described in great detail how he fought for the constitution against the Russians. He also hated the British." Yadollah laughed. So did Behrooz and I. We all knew the type: the elderly Iranian man, nationalistic, proconstitution, anti-British, and prone to great feats of exaggeration.

"Do the Americans know much about the Constitutional Revolution?" Behrooz asked.

"Not really," I said.

They looked disappointed. I assured them, however, that American scholars have done some very good work on the subject.

"Has Kasravi's book been translated into English?" Behrooz asked.

Ahmad Kasravi, the sharp critic of Iran's clerical class and a favorite son of Tabriz, wrote what still stands in Iran as the most popular history of the movement, despite attempts in the early years of the Islamic Republic to discredit him. Kasravi's history heaped praise on the Tabriz revolutionaries and the secular Constitutionalists who believed in social democratic ideas, the sorts of ideas emanating from Transcaucasia in the north. He dealt harshly with the clerical Constitutionalists, who he believed were self-interested at best and antidemocratic and reactionary at worst. Needless to say, the Islamic Republic does not care much for Kasravi's books, preferring other histories that advocate the important role Iran's clerics played in the movement.

"The book has not been fully translated," I told them, "but it is quoted often in English histories." I told them of E. G. Browne, the great British Persianist who had written a riveting history of the Constitutional Revolution.

Both of them nodded; they had heard of Browne.

I asked them if they had heard of Howard Baskerville, the American missionary who had fought, and died, with the Tabriz revolutionaries.

Vaguely, they said. "Is he a popular figure in America?" Yadollah asked.

Hardly.

Yadollah asked me to tell them the story. I gave them a brief summary of the events. Baskerville, a graduate of Princeton University, was an idealist, the kind of young man who wanted to have an impact on the world, help people, see lands far away. At the age of twenty-three he decided to go to Iran to work as an English teacher in one of the many American religious missions in the country at the time. He taught English and mathematics at the American

Presbyterian school in Tabriz during the days of the Constitutional Revolution. He was so moved by the Tabriz resistance and the Constitutional Revolution that he joined the revolutionaries. Therefore, he had to sacrifice his teaching position. He believed fervently in the right of Iranians to have a constitution and an elected parliament. His friend the British journalist M. A. Moore joined him, and both became active advocates for the constitutional cause. They proved to be skilled leaders and were given a contingent of soldiers to lead in battle against Russian and royalist forces. In one of the last stands before Tabriz fell to Russian soldiers, Baskerville was killed.

Behrooz and Yadollah seemed impressed, asking several follow-up questions: How did he die? Did the American newspapers write about it? Did he have family?

In my rucksack I carried with me the April 22, 1909, article in the London *Times* by M. A. Moore that described Baskerville's death. I read aloud from the newspaper article in English, translating (I fear badly) as I went along:

I must now chronicle the gallant death of Mr. Baskerville, an American, lately master of the mission school. Some retrospect is necessary. On March 31st, by curious coincidence, he left the fence of neutrality and decided to throw in his lot with the starving town, thereby sacrificing his appointment in the American school. . . . Baskerville was given charge of 150 men and myself 350. . . . We reached the rendezvous at eleven and had to wait for the men. We only began to move at 4:30 AM. Baskerville led 150 men to the right. By the time he arrived within range of the enemy, the number had dwindled to 9. With these he gallantly began the attack at 5:30, but was shot by a bullet through the heart when leading on. He died almost immediately.

I also showed them a copy of a letter written by the wife of the headmaster of the missionary school to Baskerville's parents. I had found the letter on the Internet, on a site called Iranian.com, a popular site for Iranian expatriates and, increasingly, for Iranians living in the country. In the letter, the woman described her conversation with Baskerville before his death. She told him that his actions would have consequences, that he no longer belonged only to himself. To that, Baskerville replied: "I know. I am Persia's now."

Behrooz shook his head. "It is a shame that more Americans do not know of him," he said.

"It is a shame that more Iranians do not know of him!" Yadollah laughed.

Baskerville lies buried in a simple tomb in a Tabriz cemetery. It is largely ignored, except for a mysterious admirer who regularly places yellow roses on the large marble stone that says simply: "Howard Baskerville: Born April 10, 1885. Died April 19, 1909."

I told them of a semihistorical fiction rendering of Baskerville in Amin Malouf's book *Samarkand*. I carried Malouf's book with me everywhere in Tabriz. It provided a dramatic rendering, albeit fictional, of the Tabriz resistance, and it came in handy as I recounted the story of Baskerville. I pulled out the book and flipped through the pages looking for the Baskerville portions. I told Behrooz and Yadollah that Malouf, a French-Lebanese writer, had won numerous awards for this novel. They looked impressed.

"This novel was set in Tabriz?" Behrooz asked.

Part of it, I said.

"I must read this novel," Behrooz said.

I pulled out my worn copy of the novel. I turned to a page on which Baskerville describes his reaction to a mourning ceremony for Imam Hossein. Baskerville speaks to an American visitor in Tabriz. It creates an evocative image of an American missionary who cares deeply about the people he has come to serve. I made a rough translation as I read Baskerville's words:

I [Baskerville] had mingled with the crowd and groans were being emitted all around me. Watching those devastated faces, bathed in tears, and gazing at those haggard, worried, entreating eyes, the whole misery of Persia appeared to me— they were tattered souls besieged by never-ending mourning. Without realizing it, my tears started to flow. Someone in the crowd noticed, they looked at me and were moved. . . .

When they saw me crying, when they saw that I had thrown off the sovereign indifference of a foreigner, they came to tell me confidentially that crying serves no purpose and that Persia does not need any extra mourners and that the best I could do would be to provide the children of Tabriz with an adequate education. . . . [However,] if I had not cried, they would never have come to talk to me. If they had not seen me crying, they would never have let me tell the pupils that this Shah was rotten and that the religious chiefs of Tabriz were hardly any better.

I closed the book. I feared that I had stumbled with a few words in the translation. I certainly did not offer the same poetry of language. Still, I could see that the young men were interested and perhaps even moved.

"Go on," Behrooz said, "read some more."

I turned to a section where the American narrator laments Baskerville's death. The passage had moved me, and I hoped it would do the same for my audience. Yadollah looked over my shoulder as I again translated. The narrator writes: "Of all those who died during the months of hardship, why have I singled out Baskerville? Because he was my friend and compatriot? Most probably. But also because his only ambition was to see liberty and democracy triumph in the rebirth of the Orient, which for all that was foreign to him. Had he given his life for nothing? In ten, twenty or a hundred years would the West remember his example, or would Persia remember his action? I chose not to think about it lest I fall into the inescapable melancholy of those who love between two worlds which are equally promising and disappointing."

I feared that my translations were inadequate. I wanted Behrooz and Yadollah to feel the emotion in the lines.

"Thank Allah," Yadollah said, "that Mr. Baskerville was really a great man." Behrooz, nodding, added: "I wish all Americans were like that." We stood up to head our separate ways, bidding one another good-bye with embraces and promises to stay in touch.

"The Strangling of Persia": A Constitutional Ending

For many Tabrizis, the Russian troops that stormed the country after Baskerville's death may actually have been a relief. In the final months of the royalist siege, the Russians had shut off all food supplies headed for Tabriz from south and north. Some residents had to eat grass. The tsar's men, at least, brought with them order and a chunk of bread and a bowl of soup, far more important for the average Tabrizi than a constitution.

Tabriz Constitutionalists, for their part, fled from their besieged city and headed toward Tehran, where Constitutionalists had fallen nine months earlier. They joined up with proconstitution Bakhtiari tribesmen from Iran's south. The sudden rush of Constitutionalists from the north and south revitalized Tehran's *anjumans*, which increased their proconstitution activity. Meanwhile, in Najaf, Iraq, home to Shi'a Islam's grand authorities, three of the most revered scholars offered religious sanction to the constitution. Just three months after Tabriz's fall, momentum again shifted toward the Constitutionalists in Tehran. Within a month they took control of key sectors of Tehran. The frightened Shah, Mohammad Ali, took refuge in the Russian Embassy. It was a de facto abdication. The Constitutionalists deposed the Shah in favor of his twelve-year-old son, an unctuous and frightened boy who wanted nothing of the job.

At this time, Sheikh Fazlollah Nouri, the anti-Constitutionalist cleric instrumental in the early bombardment of the Parliament, underwent trial as a traitor. Found guilty, he swung from the gallows at the hands of a Constitutionalist hangman on July 31, 1909, an event commemorated on the Tehran billboard.

Alas, even after Nouri's execution and the reimposition of the Parliament, Iran still had a long way to go before representative government could reach a level of maturity that would resemble a democratic society. The landed gentry packed the new parliament. Literacy rates were below 10 percent. Several formerly pro-Constitutionalist clerics turned on the Parliament. Bakhtiari tribesmen from Iran's south who supported the Constitutionalist resistance for personal reasons had little use for Constitutionalist principles after the victory. The average illiterate Iranian did not understand the constitution. He may have supported it because he thought it would put more bread on the table. Instead it brought civil war, chaos, and shortages.

Britain and Russia cooked up ways to end the Iranian constitutional experiment. Britain had come to realize that one king came to heel more easily than eighty parliamentarians with their own opinions and agendas. Into this uncertain environment another American entered the Iranian political scene and left his mark on the Constitutional Revolution: W. Morgan Shuster, a New York banker whom the Iranian Parliament retained to reorder Iran's finances. He proved to be, like the young Baskerville, an idealist who believed in the cause of Iranian independence and self-representative government. He had read Browne's dramatic and sympathetic account of the Constitutional Revolution and arrived in Tehran in May 1911 suffused with romantic visions of Iran's yearnings for freedom.

Shuster's politics did not recommend him kindly to the British and Russian legations. Early on he rankled the British and Russians with his refusal to play by their rules. In an act of great symbolic importance to Iran's Parliament, he shunned the two embassies, refusing to pay a courtesy call on either ambassador. As days and weeks and months passed with no courtesy calls, talk in Iranian political circles excitedly swirled around the American banker who feared not the British and Russian legations.

As Shuster wrote in his moving memoir, *The Strangling of Persia,* "The Iranian people were surprised to see a farangi (foreigner) who does not take orders from foreign legations." He came to the same conclusions that Baskerville had before him: Iran's kings and reactionary clerics bristled at any major reforms of the political system. As long as imperial Britain and Russia sided with the "reactionary agents hostile to any improvement," Iran would remain mired in its backward state.

Shuster, for his part, had a job to do, and he was determined to do it with efficiency. Charged with collecting taxes from Iran's wealthy elite, he soon realized that the elite viewed state taxes as a burden to be shouldered only by peasants and workingmen. He also learned that Iranian politicians, including leading Constitutionalists, not only refused to pay taxes but had an unfortunate tendency to dip their hands into public funds, a disease that continues unabated today. "Unfortunately for Persia," Shuster wrote, "the patriotism which impelled numbers of her brave nationalists to fight to depose the ex-Shah . . . did not suffice to prevent the looting of the public treasury."

Shuster pursued the tax evaders with the efficiency of a drillmaster. The democrats in Parliament supported him fully, though the clerics and wealthy landowners grew wary of Shuster's zeal. He organized a tax gendarmerie to add muscle to his demands. Inevitably, he faced confrontation with the Russians when he sought to confiscate the property of a Russian-backed Iranian Qajar prince who refused to pay his taxes and who supported Russian policies, including the elimination of the constitution.

Moscow, in retaliation for Shuster's affront to its princely ally, demanded that Iran's parliament dismiss Shuster. Britain refused to defend the American, emboldening Russia further. A crisis ensued. Russian soldiers poured into Iran's northern region and massacred Tabrizi Constitutionalists. Among those killed was Mohammad Ibrahim Qafqazchi, a Tabriz merchant who fought under the command of Howard Baskerville. Russia offered the Parliament an ultimatum: Dismiss Shuster and guarantee that no foreign adviser would be hired in the future without the consent of the British and Russian legations, or Iran would be occupied by force. To add insult to this injurious ultimatum, Russia demanded that Iran's government pay Russia 150,000 rubles in return for the cost of its invasion of Iran.

Iran's cowed cabinet accepted the Russian ultimatum and urged the Parliament to do the same. It refused. The Russians bombarded the Parliament again, and Shuster was forced out of the country. The constitutional movement never reovered from this blow.

The Parliament of the Islamic Republic of Iran

Upon my return to Tehran, I visited the Parliament of the Islamic Republic of Iran with a veteran reporter, Mehrdad Serjooie. He had told me to meet him in the public waiting room. There I sat among sun-baked laborers, chador-clad elderly women, and young, bearded youths. Most in the crowd were petitioners, who lined up to ask their local representatives for help in finding jobs, low-cost housing, better health insurance plans, or a myriad of other small and big favors. I had seen this all over the Middle East, huddled masses anxiously lining up to see important men for that important signature that would solve so many problems. I took a seat on the floor next to a middle-aged man with gnarled brown hands and gray hair on his knuckles. He repeatedly rubbed his hands together and wrung them nervously like an expectant father in the waiting room. He asked me the time on three separate occasions.

Mehrdad arrived at our appointed hour and strode through the crowd. He directed me to a glass window where I was announced as his guest. A phone call was made, and I ended up with a pass to enter the hall. A woman in a black chador, with one eye showing and a bit of the cloth in her teeth, approached me as I walked toward the entrance. She handed me an envelope. "My son, please give this letter to Mr. Shirazi. Please, my son." As she pleaded, a small crowd pushed toward me. They wanted the same opportunity as the woman. "Please give this letter to so-and-so," another woman screamed, handing me a note. A crescendo of letters came raining down on me as Mehrdad hurried me through the door. I heard the old woman's voice again outside the door: "Please, my son! Please!"

I asked Mehrdad if he knew a Mr. Shirazi. He took the letter, saying he would do his best to find the man. I imagined he would. He was like that. Once inside, we walked through security. I was told that my camera and tape recorder and bag all would have to remain behind. I was allowed only a pen and a pad. We strolled into the Parliament grounds, concrete walkways shaded by tall brown trees and grass, the high walls shading us from the din on the outside. Mehrdad walked through the halls of Parliament, introducing me around. "Meet my friend Mr. Molavi," he told Parliament members. "He writes for the *Washington Post*." He told me that he had pulled some strings to get me in. "After all, today is a closed session; the budget will be discussed."

A Parliament member with an orange-brown beard approached Mehrdad. He took him aside and whispered something in his ear. I assumed that he related an important leak to Mehrdad, who consistently scooped the competition. The deputy walked away, and Mehrdad laughed.

"You know what he just asked me?" Mehrdad said. "He wanted to know if I could get him a copy of the movie *Titanic!* He said his kids are constantly bothering him about it!"

Mehrdad knew the Parliament beat well, and he obviously relished his job, backslapping MPs just before thrusting his tape recorder in their faces for spot interviews. His dogged and tireless pursuit of the news took no shortcuts. I often looked to him for analysis also because he adhered less overtly to an ideological stream of thought than other reporters. As I questioned him about the current ideological leanings of the Parliament, he cut me off: "Afshin, look! It's Nourbaksh, the Central Bank governor! Let's grab him!"

Reluctantly, I ran behind Mehrdad, who ran after Mohsen Nourbaksh. I was less interested in the day-to-day budget minutiae and more interested in getting a feel for the Parliament. Breathless, we reached the Central Bank governor. "Mr. Nourbaksh," Mehrdad said, "My friend Mr. Molavi from the *Washington Post* would like to ask you a question."

Before I could stammer out my question, Mr. Nourbaksh had one of his own: "What is the *Washington Post* doing here in a closed-door session?" Mehrdad smiled. He knew he had pulled off an impressive feat to get me into Parliament on this day and the Central Bank governor had just affirmed it.

Throughout the day I pumped Mehrdad for information, and he rushed around, introducing me to Parliament members. One MP, a conservative who ran for the presidency in 2001, Hassan Ghaffuri Fard, complained to me that his application to attend a national electrical engineers' conference in the United States was denied because of visa problems. "I am an engineer by profession," he said. "I simply want to attend a conference. They should not deny me a visa." Another MP approached Mehrdad, complaining: "All you reporters do is chase scandal and conflict. What about the good things we do for our districts? Why don't you write about them?" The 2000 parliamentary elections were just around the corner. A female MP, wearing the chador, approached Mehrdad and reminded him of their scheduled interview. Late in the day, in a quiet moment in the courtyard, as the sun grayed, I watched Mehrdad interview a reformist member of Parliament.

"We want more freedom of the press," the reformist said, "we want to give more rights to the people. These democratic ideas are the wave of the future, and we must not be left behind. We shall fight. We shall do our part in Parliament, but there are many obstacles." As I listened to the deputy, I harkened back to Iran's Constitutional Revolution and the Pahlavi era that followed it. The Constitutionalist defeat stymied the democratic hopes of some of that era's leading intellectuals. Still, the prodemocracy aspect of the movement (as opposed to the antiking or anti-foreign power aspect) was an elite one led by intellectuals and liberal clerics. It was not until much later, starting in the 1950s, that the ideas of democracy spread among middle-class Iranians. Even then, their democratic wishes were often confused with an anti-king and anti–foreign power sentiment (the kings being the Pahlavi Shahs and the foreign powers being the British and Americans).

The defeat of the Constitutionalists in 1911 led to a chaotic period until the virtual takeover of the country in 1921 by Reza Khan, who crowned himself king in 1925. The era of the Pahlavi kings (1921–79) dealt heavy blows to the democratic hopes of Iranians, though it contributed immensely to the modernization of the Iranian state, economic development, and the growth of the middle class—all prerequisites for an effective democracy. The relatively successful economic modernization of the country created an educated modern middle class more receptive to the ideas of representative government. No longer were democratic ideas the bastion of the elite.

Modern middle-class support for the 1979 revolution proved to be critical to its subsequent success. The hope-inspiring revolution, the sort of uprising that Baskerville and Shuster would probably have supported, gave way to more disillusionment as a group of antidemocratic Islamic clerics took over the state.

Secular Iranian writers of the early 1980s, most of whom supported the revolution, lamented the course it eventually took. Ahmad Shamlu, a leftist poet and major figure in Iranian letters who passed away in the year 2000, wrote in the early years following the revolution that the king's elite were simply replaced by a clerical elite, thus inflicting a blow on working people. In the early twentieth century, the liberal Constitutionalists used Iran's clergy to help them achieve their goals, but were quick to dismiss them once the Parliament was achieved. In much the same way, secular, democratic, leftist, and Marxist revolutionaries joined with Iran's clergy to fight the 1979 revolution against the Shah. Only this time, the clergy managed to push everyone else aside and consolidate and hold on to power.[5]

I had been traveling across Iran almost constantly for two months, searching Iranian history and talking to Iranians. So much of the talk and what I saw centered on "the revolution," known simply as *enghelab* in Persian. It was time for me to visit the shrine of Ayatollah Khomeini, the most forceful figure of Iran's 1979 revolution.

[5] Interestingly, women played a key role in both the Constitutional Revolution and the 1979 Iranian revolution. And in both cases, their needs were pushed aside in the afterglow of victory.

VII

Cities: Tehran, Rey

My Tehran

I lived in a modest two-bedroom apartment in north-central Tehran when
I was not traveling. The apartment was old and worn, with tea-stained
Persian carpets and yellowing walls, but there was plenty of space and a
balcony overlooking a pleasant garden. From the roof I had a splendid view
of the brown, snow-capped Alborz Mountains. The highest peak of the range,
Mount Demavand, rose more than eighteen thousand feet into the blue sky,
a puff of white snow eternally covering its top. Mountain views, in a sense,
dictate Tehran's real estate values. The better the view you have, the higher
the price you pay for the property. Farther north from where I lived, in some
of Tehran's affluent suburbs, on clear days, the Alborz look like a painting
framed by blue air. As you move into South Tehran, where the poverty of residents increases with the lower altitude, there is little or no view of the mountains, obscured anyway by a haze of smoke.

In between travels, I always returned to Tehran, to my apartment on a quiet,
leafy street, just a five-minute walk from the noise and color of a popular shopping district. After the tragic destruction of the World Trade Center in September 2001, the shopping area near my apartment, Maidan-e-Mohseni, as it
is called, became the scene of candlelit vigils for the victims of the terrorist
assault. Those vigils were violently broken up by Ansar-e-Hezbollah hard-liners.

My grandfather used to live in the same neighborhood, before he passed away ten years ago. I bought my fruit at a nearby market from Mr. Pouron, a wiry man with dark eyes and a wide smile, who knew my grandfather well. "Your grandfather was a great man," Mr. Pouron always said. "Let me show you what kinds of oranges your grandfather liked." Sometimes Mr. Pouron scolded me like a schoolboy, "Your grandfather would have chosen better apples than that," as he emptied my sack of carefully chosen apples and replaced them with his own batch.

Near Mr. Pouron's fruit stand was a corner market run by a family of Iranian Azeris from Tabriz, my birthplace in the northwestern Iranian province of Azerbaijan. At this particular market, my birthplace and background conferred upon me a special status as a novelty item, an Iranian from America who could say a few words in Azeri and tell stories about supermarkets in the West. As a result, the market delivery boy, Abbas, was always put at my disposal during my shopping—whether I wanted him or not. The routine went like this: I saw a perfectly reachable cheese. I then pointed out the cheese to Abbas. He reached over and put the cheese in my sack. I said *chokh mamnoon*, "thank you" in Azeri, and the delivery boy laughed at the Iranian from America speaking Azeri, with the process repeated all over again for milk, eggs, and other groceries.

Down the street from the Azeri market, a small hamburger shop, Burger Zoghali, serves up flame-broiled burgers. On Thursday evenings (the Iranian equivalent of Saturday night), young Tehranis gather at Zoghali to see and be seen: boys and girls sipping sodas, munching on burgers and fries, and, perhaps, furtively exchanging phone numbers under the tables.

A short walk from Burger Zoghali, past the sweets shop selling cream-filled and chocolate pastries, the crowded bookstores, a flower shop, clothes stores, and a taxi agency, I approached Shariati Street, a broad avenue of shops and newsstands and restaurants amid a raging sea of cars, taxes, and buses, darting and slashing like professional race car drivers up and down the street. For the uninitiated, driving in Tehran is a harrowing experience. It is the ultimate example of survival of the fittest, a test of will and skill in conditions more chaotic than Rome or Cairo. Iranian drivers think nothing of reversing on highways, driving the wrong way on one-way streets, cutting off nearby drivers, and generally breaking every driving rule imaginable.

For the pedestrian to survive, a similar attitude is needed. Shariati Street, named after the 1970s revolutionary intellectual who inspired Davoud and so many of his generation, tested my crossing skills daily. Through repeated practice, I've became adept at darting across the street in and out of traffic, as if I were a figure in a video game. Once on the other side, I visited the Caravan travel agency, ate bologna sandwiches with orange soda in a nearby café, or checked my e-mail in one of the many Internet cafés along the street.

In a sense, Shariati Street and my leafy neighborhood constituted my own little Tehran. Despite the enormousness of the city (thirteen million people), most residents have their own little Tehrans: collections of neighbors and shopkeepers and bread sellers and newspaper vendors that form the bonds of community. The bonds are tight and sometimes transgress the Western rules of "keeping the appropriate distance" that I was accustomed to. For example, my flower seller routinely asked me detailed questions about my salary; a neighborhood taxi driver expressed concern about my sex life, wondering if I needed any "female services"; the local laundry guy took me aside once, after handing me my clothes, telling me to stay away from "that taxi driver," who was "no good"; a local shopkeeper told me to stay away from the laundry guy, who charged too much; fighting back tears, a local key cutter described to me his marital woes in great detail and also told me to stay away from that "pimp" taxi driver; a local street sweeper stopped me to tell me that I carried my bag too nonchalantly, an invitation to theft; and finally, the newspaper vendor calmly informed me that I was getting fat and should cut down on the sweets he saw me regularly buying.

Though it was unsettling at first, I grew to accept, and even like the frequent advice, questions, and comments from members of "my Tehran." I learned how to be appropriately evasive on uncomfortable questions and to smile and offer thanks when useful advice was dispensed. Somehow it soothed me to know that people were watching, even if it was my weight. It also told me that I am no longer the "Iranian visitor from America" but a full member of the community, who therefore should know the proper way to carry his bag and that the laundry guy charged too much.

Beyond the familiar confines of "my Tehran," the city is a massive, sprawling urban area roughly the size of New York, with a New York–style diversity and energy. Tehran is loud, brash, and aggressive; it is also charming, gracious, and sophisticated. It is fantastically wealthy and astonishingly poor. Everywhere one goes, there are people, people walking and talking and arguing and laughing and shopping and eating and reading and picnicking and, of course, telling their compatriots how to eat or sit or carry their bags properly. Then there are cars, honking and belching and swerving and speeding and darting.

Tehran is a diverse and colorful city. There are Armenian districts, Indian ghettoes, Jewish neighborhoods. There are parks for picnicking families, for artists, and even for drug addicts to congregate in. There are nearby mountain retreats, fine museums, and wonderful spots for evening walks. There is a vibrant arts scene, decent Internet connections, excellent restaurants, and fine cinemas. There is also a vigorous underworld, of prostitutes and opium addicts and alcohol bootleggers, a scene that one of the local taxi drivers knows all too well.

Tehran's sprawl is connected by wide highways that loop around the major urban centers in a complex set of overpasses and exits. The city's explosive population growth beginning in the early 1970s brought with it big-city problems: choking traffic, crowded slums, air pollution, crime. It has also spawned a diverse and talented population, a large force of skilled and unskilled labor, and a vigorous entrepeneurial spirit. Its enormous economic potential, however, has been considerably stifled by the country's poor economic management. Still, business is good in Tehran for the merchant with a storefront and goods to sell. Nontrading jobs, however, are scarce, and public squares are packed with unemployed, bored, and frustrated young men.

The city is not conventionally pretty. Its architecture is a monotony of flat, boxlike buildings interspersed with the occasional crumbling but elegant fin-de-siècle French structure and spots of glitzy high-rises. Still, in the middle of the urban sprawl, there are splendid, well-lit parks, well peopled with picnicking families and crowds of boys and girls flirting from across park benches, looking over their shoulders for the roving bands of morals police that seek to prevent such "vice." Though there are few of the great historical monuments found in other Middle Eastern capitals, there are old houses of astonishing beauty in the unlikeliest run-down neighborhoods. While cities like Baghdad or Damascus have served as capital cities and major urban centers for thousands of years, Tehran is a relatively new capital, barely two hundred years old as the seat of government, so not many of the buildings evoke history as they do in older Iranian cities like Isfahan, Shiraz, and Tabriz.

Tehran served as a base throughout my travels. Here I returned to catch up on the latest political news, the ups and downs of the reformist movement, the latest popular films. Here I was embraced warmly by a large extended family, of aunts and cousins and uncles whose hospitality, and delicious Persian cooking, refueled my energies for the next trip, the next pilgrimage. Here I visited with an eclectic group of friends and sources: a war veteran, a Western-educated political analyst, a gray-bearded conservative cleric, a historian, a street sweeper, a karaoke group ("Hotel California" was the favorite Western song at the gatherings), a hard-line student leader, and an array of bazaar merchants, government officials, students, and middle-class professionals.

Here I also booked my plane tickets, usually at the Caravan travel agency on Shariati Street, with its banks of smiling young women in blue head scarves, wearing foreign airline pins on the loose-fitting manteaus that covered their body. Sitting down at the domestic flights desk, facing a young woman with green eyes and wisps of brown hair fighting against her head scarf, I would tell her my destination. As she punched the computer keys, she would ask me of my recent travels.

"Mr. Molavi," she once said, "forgive me for being intrusive, but I think you should be careful how you hold your bag. There are many thieves, and you carry it too nonchalantly."

I smiled, thanked her, and put the bag strap over my opposite shoulder, snug against my neck and chest. "Much better," she said.

"The International Congress on the Elucidation of the Islamic Revolution and the Thoughts of Imam Khomeini"

The fax buzzed into my temporary Tehran office: "The Foreign Press Section of the Ministry of Culture and Islamic Guidance cordially invites you to attend 'The International Congress on the Elucidation of the Islamic Revolution and the Thoughts of Imam Khomeini.' When I arrived at the Tehran International Conference Center to attend the conference the following week, a burly, bearded guard with a walkie-talkie turned me away. "Impossible," he said. "You are carrying the wrong pass. You should have picked up the proper pass."

After a round of gentle pleading, he stood firm. "Impossible," he repeated. "You should have gone to the ministry and picked up the appropriate pass." He looked away, speaking into his walkie-talkie but positioning himself in front of the door, lest I make a daring dash into the conference hall.

His abrupt manner surprised me. Usually, gatekeepers are not so gruff and direct. They understand an unwritten Iranian rule: everything is negotiable. Iran, like many Middle Eastern societies, is formed around a culture in which human relations, connections, and networks often trump laws and rules. These connections, known in Persian as *ashna* and in Arabic as *wasta*, form an important part of daily life. Even without an *ashna*, a certain amount of negotiation is common. This gatekeeper, however, seemed rigid, almost legalistic, like the sort of gatekeeper found in the United States or other legalistic societies. In the West, the use of connections to accomplish goals is less overt and rarely flaunted. In contrast, Iranians often brag about their connections in high-level places and their use to achieve a certain end. President Khatami, in his efforts to avocate adherence to the rule of law, it seemed to me, was fighting against a deeply rooted cultural phenomenon. After all, by their very nature, laws are nonnegotiable. A society like Iran, one rooted in human relations and networks, would have a difficult time transitioning.

I walked away, and strolled the grounds of the conference center, with its green trees and large grassy areas, hoping to spot another entrance and a more sympathetic guard. The center, built to accommodate Muslim heads of state for an important meeting in 1997, sat picturesquely against a backdrop of the Alborz Mountains. The clean, cool air pecked at my ears. A large billboard in the distance carried a massive drawing of Ayatollah Khomeini's face and his long, flowing gray beard transposed on a blue-black twinkling night sky. Below the billboard, a sign read: WELCOME TO THE RESPECTFUL AND MERIT GUESTS OF THE INTERNATIONAL CONFERENCE ON THE ELUCIDATION OF THE ISLAMIC REVOLUTION.

I spotted no "alternative" entrances, so neither a "respectful" nor a "merit" guest, I walked back to the main guard. He was standing next to a round-bellied cleric with a tan cloak and white turban, also speaking into a walkie-talkie.

"That's the one," the guard said, pointing to me. "That's the one who doesn't have the right press card."

The cleric, who looked to be in his early forties and had a deep black beard, addressed me. "Let me see your press card," he said.

I handed it to him. It read: "Afshin Molavi, correspondent, Washington Post, America."

He examined the photo, looked at me, then looked at the photo again.

"I have come from America for this conference," I stammered, making an attempt at negotiation. "I apologize for bringing the wrong pass, but there are important issues to be discussed in this conference and I would like to report them to the world."

The cleric smiled thinly. "I must ask you a question," he said, as he stared at my press pass.

"Certainly," I said, assuming that he was about to ask me why the Western media hate Iran, a familiar question I heard from gatekeepers all over the country when they read my press affiliation.

Instead he asked: "Do you know Bob Woodward?"

"No," I said, somewhat surprised. "I have never met him."

He seemed disappointed, so I explained that I worked for the foreign desk of the *Post* as a freelancer and was therefore unlikely to meet a senior national journalist like Woodward. Still, I engaged him on Woodward, hoping it might help my cause. Had he read Woodward's books?

"No," he said, "but I saw the movie *All the President's Men*. It was a good film, much better than the filth being produced in America today."

I nodded in agreement, probably a good tactic.

Next, he said: "Why do the American media hate Iran?"

"I don't think the American media hate Iran. If you read the newspaper coverage over the last few years in most major media outlets, it has been balanced, one might even argue favorable toward Iran. Major papers like the *New York Times* and the *Los Angeles Times* have in-house Iran experts whose coverage is balanced."

"Do your editors print what you write?" he asked. "Do they twist your words?"

"No," I said. "They may change a word or two to make me look like a better writer, but they don't touch the content."

He gave me his card. "Will you send me some of your articles?"

"Certainly."

"Go in," he said. "Enjoy the conference."

The entrance hall bore the characteristic marble of conference centers in the Middle East. Groups of Iranians in beards, rumpled suits, and Nehru-collar shirts (no tie), the official nonclerical uniform of the government, shuffled around a collection of book publishers that exhibited their titles on tables.

Mostly the books concerned the life and thoughts of Ayatollah Khomeini: histories, biographies, poems of praise, political speeches, children's books, picture books, pamphlets in broken English and French, and collections of the ayatollah's writings.

I picked up a paperback biography of Khomeini and leafed through the pages. The book opens with the following sentence: "His Eminence Ayatollah Ruhollah Khomeini, the Radiant Light of Iran (May God Rest His Soul), was born in the town of Khomein. . . ." It goes on to describe a young Ruhollah, admired by his elders for his "nobility of temperament." Later in the book, a contemporary of Khomeini is quoted: "The Imam was different from the rest of the children. He was always peaceful and never took part in any of the children's fights."

A loudspeaker called the conference delegates to assemble inside the hall. I found an elevated spot with a fine view of the stage and the dignitary seats on the floor. The towering ceiling of the conference hall was a dome of silver grillwork, lending the onion-shaped conference hall a spaceship feel. At the base of the stage the ubiquitous and awkward sign greeted attendees in English: WELCOME TO THE MERIT AND RESPECTFUL GUESTS OF THE CONFERENCE ON THE ELUCIDATION OF THE ISLAMIC REVOLUTION. A large bouquet of pink and white flowers hunkered at the base of the sign.

On massive screen televisions at both ends of the hall, images of Khomeini flashed across the screen: Khomeini waving to a frenzied revolutionary crowd, Khomeini inside a car on his triumphant return to Iran, Khomeini cradling a baby, Khomeini praying, Khomeini waving, Khomeini sitting, Khomeini staring.

A group of African dignitaries in white skullcaps and colorful robes proceeded to the front row with an escort. Just behind them, a smiling African military man in a striking green uniform with a green silk shirt and black tie waltzed down the stairs as a television crew from Tanzania stumbled in front of him. Africans regularly frequent these sorts of Khomeini conferences, flown in at the expense of Iran's government to display their revolutionary sense of Third World solidarity with Africa. Across the hall, a group of Malaysian women with tightly wrapped white head scarves walked into the hall, trailed by an Indian woman in a yellow sari and yellow head scarf. In the top corner of the hall, just above the section reserved for wives of ambassadors from Muslim nations, a sea of two hundred black-clad Iranian women took their seats. Just behind me, a collection of foreign journalists from Africa, South and Southeast Asia, and the Arab world—hosted with all expenses paid by Iran's government—shuffled into their seats, waiting for the conference to begin.

As I looked around the hall at this collection of the Third World's not so finest, I heard a murmur of applause when Iranian officials entered the hall. When President Khatami entered, the applause increased, and all conference delegates stood up. The ever-smiling president waved to the crowd and took his seat next to Iran's Vice President Hassan Habibi and Ayatollah Khomeini's grandson Hassan Agha Khomeini. To his right, the leader of Lebanon's Hezbollah, Sheikh Hassan Nasrallah, fingered prayer beads.

A prominent television news anchor opened the conference with a poem in praise of Khomeini. Vice President Habibi followed by extolling the virtues of Khomeini's thought. Next up, President Khatami, in his typical manner, promoted his views on the need for democratic reform, cleverly co-opting Khomeini for his own purposes.

"Some people are misusing the Khomeini legacy," Khatami told the crowd. "The imam came to power because of the will of the people, and he governed through the will of the people. The imam was also a philosopher and a man of depth who understood that certain times require certain political systems."

The obvious implication to everyone in the hall: Khatami, as a popularly elected figure, held the will of the people much as Khomeini did as a revolutionary figure. If Khomeini still lived, Khatami seemed to be saying, he would promote democratic reform. Such skillful and delicate political arguments defined Khatami's speeches, though it reminded me once again of the difficulties inherent in promoting democracy in the long shadow of a theocracy no one could wash his hands of.

I found Khatami to be an alternately inspiring, shrewd, and exasperating political figure. He clearly believed in the principles of democracy, a free press, and civil society, yet he had to navigate in a political world crowded with powerful people who opposed those ideas. He was, by nature, a persuader and not given to confrontation. His critics often charged him with softness, too willing to talk through a problem with opponents backed by heavy hands. Yet for those who knew intimately the hard-line and violent tendencies at the core of key institutions of the Iranian government, Khatami's style of slow and consistent reform seemed ideal at the time. However, delicate balancing acts, replete with clever interpretations on the legacy of revolutionary figures, cannot work forever. They may offer a necessary introduction to more radical reform, but eventually a rupture with the past must occur one way or another. With Iran's frustrated and restive population, the day fast approaches when a reformist like Khatami might have to become a revolutionary just in order to survive.

Khatami concluded his remarks with a smile and a reminder of the need for dialogue. He thanked the attending delegates from abroad and officially announced the opening of the conference. As security officials led him out, I gathered my notes and headed for the exits with all the other delegates, to a terrace of tea and sweets. Munching on raisin cookies and honey-glazed biscuits, I met a silver-haired professor of Islamic and Middle East history from New Zealand. The professor's invitation to attend the conference had come from Iran's embassy in New Zealand. It was his first time in Iran, he told me. He taught Khomeini's writings in his political Islam classes, he said, noting that he is more of a specialist on Egyptian Islamic movements. "I am eager to learn more about Khomeini," he said, popping a cookie in his mouth. "Maybe I will be elucidated." He winked.

As we spoke, an Iranian journalist, trailed by a camera crew, approached us.

"Are you this gentleman's translator?" the journalist asked me.

"No," I said, "but if you want to say something to him, I can help you out."

"We want to interview him for television," he said.

I relayed the news to the professor, who blushed slightly at first but seemed pleased with the idea and said: "Let's do it." I passed on the professor's response to the journalist, and he told us to meet him downstairs in the studio in fifteen minutes.

"Us?"

"Yes," he said, "you will translate."

"I am not a skilled translator," I said. "You will need somebody else."

"Hamid is not here," the journalist said. "He is our translator."

Throughout the conference hall I had seen about fifty journalists with Iranian television. That none of them could translate seemed ridiculous, perhaps another sign of Iran's isolation.

As I offered countless reasons not to do it, the journalist pleaded with me. The professor looked confused by our banter. Finally, I succumbed and reluctantly turned to the professor. "We shall meet them downstairs in fifteen minutes. I shall translate for you." He smiled and bit into another cookie. The journalist scurried away. I drank another cup of tea. The conference delegates chatted. Darkness had fallen outside the hall.

We showed up at the makeshift studio, and the journalist turned to me and explained what he wanted to do. He would ask the question in Farsi. I would then translate the question into English. Then I would speak clearly into the microphone and translate the professor's response in Farsi—with the camera rolling on me! I refused immediately. I could do the first two without a problem—understanding the Farsi question and translating it into English—but I would stumble if I had to do the third, translating from English to Farsi as the cameras rolled. The Farsi language has a conversational and formal aspect. News and speeches are conducted in the more formal Farsi, a skill that I woefully lacked. It would be a pitiful display, and I told the journalist I would not subject his viewers to such excruciating pain.

We settled on a compromise: The journalist would ask the question; I would translate the question and take notes from the professor's response. Later we would piece together an off-air translation for him that could be voiced over later. We agreed, and I pulled out a notebook, somewhat annoyed that I had got myself into this mess. Before I knew it, the spotlights turned on, the professor adjusted his tie, and I began working, for free, for conservative state-run Iranian radio and television.

The first question came: "What do the people of New Zealand think of Imam Khomeini?"

I dutifully translated the question. The professor looked confused and uncomfortable. "Well, New Zealand is a small country," he said, "and we are very far away from Iran. Our people do not have much information about Khomeini," he said somewhat diplomatically.

The journalist asked the next question: "What is your interest in Imam Khomeini?"

I translated, and the professor responded: "As a scholar of Islamic political movements myself, I teach Khomeini's writings in my university as part of a course on political Islam. I am hoping to learn more about Khomeini's thought in this conference," he said. "Maybe I will be elucidated." He laughed, referring to the title of the conference. The journalist looked at me quizzically, perhaps wondering why the professor had laughed at Imam Khomeini. The professor looked at me anxiously, perhaps hoping he had not insulted anyone.

The questions improved as we went along, and I wrote down the professor's responses furiously. The interview ended in a few minutes. The post-interview translations didn't bother me as much as I expected. The journalist thanked me profusely.

The professor wondered if he could get the name of the channel on which he would appear. "We have a university newsletter," he explained. "They like to publish notices of media appearances of our university staff."

"Channel One evening news of the Vision of the Islamic Republic," I said.

He smiled, perhaps thinking of the reaction his colleagues might have when they opened their newsletter and saw the notice of his television appearance. He reached into his pocket and pulled out another cookie.

"A Jug of Love"

After the interview I moved back to the book displays in the front of the conference hall. I came across a sensually designed English booklet in gold and blue with birds, flowers, and yellow vines on the cover. The English booklet, titled *A Jug of Love*, contains a collection of Khomeini's mystical poems. They have titles like "Languid Eyes" and "The Retreat of the Drunkards" and generally follow the typical form and content of mystical poems: exaggerated expressions of love for God, descriptions of Divine love as a feeling of drunkenness, and sad laments about the futility of time spent in the mosque, rather than in direct embrace with God. The poems recall, in genre, if not in style and skill, the mystical poems that Iranians so revere—poems of the thirteenth-century Jalaladin Rumi or the twelfth- to thirteenth-century mystical poet Attar. In the book, I came across the following verses:

> *Open the door of the tavern before me night and day,*
> *for I have become weary of the mosque and seminary.*
>
> *I did not find the Friend in the books of the seminary.*
> *At the top of the minaret, I saw no sound of the Beloved.*
> *I did not uncover anything in any scholarly books.*
> *In the lessons of Scripture, I was led nowhere.*
> *I spent my life in the temple, spent my life in vain.*

I am a supplicant for a goblet of wine
from the hand of a sweetheart.
In whom can I confide this secret of mine,
Where can I take this sorrow?

In other poems, Khomeini describes the sorrow of his distance from "the Friend," whom we are to assume is God. He wishes he could be free from "the little house of the horizons," which means his earthly existence, and thereby move closer to God. The conceits he used and the symbolic language would be recognizable to all Persian readers of mystical religious poetry, but the author of the poems, a chest-thumping political leader who led a popular revolution and who once said all opponents should be "annihilated," seemed irreconcilable with the soft Sufi views.

In one sense, Khomeini, in his demands for an unbending adherence to a set of Islamic laws as he defined them, was an heir to Mohammad Bagher Majlesi, the Isfahan cleric who derided all mystics and Sufis. In fact, Khomeini's only public affectation of the mystic way was his ascetic nature as a man who subsisted on fruits and yogurt and rice and showed little interest in material gain.

In fact, the Khomeini poems might never have been intended for public use. He had written them to his daughter-in-law in response to questions she had on *erfan*, Shi'a Islamic mysticism. The poetry book, *A Jug of Love*, emanated from one of hundreds of government-affiliated organs dedicated to preserving a positive image of Khomeini. In offices across Tehran, men sit in plush offices producing works that call Khomeini "the radiant one" or "the exalted one." They also decide on the Khomeini billboards that dot the country. Somewhere in one of these many offices across Tehran, a fellow must have stumbled upon the idea of publishing Khomeini's mystical poems. After all, Iranians are a nation of poets and poetry lovers, his reasoning must have been, and every Iranian knows that the king rules the state but poets rule the hearts. So why not publish the Imam's poems?

Elegant leather-bound volumes of Khomeini's poetry ensued. A small, pretty English-language booklet of translated poems followed. The Imam was not only a great political leader and noble Muslim, these volumes tell us in their introductions, but he was also a mystical and sensitive poet. In much the same way Mao Zedong was celebrated in some posthumous propaganda tracts as a great master of calligraphy (the Chinese revere the calligrapher as the Iranian does the poet), Khomeini was posited as a great mystical poet. Indeed, Iran boasts a long and illustrious history of "ruler-poets." Both Shah Ismail Safavi and Nasiruddin Shah Qajar presented themselves as poets. More recently, however, the Pahlavi kings saw little use in presenting themselves as poets as well as kings.

The bookseller asked me if I wanted to purchase the book.

I did, yes, but first I asked him what he thought of Khomeini's poetry.

He smiled and said: "It was not his poetry that inspired us to take to the streets against the Shah."

The bookseller was right. Khomeini was renowned for his fiery anti-Shah, religious-nationalist speeches, not his Sufi poems. In a 1963 speech in the holy city of Qom, Khomeini shocked his listeners with a firm retaliation against what he viewed as government attempts, backed by Israel, to reduce the influence of Islam and Iran's clergy: "Shah . . . listen to my advice, listen to the ulama of Islam. They desire the welfare of the nation, the welfare of the country. Don't listen to Israel; Israel can't do anything for you. You miserable wretch, forty-five years of your life have passed; isn't it time for you to think and reflect a little, to ponder about where all this is leading you . . . . Israel and America do not care about you. They only care for the dollar. They will not help you if you face trouble."

Later, in a 1964 speech in response to a widely criticized decision by the Shah's government to grant American military personnel and their dependents immunity from prosecution under Iranian law, Khomeini shook the establishment with the following lines, which were sure to stir the hearts of Iranian nationalists: "Our dignity has been trampled underfoot; the dignity of Iran has been destroyed. The dignity of the Iranian army has been trampled underfoot! . . . They have reduced the Iranian people to a level lower than that of an American dog. If someone runs over a dog belonging to an American, he will be prosecuted. Even if the Shah himself were to run over a dog belonging to an American, he would be prosecuted. But if an American cook runs over the Shah, the head of state, no one will have the right to interfere with him . . . . Gentlemen, I warn you of danger! Iranian army, I warn you of danger! Iranian politicians, I warn you of danger! Iranian merchants, I warn you of danger! Ulama of Iran, maraji of Islam, I warn you of danger!" This speech earned Khomeini his long exile. The Shah, who refused advice from SAVAK officials to kill the pesky cleric, ordered him out of the country.

For the next fifteen, years, Khomeini continued speaking out against the Shah. He became increasingly more strident, calling the Shah "the strangling tyrant of history" and demanding his removal from power. In a letter in 1978, he appealed to the Iranian people: "The Shah and his government are in a state of armed rebellion against the justice-seeking people of Iran, against the Constitution, and against the liberating decrees of Islam. They are therefore traitors and to obey them is to obey the *taghut* [the devil]. Do not give them the slightest respite, and inform the whole world of their barbarous deeds with your strikes and protest demonstrations."

Khomeini was keenly aware of the traditional strain between the orthodox and the mystic, and publicly chose to embrace the orthodox. Indeed, his very assertion into the Iranian political scene differed from the world-retreating stance of the Sufi mystic. He spoke in absolutes. He commanded. He rarely quoted mystical poets. Khomeini praised Imam Hossein as a man of action willing to die for justice, not as a man who retreated to pursuits of searching the Divine through poetry or asceticism like later Sufis. Khomeini said, from the beginning, "The Shah must go." When people came to him as a revolutionary in exile, seeking deals, he said, "No deals. The Shah must go." Once the Shah departed, he insisted on clerical rule, the *velayat-e-faqih*, despite opposition from senior Muslim clerics who saw the Khomeinist idea of clerical rule as a dangerous innovation in religious law. When others opposed him, he branded them "unbelievers." He even took an extraordinary step, defrocking a recalcitrant senior ayatollah who disagreed with him, a move unprecedented in Shi'a clerical history. Khomeini was a brilliant revolutionary because he was so uncompromising. He saw the world in black and white and refused to cut any deals, forcing his will on the population. In his public stance of black and white, there was little room for the grays of the Sufi poet.

Mr. Hashemi and the Pro-Khomeini "Oppressed"

To understand the Khomeini appeal, to understand why so many Iranians had taken to the streets to support him, I decided to visit a South Tehran slum. An important part of Khomeini's revolutionary platform called for the elevation of the "oppressed" and "barefoot masses." In dramatically populist speeches from exile, distributed from hand to hand on cassette, he promised free water, electricity, and even cash from Iran's oil income, promises that many of the "oppressed" either believed or, in their dire poverty, desperately wanted to believe.

Twenty-three years after the revolution, I made a visit to the crumbling home of a proud and broken man in a South Tehran slum. Mr. Hashemi, sixty years old, welcomed me with all the hospitality I had come to expect in Iran. When I arrived, his wife laid out a bowl of bruised fruits and cups of steaming gold-red tea. She wore a long, all-encompassing black chador and plastic pink slippers with tiny rose designs. There were deep bags under her wide eyes. "Please forgive our humble home," she said as she offered me a sugar cube. It was a *ta'rof* comment typical in lavish residences, but in this case it rung true, and she said it without the usual smile. The bare walls of the small room we sat in had turned yellow and cracked. We sat cross-legged on a worn, coarse Persian carpet. Mrs. Hashemi occasionally retreated behind a door. Mr. Hashemi leaned against the bare wall, cross-legged. He insisted that I use a cushion.

I first met Mr. Hashemi at Tehran's martyrs' cemetery, a vast and haunting site where miles of tightly packed white tombstones and memorial pictures of fresh-faced boys attest to the tragedy of war. He had gone there to wash the tombs of two nephews who died in the war, a weekly ritual that he had inherited after his brother's death.

"Perhaps it is better that they were martyred," Mr. Hashemi told me at the time. "They do not have to see the suffering of our people," he said. He gave me his home address. He urged me to visit him sometime. He did not have a phone, so I met him a few days later at the government office in which he worked as a janitor/tea server. When we met there, he spoke in a hurried manner. "The minister needs his tea," he said. "I must go. Here is my address. See you on Tuesday."

I arrived at the appointed hour on Tuesday, and Mr. Hashemi invited me into a small, carpeted room with a silver samovar of tea in the corner. He wore baggy blue wool trousers with red-and-white pinstripes. His gray hair was combed to the side and looked as if it'd recently been cut. He had shaved for my visit. I asked about the health of his three children. His son, twenty-eight years old, lives at home with Mr. Hashemi and his wife, earning money as an auto mechanic/messenger/bread baker/occasional driver. "He wants to get married," Mr. Hashemi said, "but he has no money. What can we do?" His two daughters are married and live their own versions of Mr. Hashemi's hard life in different parts of the city.

Mr. Hashemi first came to Tehran in the mid-1960s. His father, an agricultural laborer in Iran's north, received a deed of land as part of the late Shah's attempt to redistribute farmland away from large feudal lords and toward peasants. Like many of the peasant farmers granted land deeds, Mr. Hashemi's father quickly sold the deed and moved to the city in search of what he thought would be good jobs for his sons. Mr. Hashemi arrived in Tehran in his late twenties.

"I became a construction worker, and I worked on many of the big buildings that were going up all over Tehran," he said, sipping tea, as his wife peeled apples. "With the money I was making, I managed to buy this small house and give a little bit of money to my father. It was not easy, but I could make a living out of it, and I saved enough money to get married. Today my son can barely survive, and he works much harder than I did. Today even government workers and professors cannot buy houses! In the time of the Shah, things were much cheaper, God bless his soul. If only the Shah were not opposed to Islam," he said, "then maybe the revolution would not have happened."

When Mr. Hashemi's father brought his family to Tehran, he was part of a massive rural-urban migration taking place all over Iran. The migration brought not only an abundance of labor but also village values to the big city. These former villagers who hosed the gardens, erected the houses, cooked the food, and washed the cars of Iran's modern middle and upper classes lived both geographically and socially apart from their masters. For many, including Mr. Hashemi, their lives revolved around long workdays, Islamic holidays, and the local mosque.

Around 1977, construction projects slowed, and inflation began to take a toll on Mr. Hashemi's income. He also began to resent the ostentatious wealth he saw in many of the Tehran neighborhoods where he labored. "Things were getting out of hand," he said. "I remember the billboards of the women in bikinis. This was not right. I did not want my mother to have to see that. There were casinos and people drinking in the street. It was uncomfortable."

As revolutionary forces gathered in strength in 1977, an overheated economy slowed new projects. At the local mosque, worshipers talked excitedly about an exiled cleric named Khomeini. One cleric told Mr. Hashemi that Khomeini had semi-Divine qualities. In one sermon, another local cleric referred to the corruption and deceit in the eighth-century court of Yazid, the Arab king who killed the famous Shi'a Muslim Imam Hossein. Everyone in the audience knew that the cleric was implicating the Shah with Yazid, the most hated leader in Shi'a historiography.

"Before I began attending the mosque lectures and talks, I never really thought much about the Shah politically," Mr. Hashemi said. "After all, I was merely a workingman and he was the king of kings. That is just the way the world was, and I never imagined it would be changed.

"When I listened to some of the tapes of the Imam [Khomeini] that were distributed in the mosque, I was deeply moved. I felt something stirring in my stomach. He was so brave to say the things he said. For the first time, I felt strong in the face of the king of kings. I felt that we had a champion in the Imam. I also felt more religious after listening to his tapes. I wanted to fight for this man I had never seen or known.

"When I look back on it now, I now realize that the Shah was not a bad leader. His only problem was that he opposed Islam. These clerics who promised us freedom and prosperity now are all after money and power. They steal our money all the time. They are not real Muslims."

And what of Khomeini? I asked.

"If the Imam were alive today, he would be deeply disappointed."

Sometimes Mr. Hashemi wonders what went wrong. "The Imam tried," he explained. "He tried to make life better for us, but all those devious people around him didn't let him. If he were still around, things would be better. I really think things would be better. We are a Muslim people. We need good Muslim leaders. That is the only way."

We talked for another hour. He asked me questions about my life in America, and I asked about his children. It got late, and I thanked Mr. Hashemi for his time.

I carried with me a small envelope of bills, equivalent to about twenty U.S. dollars, probably approximately more than one month's salary for Mr. Hashemi. I knew life was hard for him and his family, and I wanted to give him something small to ease the hardship, yet I felt embarrassed about broaching the subject. Would it hurt his pride? Was it appropriate? Nervously, I muttered something about a gift and reached into my pocket and produced an envelope.

His face turned red. "I invited you here to be our guest, Mr. Afshin. I did not have any hidden motives. You are like my own son." His wife looked on from the background, her head lowered. From the pained look on his face, I could see that he was not merely playing the *ta'rof* game of feigned refusal and eventual acceptance. He was genuinely hurt by my action.

I felt awful. My own face must have grown crimson red too because Mr. Hashemi tried to reassure me. "It's all right, you have a good heart," he said.

I mumbled an apology, thanked them profusely for their hospitality, and walked out, marveling at my insensitivity and Mr. Hashemi's profound dignity.

Reza Shah: Forgotten Shrine, Remembered King

Not far from Mr. Hashemi's home, the Shah Abdolazim shrine beckons Iranian Shi'a pilgrims to its slender, rising minarets and gold domes. The shrine is a few miles to the southeast of Tehran in the storied old city of Rey. Early-tenth-century travelers to Rey (then called Rages) compared the city with Baghdad, the pearl of the East. Rages has even been mentioned in the Bible and the old Persian Zoroastrian holy book, the Avesta. It is a city with a six-thousand-year history. In 1220, the Mongol hordes utterly destroyed it, dispersing the population to nearby villages and cities. Today Rey is a small, moderately busy city that attracts many Tehrani laborers, civil servants, and small merchants because of the lower-cost housing. It was the sort of place where revolutionary support for Khomeni was high in the 1970s.

Today's Rey resident, from what I could tell from a few days spent there, generally agrees with Mr. Hashemi. The revolution's promise of material gain, not necessarily its political dimension, attracted them. Today they fondly recall the old days, when housing was more affordable and jobs were aplenty.

The Shah Abdolazim shrine has served as backdrop for many of Iran's national dramas in the last 150 years. The Qajar king Nasiruddin Shah was assassinated just outside the shrine in 1896 after attending Friday prayers there. The assassin, who was interrogated later, said he was a follower of Jamal ad-din al-Afghani, a liberal-minded Islamic scholar, revolutionary, and inveterate opponent of the tyranny of Iran's shahs. During the Constitutional Revolution, the shrine served as a sanctuary for leading Constitutionalists. Shortly afterward it became a center of anti-constitutional activity led by Sheikh Fazlollah Nouri. In the days preceding the 1979 revolution, worshipers heard fiery anti-Shah political speeches outside the walls.

Just outside the shrine, Reza Shah, the first Pahlavi king, lies buried. Reza Shah, like Khomeini, was one of those seminal figures of twentieth-century Iranian history whose impact was immediate and far-reaching and whose long shadow will be cast on Iran's future. In an attempt to erase Reza Shah's memory, an angry revolutionary mob destroyed the mausoleum holding the late king, a man whom Khomeini referred to as "vile" and "devilish." A leading ayatollah who urged the mob to attack the shrine even suggested that a public toilet be erected above Reza Shah's grave site.

Now there is virtually nothing left of that grave site, no way to tell it was once an impressive marble mausoleum. It houses a seminary, a clerical training ground. There is of course irony in the location of this seminary. Reza Shah, during his reign, sought to dilute the power of the clergy, viewing it with open contempt as a backward and regressive force in a society that he wanted to modernize. The new seminary is located in Modarres Square, named after an ayatollah who opposed the Pahlavi dynasty. Somewhere in the courtyard leading up to the *madreseh* Reza Shah lies buried. The parallel marble pools that once led up to the marble fountains are still there, but the marble is chipped and dirty. The pools are dry, filled with dying shrubs and weeds.

Given its proximity to the Abdolazim Shah shrine, busloads of pilgrims can be seen napping and picnicking in Modarres Square, just outside the mausoleum. Interestingly, most of the women are draped in black chadors, the Islamic garb that Reza Shah had banned nearly seventy years before. Reza Shah viewed the veil as a symbol of backwardness. In one stroke, he challenged established tradition and de-veiled Iranian women.

When Reza Khan, later named Reza Shah, served as a young military officer in the Russian-trained Cossack brigade in the early twentieth century, he watched with alarm as his nation deteriorated politically, socially, and economically. Sordid prime ministers, British and Russian rivalry, corrupt and wastrel kings, profound economic degradation, widespread tribal unrest, and the disintegration of Iranian territorial integrity plagued the ten years prior to

Reza Khan's 1921 coup d'etat. The previous Shah had virtually lost control of the country. After an aborted effort by Britain to subjugate Iran fully as its protectorate, a British military officer, General Edmund Ironside, wrote about the young, broad-shouldered Cossack-trained Reza Khan in his diary: "I have seen one man in the country who is capable of leading the nation, and that is Reza Khan." Ironside saw in Reza Khan a strong man who could bring order to the disordered Iranian realm. In fact, some of the intellectual journals of the time also expressed a longing for a strong man, perhaps as a consequence of the chaos that followed the failure of the Constitutional Revolution. The poet Eshqi, an ardent Constitutionalist, wrote a poem at this time calling for "a season of blood" as a sort of cleansing of the ills afflicting Iranian society and its culture and politics. As the scholar Ahmad Karimi Hakkak notes, "[T]he conditions and the culture necessitated the need for a Reza Khan figure to step forward the way he did. If he did not exist, he would have to have been invented."

Reza Khan, like Ironside, had the soldier's distaste for Iran's corrupt politicians. In a speech to his fellow soldiers, he said: "You have offered every possible sacrifice in the defense of the land of your fathers. . . . But we have to confess that all our loyalty has served merely to preserve the interests of a handful of traitors in the capital. . . . These insignificant men are the same treacherous elements who have sucked the last drops of the nation's blood."

In 1921 he took action. The Bolshevik Revolution in Russia led to the creation of the self-declared Soviet republic of Gilan in Iran's north. The British were understandably alarmed by the Russian incursion and demanded control of Iran's well-trained Cossack brigade. Reza Khan, a rising star among the Cossacks, led a march on Tehran accompanied by Iranian nationalist politicians. Their demands: Iranian control of the Cossack brigade in order to defeat the Gilan separatists themselves. Once permission had been granted by the fearful king, Reza Khan ordered his men to arrest the cabinet. The king, who justifiably feared the ambition of this upstart general, then appointed him the commander of all armed forces. His forces crushed the Gilian separatists.

Reza Khan harbored a deep mistrust of Iran's clergy. Like Atatürk in Turkey, he hoped to curb the power that Islam held on the masses. He dreamed of setting up Iran as a republic on the Turkish model. Iran's clergy, however, feared the idea of a republic, since it could conceivably break its power base, which rested on a delicate compromise with the king; the clergy gave the king the legitimacy he needed to rule. So it forged a compromise with the rising minister of war, Reza Khan. If he agreed to become the next Iranian king, the clergy would back him with the appropriate religious legitimacy. Reza Khan agreed, and on April 25, 1926, a solemn ceremony attended by clerics, priests, ethnic and tribal leaders, and sullen princes of the old monarchy marked his coronation.

The new king, now called Reza Shah, wasted little time in molding Iran on his terms. As a nationalist, he despised Iran's backwardness and largely blamed four groups for his land's troubles: Muslim clerics, feudal landowners, dueling tribes, and foreign powers. Systematically, he attacked all of them. He took dramatic steps to limit the power of the clergy by creating state schools, thus stripping clerics of their educational role. He also replaced clerical judges with civil courts. Turning to landowners, he stripped many of their property but also took important steps toward creating individual property rights by demanding the use of deeds in all lands. He quelled tribal revolts, brutally putting down the Qashqai tribe. Though he employed severe tactics, he brought order to the restive provinces. He achieved some measure of success in distancing Iran from Britain and Russia, though his flirtations with Hitler's Germany in the late 1930s undid his efforts. For those flirtations he was pushed aside by the British in favor of his son, Mohammad Reza.

When the British shunted Reza Shah aside in 1941, he had ruled Iran as king for only fifteen years. In those years, he reunited a fractured country, helped create a middle class, ensured property rights (even if he had a penchant for amassing his own property illegally), built a solid infrastructure, and created Iran's first batch of technocrats. Simultaneously, he crushed democratic opposition, reduced the Parliament to a rubber-stamp institution, elevated the military to unprecedented levels of power, and stifled all attempts at free expression. Some of his secular intellectual supporters weathered his authoritarian nature because they shared some of the same opponents, especially the clergy and feudal landowners whom they blamed for perpetuating Iran's "backwardness."

In today's Iran, there is a mini–Reza Shah revival among middle-class Iranians. Frustrated with the current order, many Iranians see Reza Shah as a nationalist, a builder, and a patriot, preferring to forget his sometimes brutal authoritarianism in favor of his nation-building. Biographies of Reza Shah sell briskly. A trickling of Iranians knock on the doors of the seminary, hoping to pay a furtive pilgrimage to Reza Shah's unmarked tomb.

Today young clerical students shuffling across the courtyard walk over the body of the king who sought to demote their influence. Just outside the seminary, however, most residents of Rey expressed a fondness for Reza Shah. As one shopkeeper put it, "At least he built something in Iran. The guys in power today only destroy."

A few miles away from the Reza Shah shrine, the gold domes and slender minarets of another shrine, the shrine of another political figure who made an indelible stamp on Iran, beckons pilgrims from all over Iran. The shrine to Ayatollah Khomeini, the revolutionary founder of the Islamic Republic, covers an area roughly the size of the downtown district of a small European city. It was time for me to make my pilgrimage to the Khomeini shrine.

The Khomeini Rise

Ayatollah Khomeini benefited from propitious timing, an iron will, a sharp economic downturn, and a stroke of luck. When Khomeini first openly challenged the Shah in 1963, Iran proceeded on an ambitious and massive top-down modernization program that aimed at creating what the Shah called "a European standard of living." Named the "Shah and People's Revolution", and also known as the White Revolution, the plan sought to redistribute land away from feudal landlords toward peasant farmers, increase the rights of women and minorities, modernize industries, and create a powerful, centralized military.

Though the Shah's White Revolution plans were laudable socially, they proved fatal politically (and exceedingly difficult to implement). Many of Iran's clerics felt uneasy with the reforms, particularly the emancipation of women and equal rights for religious minorities. More ominously, the Shah threatened the economic livelihood of Iran's clerics, many of whom might lose some of their large landholdings to the planned redistribution. The traditional bazaar merchants also felt threatened, as their monopolies on banking and commerce gave way to new merchants well connected to the West and the Shah. Large landowners also disliked the reforms because it cut their holdings. The Shah, most of all, wanted the land reforms to be seen as a direct link to the peasants and rural workers, but shoddy implementation coupled with urban economic growth led to widespread migration from rural to urban areas. Instead of embracing the Shah, Iran's peasants who moved to the citites became key supporters of Khomeini.

The White Revolution led to the first open strains between the Shah and the clergy. Before 1963 Iran's leading clerics had developed an alliance with the Shah that offered a certain modus vivendi. The leading cleric at the time, Ayatollah Borujerdi, advocated the traditional Shi'a view of abstention from politics. The Shah showed his appreciation by paying regular visits to him and allowing a certain amount of dialogue on social and religious issues between court officials and the ayatollah. After Borujerdi died, in 1963, no single cleric emerged as the consensus *marja-e taqlid*, or leader of the Shi'a Muslims, and the Shah increasingly ignored the Islamic clergy. Khomeini, a seminary student and young lecturer during Reza Shah's assault on the country's Muslim clerics and institutions, distrusted the young Shah from the beginning, even though the new king showed less overt hostility to Islamic traditions.

By 1964 Khomeini had begun speaking out against the Shah's policies on a wide range of issues from women's rights to Iran's close ties with Israel and the United States. Around this time many Iranian nationalists also murmured concerns over the Shah's close alliance with the Americans. Khomeini's outspoken opposition to this alliance earned him nationalist credentials to go along with his religious credit. In that same year, Iran's Parliament passed a law granting immunity from prosecution for all American military personnel and their dependents stationed in Iran. Iranian nationalists saw it for what it was: a blatant violation of Iranian integrity and a reminder of the debilitating "capitulation" agreements of the nineteenth century that the British or Russians forced on Iran. Khomeini led the charge against it. In language sure to rile his supporters, Khomeini said that the Parliament "has signed the document of enslavement of Iran . . . it has given America a document attesting that the nation of Muslims is barbarous, it has struck out all our Islamic and national glories with a black line." In one of his most memorable lines, a line that went beyond his traditional base of support toward nationalist impulses in the Iranian psyche, Khomeini said: "If the Shah should run over an American dog, he would be called to account but if an American cook should run over the Shah, no one has any claims against him."

After nearly seventeen months of outspoken criticism of the Shah by

Khomeini, including thinly veiled references to the Shah as reminiscent of Shi'a Islam's most reviled figures, Khomeini's attack on the parliamentary law was the last offense. Advisers to the Shah suggested executing Khomeini or, perhaps, "an accidental death." The Shah refused, instead sending the Ayatollah into fourteen years of exile in Turkey, Iraq, and finally France. Former royalist officials now living in London, Paris, and Los Angeles still grumble about the decision not to kill Khomeini in 1964.

Though publicly the Shah tried to cultivate a cordial relationship with Iran's clerics after the Khomeini confrontation, he privately despised them just as much as his father had. During a 1963 ceremony in which the Shah handed out land deeds to peasants as part of his White Revolution, he deviated from the set public pronouncement and let fly with a blistering, unrehearsed attack on Iran's clerics that ended up heavily edited in the next day's papers. In the impromptu attack, the Shah said: "They [clerics] were always a stupid and reactionary bunch whose brains have not moved for a thousand years." He went on to describe them as "parasites" who were more dangerous than Iran's Communists. "The Red subversives have clear intentions and, incidentally, I have less hatred towards them. They openly say they want to hand over the country to foreigners, without lying and hypocrisy. But those who lie about being patriotic and in practice turn their backs on the country are what I mean by black reaction. . . these men are one hundred more times treacherous than the Tudeh [Communist] Party."[1] The Shah's off-the-cuff remarks did not make the next morning's newspapers. He censored himself.

By the late 1960s the Shah had become increasingly confident and no longer bothered to offer even a semblance of interest in cultivating cordial ties with Iran's clerics. Iran nestled into a position of chief American ally in the Persian Gulf. When U.S. President Richard Nixon visited Iran in 1971, Washington only voiced consternation about the continued, uninterrupted flow of Persian Gulf oil since the British departure from the region in 1968. Nixon, according to published accounts, looked across the table at the Shah and said, "Protect me." After that meeting Iran virtually became the U.S.-appointed guardian of the Persian Gulf region. American military supplies poured into the nation, sapping large chunks from its oil revenue and helping create one of the world's top ten military powers.

[1] As reported in Baqir Moin's excellent biography of Ayatollah Khomeini.

Just one year before Nixon's visit, Khomeini, living in the Iraqi Shi'a religious shrine city of Najaf, Iraq, had given a series of lectures titled "Islamic Government." Khomeini outlined his vision of an ideal Islamic government as one led by learned religious elites, much like Plato's idea of rule by philosopher-kings (Khomeini, who read Plato, simply replaced philosopher with cleric). Though many Shi'a scholars and clerics had expressed a desire to have a supervisory role in government, no cleric of Khomeini's stature ever called for direct clerical rule over the population. Still, though the lectures caused a minor stir among Shi'a clergy, they barely made a ripple in Iran.

In the early 1970s several key aspects of the Shah's White Revolution began to crumble. Peasants granted deeds of land had neither the managerial capacity nor the will to till their own soil. Many sold their deeds for quick profits and headed to the cities, where high-speed industrialization offered the promise of abundant jobs. When revolutionary conditions began to boil in the late 1970s, many of these former peasants formed part of the urban subproletariat that thronged to the street demonstrations in opposition to the Shah.

By the mid-1970s a diverse political opposition movement against the Shah had gathered momentum. A loose coalition of nationalists, Communists, Marxist guerrillas, liberal intellectuals, bazaar merchants, clerics, and religiously inspired dissidents raised their collective voices in opposition to the Shah's authoritarian grip on power. From abroad, in Iraq, Khomeini's voice boomed defiantly. "The Shah must go," he said loudly in his sermons distributed on cassette in mosque networks across Iran. "It is too late for reforms," he said. "The time is ripe for action. The Shah must go."

In the early 1970s Marxist urban guerrilla networks sprouted across Iran and violently challenged the authority of the government. Iranian writers quickly jumped onto the bandwagon of such groups. A culture of revolution gripped Iranian thinkers and students. As one student described it, "We saw everything as political and revolutionary. We woke up at six A.M. and went running in the mountains and saw that as a political act. We were strengthening ourselves for the inevitable revolution to come."

In the mid-1970s the government began a heavy crackdown on the urban guerrilla movements. The Shah, showing more signs of megalomania, announced the formation of a single political party of which all Iranians must become members. The opposition movement expanded and grew more vocal as the gulf between ruler and ruled widened. Throughout this period Khomeini engaged in a running commentary on Iranian affairs from his exile in Iraq. He stepped up his attacks on "the American lackey tyrant" and "the anti-Muslim king." Still, in 1975, Khomeini himself could not claim to be a national figure. Beyond political circles and urban mosque networks, few middle-class Iranians had heard of him. Events over the next few years created the conditions for Khomeini's rise.

In 1973, oil prices quadrupled, bringing Iran, and the Shah, riches beyond anyone's imagination. The Shah used much of this new wealth to go on a buying spree of American military equipment. At home, he cracked down further on any domestic opposition. Emboldened by his new position as the guardian of the Persian Gulf and flush with the new wealth, the Shah announced the formation of the Rastakhiz political party in 1975. This new party, he proclaimed grandly, would be the only political party Iranians needed. Membership in the party was not optional. Needless to say, much of Iran's growing and politically astute middle classes bristled at this imposition. Opposition to the Shah hardened.

In 1976, the Shah took another controversial step: he changed the national calendar. The Shah decided that Iranians should discard their Islamic lunar-year calendar and adopt a new calendar that begins with the birth of Cyrus the Great. Suddenly, almost overnight, Iran moved from the year 1355 to 2535. The clergy saw the move as a gratuitous affront to the faith. Iranian opposition figures proclaimed the Shah a whimsical despot. And the Iranian population largely found the change in years an unnecessary annoyance.

Shortly after the calendar change, another important event occurred, and in retrospect, it can be seen as yet another step toward revolution. In 1977, Iranian writers reconvened the Writers Association, emboldening the intellectual opposition to the Shah and culminating in the famous "ten nights" of opposition poetry in October 1977.

At about the same time Iran's once-booming economy hit a sharp recession. After years of growth and subsequent rising expectations the nation suddenly found itself facing inflation, shortages, increased urban unemployment, and an overheated economy. At this same time, the Shah began a gradual liberalization program intended to appease the rumbling opposition and new human rights-minded President Jimmy Carter. In fact, the Shah's liberalization emboldened the opposition and loosened its fears of political activity.

In this period of relative liberalization, Khomeini's voice grew louder, and the Shah asked Iraq to exile the ayatollah once again. This time the aging and intransigent cleric turned up in Paris, where he would be far from Iranian travelers to Najaf, who returned from their pilgrimages with sacks full of fiery Khomeini sermons on cassette. Paris, however, proved an even more damaging base for Khomeini. Suddenly, almost overnight, he became the sort of international figure he never could have become had he remained in Najaf. The world's journalists waited on his doorstep in a château outside Paris, reporting his every word back to an international audience intrigued by the bearded cleric with the audacity to challenge the all-powerful Shah. Perhaps most important, the BBC Persian Service, widely listened to in Iran, became a vehicle through which Khomeini could reach a mass audience unattainable by the mere distribution of cassettes in mosques.

Leaders of Iranian student groups abroad turned up to pay their respects to Khomeini. Nationalists made the pilgrimage to Neauphle-le-Château. Iran's Communist Tudeh party sent its emissaries. Western-educated technocrats like Abol Hassan Bani-Sadr and Sadeq Ghotbzadeh became Khomeini's de facto spokesmen to the Western media, effectively spinning an image of a pious, democratic-minded man of religion facing an ogrelike, authoritarian king. French journalists, especially those from *Le Monde*, fell over themselves to praise Iran's revolutionaries and attack the Shah.

Back in Iran, demonstrations turned bloody, which spurred traditional mourning ceremonies, which led to more confrontations. With the situation turning grim, a delegation of Iran's leading generals approached the Shah and asked his blessing for a massive and bloody crackdown. He refused, saying that too much blood had been spilled already. Bowing to history, the teary-eyed Shah, carrying a jar of Iranian soil, boarded a plane into an unknown exile.

Shortly before the revolution, the Shah published a volume entitled *Toward the Great Civilization*. He described his dream of Iran as "a developed and free country equipped with advanced industry and technology and a healthy and prosperous economy; a powerful society possessing human dignity to the maximum extent, enjoying individual freedom and social justice, blessed with high moral and cultural values, and devoting its creative efforts to achieving both for itself and for the world an ever greater advancement on the never ending road to perfection."

The Shah's ambitions for his land were noble. Still, he seemed to be the archetypal "nationalist" who spent more time concerned about "the nation" than he did about his people. His inability to connect personally with his population, and his unwillingness to heed their calls for more openness, proved to be a fatal political flaw, one that allowed for a mystical-looking, white-bearded cleric to ride the tide of revolutionary dissent to lead the overthrow of the nationalist but misguided and aloof King of Kings.

Eleven days after the Shah's departure, on February 1, 1979, Khomeini boarded a 747 jet from Paris with leading members of his delegation and members of the international press corps on an improbable return to Iran. Khomeini returned to near rapture in Tehran. Hopeful faces lined the streets for miles. A savior had arrived. All would be well once again in the tortured land of Iran. The newspaper headlines said it all: SHAH RAFT, IMAM AMAD. The Shah's gone. The Imam has come.

Pilgrimage: The Shrine of Ayatollah Khomeini

D riving along the Tehran-Qom highway, past billboards advertising soft drinks and signs celebrating the death of prominent "martyrs" of the Iran-Iraq war, the soft green lights of a magnificent mosque twinkle against the blue-black night sky. It is fitting that the shrine to Ayatollah Ruhollah Khomeini would be on the highway headed to Qom, Iran's ancient religious city and home of Iran's most prestigious Shi'ite seminaries. After all, Qom fathered Khomeini, the fierce, brave cleric who first denounced the Shah from a pulpit there. And it was to Qom that Khomeini promised he would return after he completed the task of overthrowing the Shah.[2]

But Khomeini was attracted to Tehran more than Qom. In Tehran, there was power. Only from there could he remake Iran and direct the "Islamic Revolution" that would dramatically change the world. And so even the geography of the shrine is appropriate: it is closer to Tehran than to Qom, perhaps symbolizing Khomeini as more populist politician than quietist cleric.

Here in the shrine erected for Khomeini, a steady stream of pilgrims touched and kissed the gold grille surrounding his tomb. Barefoot, sleeping

---

[2] The 1979 CIA report that described Khomeini as "a kind of philosopher-king who would retire to Qom after the revolution" was wishful thinking on the part of the Americans.

pilgrims dotted the massive hall, with its exposed rafters and its relatively Spartan interior. Two young seminary students in crisp brown frock coats and carefully clipped black beards sat cross-legged, fingering beads and whispering prayers. A group of young schoolgirls in light blue shirts and white head scarves sat in a circle on a red-and-blue machine-made Persian carpet, listening to their teacher tell them about "the noble Imam." Boys in dirty socks ran and slid across the vast hall. Friends gleefully dragged a cardboard box carrying one young boy across the hall by a rope. At the end of the hall, boys jostled for a position to be next in the cardboard sled.

I sat down in a corner of the shrine. Next to me, an elderly man prayed on the hard marble floor. He prostrated himself, his head touching the ground. He stood, whispering prayers. Once again he lowered his body and placed his forehead on the ground. This constant prostration—up to ten times in some Muslim prayers—reminds the believer of his submission to God.

As I watched the man pray, I remembered an interview I had read with the prominent reformist Muslim cleric Mohsen Kadivar. In the interview, Kadivar describes Islam's submission as directed at God alone. He criticizes what he thought has become submission to Iran's ruling clergy. He ardently criticizes clerical rule. For his views, he received a brief jail sentence.

But Kadivar was not a maverick. An entire generation of young Iranian clerics have rethought the Khomeinist idea of *velayat-e-faqih*. From Mr. Mohseni in Isfahan to countless other young students I met in theological schools across the country, many young clerics have drifted away from the notion of clerical rule.

These young clerics are, in a sense, catching up with the rest of the population. It did not take long for the average Iranian to feel uncomfortable with clerical rule. The executions of leading writers and former government officials in the early days of the revolution turned off many. The excessive social restrictions on the population and the drawn-out war with Iraq frustrated many more. But most important, Iran's economic troubles—the falling currency, the unemployment, the inflation, the middle class's decimation—told of an incapable government, one unable to meet the needs of its people.

Khomeini, like other twentieth-century Iranian leaders, decreed himself a patriarch, a father figure eager to guide his children down the right path. Implicit in this bargain was the patriarch's protection of the family. On this account, the family could be forgiven a certain disappointment. Nearly twenty-five years after Khomeini thundered onto the Iranian stage promising so much to so many, Iranians wonder aloud what went wrong. Those heady days of revolution that inspired Iranians to dream of an equitable, free society soon gave way to a more sobering reality: violent power struggles, the deadly 1980–88 war with Iraq, economic mismanagement and decline, continued social and political repression, and international isolation.

The children have found fault with their fathers, yet like so many children of dysfunctional families, they retain an enduring loyalty to the father figure and a therapeutic silence about his faults. In some of the unlikeliest of settings, I heard defenses of Khomeini: A whiskey-drinking professor told an American journalist that Khomeini brought pride back to Iranians. A women's rights activist told me that Khomeini was not the problem; it was his conservative allies who had directed him wrongly. A nationalist war veteran, who held Iran's ruling clerics in contempt, carried with him a picture of "the Imam."

Of course, a code of silence, a wall of censorship, still shields Khomeini. Direct attacks on the former leader in Iran's newspapers lead to swift retribution. The words alone can garner incarceration. Like the legacy of other "founders" of revolutions turned authoritarian states, that of Khomeini is jealously guarded by his loyal adherents. In the early years after the revolution, Khomeini was not the untouchable political icon he has morphed into today. Other clerics, whose religious learning far exceeded Khomeini's, spoke out openly against the system of government that he proposed and the revolution's excesses. In early 1981, Ayatollah Reza Zanjani said of the Islamic Republic and its leader: "The monopoly of judicial and theological decision-making established in Iran is contrary to Islam. The title of Guide and Supreme Guide are not Islamic. No comparison can there be between the Catholic Church with its hierarchy and structure, and the leadership of the Shi'ites. Any pretension of this sort is not Islamic."

Another cleric, Grand Ayatollah Shariatmadari of Tabriz, openly defied Khomeini and urged his followers to do the same. In response, Khomeini, in an unprecedented act, "defrocked" Shariatmadari, depriving him of his title. Needless to say, the defrocking did not sit well with Iran's traditional clerics, who viewed the title "Grand Ayatollah," achieved after more than forty years of rigorous study, sacrosanct.

When Shariatmadari's followers in Tabriz failed to put up meaningful resistance to his defrocking, a message was sent to all senior clerics: either put up or shut up. Most opted for the latter.

After the Shariatmadari episode, few clerics had the audacity to challenge the Khomeini legacy openly, that is, until Ayatollah Montazeri, a former Khomeini ally who parted from the leader over a dispute concerning the execution of political dissidents in 1988. Montazeri believed his leader had gone too far in the executions. In response, Khomeini cut him off from the family, stripping Montazeri of his title as Khomeini's successor. Khomeini spoke bitterly of Montazeri, viewing his open opposition as a betrayal of the family. Today, Montazeri is a leading clerical dissident under house arrest.

Sitting next to me, a darkly clad middle-aged woman in full chador, sat cross-legged on a carpet with her daughter. They sipped Fanta orange sodas, ate biscuits, and watched the steady stream of pilgrims walk by. The woman, sensing me watching her, did the appropriate Iranian thing: She offered me a biscuit. "Be my guest, my son," she said, reaching over with a biscuit.

Embarrassed, I refused, but she insisted.

She asked me about my camera. She must have seen me earlier taking pictures of the tomb. An automatic Minolta, my camera had a zoom focus lens that jutted out with the touch of a button; a feature that had drawn a small crowd of boys as I was taking photos. I handed the camera to one of the boys. He pushed the button, the lens zoomed out, and the other boys laughed and asked if they could have a turn.

"How much does the camera cost?" she asked.

I struggled with the question. If I told her the price (two hundred dollars), she would make a calculation in her head and marvel at the camera that cost about three times her husband's monthly salary. "I don't know," I lied. "It was a gift."

"Cameras are so expensive these days," she said. "Everything is expensive. You know, before the revolution, I ate meat three or four days a week. Now I can barely afford meat once a week. Every day prices are going up.

"What is your job?" she asked.

Having lied about the camera, I told her the truth about my job. "I am a journalist. I am traveling across Iran."

"What is your salary?" she asked. Iranians regularly ask this question.

"I don't have one," I said. "I am paid by the article." I hoped she would leave it at that. I don't like discussing my pay in America, let alone in this situation.

Undeterred, she asked: "How much per article?"

I hemmed a bit, told her the general range of pay, explained that it is small money by American standards.

Suddenly her daughter entered the conversation. "How many articles do you have to write to buy that camera?"

I told her I didn't know. It was a gift, I reminded her, staying with my story.

"You didn't even check the store to see how much the gift cost?" she asked incredulously.

These money questions made me uncomfortable, though I did not begrudge the questioners. For working-class Iranians, those who live in constant fear of running out of money to pay the next bill or buy the next kilo of meat, this obsession with the costs of goods and the salaries of others is understandable.

Still, I wanted to turn the questions back on her. I asked her why prices sailed so high.

"It's these clerics who don't care about us," she said. "They are all rich, and we are poor, so they don't care if the price of meat goes up or if the cost of an apartment rises."

Ironically, women and men like this, working-class Iranians, formed the core of the street masses that made the revolution work. For them, the revolution promised a new dawn; the cycle of endless work and little pay and few benefits would end. They would be able to make more money, eat meat seven days a week, buy bigger apartments, perhaps even buy expensive cameras with zoom lenses.

Khomeini was particularly dismissive of economics. He once dismissed an aide who spoke too much on the issue of rising prices. "This revolution," he said, "is not just about the price of watermelons." Ironically, it is precisely that—the costs of watermelons and meat and housing—that could prove the Islamic Republic's undoing. While the reformists talk of political freedom and the secular nationalists talk of separation of mosque and state, the vast sea of working-class Iranians talk of a bowl of soup, a chunk of meat, and an adequate wage. They talk of the price of the dollar to the toman and marvel at the salaries of foreigners and the prices of their cameras.

Suddenly, the woman in the Khomeini shrine stood up, gathering her chador and wrapping it more closely around her face, one end of the chador held by her teeth, only one of her eyes showing. "Will you take a picture of me and my daughter in front of the Khomeini tomb?"

We walked toward the main shrine at the center of the vast floodlit hall. Mother and daughter stood in front of the gold grille of the shrine's outer cage. I waited for a few pilgrims to pass and snapped the photo. She asked if I would take another, of her worshiping at the shrine. I agreed.

She wrapped her fingers around the grille. She whispered Muslim prayers. She began weeping and speaking directly to Khomeini. "Oh, Imam," she whispered, "Help us. We need you now more than ever."

VIII

My Friend Hossein ❄ *Hossein's War* ❄ *Journey to Ahvaz* ❄
War Miracles ❄ *Pilgrimage: War Martyrs' Shrine* ❄ *Haji Agha Abu Torabi*
and the Prisoners of War ❄

Cities: Tehran, Ahvaz, Abadan, Khoramshahr, Shalamcheh

My Friend Hossein

My final Iranian pilgrimage began on a motorcycle. I heard the buzz of Hossein's Honda CG125 outside my apartment window. He had told me he planned to bring the motorcycle, but I had not believed him. "Where will we put our luggage?" I asked.

"Don't worry, Afshin, I'll take care of it," he said. Hossein used that phrase often. When I needed new pipes for my water, he said, "Don't worry, I'll take care of it," and called a reliable plumber. When I wanted to secure an interview with a leading conservative cleric, he said, "Don't worry, I'll take care of it," and arranged the interview within forty-eight hours. He always popped up at appropriate times to lend a helping hand, and he did it stoically, quietly, honorably, without any strings attached. He had no ulterior motive; he made no effort to shake down the journalist with dollars in his pocket and no effort to push a political opinion or ideology on me. In fact, he largely shunned political discussions, though I knew he sympathized with Iran's conservatives. He valued friendship, above all, as the highest honor.

Only once did he ask me for a favor. "When you go to America, could you show my X ray to a good American doctor," he said, handing me a black-and-white image of his shattered shoulder, a relic of his days as a soldier in the Iran-Iraq war. Two operations in Germany—at government

260

expense—failed to restore his shoulder to full use. Today he cannot lift his arm to his head. Every night he goes to sleep with a dull pain. By morning the pain wakes him, amplified and throbbing. At times, he said, "it feels like I have a thousand pins poking me at once." Still, every day he wakes up at 5:30 A.M., says his prayers, goes to work at a government-run insurance firm, and refuses pain pills. "I do not want to become hooked on drugs," he told me. "I have seen too many war veterans become drug addicts. I have a family to support."

On this day of our journey he entered my apartment bearing a large box of cookies in his left hand, his good hand. "We must begin our journey with something sweet," he said, leaning in for the traditional cheek kiss that accompanies all Iranian greetings. I poured two cups of tea, and we picked at the honey- and sugar-soaked biscuits as we talked of our upcoming trip.

"I brought the motorcycle," he said, a trace of mischief in his eyes. He knew my unease about riding on the back of the motorcycle on Tehran's chaotic highways. Still, I feigned courage.

"It will be a refreshing ride," I lied.

He laughed, perhaps seeing through my poor acting job. "Don't worry, it will be fine. We can slip through the airport traffic much easier with the motorcycle."

I'd picked Ahvaz as my final destination, a southern Iranian city in the province of Khuzestan, a one-hour flight from Tehran. From there we would drive about two hours to Shalamcheh, a small town near the Iraqi border where some of the bloodiest battles took place in the 1980–88 Iran-Iraq war. On the quiet, dust-swept plains of Shalamcheh, up to fifty thousand Iranians and an untold number of Iraqis died in the kind of gruesome ground warfare not seen since World War I. "We saw the eyes of the Iraqi soldiers as they died," Hossein said, "and they saw ours."

A shrine sprang up in Shalamcheh for Iran's war dead. To get to the shrine, authorities required a special pass. When I asked Hossein if he could secure a pass for me, he said: "Don't worry, I'll take care of it." A few days later he appeared with airline tickets and a glimmer in his eye. "We are going to Shalamcheh," he said. "I told you I would take care of it.

"Hamid will be meeting us at the airport," Hossein said, referring to our other travel partner, another Basiji war veteran. I first met Hamid at the martyrs' cemetery in Tehran, where thousands of Iran's young war dead lie buried. A thirty-three-year-old recent father of a baby girl, he told me of the deaths of his two brothers in the war and talked emotionally of the day one brother's bones arrived at the front door in a box. "One day, a few years after the war had ended, a soldier knocked on my mother's door. Inside a box he carried the bones of my brother," he said, his lower lip trembling. "We took the bones and gave him a proper burial. He was seventeen years old when he died," he said. "He was a great soccer player. He could have been a member of the national team."

Shortly before our travel date, Hamid asked Hossein and me if we could change our travel plans, to go a day later. His baby daughter had fallen ill. He wanted to take her to the doctor before we left. Typically, Hossein said, "Don't worry, I'll take care of it," and set about changing our ticket dates—not an easy task given the shortage of seats on the flight. Because of what seemed like the relative ease that Hossein got things done, managing just about anything with a few key phone calls, I assumed that his status as war veteran brought him extensive connections. Veterans of the war benefit from special treatment—university slots, government jobs, airline discounts—and often call on their myriad contacts to circumvent the normal channels of the system. Families of the war dead, the "martyrs," get similar privileges and some financial compensation from the government, creating resentment among the populace, who tend to exaggerate the benefits and perks.

To change the tickets, we boarded Hossein's motorcycle one day and buzzed from my apartment to the travel agency. In the small, bright agency with 1970s posters of Swiss ski resorts on the wall and red swivel chairs splayed about, Hossein bypassed the line of waiting customers and asked for Mr. Ghazimpoor. A woman in a blue head scarf, wearing a string of foreign airline pins on her loose-fitting blue manteau, went to the back to call Mr. Ghazimpoor. A few minutes later a chunky fellow with a three-day beard and chest hair curling up to his exposed neck, entered from a back room. Mr. Ghazimpoor traded three kisses on the cheek with Hossein and shook my hand in greeting. Hossein introduced me as "the American journalist interested in our war." Mr. Ghazimpoor, also a veteran, thanked me and invited us to sit down in a pair of red swivel chairs in the corner of the travel agency.

Mr. Ghazimpoor, inevitably, offered us tea as he began pecking at a computer and trading small talk with Hossein about mutual friends and recent marriages and newborn babies. An elderly, gaunt man with spotted skin shuffled up to us, carrying a tray of tiny tea glasses that clinked with the man's unsteady gait. He reminded me of Mr. Hashemi, the tea server at the government ministry. I thanked the elderly man as Hossein explained our problem. Mr. Ghazimpoor began searching for a new ticket. With every punch in the computer, he saw booked flights. He kept grumbling, "Nothing available," to himself. He continued punching, continuing his talk with Hossein about a mutual friend who recently had surgery. "Thank God," he said repeatedly as Hossein described the friend's recovery or the healthy birth of a newborn or a recent spate of good weather. After a few minutes of searching and a few more thank God's, Mr. Ghazimpoor came up empty. "I shall put you on a waiting list," he said. "I'll check every hour or so to see if anything comes up." Hossein thanked him, and we left the agency.

I'd expected a bit more pampering from the encounter. It hardly seemed as if Hossein's treatment differed from the average customer's other than that he had a friend in the travel agency who allowed him to skip to the front of the line. In fact, a friend of my own with connections in the travel industry could easily have found us tickets (once he even offered to bump someone for me, an offer I refused). I did not say anything to Hossein, however, about the friend who might help us. It made me appreciate his efforts even more to think that he did not accomplish them with ease.

When we walked out of the agency, Hossein seemed pensive. Perhaps he was embarrassed that the ticket process did not go smoothly in front of me. After all, the ability to get things done using connections is an art that is highly praised in Iran. Having an *ashna*, an important contact in a travel agency or a government office or wherever something needs to get done, opens many doors and hangs proudly on one's chest as a badge of honor. People with large collections of important *ashnas* can become very popular— and useful. I know of one such fellow who seemingly can get whatever he wants through his cultivation of contacts over the years. Mostly he likes to use them for friends and family to ease the burden of going through the regular, inefficient, sometimes maddening process of getting passports or waiting in bank lines or, indeed, securing a seat on an airplane.

"I am sure we shall get the tickets," I assured Hossein. "With your connections, how can we go wrong?"

Just across the street from the travel agency, the window of an Armenian bakery, full of honey and chocolate and cream-filled sweets, called out to me. I insisted that we go in. Hossein, like me, had a sweet tooth, so it did not take much convincing. The pleasant bakery bustled with activity. A few metal chairs and wood tables leaned up against the wall. We ordered a plate of cream puffs laced in chocolate and two cups of tea. As we sat down to eat, Hossein said, "Don't worry, Afshin. Mr. Ghazimpoor is a good man. He will help us get the tickets."

Ultimately, Mr. Ghazimpoor (and Hossein) came through. A few days later I found myself on the back of Hossein's motorcycle, dodging traffic, on our way to the airport. As we passed billboards displaying the faces of prominent "martyrs" of the war, I held firmly to the back of the motorcycle. Haunting pictures of the war raced through my mind. The night before, Hossein had spoken to me for the first time about his own personal war experience. The images he described still chilled and amazed me.

Hossein's War

Usually Hossein deflected my queries about his war experiences. "I hope, we can sit down and talk sometime later," he would say. Whenever I tried to pin down a date, "sometime later" ended the discussion. After a while I stopped inquiring, content with interviewing other veterans. Finally, the day before our pilgrimage, he showed up at my door at dusk with a pack of cigarettes in his front shirt pocket, a sharp pain in his shoulder, and a stomachful of haunting war tales.

"I have been riding the motorcycle too much lately," he said, massaging his shoulder with his good arm as he sat down. "It puts a strain on my injury."

I brought him an ashtray and poured two cups of tea. He sat down, pulled out the cigarettes, and placed the pack on the wood table in front of him, a table covered in an early-twentieth-century Russian tablecloth that looked every bit its age. I offered him some Swiss chocolate, one of his favorites.

"This Swiss chocolate is beautiful," he said, breaking off a piece and leaning it up against his tea glass inside the saucer. "It is like medicine. It can take your mind off any pain for the moment it is in your mouth."

He asked me if I needed anything before we left on our journey. I thanked him, saying he had already done enough and I could handle anything that might come up between now and tomorrow.

Abruptly he cut to the heart of the matter. "You probably want to know why I fought in the war."

"Well, yes, that would be a good place to start," I said, pulling out my notebook.

He popped a sugar cube on his tongue and sipped the tea. He paused for a moment and then began: "Sometimes we don't do things for the sake of money or honor, but because it is just the right thing to do."

"When Iraq invaded us, it was not only invading our sacred soil but was seeking to end our Islamic revolution." He referred to the initial Iraqi invasion of southern Iran on September 22, 1980. "I was very proud of our Islamic Revolution, and I was very proud of our country and people. I simply could not stand by as that dirty thug attacked us. For me, to go to the war was the right thing to do."

He then lit a cigarette, took a deep puff, and continued. "I was only sixteen years old when Iraq invaded. There were many people of my age who began volunteering to go to the war. I wanted to fight too, but my mother objected. She did not want me to go, so I did not volunteer right away. My older brother said I was crazy even to think of fighting, but I felt differently. I felt that I needed to defend our soil and our revolution," he said, taking a sip of tea. "I believed deeply in the Imam [Khomeini] and still do. After about one year and a half I could no longer resist. I joined the Basiji fighting force and prepared for my mission."

When Iraq invaded Iran, Ayatollah Khomeini declared the defense of Iran "a holy war" and promised that all soldiers who died in the war would die as martyrs and ascend directly to heaven. The Islamic Republic founded the Basiji orders to recruit young men like Hossein and Hamid, who were not old enough to qualify for the regular military. What with vigorous recruiting in mostly lower-income urban and rural areas of Iran, employing heavy talk of martyrdom and religious sacrifice, thousands of young men like Hossein joined the Basijis. Ragtag groups of country boys and working-class urban kids, they arrived unprepared on the battlefields. In some cases, the Basijis acted as human mine-clearing fields, a key to heaven wrapped around their necks as they "martyred" themselves for this "holy war." As the war proceeded, the Basijis became more sophisticated in their training and preparation. While still shrouded in a cult of martyrdom by the government, the Basijis, who boast that they charged ahead in the battle with "no brakes," eventually came to be used as more than just mine-clearing martyrs. Moreover, many of them will say that nationalism, more than religion, fired their zeal.

Hossein's first assignment sent him to the eastern front to battle drug smugglers. "We had so many volunteers that I was not needed in the south and west, where the war was being fought. I was sent east to fight against drug smugglers. Many of the smugglers increased their operations because they thought we would be too occupied with the war. The Imam did not want us to forget our national duties to fight against drugs amid the chaos of the war."

After nearly two months in the east, Hossein received transfer orders to the war front in the west. "When I got there, I was excited. I was young and a bit eager to see the war. We had retaken Khoramshahr and other parts of Iran that Iraq had captured. We were now on the offensive. I stayed in the camp for a few days, and then I joined a larger group that was preparing an offensive into Iraq."

Had he received any training by this time? I asked.

"I knew how to use a machine gun." He smiled. "I also was given some guidance in the camp. Not much, but it was enough for me."

He pulled on his cigarette and lowered his voice to a just audible whisper. I leaned in to listen to him.

"I remember the night I was injured vividly," he said. "It was Aban 1361," he said, using the Iranian date roughly corresponding to October-November 1982. "It was about eight P.M. We were preparing for an offensive. It was cold. There were about four thousand of us. Many people were praying. Some were crying. I approached many of my fellow soldiers, and we asked each other for forgiveness for anything we might have said or done that bothered us. One young man paid off a few debts. He did not want to die in debt.

"As for me, my mind soared to Imam Hossein. I thought of his matryrdom and his bravery, and I wanted to cry, but I held it in. One of my friends, a wrestling champion named Bahram Hajalia, had just returned from an advanced scouting mission. He told us that the Iraqis were unprepared. He predicted an easy victory."

As he spoke, night approached, darkening the room. When I moved to flick a light switch, he asked that the room remain dark. The only light was the pale glow of the moon through my windows and the haze of smoke and orange ash from his cigarette. He then described, in a quietly chilling way, the offensive in which he was injured. "I was carrying a heavy machine gun and checked to see if everything was in order. By the time our commander ordered us to attack, we had cried and prayed and hugged one another. Some people expressed the hope that they would be martyred. I prayed to Imam Hossein as we began jogging toward the enemy amid about a thousand other Basijis. The jog turned to a sprint, and I ran full speed through a valley flanked by mountains. We expected to engage the enemy on the other side of the valley."

The surveillance was flawed, however. The Iraqis were waiting on top of the mountains that flanked the valley. As the Iranians approached, the Iraqis fired down on the advancing soldiers like target practice. Bahram fell early on.

"Suddenly, as we ran, a rain of bullets and firepower came down on us from the sides of the valley. The Iraqis were on the mountains, shooting from all directions. People were falling all around me. I heard screams and shouts. I saw a friend die. His head was spewing blood, and his body lay on the ground, contorted in a most strange manner. His leg was twisted in such a way that his boot touched his head. I tried to duck away into a ridge in the mountain, to get away from the fire. They were just hitting us one by one, just picking us off from their mountain positions, and there was little we could do."

As he spoke, I noticed his hand trembling, the cigarette smoke dancing nervously in quick jerks in the darkened room.

"There was also mortar fire and explosions. It was so loud, so very loud. Some of the explosions were so powerful that my body was lifted in the air. This happened about three times. I felt my rib cage shattered." Instinctively, he reached for his ribs as he spoke, perhaps remembering the pain.

"I found a spot in a ridge of the mountain base and lay on the ground. It was dark, so I waited for the Iraqis to fire, and then I would shoot at the light coming from their guns above. Some of my fellow soldiers with antiaircraft rockets and antitank bullets began shooting up at the Iraqi soldiers. I heard screams from above.

"At one point, just as I was getting up to change positions, I was hit with a bullet in my shoulder. I hit the ground. My body became warm. I tried reaching for my gun, but I could not get it. Finally, I reached it but I could not pull the trigger. I was in too much pain. After a few minutes on the ground, I realized I was hurt badly."

He paused, breathing heavily. I asked him what he thought of at the time.

"I thought of my mother, and I thought of Imam Hossein. I lay on the ground in and out of consciousness for about two hours. I was shot two more times—once in the leg, once in the wrist. I was sure that I was going to die. I was going to become a martyr."

By this time he had extinguished his cigarette, so I could see less of his face. His voice began to crack, the memories breaking his normally stoic demeanor.

"Some of my fellow soldiers saw me on the ground and lifted me up and hid me in an alcove in the mountain. A few minutes later a group of soldiers came running into the alcove with a stretcher. There was fire and explosions all around them. They put me on the stretcher and began running through the dark valley. Everything went quiet, and then the firing began again. A bullet hit one of the guys carrying the stretcher. The stretcher fell, and I lay on the ground again. The stretcher was picked up, and again we ran, and again I fell off the stretcher. This happened about three or four times. It may have happened more, but I don't remember."

He paused and lit another cigarette, his face lighted momentarily by the match. I noticed a tear rolling down his stubbly cheek. "We finally made it to a barricade. I was so cold. Someone wrapped me in a blanket. I was saying prayers. I was sure I was going to die. Then our munitions in the barricade were hit. Fire swirled around me, and the blanket caught fire. A fellow soldier lifted me up away from the burning blanket. He was about to put me in an ambulance, but it was full. They put me in the next car, a big van full of other injured soldiers. Later I found out that the ambulance that was full was shot and exploded. Everyone in that ambulance was martyred."

He was pushed into the back seat of a van with four other injured soldiers. "We lay atop one another, our arms and legs crossing, our blood mingling. Everyone was screaming and crying, and I was praying to Imam Hossein. After that, I don't remember anything until I woke up in a military hospital near Khoramshahr. I lost a lot of blood. I was very weak. I was flown from Khoramshahr to Tabriz. The Tehran hospitals were already too full of injured soldiers."

After a few days in Tabriz, he recovered enough to use the phone. He called his brother in Tehran. He told him about his injuries and pleaded with him not to tell his mother.

"When I arrived at the airport in Tehran and my brother saw me with all my bandages, he hugged me and cried. So did I. My mother cried some more when I got home. For almost three months she took care of me," he said. "May God rest her soul. She fed me like a child, and she cried all the time."

Still, despite his mother's cries, Hossein's mind turned back to the war.

"I thought of my friends and the battles, and I wondered what was happening. I wanted to go back. People thought I was crazy. It was hard to explain to them. They could not understand unless they experienced it. There was a certain mystical side to the war. I needed to get back to that."

Many war veterans, especially the religious ones, often spoke of this "mystical" aspect of the war. Sure, it was bloody and frightening and debilitating, but somehow it had a pull, "an emotional and religious state of higher understanding," as one Iranian psychiatrist who studied war veterans put it. Hossein said: "When you are faced with death every day, somehow everything else becomes so trivial. You begin to see so clearly. You become as close to God as you ever will be. I wanted to get back to that. I could not stay in Tehran and complain about the rising price of meat."

And so, his arm in a sling, he turned up at the local mosque, where volunteers were recruited for the war. A few weeks later he was back on the front lines. This time he was more careful. He stayed in the back during offensives. He ducked behind secure positions before firing on the enemy. He did not volunteer for the most daring missions. Still, he saw more friends die. He fainted several times from heat exhaustion. He drank water from a bloody stream. He exacerbated his shoulder injury and broke his ankle.

After a few months at the war front, he returned home, ostensibly for good. He had served his country and, in his view, his faith. No need to go back. He got married, had a son, and settled back down to a familiar routine of work. Still, he felt the pull, the urge to go back one last time. He volunteered again.

"By this time I noticed some of the original religious fervor declining among the troops. I fought in two more offensives in the west and went home again." This was in 1984. He did not go back. The war lasted another four years. Khomeini rejected numerous cease-fire opportunities. The slogan— War, War, until Victory—graced billboards and newspapers and government buildings all over the country.

By 1985 open demonstrations against the war had surfaced in Tehran and other major cities. The government branded the war protesters as traitors. The war would continue, Khomeini thundered, until Saddam Hussein fell.

I asked Hossein about the numerous internationally brokered cease-fire opportunities rejected by Iran.

"The Imam knew what he was doing," Hossein said. "He knew what an animal Saddam Hussein was. He knew that Saddam would only use a cease-fire to reload and attack us again. Iraq had to pay a price for its insolence," he said. "It was the right thing to do."

Today questions abound concerning the continuation of the war beyond 1983. After Iran had successfully ousted Iraqi forces from Iranian territory in 1982, a Saudi Arabian-backed plan to end the war was agreed to by Iraq. The terms were extraordinarily favorable to Iran: seventy billion dollars in war reparations to Iran paid by the oil-rich Arab gulf states on behalf of Iraq and complete Iraqi evacuation from Iranian territory. Iran dismissed the plan, insisting on Saddam Hussein's removal as head of state, a demand that Iranian diplomats knew would be rejected. When Iraq refused, Iran prepared for more war.

The Islamic Republic's war propaganda machine kicked into overdrive. Television programs showed mothers thanking God that their sons were "martyred." One woman told television viewers that she wished for the martyrdom of her two remaining toddlers, as they sat, playing with toys next to her. The government newspapers approvingly called Iran "a martyr-breeding nation." Iranian radio called Iraqi soldiers "the mercenaries of Saddam Hussein, the American-supported infidel." The following column in the government-owned *Etelaat* newspaper, published on April 4, 1983, typifies the mind-set: "There is not a single school or town that is excluded from the happiness of waging war, from drinking the exquisite elixir of death or from the sweet death of the martyr, who dies in order to live forever in paradise."

Of course, Iranian government propaganda, as usual, offered a poor reflection of reality. Most Iranian mothers don't wish for the martyrdom of their sons. Most Iranians hated the war; it tore families apart and disrupted lives. Few towns or schools saw death as "the exquisite elixir." Though the eighth-century martyrdom of Imam Houssein moves Iranian Shi'as, the war had more to do with realpolitik than religion. In retrospect, the war served an important purpose for the new revolutionary government. It gave the leaders a chance to consolidate their rule amid power struggles with leftist and Marxist guerrilla opposition groups. The war also fueled some of the genuine revolutionary euphoria felt by a certain segment of Iranians, the recently empowered urban and rural working classes. Perhaps most important, the war deflected attention from the authoritarianism of the Islamic Republic, helping silence those who opposed the postrevolution theocracy (and there were many). Akbar Hashemi Rafsanjani, the wily cleric who masterminded the war effort and has since held a variety of senior positions in the Islamic Republic, including president and parliament speaker, put it bluntly in 1985: "We have been able to use the war to awaken the people and to fight the problems that threaten the revolution."

Was the war continued beyond the necessary time in order to consolidate political power? Should it have ended sooner? Was there a colossal abuse of youthful idealism and religious innocence by Iran's leaders? These are fair questions and the piercing and painful kinds that Iranians ponder today.

Akbar Ganji, the jailed journalist and war veteran, has also raised questions about the war. He told me: "If it were truly necessary to fight the war for another ten years, we would have done so. It was our duty to defend our country. But my question is: Was it necessary to fight as long as we did?"

Hossein would rather not ask that question. "I think these discussions about whether the war should have ended sooner or not are an insult to our martyrs," he said. "Even if we find evidence that the war should have ended five years earlier or four or three. That will not return our martyrs, will it? Their sacrifice should honored. We should not talk of such things."

He stood up. He flicked a light switch. The sudden rush of light was disorienting. He blinked his eyes. "Afshin, I have talked too much. I have tired you. We have a big journey tomorrow."

He walked toward the door. He was not angry, just seemingly tired of the questions he is faced with today, questions that threaten the simple, noble goal of the war: defending the nation and the revolution and the Imam. For Hossein, that was enough. He did not need to ask any questions. Questions raise the possibility that maybe, just maybe, the estimated two hundred thousand Iranian soldiers who died after 1982 died because a political system needed them to die to maintain its hold on power.

Such thoughts grate heavily on the nerves of pious patriots like Hossein. His fellow Basijis died noble deaths. They were not pawns of political games. They were glorious martyrs, and that was the only way it could be. I heard the buzz of his motorcycle as he drove away.

Journey to Ahvaz

Before every Iran Air flight, brief prayers from the Quran are said over the loudspeaker to ensure a safe journey. The prayer is repeated in English. On our flight to Ahvaz, in addition to the prayers, the female flight attendant asked us to remember the martyrs of "the sacred defense," Islamic Republic–speak for the Iran-Iraq war. When they repeated the prayer in English, they dropped the line about the martyrs, a fact I pointed out to my travel partners.

Hamid shrugged and smiled, his auburn brown, neatly trimmed beard rising on his face toward his blue eyes. "The foreigners don't care about our martyrs anyway," he said, "so why bother repeating the line in English?"

Hossein nodded in agreement. "The Western world was against us during the war. In fact, they are the reason we have so many martyrs."

He was right. The Western world, for the most part, sided with Iraq, though several countries—especially the United States, France, and West Germany—funneled arms to both sides. Still, despite the occasional arms transfer to Iran, the geopolitical calculation in Washington and other Western capitals was the same: A victory by Iran would be unacceptable, a dangerous tilt in the regional balance of power in a region that controls nearly two-thirds of the world's oil reserves.

So in 1987 the United States implemented Operation Staunch, a plan intended to prevent an Iranian victory that included the sharing of satellite intelligence with Iraq, protection of Kuwaiti and Saudi oil tankers, and brief naval confrontations with Iranian ships in the Persian Gulf. In a moment of confusion, the United States shot down an Iranian passenger plane, killing more than four hundred on board. Washington expressed apologies for the mistake and compensated the family's victims. Iranian leaders don't buy the "accident" version of events. Washington did not help matters much with the outrageous promotion of the admiral who ordered the tragic shots.

"A country that shoots down our passenger planes certainly doesn't care about our martyrs," Hossein said. "The Americans don't care about our martyrs and injured war veterans. Don't even bother writing what I am telling you in your notebook. Your editors will not publish it."

When we stepped out of the plane in the Ahvaz airport, a blistering, hot wind assaulted us. I felt an almost immediate thirst for water. I wore short sleeves and loose-fitting cotton pants. Hossein turned to me and said: "Imagine wearing two layers of military gear in this weather. We spent more time dreaming of cold water than we did of our families."

Hamid, Hossein, and I walked across the runway toward a small, busy baggage claim area. A tall, slender man with a dark mustache approached us and greeted Hossein warmly. After a round of flowery introductions and greetings, the man, Mr. Mohammadi, led us to his car, a Peugeot with a powerful air-conditioning unit. "It is not even summer yet," Mr. Mohammadi said, wiping away beads of sweat on his forehead. "You came just in time. One month from now it will be unbearable."

Mr. Mohammadi worked with Hossein in one of the large, government-owned insurance agencies. He was the Ahvaz representative of the firm. Like most residents of Ahvaz, he is ethnically an Arab. At home, with his wife and children, he speaks Arabic rather than Farsi and teaches his children to be proud of their Arab heritage. When Iraq invaded Iran, Saddam Hussein assumed that the ethnic Arabs of southwestern Iran, people like Mr. Mohammadi, would rise up in solidarity with their Arab brothers. No such thing happened.

"We are ethnically Arab," Mr. Mohammadi explained, "but our nationality and loyalty are with Iran. Saddam misunderstood this."

Mr. Mohammadi, who lived in the heavily besieged city of Khoramshahr at the beginning of the war, helped out with the evacuation of women and children. "We arranged for bus transport. Everyone tried to push his way into the buses. When there was not enough room on the inside, people sat on top of the buses. The buses had to move very slowly, so the people on top would not fall off."

After a short drive from the airport, he pulled up to the driveway of a two-story house behind tall, whitewashed walls that exposed only the top floor. We slipped off our shoes at the door and entered a large living room with a cream carpet on the floor and red, embroidered cushions leaning against the wall. In one corner, a cluster of mock Louis XIV chairs with faux gold frames clung to the wall. We chose the floor, cross-legged, our backs supported by the wall cushions. A brown air-conditioning unit jutted out of the wall, emitting loud, whirring gusts of cold air. We drank tea and talked about our upcoming journey.

We planned to drive to Abadan, the port city that was once the pride of

Britain's Anglo-Iranian Oil Company until the nationalization of Iranian oil in 1953. Even after the nationalization, Abadan remained an important oil town, pumping and refining nearly one-third of Iran's total output before the 1979 revolution. Iraqi bombers successfully targeted Abadan refineries, hoping to choke Iran's oil flow. The city has yet to recover from the bombings. Today Abadan pumps less than what it did before the war.

From Abadan, we would go to Khoramshahr, the city that was initially occupied by Iraq and dramatically liberated in 1982. So violent were the fighting and destruction in Khoramshahr that the city came to be called Khooni-shahr, or Bloody City.

"You cannot believe the things I saw in Khoramshahr," Mr. Mohammadi said. "For almost a month Iraqi soldiers shot and killed us and raped our women. We fought back, but we were overwhelmed, until our support lines came from the east."

Finally, we would go to Shalamcheh, a stone's throw from the Iraqi border, where up to fifty thousand Iranian soldiers died. The war martyrs' shrine hugs the border with Iraq.

"Fortunately," Mr. Mohammadi said, "we won't have to face Iraqi tanks on our journey."

War Miracles

After a short tour of the city at dusk, a dinner of saffron and lemon fish with white rice in a local restaurant and a seemingly endless round of tiny teacups back at Mr. Mohammadi's home, we went to sleep on roll-out mattresses in the living room. Throughout our stay in Mr. Mohammadi's home, we never met his wife and three daughters. We heard their voices coming from the kitchen, but they never entered the living area where we drank tea and talked. They prepared the meals, but Mr. Mohammadi served us himself. This "hiding" of the women does not occur often in Iran. In most homes, even conservative religious ones, women usually eat with the men. Hamid commented on the women's issue when Mr. Mohammadi went to kitchen to retrieve our breakfast. "These Arabs are very conservative," he said quietly.

In fact, the absence of women in social situations like this one is not an Arab/Iranian division. More likely, it is a city/village or big town/small town one. Still, the fact that Hamid viewed it that way interestingly reflected the

Iranian self-perception of difference and perhaps, a self-assumed superiority over Iran's Arab neighbors and, indeed, over Arab Iranians.

With our stomachs fueled by a breakfast of eggs, feta cheese, bread, and watermelon, we began our pilgrimage. The drive from Ahvaz to Abadan is marked by a string of idle cranes, dust brown houses with baby blue metal doors, small billboards of war martyrs, dry circular fountains, and a few gutted, shuttered buildings. Ahvaz was an important logistics center for the war, and the city still bears scars from this experience. As we drove farther, through Abadan, then onto Khoramshahr and Shalamcheh, the scars got deeper, the number of gutted buildings increased, and houses with bullet holes became more prevalent.

On the highway just before reaching Abadan, a display of three destroyed Iraqi tanks sat quietly on the tan, dry landscape abutting the road, one of many reminders of the war that rocked the cities close to Iraq's border. As we approached the city, we passed by date trees swaying in the hot wind and more crumbling dust-colored homes with baby blue metal doors. Near a small religious shrine, we drove by a busy outdoor market where peddlers sold yellow apples and red pomegranates and fresh greens. On one of the crumbling, mud brick homes, I spotted a "Death to America" sign. A few houses down, someone scribbled in English: "We love Pink Floyd."

We parked the car near a dock jutting into the blue waters of the Persian Gulf, a busy dock where small wooden dhows with massive white sails floated, waiting for their next shipments. Gleaming bales of silver fish with blue eyes fell into gargantuan tanks of ice as sun-baked, coffee-skinned deckhands chatted in Arabic. Nearby, a cinema house advertised an Iranian action film. The cinema led to a road flanked on both sides by a series of photos of young, fresh-faced martyrs, like street signs.

We got back in the car and drove by the Hotel Azadi Aban. Mr. Mohammadi told us that the hotel once hosted the area's hottest nightclub. Today the club belongs to a revolutionary foundation in the name of Iran's war veterans and has a decidedly less glittering nightlife.

As we drove toward Khoramshahr, Hamid told me stories of "war miracles." One young soldier, he said, had his head blown off by a mine. His headless body then miraculously spoke and said: *"Salam alayk ya Abu Abdullah* [another name for Imam Hossein]." Next, he told me the familiar story of the bright red tulips that grew spontaneously in areas in which Iranian soldiers were martyred. I had heard these types of stories before from other war veterans, stories of graves that emitted the smell of perfume, of soldiers dreaming their own deaths exactly as they happened the next day, of apparitions of Imam Hossein appearing ahead of charging Iranian troops. I suppose all wars have their own share of miracle stories, but these Iranian "miracle" stories had a purpose. The government war propaganda machine fed and encouraged them, repeating them on television and printing them in books on the war. The "miracles" helped their cause. It made their war just; God was on the side of Iranian soldiers. For the soldiers who believed in the miracles, they offered a certain solace for a lost leg or dead brother or shattered shoulder.

As we talked of more miracles, we passed a billboard of one of the most famous of the young martyrs of the war, the young Shahid Fahmideh (the word *shahid* means "martyr"). Shahid Fahmideh, the chroniclers tell us, strapped a grenade to his body and "gloriously" knocked out an Iraqi tank in a "noble, martyr-breeding attack." For that, the chroniclers of the war celebrate his sacrifice. These chroniclers, the men and women who work in government-financed institutions, churn out pamphlets and videos and books on Iran's martyrs and "the sacred defense" against Iraq.

But there is another series of stories that the chroniclers won't write about: the young soldier who did not want to go to war but was forced into it by peer pressure; the young man who tried to emulate Shahid Fahmideh with a faulty grenade but who died less "gloriously" under the wheels of a crushing Iraqi tank; the religious young man at the war front who wondered why no cleric went to the front line to martyr himself.

The case of Mohammad from Shiraz reflects the less glorious version of "martyrdom." In an interview with a war veteran in Shiraz, he told me of Mohammad's death, asking that I not use his last name. Mohammad is celebrated in his hometown by the local chroniclers as a war hero who died in "a martyr-breeding mission" that knocked out two Iraqi jeeps and took his life in the process. The reality is far less "glorious." In reality, Mohammad died inside a grenade hole while going to the bathroom. Iranian soldiers used the holes made by grenade explosions as makeshift toilets. While using one of these toilets, Mohammad fell victim to an Iraqi cluster bomb. "You must not use the last name because it will disgrace his family," the soldier said. "Everyone thinks of him as a hero, but he was just a scared soldier who wanted to go back home, like many of us."

The bottom line: Not every war death shines with glory. Not everyone dies a "sweet martyr's death" with lips parted in a smile, as one oft-published picture shows, or a noble, "martyr-breeding" death that includes taking out a couple of enemy soldiers in the process. In Hamid's and Hossein's personal stories, sweetness garnered few paragraphs. Hamid split his chin open when his jeep flipped over and tumbled down a ravine. A friend of his crushed his ribs in that same crash. "For nearly a year, it hurt him every time he took a breath," Hamid explained. The sting in Hossein's shoulder reminds him every day of the pain of war. One of Hossein's closest friends will never have the joy of becoming a father: Saddam's chemical attacks made him sterile.

A large sign on the road notified us that Khoramshahr, the city devastated by the initial Iraqi invasion, was close by. ENTER WITH RELIGIOUS CLEANLI-NESS, the sign said, referring to the cleanliness one must have when entering a mosque for prayer. The chroniclers declared the city holy ground.

Everywhere we drove by shells of buildings, skeletal reminders of the Iraqi bombings. In the distance I spotted an idle Ferris wheel. We drove over a recently reconstructed bridge, freshly painted with sea blue railings.

"The Iraqis held this city for twenty-one months," Mr. Mohammadi said. "You can't imagine what they did here," he said, shaking his head, "you can't imagine." We drove by more gutted buildings and an entire block of leveled houses. "The city is only just recovering," he said, twelve years after the war ended.

"The center of the city has shifted," he said, "because the old city center has not been reconstructed. We are now driving through the old city center," he said as we drove through eerily quiet streets.

Emerging from the silent city center, we got back on the main road, just a few miles away from our destination, the war veterans' pilgrimage site. A two-lane highway flanked by vast, tan, shrubby emptiness led to the shrine. "There were many villages along this road before the war," Mr. Mohammadi said. "Now there are only mines." A dangerous collection of nonactivated mines lurk beyond the recently reconstructed telephone cables flanking the highway. An overturned Iraqi tank, buried halfway into the ground pokes out of the ground in the distance, casually left there because of the enormous expense of moving it. Perhaps the mines made it difficult to move the tank or, better yet, set up a propaganda memorial around it.

"We are almost there," Mr. Mohammadi said as we approached a small outpost manned by a lanky teenage guard with sun-baked cheeks and a rifle. The car slowed. The guard glanced at the license plate. Mr. Mohammadi rolled down the window and showed the guard an official permit to enter the war martyr's shrine. The sky draped over our heads was pale blue, as if tired from heat and war. An overturned jeep and a large chunk of an old, rusted pipeline dotted the landscape ahead of us. The guard looked into the car and disinterestedly waved us on. It was too hot to show emotion.

Pilgrimage: War Martyrs' Shrine

Our car rumbled to a stop amid a rocky dirt parking lot. There was only one other car there, a rusted white Toyota pickup truck. At the entrance to the shrine, a sign in Farsi read: SHALAMCHEH: WELCOME TO IRAN'S KARBALA. The word "Shalamcheh" in the sign was written in green letters, with red, painted splotches dripping from the word like blood. Karbala, which is now in Iraq, is where the eighth-century martyrdom of Imam Hossein took place. The Imam Hossein shrine in Karbala draws Shi'a pilgrims from around the world.

Just beyond the bloody sign, a small prayer area awaited with rich Persian carpets laid out directly onto the concrete. A crude aluminum ceiling, crisscrossed by steel girders, protected worshipers from the blistering midday sun. The prayer area included a small billboard with pictures of martyrs. I looked at some of the photos of these dead young men.

Rahim Ahvazi had a fresh, earnest face with soft eyes.

Abdul Said Rashid wore a fat 1970s disco collar and had a dark goatee.

Mohammad Taghimi Azimi looked like a film star with a broad, curling black mustache and his dapper military uniform.

Ali Reza Dezfuli was a young man, who looked no more than sixteen, with a hard, cold stare and a severe bowl haircut.

On and on the photos went, eventually leading to a display of gruesomely dismembered bodies, of dead young men with their intestines on display and their heads nearly sliced off, the sort of shock photo that human rights groups use to criticize the use of torture. Just off to the side of the shock photos, there was a picture of a woman cleaning her martyred son before burial, accompanied by a letter she supposedly wrote. The letter reads in part: "Let our enemies know this. We are not afraid to martyr our sons for the cause."

Just below that letter was a photo of a young man with bullet holes in his bare chest, yellow flowers scattered around his neck.

From the prayer area, we had a clear view of the shrine: an open-air dome of green steel girders covering a five-foot-tall glass coffin surrounded by an assortment of flapping Iranian flags and black-and-white flags with religious sayings. Set amid a dust-swept desolate landscape, the open-air shrine had a quiet somberness about it. Hossein, Hamid, and Mr. Mohammadi decided to say their noon prayers as I walked toward the shrine.

Air sounds whooshed by my ear as I approached the glass coffin. Inside the coffin display, I saw a collection of war paraphernalia: helmets of fallen soldiers, dusty boots, bloodstained headbands, a rusted AK-47, and worn soldiers' diaries. There was also a picture of Ayatollah Khomeini and hundreds of small-denomination bills scattered inside the coffin. Like all religious shrines, this martyrs' shrine allows pilgrims to make donations for the shrine's upkeep and for charitable purposes. I dropped a bill in the slit at the top and watched it land on a soldier's helmet. All around me, I heard the pop of flags flapping in the wind. Hamid and Hossein soon joined me at the shrine. Mr. Mohammadi stayed a few feet back, leaning up against one of the steel girders.

I watched Hamid and Hossein as they looked into the glass coffin. They stared at the display of helmets and guns and boots, their faces drawn, their lips taut, their foreheads crinkled. Hossein put two fingers on the glass coffin and began whispering prayers. Hamid raised his hands to chest level, palms toward his face, and closed his eyes, singing verses from the Quran. Mr. Mohammadi approached the coffin, his hair and loose shirt flapping in the hot wind, and joined the prayers.

After the prayers ended, we all looked into the glass case in rapt contemplation. I wondered what emotions must be running through Hossein's mind, wondered if he recalled martyred friends or his own near-death experience. Hamid slipped a bill into the slit of the glass coffin. Hossein broke the silence, asking me if I would like to walk to the Iraqi border. "It is only a few minutes from here," he said, pointing to an outpost in the distance where a single Iraqi flag fluttered in the wind. "We can take you there."

We walked in silence over dirt and scrub and rocks toward the border. In the distance, I saw an Iraqi soldier in a lonely outpost, less than a thousand feet away. He had a gun slung over his shoulder. He waved at us. An Iranian guard, another teenage boy with a peach-fuzz beard and a long gun, called out to us from the Iranian post that faces Iraq. Hossein told the Iranian soldier that we were war veterans walking up to the border. He pointed in the direction of the Iraqi outpost, where the young soldier with a gun waved at us again. Mr. Mohammadi reached into a bag he carried and handed the guard a pair of small insurance company clocks as a gift. Many war veterans, I was told, bring sweets and fruits and gifts to the young guards as gifts for manning the martyrs' shrine. The young guards often share their booty with the Iraqi guards on the other side of the border, a poignant reminder of simple humanity obscured by power politics. Perhaps the Iraqi guard's waves sent thanks for leftover gifts he expected to receive later.

The Iranian guard apologetically told us we could not go any farther. "Last night, we caught two 'hypocrites' crossing the border," he said referring to the Iraq-based armed resistance group known as the Mojahedin-e-Khalq, whom the Iranian government calls *monafeqin,* or hypocrites. Most Iranians seemed to agree, there being little support for the Iraq-based group that once fought with Saddam's soldiers against their fellow Iranians.

Hossein did not protest. He understood that a soldier should follow orders, and we turned back. We looked over at the Iraqi side, and the soldier waved again. As we walked, Hossein quietly said: "Many of my friends died on this soil we are walking on now. We are walking on thousands of martyrs."

Haji Agha Abu Torabi and the Prisoners of War

When we returned to Tehran, Hossein took me to a downtown mosque where I would meet Haji Agha Abu Torabi, a conservative cleric who spent eight years in an Iraqi POW camp. Haji Agha, as Hossein called the cleric, served in Iran's Parliament and had close ties to Iran's Supreme Leader, Ayatollah Ali Khamenei, whom Hossein reverentially called Agha. Haji Agha also served on the Clergy Court, the conservative body that jailed reformist clerics like Mohsen Kadivar and the prodemocracy cleric Abdollah Nouri.

Before we visited with Haji Agha, Hossein invited me to his home to watch an Iranian film on video titled *From Karkheh to Rhine.* The film depicts the lives of Iranian war veterans waiting hopefully in a hospice in Germany in the early 1990s for the operations that might restore their sight or repair their torn legs or soothe their withered bodies, burned by Iraqi chemical attacks. At the entrance to his house, I slipped off my shoes, looking up at a small picture of Khomeini pasted on the wall. Hossein's wife, a sweet-faced woman in the traditional chador, offered me tea and fruit. His elderly father, who lived with them, greeted me, before retreating to the back for a nap.

In the movie, there is a scene in which one of the veterans watches a video replay of Khomeini's funeral. Melancholy music emerged. The veteran shook with deep sobs. He grabbed at the television, touching it and crying. The scene in the movie seemed overly melodramatic, almost contrived. I looked over at Hossein to gauge his reaction. His chest heaved. His eyes teared; his hands shook: the same reaction, but less dramatic.

After the movie ended, we ventured on the back of his motorcycle to the Imam Hossein mosque, where we were to meet Haji Agha Abu Torabi. Inside the mosque courtyard, we walked toward a simple white door. When we opened the door, I saw a group of men, mostly with beards, sitting cross-legged on the floor, all eyes fixed on a slim elderly cleric with a black turban, Haji Agha Abu Torabi.

The cleric stood and insisted that I sit at his right. We exchanged Persian greetings as Hossein told Haji Agha a bit about my background.

"Mr. Molavi, if you do not mind, I have some business to take care of. But please remain seated, and we shall talk soon."

The men sitting in the semicircle around Haji Agha then came forward, one by one, asking the Parliament member and cleric for assistance with various issues: an insurance policy, his attendance at a crafts fair for war veterans, a message of thanks from a group of POWs to Khamenei, a whispered request for financial assistance. Haji Agha dealt with all the petitioners quietly and attentively. He took their names and addresses. He made promises. He agreed to attend the crafts fair.

When the petitioning ended, Haji Agha turned to me and said: "So, I hear you have been to Shalamcheh?"

Yes, Haji Agha, I had.

"Our martyrs fought with great courage there," he said.

Yes, I knew.

"Sometimes," he said, "I wish I were also martyred. To be closer to God. Instead, I was taken to prison."

I asked him why he had gone to the war. Most men his age (he was in his late forties then) had stayed home.

"I wanted to defend our soil and defend our revolution," he said. Then he laughed, saying, "But I was taken to prison very early on, in one of the first offensives. When the Iraqis first captured me, I was wearing a soldier's uniform. They asked me who I was. I only told them my name. I did not tell them I was a cleric. They especially liked to beat clerics and insult our religion. They found out I was a cleric, and they beat me on the head with a metal rod, laughing as they insulted Imam Hossein." He raised his turban to show a wrinkled wound on his balding head, a reminder of the beating.

"Life was not good in the camp, but we did our best to keep up the spirits of our soldiers. We organized plays. We talked about religion, about our families. I led quiet prayers. If the Iraqis saw us pray, they beat us. One time they asked me to curse Imam Khomeini. I refused and they beat me."

Hossein clenched his fists as Haji Agha continued. "Yes, but thanks to Allah, we returned home. I wanted so badly to return home, to participate in Iranian society again, to help my fellow countrymen. And now my days are filled with Parliament debates and my official role, but it is these informal gatherings I like best, where I can talk to fellow war veterans and prisoners of war. If I can help them, I am truly happy."

He invited us to join him for prayers, and we did, in a massive hall, where hundreds of worshipers waited for him to lead them. He invited me to the front, but I preferred to do my prostrations in the back. So did Hossein.

After the prayers a small crowd gathered around Haji Agha, asking him religious questions, which he answered for up to an hour. When we left, we bade him good-bye; he insisted that I come back again, and I did. Over the next few weeks, I saw Haji Agha two more times, once at a dinner hosted by a prominent bazaar merchant and the other time at his book-lined office of POW affairs.

In that meeting, he told me: "I know you do not agree with some of the conservative views. I know your sympathy lies with the reformists and the students. But you have shown a willingness to listen. This is good. We Iranians do not always listen to each other. Too often we are yelling at each other. You have come to Iran and listened. You will go home and make your conclusions. That is fine. But most of all, you listened."

A few months after I left Iran, Haji Agha Abu Torabi, driving his own white Paykan, died on the road to Mashhad, where he planned to make a pilgrimage to the Imam Reza shrine.

IX

Cities: Tehran, Damascus (Syria)

Storming the Gates with the Software Engineers

Outside the German Embassy in Tehran, a small crowd of Iranian software engineers huddled anxiously around a security guard. "Please, let us in," one of the young Iranians pleaded with the guard. "We just want to find out if it's true!"

The guard refused sternly. "Come back tomorrow," he said. "Everyone has left already."

The young man persisted. "Surely, there must be someone still in there, anyone? Please, let us just take a look!"

The guard, a meaty middle-aged Iranian with a tattered rifle slung over his shoulder, refused again, staring down the mostly recent university graduates in their mid-twenties. "No, it is impossible," he said. "Out of the question."

Two more breathless young Iranians approached the crowd of about thirty. "Is it true?" they asked urgently. "What have you heard? What? Tell us!"

A tall young man, a leather laptop case slung over his shoulder, responded: "We don't know yet. This gentleman," he said, pointing to the guard, "won't let us in to ask." The two newcomers sighed, their hands raised in the air, their eyes begging the guard.

"No," the guard said flatly. "I'm sorry. It is against the rules. How can I let you in when everyone has left?"

"You're lying!" one of the software engineers shouted defiantly. "We'll just wait out here until one of the diplomats walks out! It's only five o'clock. They can't all be gone!"

So they waited for up to an hour for a German diplomat, a secretary, anyone from the inside to walk out the door, to confirm the breathtaking news: Germany, they had heard, was ready to open its doors to Iranian software engineers.

For the Iranians assembled outside the embassy, many of them unemployed or underemployed, the German opening could change their lives. A lack of jobs at home and the promise of professional advancement and riches abroad have sent these software engineers, like many of the country's educated elite, looking for a way out. The news of the potential German opening traveled fast in their tight-knit community. In Internet cafés and university computer labs, by E-mail and telephone, the news had sent them scurrying to the embassy and the standoff with the intractable guard.

"You are wasting your time," the guard said. "I told you they already left."

The software engineers held their ground. "We shall see," one of them said with steely determination. "We shall see."

As they waited, conversation drifted to the recently launched Microsoft Windows 2000 software package. "It's too many megabytes," one of the young men said. "I had to erase half of the applications on my hard drive so that it would fit!"

Another said mockingly: "Windows 2000 is fine. You just need a new computer! Your computer is from the era of Nasruddin Shah," referring to the nineteenth-century Iranian king, eliciting loud chuckles from the assembled software engineers.

Suddenly one member of the waiting group said: "Do you think it's a hoax? Like last time." The crowd sighed, almost in unison. A few months earlier, a rumor had spread by E-mail that the Swiss Embassy, which represents American interests in Tehran, was taking applications for computer software engineers to work in the United States—in Silicon Valley!

"No, this can't be false," one said. "It was printed in a German newspaper."

Heads turned to the young man with the new information. "What? Where?" A cacophony of voices asked for the Web address of the newspaper, but he could not remember it. More sighs.

"Besides, none of you reads German," he said smugly, hinting that his knowledge of the language would make him a virtual lock for one of the highly coveted visas.

Three more software engineers jumped out of a car. "What's happening? Is this the line for applications?"

The tall boy with the laptop, the de facto group spokesman, replied with his usual line, pointing to the guard: "This gentleman won't let us in to find out." He said "gentleman" in a mocking tone.

The group shuffled angrily, all eyes on the guard. Suddenly, the guard snapped. "Attention, everyone! You must leave the area now or I'll call my supervisor!" He reached for his walkie-talkie. "This is not right! I told you that everyone has gone home! You must all leave the area!"

The tall young man stepped in. "Calm down. We are sorry. We are leaving." He turned back to his sullen fellow software engineers. "Let's go. We're giving the poor guard a heart attack."

One by one and in small groups, the software engineers retreated. As the crowd dispersed, one young man called back at the guard: "I'll be back here at eight A.M. tomorrow. You'd better let me in!"

The guard touched his gun.

Children of the Revolution

At an Internet café in an affluent section of Tehran, I met with two of the software engineers who had gathered outside the German embassy gates a week earlier. We sat on tall black chairs around a tall glass table as young Iranians surfed the Web on four computers set up against the wall. Web sites for Britney Spears, Timberland shoes, skateboarding, and the Los Angeles–Iranian pop music scene flashed across the screens. Two teenage girls typed messages, giggling. They were in a cyberchat room that linked them with other teenage girls in America, Britain, Hong Kong, India, and somewhere they had never heard of, the Cayman Islands. The correspondent from the Caymans was particularly emotional about the subject in discussion, teen hearthrob Leonardo DiCaprio. "I love him! I love him so," the Cayman Islands message went. The London correspondent piped in with her own message: "Do you love him more than David Beckham?" Cayman's response? "Yes!!!! Way, way more!!!"

The Iranian girls at the café thought that Cayman *khanom* (Mrs. Cayman), as they called her, was a bit too obsessed. "This girl is strange," one of them said. She began typing a response to Cayman *khanom,* taking the high road: "I am also love Mr. DiCapro, but I love how he is good actor. Very good actor [*sic*]." She pressed the key to send the message. She grinned with a smug satisfaction.

Nearby two boys in their early teens were surfing a skateboarding site. "Wow! Look at that one," one of the long-haired boys said. "How did he do that?"

In a corner of the room a middle-aged man checked on his stock portfolio from an American on-line stock-trading site. Iran's gray-bearded Supreme Leader, Ayatollah Ali Khamenei, a regular critic of "Western cultural imperialism," looked down upon the Web surfers from a framed photo high in one corner of the café.

The two software specialists and I ordered Nescafé, which was served with thin wafer cookies on the side. Madi, a twenty-seven-year-old graduate of Tehran University, was clean-shaved with a mop of unruly black hair atop his round face. His university classmate Pooya was a slightly built twenty-six-year-old man, with bright eyes and a dimple that appeared at the top of his right cheek when he laughed. Neither of them had studied computing or software at the university—Madi is a biochemistry graduate and Pooya a civil engineer—but both had learned software packages in their free time, spending hours behind the computer between classes and on weekends. Since graduation they had continued studying, setting up a group that met regularly to teach one another new programs.

One day, in 1993, they signed up for a specialized software course at a local cultural center. "The teacher was a middle-aged man who had studied in America in the mid-1980s," Madi explained. "He was so out of touch with the latest trends that it was comical. We students knew far more than he did, so we developed a game in class to entertain ourselves. Every session one of us would ask him a very technical question that had no meaning whatsoever. He would fumble a bit and say, 'We will get to that question in a later session.' We all had visions of the poor guy going home that night to study the answer to that meaningless question."

Pooya smiled. "Madi put that poor fellow through a great deal of trouble with his questions. I almost broke down once, to tell him that we were just fooling with him, but the other students didn't let me."

Today they both teach an evening course on basic computer skills at the same cultural center. "Every one of my classes is oversubscribed," Madi said. "The students are diverse. I teach housewives, children, university students, even a man in his eighties. The elderly man said he wanted to learn how to send E-mails to his grandchildren in America. One of the younger students wanted to learn how to type faster, so he could send out more E-mails to his cyber girlfriends around the world! I sent him to a typing class instead."

Both of them held day jobs as well, Madi at a pharmacy and Pooya with an engineering firm. They also had weekend jobs, providing computer support to private-sector companies. "We do all the basic computer stuff an office needs," Pooya explained. "It is very simple work. Most of the people in my office do not even know how to send E-mail, so we do it for them."

So why did they want to go to Germany?

"In Iran the work is very basic and the pay is very low," Pooya said. "We cannot survive on our salaries alone. Even with pay from the night classes and the weekend job, I cannot afford to buy a car." The two young men, like many Iranians in their mid-twenties, including some married couples, still lived with their parents. "We are stagnating professionally and suffering economically. That's why we all want to go to the West. Our biggest dream is America. Silicon Valley. But we'll take whatever we can get. I currently have an application in the works for Canada."

Madi agreed. "There is no future for us in Iran. This is not a country that treats its professionals well. It is a great place for the businessman or the trader. You can make a lot of money if you know the right people and trade in the right goods. But for the educated? It is terrible. I make about one hundred and twenty thousand tomans a month [approximately $175] with three jobs. How can I rent an apartment, buy a car, and get married with that salary? I don't want to leave Iran, but I have no choice."

What of the German rumor? Did it turn out to be true?

"Partially, yes," Madi said. "Germany has expressed an interest in software engineers, but Iran was only one of the countries mentioned. It is still unclear how many Iranians they will invite to apply, but I am sure they will be overwhelmed with Iranian applications."

Madi and Pooya represented a troubling aspect of Iran's economy, the massive brain drain of the country's educated professionals to foreign countries since the 1979 revolution. A distorted, anemic economy that favors the trader and speculator has sent many of Iran's elite professionals outside the country. Iran has one of the highest rates of brain drain in the Middle East. Nearly one in four Iranians with a college degree works outside the country. In the year 2000, more than two hundred thousand Iranians emigrated.

The first wave of the brain drain occurred shortly after the revolution as Iranian technocrats fled the country. They were disillusioned by the authoritarianism of the new government, angered by the government's emphasis on religious purity over technical skill, and fearful over the war with Iraq. Since then, as Iran's economy has shown little sign of improvement, Iranian professionals have steadily left the country, employing their skills successfully throughout the West. Major American cities—especially Los Angeles, San Francisco (including Silicon Valley), New York, and Washington—host a wide range of highly successful Iranian immigrants. Success stories of Iranian dot-com millionaires and celebrated surgeons filter back to Iran, further enticing Iranian youth with dreams of the West. Sometimes the stories are greatly exaggerated. "Is it true," Madi asked me, "that there are more Iranian millionaires in America than American ones?"

Though Madi and Pooya might be gullible enough to fall for some of the urban legends surrounding their compatriots in America, they understood the implications of their decision to leave the country and its effect on their generation's psyche. "We know that by leaving Iran, we are in a sense abandoning our countrymen," Pooya said. "The educated elite should stay to help build the country. But our country doesn't want us. How else can you explain the fact that a taxi driver makes twice as much money as a physics professor?"

"It's not only jobs or money," Madi said. "Our generation is obsessed with the West. In the schools of the Islamic Republic we were constantly told that the West was bad and evil. But on satellite TV and on the Internet and in magazines, we saw a different West. We saw a land of freedom—both political and social—and a place of economic security. We heard so many success stories of Iranians living in the West, especially America. Many of the dreams of the people of my generation are wrapped up somehow in going to the West.

"Still, our departure contributes to a seemingly never-ending cycle. If Pooya and I leave the country, our younger brothers and sisters, who are also educated, will want to follow us. We'll send back pictures of us at our desks, on the beach, in front of tall buildings, and our younger relatives who see those pictures will also burn for a chance to see the same beach, work in the same office, ride to the top of the same tall building. It is a cycle of departure and longing for departure. It can be broken only when this economy is taken away from state control and the natural talents of our people can progress in a competitive market."

Madi breathed in deeply. Pooya nodded his head, looking at his friend appreciatively, as if to say, "Well put." We finished our coffee in silence, the sound of the giggling girls in the Leonardo DiCaprio chat room filling the air.

Calculating quickly in my head, I realized that Madi had been six years old at the time of the revolution and Pooya must have been five. In a sense, they were just as much "the children of the revolution" as the 55 percent of the population born after 1979. All told, nearly two-thirds of all Iranians are under thirty, making it one of youngest populations in the world. This mass of youth—unborn or unwitting at the time of the revolution—was expected to become the vanguard of the Islamic Republic, "the future foot soldiers for Islam," as Khomeini put it. Instead most of them have become the vanguard for change. Iranian youth voted overwhelmingly for the reformist Khatami in 1997 and 2001, and they are today displaying impatience with the slow pace of change. More important, their acts of daily defiance against the rigid rules that govern their lives have chipped away at the power of Iran's ruling conservatives. Each act of defiance emboldens another.

Madi and Pooya, however, were in no mood for a fight. They were, in Lenin's famous phrase, "voting with their feet." The two young men flew to Damascus, Syria, in what has become a contemporary rite of passage for the young Iranian educated elite, the Canadian Embassy visa pilgrimage. The Canadian Embassy in Damascus processes all the Iranian work visa applications. Canada has opened its borders to Iranian professionals, especially computer specialists, engineers, and doctors. Every day the Canadian Embassy receives hundreds of applications from Iranians. Both Madi and Pooya passed the first cut. They were waiting to be called back to Damascus for a personal interview that would determine their final status.

"The visit to the Canadian Embassy is our generation's pilgrimage," Madi said, shrugging his shoulders. "It really is. You will see what it is like soon. You will see." I had told them of my plans to chronicle an Iranian visa seeker on his visit to Damascus. The pilgrimage, though not a traditional one and not on Iranian soil, seemed to define something about Iran's children of the revolution, and I thought I needed to understand it. I was to leave in a few days.

"It is a very sad thing to see," Pooya said. "Our best minds are lined up outside the Canadian Embassy like common beggars. If you are an Iranian nationalist, you should cry at the sight." I told them that the scene outside the German Embassy could be seen as equally sad. "Yes, that was bad too," Pooya admitted. "I suppose we looked pretty desperate."

We ordered another round of Nescafés. Inevitably talk turned to the revolution, a subject of conversation that is seemingly inexhaustible in Iran. Madi's father supported the revolution, he told me, but he couldn't figure out why. "My father thought it would bring greater democracy to Iran, but from my reading, I know that the leading revolutionary figures were either Marxists or mullahs. What kind of democracy could they produce?" Madi's statement reflected a recurring sentiment among the children of the revolution: a difficulty in understanding the revolution's motivations, a distrust of Iran's clerics, and a skepticism toward some of the leftist ideals of their parents.

"One year after the revolution," Madi said, "as it became clear that the clerics would take over and democracy would be sacrificed, my father turned against the government. Still, sometimes I have heated arguments with him. I become angry. I say: 'How could you have been so blind? The leftists that you supported were all stooges of the Soviet Union, and the clerics that you cheered for never had any experience with democracy!' "

Pooya interjected: "You must be fair, Madi. Not all the leftists were Soviet stooges, and there were many, many Iranians who fought for the same reasons your father did: democracy and freedom. If we'd lived in those days, we would probably have been revolutionary too. The Shah was a dictator. He did not allow for any political freedom. He forced people to choose revolution. Our parents' generation was also politically unsophisticated, so they chased after every utopian idea there was. When there is no room for dissent and no room for political freedom, it doesn't take much to get people excited about change. They will follow anyone who calls for equality and democracy whether he is a mullah or a Marxist."

He continued: "You know, Afshin, our generation is not as political as were our parents, who were obsessed with Che Guevara and leftist politics. You see, times were different. They had jobs and some economic security, so they had the luxury to be fashionable leftists. We don't have that, so we want very basic things: a good job, a living wage, and some personal freedoms."

Madi interjected defiantly: "I long for the Shah. I wish he still ruled Iran. There were jobs and social freedoms at least. Now we have neither political freedom nor social freedom. At least the Shah allowed for religious freedom!" He looked at Pooya meaningfully, his stare lingering longer than normal. "This is something that *you* should appreciate."

Pooya fidgeted with his coffee spoon. Then he said: "Yes, you are right, Madi. Religious freedoms are very important." He then looked at me and said: "I am Jewish. That is what Madi meant."

I had not known Pooya was Jewish. Like most of Iran's thirty-five thousand Jews, the largest community of non-Israeli Jews in the Middle East, Pooya seemed well assimilated. Iran's Jewish community dates back more than twenty-five hundred years, even before the rise of Cyrus the Great. Still, despite their assimilation, the revolution created strains in the Jewish community.

"It was not easy for us in the early days of the revolution," Pooya said. "We were not persecuted, of course, but we felt uneasy. You know what I mean, right?" He whispered the last sentence, looking around as he spoke. I knew what he meant. Ayatollah Khomeini, then the new leader of Iran, regularly cited the state of Israel and Jews as international conspirators in plots to destroy Iran. Revolutionary tribunals branded former government officials as "Zionist agents." One ayatollah gleefully told a crowd that the revolution humiliated the Jews and the Bahais (a persecuted religious minority that first emerged in the mid-nineteenth century as an Islamic reform movement and that today preaches a religion of universalism and peace).

"I was too young to remember much," Pooya said, "but I do remember a loud argument between my parents over my father's gold necklace with the Star of David on it. My mother told my father to stop wearing the necklace. She thought it might cause problems. My father, however, refused to take off the necklace. He said that he was a proud patriot of Iran, and no Iranian government could ever tell him otherwise. He kept saying that he was an Iranian and very proud! He was yelling it loudly. My mother cried. She said that it would only be temporary, in case the new government checked for these things. But my father refused. In the end he turned out to be right. Nobody bothered him."

Nevertheless, the unease that settled across the community sent many

Iranian Jews to the exits. A large group of them moved to the United States, especially Los Angeles. Pooya's family, however, went about their business as usual, and he, like most Iranians his age, remains intensely nationalistic about his country, though skeptical of its government. "I love Iran," he said. "This is my country. All my dear friends are here. I do not equate the country of Iran with the government of Iran. However, my father, it seems, has lost some of his former patriotism since the revolution. Today he talks more of his faith than his country. He has become more Jewish than before. He reads the Torah much more so than before."

Madi stirred his coffee, leaned into the table, and whispered to Pooya: "Why don't you ask Afshin about that issue we discussed?"

Pooya shot a sharp glance toward his friend. "It is best if we do not discuss these things," he said.

"You can trust him, Pooya," Madi told him. "Don't worry."

"I don't want to do it that way," Pooya responded testily. "It's nothing," he said, turning to me. "It's really nothing."

Visibly annoyed, Madi leaned in and whispered to me: "Pooya wants to know about the Jewish groups in America and Europe that might help him get a visa. Have you heard about these groups?"

"No!" Pooya said in an agitated whisper, startling the giggling girls amid their Leonardo DiCaprio cyberchat. They looked at us. Instinctively we all reached for our coffee mugs, trying to act casual. They turned back to the monitor, with one of them shrieking: "Ohmygod, look what Cayman *khanom* has written now!"

Madi stirred his coffee again. "I'm just trying to help," he said. "You should use every opportunity you can get. Maybe Afshin can pass on a letter for you to one of the groups."

"I don't want to do it that way," Pooya said again, visibly angry. He took a sip of coffee and said: "If I make it to Canada or Germany or America, I should like to know that I made it because of my skills, not because of my religion. I don't want religion to have anything to do with it. I don't want to use religion for anything. I just don't want it that way."

Madi nodded in understanding, reaching for his coffee mug. Pooya breathed in, as if a burden had been lifted from his shoulders. The giggling girls pecked at the computer. I put away my notebook. Ayatollah Khamenei's picture still looked down on us from the wall.

Visas and Billboards

As Iran Air Flight 517 to Damascus taxied into position before takeoff, Maziar, a thirty-five-year-old engineer and Canada visa seeker, pointed to the front of the plane. "Look at that," he said, gesturing toward a large group of elderly, mostly working-class Iranians wedged into the first twenty rows. "All those people are doing the pilgrimage to Hazrat-e-Zaynab [an eighth-century Shi'a saintess and sister of the revered Imam Hossein, who lies buried in an exquisite Iranian-funded shrine in Damascus]. They are religious pilgrims." I looked closely at the crowd, scanning the weather-beaten, wrinkled faces, stopping at a man with a striking resemblance to Mr. Hashemi. He was putting his suitcase into the top rack, something Mr. Hashemi probably could not have done with his recent bout of arthritis (he'd had to give up his job as a tea server at the ministry, I had heard, but a friendly deputy minister ensured that he would remain on salary even while staying home).

"Now, look around you," Maziar said. I saw a group of mostly young Iranians, early twenties to mid-thirties, scattered throughout the back of the plane, near where Maziar and I sat. "We are economic pilgrims," he said. Maziar, like Pooya and Madi, understood the implications for his potential departure. "I should like to stay and serve my country," he had said earlier as we boarded the plane, "but there are no jobs. I have a wife and a child. What can I do?"

Sitting on the blue metal chairs at Mehrabad Airport in Tehran, we spoke almost continuously for an hour before the flight, not stopping as we boarded the shuttle bus and into the plane. "I am carrying with me a document from Canada attesting to my qualifications as an engineer," he said. "This is a very important document. It means that I am almost assured of acceptance in the first round."

He showed me a picture of his three-month-old daughter. "When I put her in my arms, I know that I must leave. I cannot give her everything she deserves in Iran." Before the flight we fell into an easy camaraderie even though we had met only once before, when he had agreed to my request to follow him on his visa pilgrimage because a mutual friend had asked him to. At first I wasn't sure if he was happy about the prospect, but his loquaciousness in the early part of the trip eased my concern.

He had soft black eyes and a bushy black mustache, but his face looked younger than his thirty-five years. If he shaved the mustache, I thought, he could pass for a twenty-five-year-old. He laid out reasons for his visa pilgrimage: "The average engineer makes approximately one hundred and fifty to two hundred and fifty dollars a month, slightly less than the monthly income of a taxi driver. Average monthly expenses for a middle-class family of four far exceed that salary range. I have a baby daughter to support and maybe another one coming soon. Economically it is very tough to survive, and I don't have much family financial support. I don't want to be one of those people who hold two or three jobs to survive. Besides, I don't like the social restrictions we are living under. My wife does not come from a family that veils. She doesn't like the forced veiling.

"Every year I told myself that the economy would get better, and every year I waited and waited and did not apply for the Canada visa. Already three of my classmates are in Canada. This year I am doing it. I shall put in my application. The rest I leave to God."

The airplane rose into the night sky, a smooth takeoff. The group of pilgrims in the front praised God. One of them, a gray-haired, gray-bearded man holding blue prayer beads, unfastened his seat belt, stood up to face his fellow pilgrims, and urged them to say a *salavat* (prayer) for the Prophet Muhammad and his family. They dutifully complied: "Blessings and greetings to the Prophet Muhammad and the family of Muhammad." A few of the young economic pilgrims joined them in prayer.

Among the visa pilgrims, Maziar was one of the oldest. Most were in their early and mid-twenties. I sat on the aisle. In a nearby row, three young visa pilgrims, Ali and his cousin Nazila and another woman, Niloofar, unfastened their seat belts and leaned in for a conversation. Surprised to hear that Maziar was on his first visa run, they traded "war stories" of visa rejections by various European embassies.

The Americans and the British were the worst, they thought. "They almost seemed to enjoy rejecting us," Nazila said. She shook her head and said: "That guy in the American consulate in Dubai is the worst of the worst!" Her comment was received with much head nodding from the other two.

"Yes, you should avoid Dubai at all costs," Ali said. "Use the American Embassy in Abu Dhabi. They are much friendlier," he added.

Niloofar had even better advice. "Try the American embassies in Eastern Europe," she said. "It's not difficult to get a visit visa to Romania or Bulgaria, and the advantage is that the American consular officials are not accustomed to seeing educated Iranians, so they are not inclined to reject us." Good idea, everyone said.

Ali leaned forward to tell a joke. "Did you hear the one about the young Iranian who went to Dubai for a visa and threw his passport in the Dubai creek?" Nazila nodded in knowing appreciation, but the rest of us were eager to hear the joke. "This poor fellow was rejected by every consulate in Dubai: the French, the Italians, the Germans, the Americans, the British, the Eastern Europeans, even the Chinese and the Africans! So he walked along the Dubai creek and dejectedly sat on a bench. He opened his passport and flipped through all the rejection stamps. In a moment of anger he threw his passport into the waterway that intersects the city. A few minutes later a fish jumped out of the water and handed him back his passport. He opened the wet pages and saw a new stamp: 'Rejected for entry into Dubai creek.'" They laughed bitterly.

"That's a good one," Maziar said, "but also sad, so sad, is it not?"

The plane landed bumpily in Damascus, and the tires shrieked loudly as the jumbo jet slowed. An Iranian nearby joked that the pilot must be in a hurry to have a drink. (Syria, unlike Iran, does not prohibit alcohol consumption. Many Iranians waste no time, drinking beer at an airport bar shortly after arrival.) "I am myself in a hurry to have a drink," another Iranian quipped.

At the baggage claim, several young visa pilgrims exchanged phone numbers and wished one another luck. Niloofar planned to make a visit to the Zaynab shrine before going to the Canadian Embassy. "I shall pray for my visa," she said.

We pulled our bags from the conveyor and walked into the Damascus midnight air underneath a large yellow airport sign that read WELCOME TO ASSAD'S SYRIA. Pictures of the late Syrian president Hafez Assad, with his thin, gray mustache and his long head, dotted the airport. The image disconcerted me for a moment. I had become accustomed to seeing gray-bearded, turban-wearing Iranian clerics on the walls, not mustachioed, tie-wearing Arab autocrats. We hailed a taxi and headed for our hotel. Along the wide, quiet, tree-lined highway into the city, we passed several Assad billboards.

As Maziar dozed, I ruminated on the totalitarian impulse to paint cities with pictures of the Leader. In Iran, pictures of Ayatollah Ruhollah Khomeini and his successor, Ayatollah Ali Khamenei, are seen in public places and on billboards all over the country. On one stretch of Tehran highway, small drawings of the two men run across a long green wall, alternating one, then the other, so the bored passenger looking out the window can be reminded continually of the faces of his leaders past and present. It was no different before the revolution, with pictures of the Shah seen everywhere.

The effect of the towering face painted on the wall or on the grand billboard looming out over the highway is curious. For the first-time visitor, the pictures are jarring, a stark reminder of who's in charge and the nature of government. There is latent threat in the pictures, but there is also dark comedy. Tourists to Iran often stand in front of the large billboards of Khomeini, smiling, as their friends snap photos. Back home, in Frankfurt or Rome or Tokyo, the tourist laughs, as he shows his friends the picture, a backpacking foreigner standing in front of an angry-looking cleric. His friends nod in appreciation, wondering if they too might one day go to Iran or Syria and take an "exotic" picture with an autocrat on a billboard.

For the resident, there is nothing "exotic" about the pictures. They become just another part of the scenery, neither particularly threatening nor inspiring. The taxi driver who drove by the photo of Assad every day could not possibly be "inspired" each time he saw his leader, even if he had been a big supporter. The same goes for Khomeini or Saddam Hussein or Stalin or Castro or any number of rulers whose visages peer or once peered over their populations. Then again, perhaps that is the unintended result of the billboards and the photos: They train the eye to feel a certain normality in the photos. The Islamic Republic will be here as long as the sun shines on Khomeini's billboard beard.

On the other hand, the billboards also become the face of government mismanagement. A bad experience at the passport office blemishes the billboard. A rough encounter with the police tarnishes the billboard. High electricity bills or the rising price of meat are blamed on the men on the billboards. In a struggling economy like Iran's, the faces on the billboard come to represent all the impediments to a better life. The billboards become guilty, and in Iran, people do not shy away from pointing the finger.

Iran is not a police state the way Syria is. Iranians are far more willing to criticize their government publicly than are Syrians. The Syrian taxi driver rarely talks politics; the Iranian will talk of nothing else. In Iran one does not get the sense of an overwhelming intelligence presence monitoring every word one utters. One does not feel stifled as one does in Damascus. (To use the Internet in Damascus, I had to go the state library, register my name, and list all the Web sites I planned to view. As I wrote out my addresses longhand on a bureaucrat's form, I thought of the giggling girls at the Internet café in Tehran.) Yet despite the active civil society of student protesters and political associations and the general willingness (and loquaciousness) of the Iranian people to criticize their ruler openly, Iran's government has totalitarian elements, especially the elevation of the Supreme Leader Ayatollah Ali Khamenei to an almost untouchable political icon and, of course, the billboards dotting the country.

As we drove into a neon-lit circle in downtown Damascus, under another massive billboard of Assad, I stumbled upon an idea: Iran's relative liberalization since the election of Khatami in 1997, especially the opening of the floodgates of criticism, undermines the faces on those billboards above the roads. The Assad billboards, however, were not indicted in the same way because the political culture of Damascus was more stifling, more conducive to the totalitarian face on the wall. When Iran's liberalized press criticized Iran's conservative ruling clergy in that moment of press freedom from 1997 to 2000, the targets of the article stared down at people from the billboards. When the taxi driver fills a passenger's ear with stories of "those thieving mullahs," the passenger need only look up to the sky to see whom he is talking about. When radio show hosts take phone calls from listeners who spew invective against the poor state of the country's economy, the billboards above the road must shake just a little. Suddenly the people—not the political activists or reformist intellectuals, but the average people—pine for the old billboard, for the clean-shaved, dapper Shah who provided a strong economy. They seem to forget that once the Shah's face on billboards across the country was the source of all their troubles, and they forget their view that "if only the king would go and the Imam [Khomeini] would return, all would be well."

When the Shah, responding to the unrest, partially liberalized the Iranian polity, he might as well have taken down his face from the wall. What I mean by this is: If you are going to put up totalitarian-style billboards all over the country, you'd better be a fully totalitarian state. Partial liberalization only engenders demands for more liberalization and ultimately for full liberalization. The faces on the billboards and the statues on the streets become merely marked men, filling up airspace for a few years until new billboards crop up or, better yet, are replaced by ads for chicken and soap. Iranian chicken and soap producers, it seemed to me, should be more optimistic than their Syrian counterparts.

"In Damascus, I Can Breathe"

The taxi driver dropped us at a small hotel in a slightly seedy district in downtown Damascus. The hotel clerk, a round man with a brown beard wearing a narrow brown tie and brown slippers displaying chunky toes, helped us with our bags. *"Khosh amadadeed,"* he said in Farsi, with an Arabic accent, using the familiar welcome phrase that he had learned from his regular Iranian guests. The hotel was popular with Iranian pilgrimage tours. Maziar and I had arranged a package deal with a tour agency that specializes in religious pilgrimages. Many of the young Iranian visa pilgrims use these tour agency package deals because they offer the most economical means of travel.

"Your bus for pilgrimage ready nine o'clock," the hotel clerk said in broken Farsi. "Breakfast, eight o'clock." We thanked him and retired to our room. Two iron beds with thin mattresses and heavy blankets greeted us. Maziar was not pleased. "I asked for a three-star hotel. This is not right," he said. "This is not right. I shall talk to somebody tomorrow." Outside, I heard the occasional beat of a honking horn as I tried to sleep. The coarse blanket itched my body, and unable to sleep, I dressed and walked downstairs to the small lobby decorated with gold teapots and colorful Arabic textiles on the wall. The bleary-eyed clerk smiled and looked at his watch. It was 1:30 A.M. "Bar is closed," he said in English. "All bars closed. No drink."

I asked him why he assumed I wanted a drink.

"All Iranians want drink," he said somewhat testily. "Sometimes even the religious man want drink. You no can drink in Iran. You drink here."

His summary was right, in a sense. Curbs on social freedoms tend to create a larger appetite for contraband, whether it be sex or whiskey. I have lived twice in societies that curbed social freedoms—Saudi Arabia in 1993–94 and Iran 1999–2000—and know from experience that deprivation can breed unhealthy bingeing when one is abroad. It is not without cause that a stereotype of the whiskey-swigging, womanizing Saudi exists in major European capitals. Iranian men, more impoverished than the Saudis, must do their drinking and womanizing in less expensive spots, in Damascus or Istanbul or Dubai.

"Sometimes the Iranian man drink too much," the hotel clerk added. "He come here at night and he fall down and he can no stand up. This no good. Drink is against Islam. You Iranians no good Muslims," he said in a scolding tone. I noticed that he had a brown mark on his forehead, the sign of a pious Muslim, created by repeated prostrations of the forehead to the ground.

"Iranian man also go after woman. They always ask, 'Where find woman?' Not far from here, there is woman in hotels," he said. I assumed he meant prostitutes, but I wasn't sure.

"Yes, women for money! From Russia, from Lebanon, from Afghanistan. Too much woman!" He looked at his watch. "Now available woman. One hour more." Despite his aversion, he was a professional, a helpful clerk who thought he should please the customer, so he pointed to the streets I should avoid and the ones that might interest me. I thanked him politely (what else was I to do?) and went back upstairs to sleep.

The next morning we joined the large crowd of religious pilgrims in the cramped breakfast salon. Gray-haired men with round paunches and heavily veiled women ate breakfasts of eggs, bread, feta cheese, and sweet tea. Syrian waiters in stained shirts rushed around, delivering metal pots of tea and white slabs of feta cheese to the tables. After a short wait Maziar and I were seated. A waiter dropped a long piece of flat bread on our table. I looked around the room at a sea of gray-haired men and chador-clad women. Maziar and I were by far the youngest in the room, by at least twenty-five years.

Seated next to us, a man in the baggy pants and the conical white cap of a rural worker scooped up his egg yolk with a piece of bread as he described his yearlong pilgrimage tour. "I visited Karbala and Najaf this year," he told us, referring to the shrines of the Shi'a imams Hossein and Ali, "and I visited more than twenty *imamzadehs* [shrines of family members of the twelve sacred Shi'a imams] in Iran in this past year, and after I visit the Zaynab shrine, I shall, Allah willing, go to Mecca.

Maziar and I expressed our hope that his pilgrimages would be accepted by God: the typical rejoinder.

"God willing," he said. "My sons are your age. I hope they will come to pilgrimage here soon. May your pilgrimage also be accepted."

He stood up and offered us the remainder of his tea, perhaps having noticed that our pot of tea had not yet arrived. We declined with appropriate *ta'rof.* Just then a plate of runny eggs slammed against our table, followed by a rusty pot of tea.

After breakfast I lingered in the lobby as Maziar gathered his papers for the Canadian Embassy visit. A group of elderly, plump Iranian women in dark chadors chatted about their coming pilgrimage with a thin, blue-eyed, middle-aged Iranian wearing a wide-banded gold watch. "Respected ladies," he said, "I pray to God that your pilgrimage will be accepted. I hope your breakfast was suitable. The bus will be here in ten minutes. Remember to pray for me!"

He smiled, walked away, and approached the front desk clerk, who looked like a younger version of the paunchy, bearded clerk of the night before, including the brown prayer spot on his forehead. The Iranian with the gold watch spoke animated, albeit broken, Arabic in a Farsi accent with the hotel clerk. "How many, my friend? What about group for tomorrow, my friend? Do you have room next Wednesday? I am need just one room, my friend! Please, I know you can do it!" He patted the clerk on the shoulder. "I bring you pistachios," he said. "Many, many pistachios!" The clerk smiled, jotted notes on his pad, and assured him he would check into the room assignments.

The Iranian walked away from the desk, lighting a cigarette, and sat down in a chair next to mine. Strapped to his waist was a mobile phone, which I thought peculiar because Damascus did not have a mobile system at the time. I asked him about the phone.

"It is the phone I use in Tehran," he said.

Did it work in Damascus?

"No." He laughed. "Nothing works here."

He inhaled the cigarette deeply, and smoke emitted from his thin nostrils. He was fair-skinned and light-haired, slightly balding at the top. His thin hairs were slicked back, giving him a faintly seedy look. His skin was sallow yellow, like the color of his teeth. His eyes constantly shifted around the room. He asked if I was staying in the hotel. What part of Iran was I from? What was my name?

"Ah, yes," he said, "you were booked by the Zafar tour agency. I am Ahmad," he said, offering his thin hand in greeting. "Is your friend with you? Are your accommodations OK? If you need anything, let me know."

Apparently he worked as a fixer in Damascus with several of the Tehran tour agencies, including the one Maziar used. "I spend six months here and six months in Tehran. I like it here. In Damascus, I can breathe, have a drink, you know how it is. You are too young to remember, but Damascus reminds me a bit of Tehran under the Shah. There is the same sort of stranglehold on talk of politics, but at least you have personal freedoms. You can get a drink, go to a cabaret, have a little fun."

He puffed his cigarette, his gold watch glinting. "Life cannot be all just mourning for the imams and religion as those clerics want. I am a religious man," he said. "I go to pilgrimage. I pray. But that does not mean I cannot breathe a little. Everybody needs to breathe, no?" He looked at his gold watch, muttered, "five minutes," under his breath, and looked around the lobby at the gathering tide of elderly pilgrims.

"In Iran, in the time of the Shah, we had social freedom. You are too young to remember," he repeated, "but I recall when Frank Sinatra came to Tehran. It was wonderful. Many international actors and actresses visited us. Jackie Onassis came to Tehran! She bought jewelry from Mozaffarian [a prominent Tehran jeweler]. They all came. The Americans loved Iran!

"Today we can write political articles until we are choking in newspapers, but if I want to have a drink in a bar, I must go to Damascus. If I want to go to a nightclub, I must go to Dubai. Many of the Iranians who come here drink whiskey to their eyeballs. The hotel clerks ask me, 'What kind of Islam is that?' I don't know what to say. I am a Sufi. They do not understand, so I point to all of the religious pilgrims, the elderly people who do their pilgrimages, who are pious. I do not want them to have a bad impression of Iran. We are Muslims after all, but still, we need to breathe, don't we?"

He stood up, and stubbed his cigarette into an ashtray. "The bus should be here soon," he said, then added with a smile, "but I assume you won't be on it. You will be going to the Canadian Embassy, no? All you young people go to the Canadian Embassy. I wish you luck. Remember, if you need anything, I am at your service." He hurried away and stepped to the front of the lobby to make an announcement: "Attention, everyone! Everybody must be inside the bus in five minutes. Let us say a prayer for the Prophet Muhammad and his family!" The group moved out in small steps, muttering the familiar *salavat* as they walked. The man in the gold watch disappeared into the bright morning light.

The Canadian Embassy Visa Pilgrimage

A few minutes later Maziar and I hailed a taxi to the Canadian Embassy. The driver, a young man, turned back to us and said in Arabic, "You must be Iranian."

I tried to engage the driver in a political discussion. On previous trips to Damascus I had no luck with these attempts. With my experience in Iran, where every driver is a loud political critic, I thought I'd try again. The Damascus taxi driver was not interested. "Assad good," he said in English. "Very good. Number one." He then raised the volume on his Arabic pop tape, as if to say that would be the end of the discussion.

The taxi dropped us off in front of the Canadian Embassy underneath a clear blue sky with café au lait mountains in the distance. A line had formed outside the embassy gates. I saw many of the same faces that had been on the airplane the night before. Ali and Nazila waved from the middle of the line. Nazila had removed her head scarf. She wore a long coat and black jeans.

"Afshin, please come here!" she said. "Hurry."

We greeted each other with the usual elaborate pleasantries. She handed me a document and asked me to check the spelling and grammar on her visa application form. It looked fine, only a few minor corrections needed. Ali asked if he could "possibly trouble me" to do the same. His required a bit more work, so I crouched at a nearby table (curiously there were no chairs, just a worn table) and made the corrections. Soon word spread among the visa applicants that an Iranian from America was in their midst, and a small group formed around me, with people asking me if they could "trouble me," if they "could impose terribly upon me," or if they could "with great apologies burden me" with their applications.

After half an hour of spelling corrections, the line toward the embassy began to move, and the visa applicants rushed back into place. At the front of the line applicants were handing their documents to a burly blue-eyed Syrian guard. He collected them and handed them inside the gate to another guard. No Iranian entered the embassy grounds.

Maziar felt introspective as he waited to hand in his completed form. "Look around you," he said, "These are some of the best and brightest young minds in Iran, and they are here lined up outside the Canadian Embassy begging for a visa. This is so sad."

I asked him how he felt about his own prospects.

"They never reject engineers with my kind of experience in the first round. I shall be concerned about the second round."

As we inched closer to the front of the line, people gathered around a just-posted notice on the bulletin board. They were yesterday's applicants, huddled at the board, hoping to see that they had made it past the first round of vetting (the Canadian Embassy offered next-day notice for first-round cuts). I heard shrieks of joy and hugs as people spotted their names on the list. The remaining young men and women continued looking, scanning the lines, checking to see if their applicant numbers matched the ones on the list. There were a few sighs of relief as two more applicants walked away from the board.

Those left behind kept searching, hoping to find something on that paper on the wall that simply was not there. A young woman wiped away a tear. A young man cursed loudly. Another young man insisted that there must be a mistake. "This is impossible," he said. "I am an accredited engineer! I am an accredited engineer. I have papers. This is a mistake."

Maziar looked on with concern as the rejected engineer walked toward the embassy and was stopped by the Syrian guard. "This is a mistake!" the young man repeated. "A terrible mistake." As he walked away from the embassy, he shook his head and kept muttering, "But I am an accredited engineer, an accredited engineer."

A few minutes later Maziar dropped off his application with the Syrian guard. We bade good-bye to Ali and Nazila and decided to walk back to the hotel. A few hundred yards down the road from the Canadian Embassy, we happened upon the embassy of the Islamic Republic of Iran. There were no lines of young people waiting outside the embassy. We laughed at the obvious irony.

After a short walk we approached the gates of Damascus University. I saw clusters of young men in jeans and clunky black shoes and young women—some veiled, some dramatically unveiled—stroll the stone walkways of the campus. Two young women in tight-fitting black jeans and heavy makeup walked past us. Just behind them three young women in head scarves and long manteaus chatted amiably. Noting the juxtaposition, Maziar said: "That's how it should be. Women should be given a choice. The Iranian way, in which we force our women to veil, is wrong. The Turkish way, in which they force their women to unveil, is also wrong [Turkey bans the head scarf on college campuses]. Women should have a choice."

We sat down on a green park bench on the university grounds. The delicate scent of mint perfumed the air. I asked Maziar about his earlier comment, his sadness at seeing his country's elite lining up outside the embassy.

"Yes, it's sad, of course, but we are the lucky ones. We have an education. We have some hope of going abroad. For those without education, it is very difficult. Many young people try to smuggle themselves into Western Europe illegally."

He was right. I told him of the hundreds of Iranian young people who fly into Bosnia every month, hoping to cross into Western Europe overland. The ones who do make it live the lives of refugees in European shelters. "We get three meals and free education," one of the young Iranians who had made it as far as Holland told me. After a year in Holland, however, he became homesick for his mother and flew back, a normal nineteen-year-old's reaction. Several of his friends stayed on and eventually landed jobs and residence permits. He wondered if he had made the right decision.

"Yes, I heard about this Bosnia route," Maziar said. "It is very dangerous too." We both had read the newspaper story about the twenty young Iranians who died in a capsized boat while trying to cross a river in Croatia.

"What have we come to?" he said, shaking his head.

A Syrian professor with a thin mustache who wore a narrow tie walked past us, peeling an orange. A student, a woman with long black hair, approached him. They talked about the day's lecture.

Maziar and I watched the campus life in front of us: a boy reading under a tree, students being flirtatious, a professor surrounded by three head-nodding students. We talked little. My mind raced with what I had seen in Damascus so far, and I broke the silence by telling Maziar about my conversation with the hotel clerk ("Iranians drink too much"), about the man with the gold watch ("In Damascus, I can breathe"), my ruminations on billboards and on the stifling nature of Syrian politics versus the relative dynamism of Iranian. I told him about the excitement Iran has engendered in the West as a great hope for democracy in the Middle East. I told him of my own view, born of months of travel throughout Iran, that Iranian civil society had made genuine progress, but that the progress was intangible to the people. The real tangible things were jobs and social freedoms and a decent living wage.

He listened quietly, perhaps sensing that I had much to let out.

I continued my soliloquy, saying Iran's political development is important because it gets the nation closer to what it really needs, a truly democratic system with an open society that allows for debate and government accountability. But its closed economy, which stifles opportunities, and its strict rules on social freedoms make daily life arduous. The attempt by the government to control morality is eminently antidemocratic because it prevents human choice, and that is, in my opinion, the most profoundly exhilarating aspect of democracy and open societies: It gives people choices. I get the sense that Iranians at bottom just want more choices, whether they are for more social freedoms, more political freedoms, or both.

Authoritarian systems, however, have a way of distorting everything, I continued. They distort the economy, the culture, religion, and human choices. As a result, the natural order of things is disrupted. People react against the system: They drink too much when they go abroad, or they become irreligious or fundamentalist or Marxist, they stand outside embassies begging for visas, or they give their lives to cross a surging Croatian river because of some utopian hope that they may realize on the other side of the river.

Maziar turned toward me, as if to say, "Go on, I'm listening."

This disruption, this unnatural state of things won't end until the political system is opened further, until the economy is liberalized, until social freedoms are safeguarded. Unless these happen, there will be more Iranians dying in Croatian rivers, more lining up outside embassies for visas, and more protesting the current order back in Iran. I am not sure if the cycle will end soon, but the only way it will end is if people are given choices on how they want to live and how they want to be governed.

Interestingly, young Iranians, it seemed to me, are less idealistic than their parents' generation and, in fact, less so than their culture. This is good. Iranians have constantly sought the ideal at the expense of the real, in their art, poetry, architecture, even politics. In a sense, the *velayat-e-faqih,* the system of rule by clerics, is a Khomeinist ideal based on the view that a just man of religion will guide his flock to the right path. Traditional Iranian art, with its bright colors and exaggerated beauty, represents the ideal at the expense of the real. The socialist utopia politics of the 1970s is yet another manifestation of this constant quest for the ideal.

But today's young Iranians seem better grounded. They seem to understand intuitively that the ideals in life that matter are choice and opportunity. This visit to Damascus, this effort to secure a visa and go to Canada, at bottom comes down to choice and opportunity, does it not? I breathed in, wondering if I made any sense, wondering if my mad rush of thoughts about Iran while I sat on a green bench in Damascus University made any sense at all.

"Yes, it does," Maziar said, stroking his mustache. "Yes, it does. You must write these thoughts down," he said. "I think you are beginning to understand us."

I demurred, expressing my hope that I had not bored him. I felt faintly embarrassed by my outburst. I suggested we move on to do some sightseeing.

Over the next few hours we visited old, impressive mosques, small, elegant churches, a fashionable Armenian district, and the twisting alleyways of the central bazaar. We returned to our hotel in the evening. When we entered the lobby, the thin man with the gold watch was arguing with the hotel desk clerk, a cigarette dangling from his lips, a pencil in his hand, furiously writing something on the hotel ledger.

"We promised you fifty, not sixty-five. We cannot pay for the extra rooms if we did not use them!" he said, to the obvious chagrin of the hotel clerk with the brown spot on his forehead. As we walked past, the Iranian smiled at us—"So, are you going to Canada or not?"—before continuing his argument with the hotel clerk.

That night after dinner Maziar and I headed for a nearby bar. As we walked toward the bar, past some of the seedier hotels, young Syrians approached us quietly, whispering in Arabic, "Woman, woman, would you like a woman?" A few of them approached us, and spoke in Farsi: "Fine women. Special price for Iranian boys! Come in. Very cheap! Very nice Russians, Lebanese, anything you like."

When we sat down in the bar, Maziar said: "I think this area is their version of Shahr-e-Now," referring to a red light district in prerevolution Iran. "That travel agency really gave us the business! I'm sorry. If I'd known, I would not have booked a room here." I told him he worried himself for no reason. The district had a certain roguish charm. I genuinely liked it.

We sat on chairs at tea-stained flat wooden tables, sipped cold Syrian beer, and ate green olives. Smoke filled the room. Old men in tattered sweaters sucked on sheesha pipes. Younger men in blue jeans, smoking cigarettes, huddled around a car magazine. A group of four young Iranian men, other visa seekers, sipped beer. One of them approached us to ask if we would like to join them at a cabaret. "There will be Russian women dancing," he said. After a few drinks Maziar and I, tired from a long day of walking, went back to our hotel.

The next day Maziar made the first cut. We spotted his number on the white paper attached to the embassy's brick wall. He smiled and breathed in deeply. I congratulated him. He reached out to embrace me. Perhaps he had been more nervous than he let on. He was allowed into the embassy grounds to fill out a series of forms. If he made the second cut, to be determined in twelve months, he would be called back to Damascus for a personal interview.

While Maziar went inside the Canadian Embassy to get the forms, I met a teary-eyed young woman who had failed to make the cut. She still wore the head scarf and manteau, the Iranian female uniform of the Islamic Republic, even though several of the Iranian women had taken advantage of Syria's relative social freedom and discarded them.

"I want to live in Canada or America so badly. It is like a dream to me," she said, adjusting her head scarf. "I don't want to go back to Iran. I want to go and study pharmacy. I want to be a pharmacist. Why wouldn't they accept me? Why?"

She walked away, her shoulders shaking, her silhouette getting smaller against the horizon. To her right, a few hundred yards away from the Canadian Embassy, she passed by the embassy of the Islamic Republic of Iran. She paused, looked at the black gate, then continued walking, her head scarf blown down by the wind.

Farewell, Iran

When I returned from Damascus, I began my preparations for my departure back to the United States. Surely it would not be the last time I visited Iran, but somehow, I felt melancholy. I found myself lingering a little bit longer over cups of tea with friends, wandering deeper into the bazaar, spending hours on the telephone bidding adieu to new friends in distant cities. I spoke with Davoud, Mr. Zari, Mrs. Teimouri, Mr. Mohseni the cleric, Mr. Mohammadi in Ahvaz, and many others. On my last few days I went shopping in the local markets, just to hear Mr. Pouron, the fruit seller, scold me one last time about my poor choice in fruit and to watch the Azeri boy scurry across the market, grabbing cheeses and milks that I surely no longer needed. I did not say good-bye to them. I could not bring myself to it.

Hossein, the war veteran, insisted on driving me to the airport. Hossein, ever the good friend, was like that. At six on a warm late-spring morning, he buzzed my door, his white Paykan churning outside my building. I had been up since three, unable to sleep. Had I seen everything I needed to see? Had I talked to enough people? What was this sense of loss I felt?

We drove in silence, past the billboards displaying Iran's war martyrs, past the dirt-colored apartments jutting out over the highways, past buzzing mopeds, and bleary-eyed laborers. At the airport Hossein parked the car. I watched everything closely as we walked to the terminal, hoping to imprint permanently images of Iran, of my journey, into my mind. There was something special about this trip, this journey of discovery. I'll be back, I thought, but it won't be the same.

At the terminal Hossein and I embraced. Neither of us engaged in the usual *ta'rof* pleasantries. We simply said good-bye. He knew that Iran had cast a spell on me. He knew I would be back.

Just before we parted, Hossein said to me: "Just remember, Afshin, please remember our martyrs." I assured him I would. "Also, remember one more thing," he said.

Yes, what was it?

"Do you have your notebook?"

Yes. I pulled one of the nearly fifty notebooks I had filled out of my bag.

He took the notebook from me and began writing. He then handed me the notebook.

In it he had written, in Farsi, *"Zendebad Iran."*

Long live Iran.

INDEX